# SALVAGE

#15
BEWITCHED AND DISTORTED

AUTUMN/WINTER 2024 | SPRING/SUMMER 2025

# Contents

SALVAGE EDITORIAL COLLECTIVE
**Bewitched and Distorted: Perspectives #15**　　　　Insert
History is fast, *Salvage* production slow: a time capsule from instants before the MAGA dispensation.


ABDALJAWAD OMAR
**The Anxiety of Liberation**　　　　7
Reflections on rupture and the weight of history. The courage to be afraid.


RICHARD SEYMOUR
**The Atrocity Exhibition: On Perpetrators**　　　　21
Shame amid the shameless: how to both deny and enjoy sadism.


JOSEPH DAHER
**Hamas After 7 October**　　　　47
Towards the most scandalous transgression: actually understanding the designated enemy.


BARNABY RAINE
**What Do People Panic About When They Panic About Anti-Semitism?**　　　　67
Once more on diasporaphobia and the genocidal negations of Zionism.


GHALYA SAADAWI
**Against History: Art, Culture, and Business-as-Usual Under the Gazan Genocide**　　　　89
Under the shadow of genocide, what price proud aboutness? Art is not only about, but of, and in.

ANDREAS MALM
**The Politics of Life**     109
The tanks are still there, and still we must bang loudly upon their walls.

JULES GILL-PETERSON & SOPHIE LEWIS
**The Politics of Childhood: A Conversation**     117
Won't somebody please, please think of the children?

REBEKAH DISKI
**The Full Force of the Law: Protest and Repression on a Scorched Earth**     135
Reports from and on the incarcerated, amid the fog of the reaction-legality-emissions nexus.

NICK DYER-WITHEFORD
**Biocommunism**     143
'No cookbooks for the future' doesn't mean we shouldn't consider how we might write recipes, or with what ingredients.

DAISY LAFARGE
**The Sick Rose**     161
Art.

DUNCAN THOMAS
**Kind of Blue: A Short History of Tory Decline**     177
There Is No Alternative cuts both ways. The Tories clutch the monkey's paw.

HAN DEE
**Trieste: Where Mad Minds Can Fly**     209
A dossier and time capsule on Democratic Psychiatry, starting with a no.

JONAS MARVIN
**The Medical Law of Accumulation: Putting the Sick on the Line**     245
Body and mind, health and unhealth as battlefields in the class war.

CHINA MIÉVILLE
**Beyond Folk Marxism: Mind, Metaphysics and
Spooky Materialism** 261
Struggling back to first principles, and against common sense, which
even on the left is no comrade to truth.


DANIEL ANDRÉS LOPEZ
**The True Infinite and the Republic of Virtue** 313
Necessary theses on love, desire, the concrete and ideal,
to recharge flailing philosophies. Because we need to stop failing.


SUSANA CALVO
**The Arrendatario** 361
Fiction.


**About the Contributors** 366

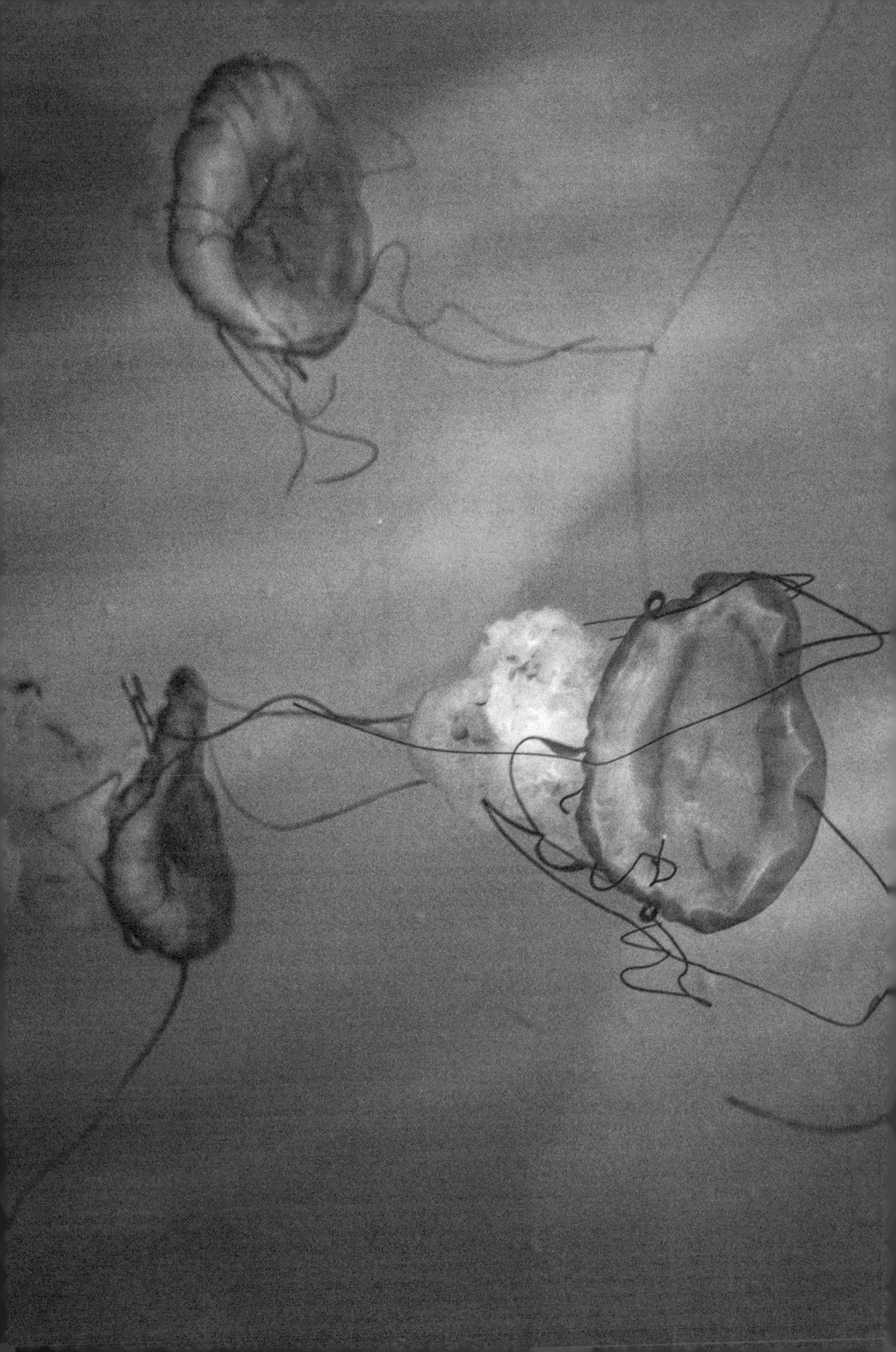

ABDALJAWAD OMAR

# The Anxiety of Liberation

I cannot pinpoint the exact moment the realisation dawned on me that for many Palestinians, the process that might end the occupation is fraught with anxiety and fear. It is not only a panic that emanates from the brute force of Israel's military – its capacity to kill, maim, destroy, and imprison – but also at the real potential for liberation itself. Nor can I remember when I first understood that while resistance embodies hope – opening countless possibilities and expanding the horizon of political potential – it simultaneously brings forth a terrible anxiety about the prospect of liberation, especially when it appears visceral and real.

For a people living under the relentless brutality of colonial rule, the notion of freedom itself is exhilarating and charismatic. It draws and mesmerises, reimagining the possibility of a different world, a different life, a different order. It creates the conditions for the heroics of declaring one's death before its actualisation, for becoming a revolutionary, a martyr, or a prisoner, to enact courageous acts despite the breakdown of metanarratives in the contemporary landscape. It means realising you are doomed yet walking proudly in the stretch of time between this declaration of rebellion and its inevitable realisation in the gallows of Israeli jails and its high-tech machinery of assassinations. The power to radically unthink the world means, at times, allowing the imaginary to invade you, to simultaneously unthink the world and daydream, to be playful with images rather than bound by logical worlds and words. I won't lie to you; to resist cannot be reduced to a single register, nor can it be encapsulated in one experience or one form. However, resistance is a form of subjective destitution, becoming a slave and servant of the imaginary.

When liberation is invoked, fighters in the West Bank speak of praying freely in the environs of Al-Aqsa Mosque, without the oppressive presence of the Israeli gendarmerie. The nonbelievers dream of the beaches and mountains of Galilee, intact and unblemished. Meanwhile, intellectuals fret over the nature of the political system that might arise if Zionism indeed implodes as a system of Jewish Supremacy across Palestine. They debate endlessly about a new structure, a new relationship between those who will hold power and those who will not. A friend of mine who loves the expansive and solemn quiet of Al-Naqab desert rather than the greenery of Galilee says, 'Believe me, if Palestine is liberated, all we will get are private and lofty beaches for the haves, and poverty for the have-nots'. Cynicism dominates his thinking, and with his realistic tone, he doubles down, 'Palestine will be plentiful but only for the few, precisely like everywhere else'.

Some Palestinians, haunted by the spectres and failures of post-colonial regimes, caution against the rise of a new bourgeoisie that might seize power. After all, when we erected a neocolonial but self-governing entity, the Palestinian Authority, we ended up being captive to the whims and interests of a new comprador class invested in capturing the feeble Palestinian economy and perpetuating its monopolisation of key sectors; importation and services. Others entertain the notion of uniting the region under the banner of an ethical and religious state, inspired by Islamic teachings, presenting a counter to the eroding edifice of liberalism and individualism – a state that would formulate a new order grounded on the long historic edifice of Arab and Islamic tradition. Some dream of resurrecting the vision of a unified Arab Nation or Greater Syria, while others worry about the prospects of a democratic and equitable state for all – including our once-settlers – as means to reformulate the relations between Israelis and Palestinian in the stretch of land between the river and sea. A few contemplate liberation as the negation of the state concept itself, asking: why create another feeble state when the world craves something more radical, something that expands the human horizon? They suggest that perhaps Palestine should remain a laboratory for novel ideas and groundbreaking social experiments.

Amid the ceaseless flow of images, desires, whims, and intellectual disputes, there emerges my mother's simple, almost absurd question: 'When will they leave us alone?' It slices through the dense fog of future projections, a question both poignant and frustrated. This question, echoed by countless voices, was even articulated by the current president of the Palestinian Authority, who raised the same question in his speech following the widespread protests of May 2021.

After the breakout of the protests, Abu Mazen was compelled to assert his presence and to prove his relevance as a political voice. To ease the tension surrounding his role as a subcontractor of the occupation, he was forced to give a speech, a performative act he otherwise avoids. He hoped that this symbolic display of empathy with the protestors would prevent the protests from turning against the PA itself. A classic political manoeuvre of his brand of pragmatic authoritarianism. He addressed the Palestinian people and the broader world, uttering a phrase that embodied the impatience of my mother in Arabic: 'Enough is enough, get off our chests, get off our chests.' In fact, Abu Mazen used the phrase *Tafah al-Keel* at the opening of his remarks, which can be translated as 'enough is enough', but more literally means 'the measure has overflowed'.

The speech was met with derision and mockery on Palestinian and Arab social media. Users highlighted the paradox of Abbas' position: a leader who, through security cooperation with Israel, permits the continuation of the Israeli occupation in the West Bank and its siege on Gaza. In a world where no power or occupation recedes without resistance, his plea rang hollow, and the president was lampooned. As many Israeli experts on Palestinian affairs would confirm, Abu Mazen's very presence is contingent on the forces that he ostensibly decried in his speech – the US and Israel.

However, the chiasmatic pull of liberation is entangled with an almost opposing yet equally forceful sway, a pull in another direction, especially at the very moment when the world seemed to be changing, and the potential for liberation was not merely a distant musing but enacted, however fleetingly, for dozens of hours beginning on 7 October. For a couple of days in October, it appeared truly possible. The dread and anxiety of liberation were not confined to an intellectual exercise, nor stuck in the domain of fantasy and imagination or only as a matter of intellectual debate. It was real, and like everything real, it was also a test.

Palestinians outside of Gaza woke up on the morning of 7 October to see white Toyota pick-up trucks in the settlements that surround the Gaza Strip carrying Palestinian fighters. At that moment, the words of Lenin struck a chord with me, 'There are decades where nothing happens; and there are weeks when decades happen.' Although in Palestine decades, weeks, minutes and seconds always find a way to collapse on each other. Something radical is always happening somewhere in Palestine. But this was different. It was not the first time Palestinian fighters infiltrated or breached Israeli garrisons and walls, nor the first time Palestinian fighters used paragliders, nor the first time that Palestinians fighters returned to their old villages and the relics of a life that could have been; a long lineage of operations since 1948 did the same. But this time something different was happening, and it is still happening.

In the Palestinian revolutionary tradition, a resistant event holds dual meaning. The word in Arabic for such an event is 'amaliyya, closely translated into 'operation'. This word implies both an event and a process. It suggests that each operation carries the potential for its repetition in time, embedding within it the seeds of continuity and an ability to maintain the capacity to resist, one 'amaliyya bequeaths another in succession. It also insinuates a rupture, a moment where the fabric of colonial power is broken, and assurance of the smooth running of the regime of terror is fractured. An event that also inscribes a long history of stone throwing, spontaneous demonstrations, the excitement of running from soldiers and almost getting caught, the horror of actually getting caught, and the ability to breach walls and jump over the implausible, to win little fights, or throw molotov cocktails at heavily armoured vehicles.

In a class on the modalities of power practised by Israel in Jerusalem, my professor described a scene that perhaps defines the moment when Palestinians come to realise their role as disruptors, as saboteurs, as those who naturally tilt towards the need and role of instigators. In the alleys of the old city, children, with a blend of innocence and audacity, mounted their bicycles and rode through the narrow streets. Like all children, they wanted to make noise. But my professor, a logical explainer of emotions and phenomena, was captivated by their playful teasing of soldiers and policemen. They would ride their bikes, honking and accelerating, almost hitting a policeman, only to stop just before the collision, precisely at that critical moment before zero-distance, where our bodies intimately collide with our heavily armed oppressors and for a moment we are rendered equal – a human colliding with a human.

Perhaps that's exactly why governments are suspicious of this identitarian category called Palestinian. After all, we were the pirates of the skies in the seventies, the instigators of revolts in various neighbouring countries, the organised voice of the era of Arab nationalism and Marxist politics, the orchestrators of 7 October that is bringing the region to the verge of an all out war. We serve as constant reminders for the Arab masses, either tired and exhausted by their own authoritarian regimes and civil wars or immersed in the bountiful spoils of oil money and life under Pax Americana, that something remains to be done, something is not adding up, that the order they live under is oppressive, no matter what they tell themselves.

The question that haunts us more than any other is not, *why do people not rebel?*, but, *why did the rebellion arrive too early or too late?* We assume that rebellion will take place, and when it occurs we only question its timing. Maybe it should have been postponed slightly, as many have proclaimed 'we were not ready for 7 October', or maybe it should have happened a long time ago, but the first question is always why now? The rebellion is weaved into the daily rhythms, yet it also survives as a spectre, as an event that will certainly arrive, either arriving too early or too late, but always arriving; after all, something radical is always happening somewhere in Palestine.

Palestinians, haunting the corridors of power, have always possessed the uncanny ability to overturn the very tables from which they've been systematically excluded, to unsettle the global order that has persistently sought to discard them. But let's not indulge in fetishisation of the figure of Palestinian revolutionaries in their different historical variants. 7 October ruptured the timeline of setbacks and defeats – a singular event in more than seventy years that cracked open, if only for a fleeting moment, the (im)possible dream of liberation. And yet, the expected insurrection in the West Bank stutters, hesitates to fully materialise. In the fractured landscapes of 1948, Palestinian villages remain ensnared in an unyielding cycle of fratricidal violence, barely interrupted, as they confront the insidious rise of organised criminal syndicates – networks that have pulled their youth into the dark abyss of crime. Meanwhile, in Jerusalem, silence cloaks the pain, and that pain in turn conceals the laborious work of denial, deflection, and the myriad modes of forgetting that obscure the horrors of Gaza. And yet, daily rhythms persist, under the weight of heavy breaths.

The questions now proliferate, multiplying in the shadow of an eternal presumption of rebellion – always on the verge, arriving either too early or too late, yet inexorably arriving. Palestinians outside Gaza find themselves grappling with a gnawing inquiry: 'Who are we?' This question reverberates through collective consciousness and the urgency of the Present. It interweaves with the daily rhythms of a life many cling to, the privilege of an Israeli citizenship that has dismembered some, the consumerist spaces of American-style malls and fast food restaurants in the West Bank that have satisfied some, and the privilege of traveling across all of Palestine, from the river to the sea, by holding a Jerusalem residency permit that have satisfied others. The question looms large: 'Do we truly want liberation, after all?'

## The Fears and Anxieties of Bare Life

Palestinians are caught in a bind, encapsulated in the words of a friend who holds Israeli citizenship. He jokingly asked me, 'Do you think that my graduate diploma would count if Israel disappears?' This humorous remark reveals a deeper existential anxiety. At its core, the joke is not merely about the practical concerns of recognition in a post-Israel scenario. It points to a profound unease about the uncertainty that liberation might bring. The diploma, a symbol of personal achievement and societal validation within the existing order, becomes a metaphor for the individual's and the Palestinian collective place and identity in a potentially new and radically different reality. My friend who worked hard to become a doctor and who devoted much of his life to integrate himself in the Israeli hospital where he works, was worried. What will happen to the world Palestinians habituated themselves to, if this world disappears? What of the plans and personal ambitions of a multitude of Palestinians in their various geographies, the homes and houses that were built in villages and towns across historic Palestine?

These hard choices are made amid the everyday normalisation of the existing order, especially for specific classes and categories; the laborers in Israel's first world market, the bureaucrats in the corrupt and collaborationist regime of the PA, the CEO's of international brands boycotted after the eruption of the war such as Coca Cola, KFC and Popeyes. The middle class and upper classes of a Palestinian society that relish in what many friends of mine call the 'privilege' of an Israeli passport, or the privilege of VIP treatment at Israeli checkpoints.

7 October reminded all of them that the world they know, the routines they have cultivated, and the daily rhythms of their lives

can be fractured, and indeed deformed. But yet this is deeper than simply the loss of material or symbolic privileges, or the possibility of upending their daily rhythms. The possibility of liberation, its real opening on 7 October, cuts through the very world many of us have frustratingly and hesitantly adapted ourselves to.

The land between the river and the sea is saturated with anxieties that traverse its entire breadth, manifesting in both the oppressed and the oppressors. There is the existential anxiety of our enemies – those who, in the name of this very anxiety, claim the right to obliterate us, to erase Palestine and Palestinians from the map. This anxiety has been weaponised, transformed into a political currency that galvanises their society into a perpetual state of war, or readiness for war. This anxiety does not simply move in one direction; it oscillates, creating a feedback loop of dread and materialising in Israel's yearly strategic conference where threats are on display and Israel's capabilities are spoken about out in the open. On one side, there is the anxiety to end all wars, an anxiety to achieve peace, especially if peace does not mean total submission to Israel and its hegemony over the entire Middle East supported by American military bases dotted across the region. On the other side, there is the anxiety stemming from the very real prospect of the collapse of the colonial enterprise at the heart of the Arab world. A lingering dread permeates the air in Israel – a fear that all the atrocities, the systematic erasure of a people, the shattered homes, the relentless flow of blood, will one day demand retribution. It's a fear that trembles at the edges of Israeli consciousness, a fear that refuses to be fully acknowledged, yet it pulses beneath the surface. This fear whispers that the reckoning might come, or is coming, that the crimes committed in the name of power and survival will one day rise from the shadows to exact their due. But the settlers and their fears are not the object of this piece.

The existential fear that grips Palestinians is not an abstract anxiety but a visceral terror, anchored in the stark realities of history and present experiences with our current adversaries. This fear is not a nebulous dread but a concrete response to the ongoing brutality that has defined our existence under Israeli domination.

Seventy years after the first widespread ethnic cleansing campaign, the spectre of another, even more intense wave of violence looms large, made palpably real by the daily atrocities and the overarching threat of erasure. The daily massacres, the systematic destruction of Gaza, and the overt declaration of a 'Nakba 2.0' on live television are not just warnings but lived experiences, reinforcing the fear that the horrors of the past are not only being repeated but amplified and that they are here once again in their full force. This is a fear with substance, a fear with a history, and a fear that, given the current trajectory, could very well define our future, or lack thereof.

The second, and paradoxical, anxiety is one that eludes tangible grasp, an anxiety not of an identifiable threat but of the potential cessation of life within the precariousness of a terror regime. It's a dark irony, perhaps a cruel twist, that within Palestinians there festers a fear of losing the very uncertainty that the occupation breeds. This is the anxiety of life without occupation: the unending questions that haunt daily existence. 'Who will be arrested next? Will today's passage through the checkpoint end in my death or arrest? Is that checkpoint even open? Or is it closed so the settlers can pass undisturbed with green plated number plates?' And, perhaps most piercingly, 'who will they kill today?' This is a daily reality that empowers a regime that thrives on unpredictability, leaving its victims in a perpetual state of not knowing, yet paradoxically fearing what might happen if this very habituated unpredictability were to cease.

But here's the rub: if my mother's desperate pleas materialise, if they truly 'fuck off' – who would bear the blame for our inadequacies? Who would we indict for the insidious infiltration of consumerist ideologies, for the stark amplification of material and class fissures? Who would we hold accountable for the surge in criminality, for the rot of political corruption that seems to fester unchallenged? What excuses would my students offer for their tardiness if no checkpoints, no new martyrs obstruct their path? And, more profoundly, what would become of the intricate web of narratives constructed upon the supposed invincibility of Israel, should liberation be achieved? The Palestinian security officer who tortured a fellow fighter, the political figure fattened by the ceaseless flow of CIA funds, the secretary who silently loathed the politician she served – what stories would they craft for themselves, what truths could they possibly speak to us?

The emergence of the Palestinian Authority and the establishment of self-governing mechanisms in the land between the river and the sea provided us with a revealing glimpse into potential futures. Almost immediately following the rise of the PA, the discourse began to shift. Many Palestinian intellectuals urged critical reflection, suggesting that we should no longer use Israel as a hanger for all our problems – an object upon which we project all our issues. The challenges we face, our shortcomings that render us human, the patriarchal structures and social and economic injustices, and the various marginalised groups within our own social fabric are ours to confront and own. Many made the plea; 'please put the occupation aside'.

The Oslo moment, in its dizzying paradox, was the juncture where we found ourselves given permission to blame ourselves for our flaws – yet without the consolation or reality of liberation. It was an epoch of confusion, where the old questions lost their edge, their ability to cut through the noise, and new questions arrived bearing unfamiliar, sometimes disorienting, answers. The occupation, once the omnipresent shadow over our lives, seemed to recede, relegated to the hilltops, the checkpoints that girdled our villages and towns. It was no longer the spectre in our daily lives but became a distant, albeit still menacing, presence – obscured by the ministries that flew the Palestinian flag in Ramallah. This was the historical moment where self-blame became permissible, even normalised, as the occupation slipped from the foreground of our consciousness, becoming the first thing we deliberately chose to obscure in our answers. In this mood of disorientation, where simple is made complex and complexity is simplified, I clung to my own answer: 'occupation might not be everything, but its trace is in everything.'

## Decisions and Regrets

I know a Palestinian girl from Nazareth who, faced with the unbearable calculus of love and legality, decided to turn away from the 'love of her life' because he is marked by the wrong geography – his identity card, that small piece of paper, signifies his origin in the West Bank, and thus, he is expelled from her future. I know another girl who, embroiled in the slow-motion torment of waiting, cuts ties with her beloved, a political prisoner, because she cannot endure the indefinite suspension, the endless deferral of a time when they might actually, physically, be together.

These decisions, fraught with the cruel arithmetic of a political order that scripts the possibilities of intimacy, leaves behind a bitter residue, a sediment of loss and redefinition, of a pragmatism that forces us to betray love, to betray values we thought would endure despite social and daily costs. These are not just choices; but redefinitions of selfhood under duress, where the pragmatic and the heartless coalesce in a stark affirmation of survival at the expense of all that we thought we could be.

These acts, seemingly personal, are deeply political, inscribing on the self the cruel imperatives of a life lived under occupation. They mark a dismemberment – not just of relationships, but of the self from the collective, of love across colonially imposed borders. These choices, forged in the crucible of oppression, resonate with the profound ache of the unchosen, of the possibilities foreclosed, and, in this, they define those who make them in ways that are both brutally real and inescapably political. Liberation would mean an endless stream of regrets, of choices that should have not been taken, of other choices that should have been made. The very frame through which many of the decisions, dreams, life-plans Palestinians made would radically change.

The decision to emigrate, to leave behind a homeland that, once forsaken, might shatter the certainty of ever returning. The choice to declare ourselves a defeated nation and people, a declaration that lingers with heavy political consequences for those who have found solace in the embrace of defeat as a familiar lover and who now attempt to eternalise our defeat. To betray the revolution in the name of the nation as the Palestinian Authority embodies. Or the choice to speak Hebrew more fluently than Arabic, to tether one's existence to the validation of Ashkenazi approval by professing a hesitant loyalty to a state that, by a mere historical accident, did not banish the lives of you or your family.

There is solemnity that comes with the life we know, as brutal and horrific as it is. Palestinians have much to lose, and a very historic opening. The real and tangible feeling that Israel is defeatable comes with an endless stream of possible regret for choices made under the stress of an existing and seemingly all powerful order. Palestinians have recreated themselves endlessly under the existing order, and in many instances their choices were choices that dismembered and evacuated the real potential for liberation.

**Resistance and the Courage to Be**
A friend of mine left Palestine, seeking a place more relaxed and quiet and less uncertain. This friend went through his own political breakdown after 7 October and its aftermath, calling me to discuss the catastrophe in Gaza – the endless flow of blood, the visceral return of what he insisted is a new Nakba. I must confess, I was never fond of the overuse of the word. I told him, what happened and is happening in Gaza is indeed a disaster, but it's not yet a Nakba. He was surprised by my words, 'What do you mean?' The Nakba assumes defeat, I explained. As a concept and historic experience, it is intertwined with the notion of defeat. It was both a disaster, leading to the destruction of homes, villages, and worlds, and a defeat, in so far as Israel was able to birth itself on the ruins of our lives. This disaster might become a Nakba, but it's not a Nakba yet. In fact, the disaster could induce a slow yet irreversible process of Zionist unraveling. By the end of our conversation, he confessed to me 'I just don't believe that liberation is possible, after all. I am afraid of liberation. What does this make me!'

At a recent conference held at Birzeit University, a critical perspective was raised regarding the events of 7 October. The argument put forth was that the operation should have been subject to more thorough planning, with a comprehensive political program in place and it should have anticipated the response from Israel, which has since escalated into a full-scale genocidal campaign. To plan out and execute an operation, and to anticipate reactions, and to advance a political program. The burdening of any action with a methodical, calculated scheme that anticipates every possible scenario belies the inherent fragility and fogginess of war. It is always easier to critique in hindsight. This burdening appears more as a manifesto against 7 October itself rather than a critique of its specific edges or execution or the responses of the adversary. The more you impose an overwhelming burden on any policy, act, or action, the more you are implicitly mounting an argument against its viability, demanding from it what it does not necessarily answer.

The slow dismemberment and unbecoming of Palestine, coupled with the emergence of new modes of existence under the sovereignty of Israel or as extension of *Pax Americana*, marked prior to 7 October, and a similar logic was prevailing in Gaza. Hamas concluded agreements to allow more workers to enter Israel, and the entire possible future looked as if it was centered on material and economic survival. It is paradoxical that at the very nadir of Arab and Palestinian weakness – amid disunity, collaboration, accommodation, the grind of everyday survival, normalisation, and the global indifference – the most significant Palestinian ʿamaliyya materialised. It was a moment that dared to disrupt the script, injecting chaos into the very marrow of stagnation, compelling a re-engagement with the cause by proposing a solution – one that was as incendiary as it was unexpected. The weakest moment, birthing the most potent act; a defiance of history's deterministic whispers.

The operation was nothing short of a seismic rupture in the geopolitical and psychological landscape, a moment that shattered the carefully constructed perceptions of the imperial managerial class and Israel's own myth of invincibility. It wasn't just an act; it was an opening – a door flung wide open to challenge the status quo. This singular event triggered a cascade of shifts: psychic, social, economic, political, and strategic. It was, in essence, a manifestation of the courage to be, a defiant affirmation of existence in spite of all the sacrifices it also demands. Paul Tillich writes that courage is the affirmation of an essential nature. It is not surprising, therefore, that at this critical juncture many in Palestine are asking themselves, 'who are we?' And, perhaps also, 'what has become of us?'

RICHARD SEYMOUR

# The Atrocity Exhibition: On Perpetrators

'It is clear to everyone today that the right-wing was right regarding the political issue and regarding the Palestinian issue. Today it is simple, you go anywhere and they tell you to destroy them. In the kibbutz, they tell you to destroy them. My friends at the state attorney's office, who've fought with me in political issues, in debates, said to me: "Moshe, it's clear that we need to destroy all Gazans."'
– MK Moshe Saada, *Channel 14*, 2 January 2024

I.
What can the captives of Sde Teiman have thought when, on 29 July 2024, protesters flooded the military base? Lying bound, blindfolded and face down on the floor, having suffered torture and rape at the hands of their jailers, they would have heard the assembled crowd riot not for prisoner freedom but for jailer impunity.

Earlier that month, Israeli soldiers from a unit known as Force 100 at the Sde Teiman military prison in the Negev had dragged a prisoner up from the floor, concealed him from CCTV behind a wall of shields, and gang-raped him. What they did left him unable to walk, with a ruptured intestine, severe injuries to his anus and lungs, and broken ribs.

The assault was hardly unique. Sde Teiman is one of the worst of what B'TSelem calls a 'network of torture camps' run by the Israeli military. Prisoners spend their days blindfolded, shackled, often in diapers. They are routinely beaten, sleep-deprived, burned with cigarettes, electrocuted, held in stress positions or sodomised with blunt objects. Palestinians call places like Sde Teiman 'death camps': as US journalist Alex Press points out, nine prisoners died in Guantanamo over twenty years, compared to sixty detainees killed in Israeli prisons over a period of ten months.

The prisoner was treated in a civilian hospital, where staff leaked details of his injuries to Physicians for Human Rights. The CCTV footage of the assault was broadcast by Israel's *Channel 12*. On 29 July, evidently in an effort to contain the diplomatic fall-out, Israeli military police were sent to the base to arrest nine soldiers. As *CNN*'s Jeremy Diamond put it, this marked 'an extraordinarily rare pursuit of accountability at the Sde Teiman facility'.

The soldiers barricaded themselves in the facility and pepper-sprayed those sent to arrest them. When news of the arrests broke, protesters – including soldiers from Force 100 and Knesset members like Heritage Secretary Amichai Eliyahu of Jewish Power and Likud's Tally Gotliv – broke into the base and occupied in protest while police looked on impassively. Protesters accused the Military Advocate General of being a lover of 'Nukhba'. (Technically, Nukhba references the naval unit of Hamas's military wing. But, as B'TSelem documents, the prisoners are mostly civilians picked up on a variety of pretexts, sometimes simply for expressing sympathy for the plight of their fellow Palestinians. 'Nukhba' has become a term of racist contempt.)

When Israeli rightists speak about the torture of Palestinians, nothing, not even their relish, puts a dent in their sense of wounded rectitude. Gotliv, broadcast live from the protest, bitterly gurns in a manner sorely redolent of Unionist politicians during the 'Troubles'.

Those who 'raped, slaughtered and abused our people have found a new method', she rages. 'They go and whine and snitch that some soldier touched them.' In the television studios, *Israel Yalom* journalist Yehuda Schlesinger says the 'only problem' with the rape is that it is 'not standard state policy' because 'in general they deserve it, and this is great revenge'. A mask-wearing soldier from Force 100 is invited to a panel discussion to berate the journalists for releasing 'edited' footage. In the Knesset, Likud politician Hanoch Milwidsky stertorously urges his colleagues to go on a legislative 'strike' until this 'crazy' situation is resolved. Asked by Palestinian legislator Ahmad Tibi if it is permissible to insert an explosive into a person's rectum, Milwidsky shouts: 'Yes! If he is a Nukhba, everything is legitimate to do! Everything!' Among the general public, 65 per cent of Israeli Jews oppose prosecution of the soldiers, just as they had previously opposed the prosecution of Elor Azaria, caught murdering a Palestinian man in Hebron in 2016. In such a militarised society, impunity is a national value.

It is vanishingly unlikely that any soldier will be prosecuted. The main culprit, Meir Ben-Shitrit, was released early. His interrogators, he said, were 'really nice … You see the support … With a hand on their heart, like, telling you "thank you"'.

> 'A second later I accidentally ran over him with a Merkava Mark 4 tank weighing 65 tons, 1500 horse power :)'
> – Israeli soldier, Daniel Lurie, posting footage of a dead Palestinian, 4 March 2024

II.
It is the world's first live-streamed genocide. Its victims, says International Court of Justice prosecutor Blinne Ní Ghrálaigh, are 'broadcasting their own destruction in real time'. Might it also be the world's first shameless genocide?

For while Palestinians document their daily terrors in the wan hope of eliciting aid from the outside world, Israeli soldiers gleefully post evidence of their own war crimes. They can be seen snickering as they blow up civilian buildings, pawing through the possessions of murdered or expelled Palestinians, giggling as they parade in stolen lingerie or dress up as a Palestinian school kid, and performing skits in the desolate, dust-caked ruins of playgrounds and classrooms as though to affirm the old hymn of the Israeli far-right: 'there are no children left in Gaza'.

Their leaders, political and military, have declared their genocidal intent so audibly – remembrance of 'Amalek', fighting 'human animals,' making Gaza a 'slaughterhouse', erasing Gaza 'from the face of the earth', no 'innocents' in Gaza – that even the cautious ICJ felt compelled to grant South Africa's application to prosecute the state of Israel on charges under the Genocide Convention. Their civilian supporters rave at the Karam Abu Salem crossing to block aid trucks trying to relieve a population on the brink of starvation and epidemic. They riot for impunity for torturers and rapists. They swagger and strut, like children imitating the fabled omnipotence of adults, soliciting, and seemingly revelling in, global disgust.

We cannot be touched, they seem to say, by the shaming gaze of the world. An example of this sort of gaze is given by Jean-Paul Sartre in *Being and Nothingness*: the person caught peeping through the keyhole, once caught up in the act, is suddenly touched in the core of his being. The inefficacy of this gaze, Sheldon George argues in *Trauma and Race*, is terribly dangerous: the person without shame is capable of limitless savagery. And that is exactly what is implied by the apparent impotence, both in Israel and its patron states, of the once regnant discourses of law, democracy and human rights.

And yet, there is also a curious game of revelation and concealment in Israeli public discourse, of flaunting it and burying it. There has been, amid all the macho braggadocio and public sadism, an extraordinary degree of official censorship. Most foreign press have been prohibited from entering Gaza. An unprecedented 116 journalists, mostly Palestinian, were assassinated in just ten months. Israel shut down *Al Jazeera*'s office, blocked its websites and outlawed the use of its footage by domestic channels. Within Israel, journalist Anat Saragusti writes, the IDF line rules: 'Hebrew-speaking Israelis watching television news are not exposed at all to what's going on in Gaza'. Domestically, the state has cracked down on what meagre, generally apolitical dissent there is – since Operation Cast Lead, Israeli wars have been supported by at least 90 per cent of Jewish Israelis. Nor has Israel spared any effort to get social industry bosses to extirpate pro-Palestinian sentiment on their platforms: Meta has a pattern of assenting to 81 per cent of requests received from Israel to remove content, and Human Rights Watch has documented pervasive censorship of Palestine content on both Facebook and Instagram.

Even those cackling memes posted by Israeli soldiers generally don't document their most serious crimes, from the sniping of children and grandmothers, to flour massacres, to the mass graves discovered at hospitals destroyed by the IDF. And they appear to be designed more for a domestic Israeli audience than for a world that 'wouldn't understand', a way of soliciting complicity through enjoyment: 'blutkitt' as Nuremberg prosecutor Leo Frank called it. For international audiences, there is denial: 'there is no limit to how much we do to protect innocent civilians', a Kahanist soldier tweets in English. In Hebrew, responding to an Israeli drawing attention to the sniping of civilians, he brags: 'I am proud to serve in the most valuable army in the world.' These videos are, moreover, tacitly licensed from above. The IDF, rather than treating such production as embarrassing exuberances to be controlled, busied itself with producing its own gore porn through an unofficial and initially disavowed Telegram channel known as '72 Virgins'. This was, if anything, more explicit than the material produced by the soldiers. 'Burning their own mother … You won't believe the video we got! You can hear the crunch of their bones.' 'Exterminating the cockroaches … exterminating the Hamas rats'. 'Garbage juice!!!! Another dead terrorist!! You have to watch it with the sound, you'll die laughing.' Only after several months of indifference, and only following the ICJ's provisional ruling against Israel, did the IDF leadership finally urge soldiers 'not to film revenge videos'.

The soldiers, the military leaders, the journalists and politicians behind this genocide yearn to shout it from the rooftops, but dare not tell the whole truth. They want to brag, while also protesting their innocence. This is a vital clue not to take at face value the Israeli performance of invulnerability: the shamelessness of Israel's genocide is far more contradictory than it appears.

> 'To wipe off the memory of Amalek! To take revenge on the gentiles!'
> – Israeli soldier, upon blowing up a Palestinian house, 4 July 2024

III.

Genocide is habit-forming. Erwin Staub, in his work on the psychology of perpetrators, points to a 'continuum of destruction' wherein annihilation is prepared by 'a history of aggression'. As perpetrators hurt their victims, they form the dispositions giving rise to motives for further killing. Having killed makes it easier to kill, just as being victimised makes one easier to victimise. A participant in My Lai quoted by Robert Jay Lifton in *Home From the War* says: if we shoot and bomb them every night, 'how can they be worth so much?'

A population must be prepared for the psychological rigours of an extermination campaign through a long process of brutalisation. It must also be willing to bear the costs. For, whatever their formal rationales, genocides are expensive outbursts of ensanguined exuberance. As Staub points out, comparing the Cambodian, Armenian and Nazi genocides, they impair the fabric of society, destroy essential functions and waste desperately needed resources. Raul Hilberg draws attention to the financial strain of the Holocaust and its burden on a 'bureaucratic machine that was already straining to fulfil the requirements of the battlefronts'. A study of the macroeconomic toll of genocides by Dimitrios Soudis et al shows that the destruction of total factor productivity leads to plunging activity in the first years and no recovery thereafter as long as destruction goes on. As one would expect, Israel's economy has been severely damaged by its genocidal war, its credit-rating downgraded, and tens of thousands of businesses made bankrupt. The total costs of the war may exceed $55 billion according to the Bank of Israel. Were it not for $17.9 billion in aid from the United States through the first year of war, the situation would be worse. Tellingly, none of this was sufficient to diminish support for the genocide.

The process by which a population is so conditioned is sometimes called 'genocidal priming'. According to Alexander Laban Hinton's study of the Cambodian genocide, *Why Did They Kill?*, this is enabled by cultural models of 'disproportionate revenge' which can be activated in the moment of mass killing. Hinton describes the popular Cambodian story of Tum Teav, in which King Reamea exacts revenge on a disobedient governor by obliterating seven generations of his family line. In the Gaza genocide, the Biblical story of Amalek plays an analogous role. For while it hardly created Israel's militarism, pervasive racism and intensely violent relations with Palestinians and the wider Middle East, in this genocide it has functioned as a symbolic node: gathering, channelling and justifying the society's killing energy.

'You must remember what Amalek has done to you, says our Holy Bible', Benjamin Netanyahu reminded the Israeli public in his speech announcing the invasion of Gaza on 28 October. 'And we do remember.' In a letter sent to soldiers and officers five days later, he repeated the reference. Netanyahu, a sophisticated operator, would have understood how the Israeli Right and, more importantly, the soldiers would take this. According to the Bible, the Amalekites were a nomadic tribe inhabiting the Negev and Sinai, who had ambushed the Israelites on their exodus from Egypt. Ignoring all customary laws of war, they attacked without cause and targeted the weakest first. In the passage from Exodus (17:14-16) referenced by Netanyahu, the Israelites are commanded to 'blot out' all memory of Amalek. Not once, but repeatedly: 'the Lord will fight Amalek generation after generation'. The command is repeated in Deuteronomy (24:17–19) with the injunction: 'Don't forget!' One is to remember to blot out the memory. In 1 Samuel 15:3, King Saul is ordered to destroy Amalek, and to 'slay both man and woman, infant and suckling, ox and sheep, camel and ass'. When Saul disobeys by allowing the Amalek king to survive, he forfeits his kingdom and the prophet Samuel hacks the king to pieces in a public square.

Biblical sources yield to interpretive commentary, and it is not incumbent on any believer to construe this as a divine command to commit genocide. It may be interpreted, Israeli philosopher Avi Saga points out, as 'the embodiment of a metaphysical struggle taking place in the divine world'. Or, as Joshua Cohen notes, Amalek may be construed as the 'spirit of military aggression', so that believers are enjoined to 'forsake the ways of war'. The Israeli and Jewish Right is more literalist: the Palestinians are the descendants of Amalek. 'The Arabs engage in typical Amalek behavior', Likud's Moshe Feiglin told former IDF soldier Jeffrey Goldberg. 'I can't prove this genetically, but this is the behavior of Amalek.' Benzi Lieberman, chairman of the council of settlers, was no less blunt. 'The Palestinians are Amalek! We will destroy them. We won't kill them all. But we will destroy their ability to think as a nation. We will destroy Palestinian nationalism.' 'Amalek is simply reality', writes the American Orthodox rabbi Daniel Lappin, scoffing at the 'doctrine of "proportional response"'. 'There are nations whose ideas are so evil that we cannot live with them – either they survive, or we do.' Shortly before Netanyahu's speech, Likud MK and former *Israel Yalom* editor Boaz Bismuth had raged against 'the cruel and monstrous "innocent citizens" from Gaza'. It was, he said, 'forbidden to show mercy to cruel people, there is no place for any humanitarian gesture – the memory of Amalek must be protested.'

After Netanyahu's speech, the destruction of Amalek immediately had a practical relevance. This was understood by the Israeli soldiers singing and chanting 'we know our motto: there are no uninvolved civilians' and calling 'to wipe off the seed of Amalek'. It was grasped by Colonel Yogev Bar-Sheshet, deputy head of COGAT, who told soldiers: 'Whoever returns here, if they return here after, will find scorched earth. No houses, no agriculture, no nothing. They have no future'. Colonel Erez Eshel likewise exhorted: 'Vengeance is a great value. There is vengeance over what they did to us … This place will be a fallow land. They will not be able to live here'. Yair Ben David, Commander in the 2908th Battalion, referenced another Biblical story of revenge when he said that the IDF had 'entered Beit

Hanoun and did there as Shimon and Levi did in Nablus.' As South Africa's application to the International Court of Justice points out, the relevant passage from Genesis (34:25) explains: 'Simeon and Levi ... took each his sword, came upon the city unmolested, and slew all the males.' All of Gaza, David said, 'should resemble Beit Hanoun'.

Soldiers were urged on from all sides. Finance minister Belazel Smotrich urged them to 'blot out the remembrance of Amalek'. The deputy speaker of the Knesset wrote of 'erasing the Gaza Strip from the face of the Earth'. On the Israeli television channel, Kan, children sang a 'Friendship Song' about the 'annihilation' of Gaza. On the eve of invasion, soldiers were addressed by a 95 year old veteran of the Nakba, who said: 'wipe out their memory, their families, mothers and children'. Israeli president, Isaac Herzog, gave him a certificate of honour. Right-wing rabbis urged soldiers to take pleasure in the destruction. 'War', said rabbi Yigal Levinstein 'is a great thing.' Early in the assault, IDF rabbi Amichai Freedman said that, apart from the Israeli dead and captured, the war had given him 'the happiest month of [his] life'. Soldiers must loot, said rabbi Yitzchak Sheilat, from the settlement of Ma'ale Adumim, because 'all the spoils must go to the king'. An Israeli soldier stationed in the north told *Ha'aretz* that a settler rabbi had said 'we need to destroy and shoot everyone', and that the rules of engagement were 'a distorted Western morality'. Orthodox rabbi Shmuel Eliyahu exhorted soldiers to ignore 'the rules of war', since 'Arabs in Gaza do not observe international conventions.' Here was a veritable, collective foghorn of genocidal priming, blasted from every quarter of church and state.

'If you gave me a button to just erase Gaza tomorrow, every single living being in Gaza would no longer be living tomorrow, I would press it in a second. I think most Israelis probably would.'
– Israeli podcaster Eytan Weinstein, 3 September 2024.

IV.

Such priming would be unnecessary if soldiers could be trusted to spontaneously avail themselves of the pleasures of transgression. Even in war, as military historian Richard Holmes documents in *Acts of War*, soldiers are often reluctant to kill the enemy. In Israel, while outright refusal to serve is a rare and valuable commodity, there are historical patterns of 'grey refusal' where soldiers persuade their commanders to let them off an operation for which they are not psychically prepared.

Even those who are politically ready to murder may still need permission to ignore their conscience, and assurance that they will not be personally culpable. It is vital for Israel's war on Gaza that there are no written rules of engagement. Field commanders and soldiers enjoy tremendous latitude in interpreting and implementing what are nonetheless military orders. What is mandatory, as Raul Hilberg suggests in his analysis of Nazi perpetrators, is 'also a mandate', containing 'broad authorisations'. The bureaucratic killer, for instance, 'clung to his orders' less out of fear of superiors than because 'he feared his own conscience': hence the 'many requests for "authorisation"'. This enables the murderers to say they had 'no choice', that their actions had nothing to do with personal malice, and that they were conscientious professionals coping with a difficult situation.

Such, indeed, is the familiar rationalisation. At South Africa's Truth and Reconciliation Commission, the apartheid state's torturers and hired assassins saw themselves as committed professionals waging war against an evil, godless, 'revolutionary onslaught'. Yet, reviewing the testimonies in *Violent Accounts*, Robert Kraft points to the latitude afforded those waging war on the anti-apartheid movement. Captain Jeffrey Benzien, for example, referred in his testimony to the 'unwritten word', the implicit, privately given instructions that allowed 'any method': including his own preferred method of water torture. Hilberg, likewise, describes how many of the instructions given in the preparation of the Final Solution were delivered privately, verbally, and not in official headquarters. The logic is that of the dirty secret, binding superiors and subordinates in a programme of atrocity, both legalised and illicit. In Gaza, there is 'no direct order to take revenge', a refusenik observes. But day to day decision-making is not determined by overt orders, but by what those orders are tacitly understood to mean. 'You fill in the blanks', another refusenik observed. If shooting was 'forbidden' on certain humanitarian routes but not expressly forbidden elsewhere, then it was 'permitted'. Israel insists that all its operations are signed off by attorneys from the IDF's Dabla unit, the international law department. This assiduous legalisation only subverts the law's usual role in sublimating the drives, turning them into the empty rituals of the death-drive.

Take, for example, the routine destruction of Palestinian homes in Gaza. One of the main justifications for this is that once a house has been used by the IDF, they must leave behind no 'intelligence markings'. Therefore, since soldiers are ordered not to leave the house as it was found, they burn them down. This, apparently acting on a narrow military rationale, also facilitates the informally stated goal of reducing Gaza to 'scorched earth', 'fallow land'. Or consider the forced starvation in Gaza, whose 'rigour, scale and speed ... surpasses any other case of man-made famine in the last seventy-five years' according to Alex de Waal. The siege on Gaza began following Israeli 'disengagement' in 2005. After which, in the words of Ariel Sharon advisor Doc Weisglass, Israel put 'the Palestinians on a diet'. The resulting de-development, plunging 80 per cent of Gaza's population into poverty, destroying the sewage infrastructure and leaving 4 per cent of the fresh water drinkable, was expedited by the use of a literal 'calorie counter' to precisely calibrate how much aid would get in. The stranglehold was further tightened by rules prohibiting 'dual use' items, a category interpreted extremely broadly by soldiers inspecting aid trucks.

Since defence minister Yoav Gallant announced a total siege on Gaza's 'human animals' in October 2023, the policy of starvation has been organised through these same bureaucratic rules. Israel claims to be using the same list of banned items that it has since 2008. But when aid workers ask for clarity on what is and is not allowed, Israeli authorities reportedly say it is 'an individual determination'. Soldiers, thus instructed, are equipped with 'broad authorisations' to create the state of biological emergency in which, as they know, the starving body takes forty days to die, eating its fat reserves, muscle mass, and heart to keep the brain alive. The brain finally eats itself. The body sickens and dies of what the World Organisation Against Torture calls 'torture in slow motion'. The moral hardness of each decision to deny a truckload of aid for containing a 'dual use' item like scissors, abetted by orders from above, flows into a strategy demanded by Netanyahu of senior advisor Rod Dermer: to 'thin' Gaza's population 'to a minimum'.

> 'I am unable to sleep if I do not see houses being destroyed in Gaza. What do I say? More houses, more buildings. I want to see more of them destroyed. I want there to be nothing for them to return to.'
> – Israeli journalist Shimon Rifkin, *Channel 14*, 13 December 2023

V.
Not all perpetrators are equal, or equally engaged, and the psychological challenges that come with killing in the field can be avoided by gamifying the slaughter. In the first weeks of war before the ground invasion, Israel relied almost entirely on aerial bombardment guided by the AI targeting system 'Habsora' ('Gospel').

With inputs from intelligence sources, satellite imagery and mobile phone signals, the system routinely generated hundreds of fresh targets. The 'power targets' were those that did the most civilian damage: a high-rise building where a junior government official is said to live, a university, a bank, or a government building. During the first five days, Israel trooped a total of 6,000 bombs weighing 4,000 tons on Gaza, half of them aimed at 'power targets'.

The automation of death has been a goal of the US military since 2004. The aim has been to progress from 'man-in-the-loop' technology, where a human decides what the technology does, to 'man-on-the-loop' system where a human can intervene but does not regularly make decisions, to full automation. In full automation, AI would have to distinguish between civilians and combatants. Even the Geneva Conventions cannot specify such a distinction, requiring that belligerents use common sense – which, of course, AI cannot even simulate. Habsora is man-in-the-loop automation: commanders decide which of the machine's targets are to be obliterated. The feted precision of AI targeting has been shown to be a myth: a target recognition programme that was claimed to have 90 per cent accuracy turned out, with a small tweak, to be closer to 25 per cent accuracy. This does not even take into account the 'reference class' problem, where everything depends on what data is deemed relevant enough to feed to the machine, and how its elements are classified. The subjective inputs are inevitably contaminated by ideology and guesswork.

The chief tactical virtue of automation is not accuracy, but the inhuman speed with which it establishes probabilistic connections between datasets, enabling the aggressor to, as Maj. Matthew Volk of the US Air Force puts it, 'create multiple dilemmas across multiple domains at an overwhelming speed'. Its virtue is damage, not accuracy: the targeting system provides a pseudo-rational occasion for attacking, but the precise target matters little when the weapon is a heavy munition causing destruction over a wide radius. As IDF spokesperson Rear Admiral Daniel Hagari put it: 'right now we're focused on what causes maximum damage'. The overt rationale is, per the 'Dahiya doctrine' – named after a Beirut neighbourhood that the IDF destroyed in 2006 – to 'create a shock' in Palestinian civil society by destroying infrastructure and causing mass death, leading them to 'put pressure on Hamas'.

Here, at last, is the automated apotheosis of the doctrines of Italian Fascist General Giulio Douhet. For Douhet, since war in an era of mass democracy was between peoples, the most expedient way to win was to destroy the civilian infrastructure and terrorise the population of the enemy. As Thomas Hippler points out, in *Bombing the People*, this wasn't simply a nasty emanation of fascist will-to-power: it could be traced directly to the ideas of the nineteenth-century pro-colonial Left. Tested in the colonial frontiers, by the French in Syria and the British in Iraq, Yemen, Egypt and Palestine, the use of terror bombing from the air recommended itself because it cost substantially less than ground forces. It formed the basis of the area bombing of Dresden and Hamburg in World War II, as well as similar practices by the US in Korea and Vietnam, and is the original source of the Dahiya doctrine. And the defence, from Italy in Ethiopia, to the US in Vietnam and Israel in Gaza, is always that the enemy has illegally ensconced its operations in the civilian population.

As a factor in perpetrator psychology, two things about digital Douhetism are instantly arresting. First, it does not work on its own terms. The historical record, documented in gruelling detail by Marilyn B Young in *Bombing Civilians* and Robert Pape in *Bombing to Win*, is clear on this point. The idea that punishing civilians to the point of social and economic collapse will lead to a civilian revolt against the leadership and suit for peace is illogical – civilians tend to despise the bombers, not their leaders, and practise stoical resilience, not collapse – and empirically unsubstantiated. Why, then, continue to do it? The question only makes sense if we assume that the goals are rationally coercive. The orectic conditions of warfare for any national ruling class, especially genocidal warfare, include surplus cruelty as an end. All enemies, as phobic objects, elicit both desire and disgust, and the Palestinians are a particularly *extimate* enemy for Israeli society: its constitutive other. In any apartheid society, the felt plenitude of racial superiority depends on the existence of those who are most hated. Without their phobogenic objects, those racially marked bodies who are supposedly poor-in-world, the rulers would face a terrifying impoverishment of their own being. There would be nothing to sustain their superiority. They need those whom they most want to destroy. The flame of Zionist messianism may well have flickered out decades ago were it not for the recalcitrant and evidently unbearable existence of the Palestinian people. The advantage of digital Douhetism is that it delegates this libidinal economy to a series of objectified statistical operations, giving it the appearance of a militarily rational determination.

Second, just as the other violent abstractions of capital relieve agents of responsibility for denying someone insurance or a mortgage, AI bombing abstracts the bombers away from the killing situation. The 'self-traumatised perpetrator', made famous by Lifton's studies, is averted when perpetrators operate a game-like interface, manipulating fungible digital objects. The computer scientist Noel Sharkey describes the moral effect of the resultant '"Playstation" mentality', quoting a young drone 'pilot' based in Nevada. 'I thought killing somebody would be this life changing experience', he said. 'And then I did it, and I was like "All right, whatever."' It was 'like squashing an ant': 'you kill somebody and it's like "All right, let's go get some pizza."' The operator, spared the laborious task of reckoning with his victims, exempted from weighing ideological justifications that have been rendered as a series of technical, algorithmic functions, can kill without emotional involvement – and then get some pizza.

> 'They had a ball! Obviously they can't say that today! Nobody failed to turn up ... I want to repeat that people today give a false impression when they say that the actions against the Jews were carried out unwillingly.'
> – Krakow police officer, quoted in Ernst Klee et al, *The Good Old Days*.

VI.

And yet, manifestly, Israeli society and its military do not fully want to disown their libidinal involvement in the genocide.

Consider the wild, wild joys available to the well-built young men who occupy most of the combat positions in Gaza. The shots of adrenaline, intoxicating sensations of omnipotence, the comradeship, the singing, the incondite wisecracks, the explosions, the occasional brush with death, the technological priapism, the freedom to decide who gets to pass, cowering and desolate, with a mere insult or roughing up, and who gets to die, and all of it officially sanctioned as justified revenge: these lads will never again experience anything like it, whether on patrol or scratching for a living, a purpose, or a scintilla of political hope in an increasingly unequal, pessimistic and precarious society.

The Israeli Defence Force is still a draft army, and to that extent still the 'people's army' of David Ben Gurion's design. It is, arguably, the last recognised social contract in Israel, the surety of its herrenvolk democracy. It structures the education of young Israelis who, explains Haim Bresheeth-Zabner in *An Army Like No Other*, are inducted into the collective memory and myths of the Zionist state from the age of eight. Their military training begins at the age of fourteen 'when high school kids join the Gadna (acronym for Youth Battalions)', until they are ready for the draft at the age of eighteen. As a draft army, it guarantees employment to young Israelis, the median age of the grunts being just twenty. It doesn't offer much remuneration for draftees: even on the frontline the monthly wage is 2,400 NIS, which is just over five hundred pounds. What it does offer is a matchless opportunity for hell-raising adventure.

In the ordinary routine of patrols, arrests and manning checkpoints, boredom and moral numbness are combined. The rituals of oppression identify the Palestinians as a threat to be managed and punished, but there is only sporadic opportunity for recreational harassment or killings. A junior commander, explains Erella Grassiani in *Soldiering Under the Occupation*, may order soldiers to hold Palestinians at a checkpoint for a few hours, for no better reason than to break the monotony. In recent years, soldiers in the West Bank have been able to enliven their day by forming irregular militias with settlers and assaulting a Palestinian community whose land and resources are wanted by the colonists.

Now, at last, they are in a war where almost anything goes, where there is no shaming gaze. There is a tremendous surge of omnipotence. 'Imagine how powerful I felt all the time', an Israeli perpetrator of atrocities during the First Intifada once explained. 'I could kick anyone in the head and nobody would talk. I could do anything ... The moment you pass from Israel to Gaza you are the law, you're God.' 'The bottom line, when I think about it', another says, 'it's like I was a Nazi.' This sense of power is revealing because, relative to today, the soldiers crushing the Intifada were limited in what they could do. The Israeli Prime Minister Yitzhak Rabin had exhorted soldiers to break the Palestinians' bones, and in the first three months of the uprising Israeli soldiers fired more than a million bullets to quell it. Yet, in other ways, as in the use of non-lethal plastic or rubber-coated bullets, their kinetic range would be regarded as miserly by today's soldiers. Neve Gordon's conceptualisation of the occupation partly explains the shift. Prior to Oslo, Israel was more directly engaged in the daily running of Palestinians' lives, attempting to drain the energies of Palestinian nationalism through control of welfare, health and economy as much as through direct violence: in Foucauldian terms, its dominant mode of power was disciplinary. Especially since the 'disengagement' from Gaza, Israel has reverted to a form of sovereign power in which the West Bank and Gaza have been ghettoised and policed with more lethal, long-range violence.

Today's soldiers thus go to war much more empowered with death-dealing capacities. In Gaza, there is no need for rubber coating on the bullets. In the West Bank, meanwhile, soldiers and settlers have been given the opportunity to escalate their pogromist offensive: B'TSelem has documented hundreds of attacks on West Bank Palestinian communities since 7 October 2023. Among those fighting today is a much higher share of those classified by Yoel Elizur and Nuphar Yishay-Krien, in their analysis of the Intifada's suppression, as 'ideologically violent'. Jewish Israelis of age to join the military are overwhelmingly right-wing, overwhelmingly opposed to any Palestinian state, and over-represented among both the *dati leumi* (religious right) and the secular far-right. What Lifton calls the 'atrocity-producing situation' does not so much cause, as liberate, their appetite for destruction.

> 'Within a year we will annihilate everyone'
> – Childrens' choir organised by Israeli propaganda group, *The Civil Front*, 19 November 2023

VII.
In sanctioned interviews, soldiers are strenuously well-mannered, calm and reflective. They express their humane concern for the Palestinians, before briskly mentioning the usual flaccid rationalisations. An Israeli 'leftist' soldier tells *CNN* that it is a 'complex situation' and he favours a two-state settlement. Nonetheless, he is '100 per cent sure' that he is 'on the right side of history' and 'trying to defend people' in fighting this war. 'Nobody wants to kill an innocent civilian, an innocent woman, an innocent child', another soldier wearily explains, 'but if we have to fight a war, there are casualties.' Strikingly, interviewees never appear to have witnessed or participated in any war crimes. None of them, for example, had stripped, tied and shot or beheaded any of the hundreds of bodies discovered at mass graves at the Nasser and Al-Shifa hospitals, or any of 140 mass graves counted by Euro-Med Human Rights Monitor. None of them had run over zip-tied Palestinians with their tanks, or sniped any of the children seen by Dr Mark Perlmutter with 'dead-centre' shots to the head. A non-commissioned officer tells the *Guardian*'s Jason Burke, 'I didn't see dead children or women and that helped a lot'. Whatever the literal accuracy of this claim, which there is reason to doubt, the vast majority of those killed by Israeli soldiers are women and children.

Perpetrator testimony is notorious for scotomising distressing details. Kraft describes the role of benign self-concept, among the apartheid state's perpetrators, in shaping and deleting memory. An example of this in Gaza would be the soldiers' astonishment, during the November 2023 ceasefire, when civilians emerged from their 'basements': 'We didn't even know they were there.' That they did not 'know', even though they had every reason to know, is significant. And, in a case of broken kettle logic, another soldier explained that anyone who remained behind after evacuation orders was a legitimate target anyway: 'What am I going to think? That they're not supporters of Hamas? What are they doing there then?'

Israeli refuseniks, and those who have broken from the 'displaced responsibility' and 'empty justifications' that Gillian Slovo discerned in South Africa's perpetrators, tell a different story. There is 'total freedom of action', explains a soldier to *+972 magazine*. If there is 'even a feeling of threat', there is 'no need to explain – you just shoot.' If someone is looking out of a window, you shoot. Even if you're 'bored', you shoot. 'Shoot a lot, even for no reason', another explains, 'anyone who wants to shoot, no matter what the reason, shoots'. Commanders encourage it. The shooting is 'unrestricted', 'crazy': shooting with 'machine guns, tanks, and mortars', everything goes. They shoot 'as they please with all their might'. 'It's permissible to shoot everyone, a young girl, an old woman.' Even they, however, occasionally offer familiar rationalisations, involving the iniquity of the enemy: Hamas members 'walk around without their weapons' making it impossible to distinguish between civilian and combatant. This is redolent of the 'unfairness' experienced by US troops in Vietnam: 'We give the medical supplies and they come and kick our ass'. As though their enemies were supposed to make it easy for them.

In his analysis of US atrocities in Vietnam, Lifton draws attention to the 'all-encompassing absurdity and moral inversion' experienced by troops responding to an 'informal message ... to kill just about everyone'. This 'all-encompassing absurdity' may, though, be deferred for as long as the killers believe in the ideological justifications for what they do. The troops in Vietnam suffered in part because they scarcely believed the official story that they were there to defend a people's freedom against communist aggression, and had barely any sense of the war's strategic goals. Israeli soldiers, likewise, can hardly believe they are in Gaza to liberate the hostages and 'destroy Hamas'. They have killed more hostages than they have liberated, and after ten months of carnage a *CNN* analysis showed that only three of Hamas's twenty-four battalions had been 'destroyed'. But since the real justification for the war is limitless revenge, annihilation and conquest, this hardly matters. The absurdity has already been scripted, and folded back into an officially sanctioned moral inversion.

The inversion of morality is not, however, the same thing as amorality. In his work with violent offenders, psychoanalyst James Gilligan finds that they are obsessed with moral questions, particularly of when and under what circumstances violence is justified. They have simply flipped conventional morality on its head, with their own antisocial 'value system' that venerates Nazis and Satan-worshippers, and takes pride in being 'the baddest motherfucker you ever saw'. David Keen, analysing the atrocities in Sierra Leone, finds the same pattern among the RUF rebels: they 'turned law and morality on their heads'. In their 'perverse', 'upside-down world', they rewarded rape and mutilation and punished those who refused: hence 'the strange shamelessness of the rebels' enclosed world'. A similar shamelessness was expressed by apartheid police officer Paul van Vuuren when he explained to South Africa's Truth and Reconciliation Commission why he enjoyed torturing and killing ANC activists: 'It was the enemy we were killing. I felt I was busy with big and important things.' Alongside the sanctioned enjoyment in doing 'big and important things', there is the illicit enjoyment in the chaos for its own sake. A veteran who served as a medic in Vietnam expresses anguish over the fact that he was 'pleased at the ugliness of what I saw … I liked it. I enjoyed death.' And then there is what Edward Weisband calls the 'macabresque', where the cruelty has a deliberate and gratuitous theatricality belying its strategic rationales.

Shamelessness is powered by shame. Not moral shame, but the shame of weakness which Elizabeth Young-Bruehl finds to be at the heart of prejudice. It is the feeling of being 'disrespected' which Gilligan says lurks behind almost every violent outburst among the offenders he works with. This sensation is said to be experienced as a 'death of the self' which can only be remedied by an immediate and overwhelming self-assertion. Kieran Mitton, describing the atrocities of soldiers in Sierra Leone in *Rebels in a Rotten State*, notes that the forced child recruits who had suffered abuses as part of their induction were more cruel than the adults. And yet, the more 'extreme acts of violence from young fighters' also seemed to emanate from 'an inner moral conflict': the atrocity that momentarily obtunded shame also deepened the sense of shamefulness that was to be metabolised through further transgression. Atrocity, then, becomes the motive for further atrocity. In Lifton's account, even the effort of justifying one's atrocities demands further atrocities. A My Lai participant recalls firing into the crowd 'in the excitement', feeling briefly horrified as 'a few people go down', and then to justify it or even make it seem logical, doing it 'more ... maybe do it repetitively just to make that appear to be ... some part of your make-up.' The 'shame-free zones' described by Keen are actually zones where shame is the overriding emotion and motive.

The role of shame in Zionist ideology is well-documented. At times, the founders of Zionism sounded like antisemites as they scorned the Jewish diaspora. Theodor Herzl was repelled by the 'revolutionary proletariat' and the 'terrible power of the purse'. Revisionist Zionist Ze'ev Jabotkinsky reviled the 'ugly, sickly' 'Yid', just as Labour Zionist Nachman Syrkin derided the 'puny, ugly, enslaved, degraded and egoistic Jew'. Diaspora Jews were 'disgraced and ridiculed' for being 'weak' and 'ugly, and as a result immoral as well', according to novelist Yosef Hayim Brenner. The answer to shame was the 'masculine beauty' (Jabotinsky) of the 'great, beautiful, moral and social' Jew (Syrkin) of the nationalist future. Big, beautiful, strong Jews who would never again be mistaken for victims. Ben Gurion, as the Second World War began, was 'choking with shame' at what was happening to the Jews in Germany. 'We do not belong to that Jewish people ... We do not want to be such Jews.' Hence, according to Jacqueline Rose, the cruel shame and silencing with which Holocaust survivors were treated in Israel after the Nakba. This was to be a nation for the strong, not the weak.

Israeli soldiers in Gaza hanker for revenge over a burning shame felt, not for anything Israel has done, but for the cracks in the defences exposed by Operation Al Aqsa Flood. 'Everyone in my unit knew someone who was a victim on 7 October', a reservist explains to the *Guardian*. They thus take pride in their exaggerated cruelty. As Gaza descends into mass starvation, an infantryman films himself setting fire to food and water supplies in Shujaiya. Another soldier stands next to dead Palestinian bodies with a sign advertising his barber shop back in Israel: the accompanying song calls Palestinians 'animals' and 'Amalek'. Another, in footage of a dead Palestinian seen through a tank window, boasts of running over the corpse with his tank. Through such productions they construct a dangerous illusion, in which ordinary morality is for people weaker and more servile than they are.

There is something in these performances that recalls an established tradition since 1948, described by anthropologist Sophia Goodfriend, of Israeli soldiers taking photographs as trophies and evidence of conquest. Yet all of this is staged with an air of conscious defiance and resentment, and contradictory self-justification, suggesting that the perpetrators are not only aware of but are abidingly preoccupied with how wretched they have become. Even the weak, jock humour on display in these memes and taunts reeks of an effort to overpower conscience, similar to the uneasy jokes after the My Lai massacre recounted by Lifton: 'ha ha, they were all women and children'.

☭

'Shame is already a revolution of a kind'.

– Marx, in a letter to Arnold Ruge, 1843.

VIII.

To speak of moral inversion implies that the readiness to commit atrocities is necessarily achieved *à rebours*, as a deviation from the norm. It suggests that the perpetrators have been socialised in a world where such things are not permissible, making them vulnerable to what David Wood calls 'moral injury'. That is generally the case. 'Ordinary men', as Christopher Browning calls them, can only be turned into genocidal killers through trained obedience, group conformity, and intense ideological drilling. Indeed, there is some evidence of trauma among the perpetrators of the Gaza genocide. Among the thousand new wounded soldiers removed from the frontline every month, according to the IDF, 35 per cent complain about their mental state, with 27 per cent developing 'a mental reaction or post-traumatic stress disorder'. In an interview with *CNN*, Israeli soldier Guy Zaken described how he could no longer eat meat, having 'run over terrorists, dead and alive, in the hundreds' with his tank. 'Everything squirts out', he added. Another soldier,

Eliran Mizrahi, took his own life before he was due to be redeployed to Gaza. Horrified by what he had seen and done, he said he felt 'invisible blood' coming out of him: out, out, damned spot.

But it isn't always so. Among those fighting in Gaza are soldiers from Israel's Netzah Yehuda battalion, an all-male ultra-Orthodox unit of volunteers recruited from the arrogant, racist, power-drunk far-right settlers and Hilltop Youth – notorious for the murder of unarmed civilians, the killing of suspects in custody and the rape and torture of Palestinians. They have been raised on eliminative racism from the nursery, their native moral capacities broken and deformed long before they learned how to hold a weapon. And while they are not representative of the whole, they are the extreme end of an army, indeed a whole society, that is thoroughly enraptured in its genocidal mania. The regime of moral inversion, while it temporarily overrides the difficulties that most people would have with killing – helping to make it enjoyable and an achievement – also empowers those who were already hankering for the adventure of mass murder. The 'ideologically violent' perpetrators are in command, they enjoy what they're doing and they have the limitless support of the Knesset, the media and the wider public. There is no reason for the perpetrators ever to experience the gift of a shameful self-revelation and start fragging superior officers. After all, there are Nakba perpetrators alive today who still have no regrets.

There is a great difference between an army of this type, and one composed of 'socialised warriors', as Lifton calls them, whose spirit of slavishness recalls Karl Liebknecht's 'obedience of the corpse'. For there is no hint of slavishness in the Israeli rank and file, who want to go further, faster than the senior chain of command. *Ha'aretz* reported in March 2024 that junior commanders and soldiers routinely disobey orders. It cited General David Bar Kalifa's handwritten order to take revenge on Palestinian civilians and Brigadier General Barak Hiram's destruction of a university in Gaza as examples. Yedioth Ahronoth reported that the IDF leadership was infuriated by some of the destructive behaviour, like the blowing up of a Hamas legislative council building, because it vaporised vital military intelligence. The rank and file clearly have the initiative. In their video dispatches from the front, they still agitate against what they call excessive 'restraint'. They demand the full recolonisation of Gaza. They call for annihilation. In one case, a masked soldier demanded Gallant's resignation and threatened a putsch: 'We the reserve soldiers do not intend to hand over the keys to any Palestinian Authority', he said. 'You cannot win a war. Resign. … We will listen to one leader, and it is not the minister of defence, and it is not the chief of staff, it is the prime minister. … Here I tell you, did you want a military coup?' The video was shared by Netanyahu's son. The attempted arrest of Force 100 soldiers, and their violent resistance, showed that they will not suffer restraint. Nor will civil society, in which the IDF is so firmly embedded, tolerate it.

After fifteen months of genocide, the Israeli government finally acceded to a ceasefire, coerced by an incoming Trump administration. Netanyahu had bedded in for a long war of attrition, but had increasingly exhausted every last military and strategic rationale for prolonging the war. The Israeli security establishment dissented, critical of the government's lack of planning, and angry that the government's unwillingness to investigate war crimes leaves the leadership vulnerable to ICC arrest warrants. Yoav Gallant, who had promised war on 'human animals', was fired in November 2024 after months of opposition to Netanyahu's plans for 'total victory', and preference for a tactical truce to return the hostages. The Israeli public, though largely unmoved by the plight of Palestinians, no longer thought the war was winnable. Yet their dissent came from the right. If an election were held tomorrow, polling suggests, Naftali Bennett – who claimed that too much aid was allowed into Gaza – would be Prime Minister.

Until he agreed to a ceasefire, Netanyahu, who had waged a demagogic battle against the military leadership and aligned himself firmly with the far-right, retained the support of the soldiers. For him, the genocide was a superstructural response to an intensely superstructural crisis, consolidating his leadership while temporarily abating the centrifugal political forces rending Israeli state and civil society. Satellite evidence compiled by Forensic

Architecture showed that the IDF was building infrastructures for a prolonged occupation, suggesting that any ceasefire would be partial, provisional and temporary, a prelude to colonisation. Crucially, for as long as Netanyahu wished to prolong the war, with whatever scant rationale, the outgoing Biden administration continued to arm it and pay for it unconditionally and to support Israel with military deployments in the Mediterranean and the bombing of Yemen. It is deeply ironic that Trump, whom the Israeli far-right wanted to win, finally imposed the ceasefire that saw them quit the government: a ceasefire that, however precariously, represents a political defeat for the state of Israel, a danger for Netanyahu, and a demoralising blow to those who looked forward to building their neighbourhoods on Gaza's ruins.

Yet, even if the occupying army is exhausted by war, many of the perpetrators are still excited, still on the spiral of shameful shamelessness, their thirst for revenge still not slaked. On the streets, their civilian counterparts are furious, raging against the ceasefire and the traitors. Far-right politicians who remain in the government assure them it's in hand: the war will continue and lead to the 'gradual takeover of the entire Gaza Strip', Smotrich says. This is among the reasons why the peace is precarious: Israeli society is weary but has not yet been divested of its cruel fantasies. Like all perpetrators, they need to be released from their illusions. Their experience of moral injury would be, not a spiritual misfortune as Wood would have it, but the beginning of sanity. They need the crisis of confidence concomitant upon ideological collapse. They need the liberation of defeat.

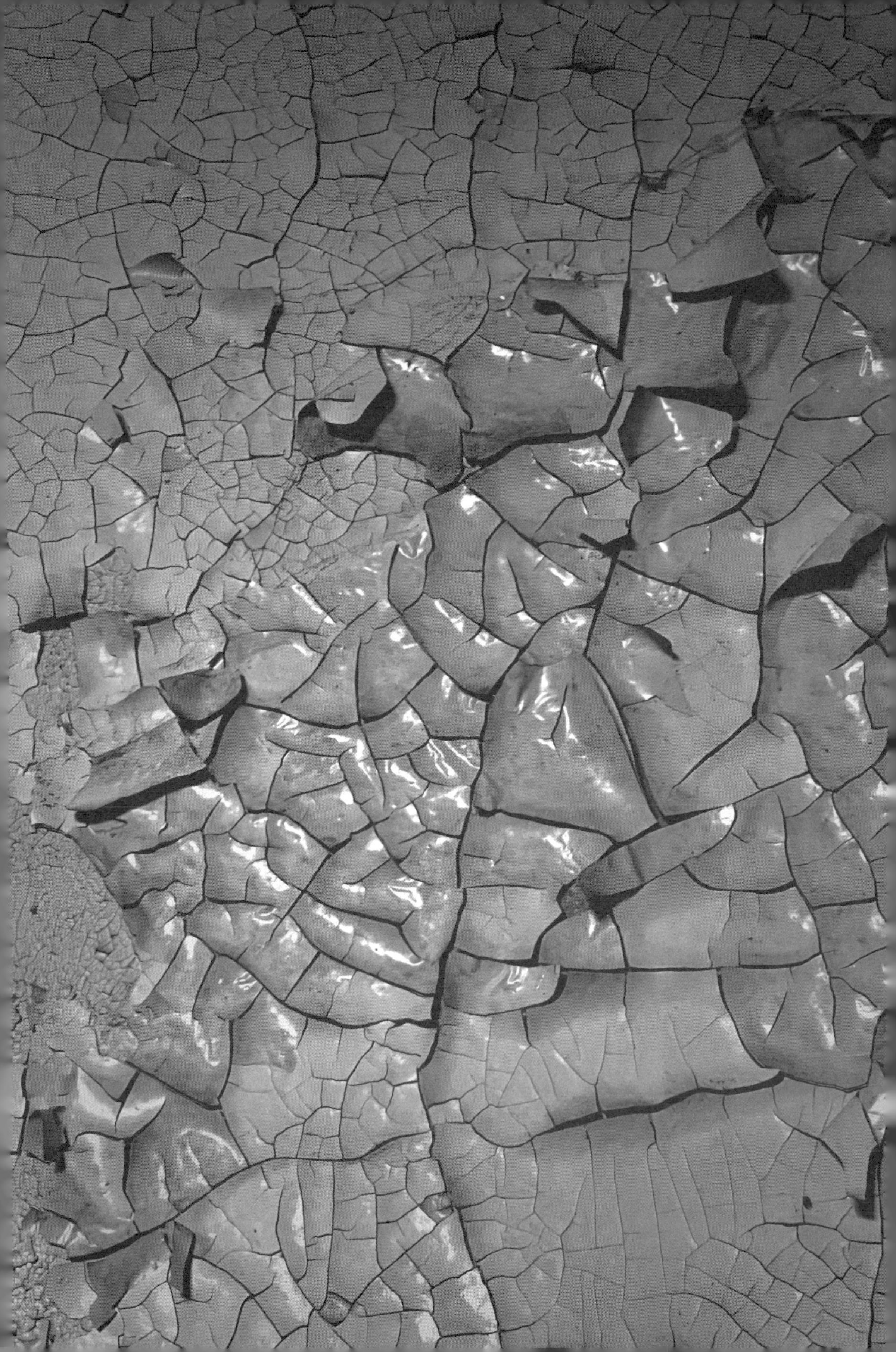

JOSEPH DAHER

# Hamas After 7 October: Resistance and Challenges

Following Ismail Haniyeh's assassination by Israel in Tehran on 31 July 2024 he was succeeded as head of Hamas' political bureau for the whole movement by Yahya Sinwar, who had led Hamas' political bureau for the Gaza Strip since 2017. According to Osama Hamdan, a senior Hamas official in Beirut, speaking to *al-Jazeera*, this choice was adopted 'unanimously'. Sinwar himself was killed by Israeli occupation forces, apparently unaware of his identity, on 17 October 2024.

Contrary to expectations, expressed in the Western Media and the White House, that Sinwar's killing represented an opportunity to end Israel's continuous genocidal war against the Palestinians in the Gaza Strip, the negotiations for a final ceasefire between Israel and Hamas did not reach a conclusion until January 2025. After the assassination of its chief negotiator, Haniyeh, and then the killing of both his successor and Hassan Nasrallah in Lebanon, Hamas was rightly suspicious of the idea that Israel had any intention of entering talks in good faith. The group insisted that it would not participate in talks unless Israel halted its operations in Gaza and called for a return to the ceasefire deal proposed by President Joe Biden on 2 July 2024. Instead, Israel added new conditions and still insisted on its right to maintain its troops in Gaza, along the corridors of Netzarim, in the centre, and of Philadelphi, on the border with Egypt, as well as at the adjacent crossing point of Rafah.

Moreover, Brigadier General Elad Goren was nominated as head of the re-established Israeli civil administration in the Gaza Strip. This is a new position within the Coordinator of Government Activities in the Territories (COGAT) unit – a Defense Ministry unit responsible for coordinating civilian and humanitarian affairs in the occupied West Bank and Gaza Strip. Existing since the end of the Six-Day War of 1967, this unit was denounced by the International Court of Justice (ICJ), in its advisory opinion of 19 July as a continuation of the Israeli occupation in Palestine.

At the same time, a large military operation was started at the end of August in the occupied West Bank, with massive violence, on a scale not seen there in twenty years. Within a few days, neighbourhoods of several cities had been targeted, dozens of civilians had been murdered, displaced, and besieged, and swathes of civilian infrastructure was destroyed. This followed months of escalating violence against Palestinians by the Israeli occupation army and settlers in the West Bank, where they had assassinated more than 840 people since 7 October. Israeli authorities also seized more than 2,000 hectares of land, declared them state property, and gave Israeli Jews exclusive rights to lease them. Israel also transferred vast swaths of sovereignty over the West Bank from the military to the far right-dominated civilian government and its ministries, granting the latter full authority over the acquisition and development of new settlements. The main objective of the Israeli strategy in the West Bank is its annexation, by dispossessing the Palestinians and confiscating their lands. Israeli violence in the West Bank against Palestinians actually increased after the January 2025 ceasefire in the Gaza Strip.

In this context of continuous genocidal war against the Palestinians – only paused, and precariously so, by the ceasefire – Hamas is facing difficult challenges regarding its future in the Gaza Strip and relations to its popular basis, as well as its regional alliances and collaborations. This said, before addressing the issue of the Hamas movement and its future, it must be clearly stated that any serious and honest criticism of this party cannot be developed without the premise of both clear opposition to the racist and colonial apartheid state of Israel and the denunciation of the genocide, and support for Palestinian self-determination and their right to resistance.

## Hamas' popular basis, between expansion and criticisms

Like Islamic fundamentalist parties, Hamas's popular constituency is not based on a single social class. Hamas' base developed in two waves, first when it joined the struggle against Israel in 1987 and pursued military resistance in the 1990s and 2000s, and second when it took over the Gaza Strip in 2007. The military resistance of Hamas, its opposition to the Oslo agreement and Israeli repressive policies, alongside its networks of social charity organisations, – based on the former networks of the Muslim Brotherhood (MB) and al-Mujamma al-Islami – and mechanism of Islamisation of the society, have enabled the Palestinian Islamic movement to build a large popular constituency. This constituency hails mainly from the working classes of the Palestinian population of the occupied territories, while also maintaining links with more traditional bourgeois and petit bourgeois forces.

The Palestinian Islamic movement has indeed historically enjoyed the general support and the sympathy of businessmen, landowners, merchants and shopkeepers. Hamas, and earlier the MB in the occupied territories, has usually included merchants, business people and sections of wealthy Palestinians. The first (undeclared) head of the Hamas movement, in power until 1993, Dr. Khairy Hafez 'Uthman al-Agha, was, for instance, a businessman and held a PhD in business administration. He was a member of the Palestinian Muslim Brotherhood movement in his youth and spent the larger part of his life – from the 1950s – in Saudi Arabia, and also died there.

At the end of the 2000s and beginning of the 2010s, Hamas was able to nurture a new generation of businessmen in Gaza who were linked to the party through the expansion of the tunnel system, while weakening the older generation of traditional businessmen often connected to the Palestinian Authority (PA). Most of the tunnels were funded by private investors, usually Hamas members who partnered with families straddling the border. An International Labour Organisation report cited the emergence of 600 'tunnel millionaires', many of them seeking somewhere to park their profits, who invested first in land and then in hundreds of luxury apartment buildings. The Al-Qassam Brigades, Hamas's military wing, established oversight over much of the tunnel network, taking over from a disparate network of clans and other political parties.

At the same time, the Al-Qassam Brigades have developed financial schemes and investments outside of the Gaza Strip through various networks of businessmen. According to the US Treasury, Hamas had established by 2022 a secret network of companies managing $500 million of investments in companies from Turkey to Saudi Arabia.

The social background of the leadership in the Gaza Strip, historically predominantly composed of people from petty-bourgeois and lower-middle-class origins and largely from refugee background, was more conducive to its spread than the West Bank leadership, which was initially mostly from a wealthier social background among the bourgeoisie and traditional elite.

One key feature of Hamas is that a large majority of its leadership and cadre have high levels of education and tend to come from liberal professional layers. There may also be a certain 'petit-bourgeois' mentality among many of Hamas' employees developed through becoming salaried cadres, particularly among those in leading positions in the administration of the Gaza Strip, who are largely from a proletarian background. This dynamic is, however, greatly reduced by the political and social reality of Gaza, characterised by a murderous siege and continuous wars by the Israeli occupying army, maintaining a relatively important link between local Hamas cadres and the Palestinian working classes.

In contrast to other Islamic fundamentalist movements in the region, it is important to note that the process of bourgeoisification of the Hamas leadership has been more limited. This is connected to the limitation of significant capitalist development in the Occupied Territories, and more particularly in the Gaza Strip since the imposition of the Israeli siege of Gaza in 2005, as well as the de-development policies imposed by Israeli occupation authorities.

Israel has pursued a policy that limits any form of indigenous economic and institutional development that could contribute to structural reform and capital accumulation, particularly in the industrial domain. Israel hinders the Palestinians from developing any industries that could possibly compete with Israeli industries, thus increasing and maintaining the Palestinian economy's dependence on Israeli imports. The Palestinian conglomerates dominating the Palestinian economy in the West Bank are mostly based in the Gulf. The PA's economic strategy has been to strengthen these conglomerates, thus widening inequality levels in Palestinian society.

What has been the effect of 7 October 2023 on this profile? In the past year, Hamas has witnessed an increase in popularity in the West Bank and among Palestinians in neighbouring countries. According to Public Opinion Poll 93 conducted in the Occupied Territories (West Bank and Gaza Strip) in the end of September 2024 by the Palestinian centre for Policy and Survey Research (PSR), a majority of 54 per cent of the public support the 7 October attack and nearly 68 per cent believe it has placed the Palestinian issue at the centre of global attention. In this same poll, Hamas is the political party most preferred by the respondents, reaching 36 per cent, followed by Fatah (21 per cent), 6 per cent selecting third forces, while one third said they do not support any party or have no opinion. This demonstrates the continued popularity of Hamas among Palestinians and the continued weakening of support for the PA, with a majority of Palestinians increasingly voicing support for its dissolution or deep reform at all levels. Similarly in neighbouring countries, there have been displays of support for Hamas and new campaigns of recruitment, notably in Lebanon where the party's presence and institutions have been strengthened in the past decade as the relations and collaboration with Hezbollah and Iran increased considerably.

This said, Hamas' popularity in the Gaza Strip, its historical bastion, is more complex and nuanced, especially under the impact of genocidal war and massive destruction. In the polls mentioned above, support for Hamas in the West Bank has systematically been higher than in the Gaza Strip. This was already the case prior to 7 October, but this dynamic has been reinforced since. Hamas' rule in Gaza since 2007 has been marked by authoritarian and repressive practices, leading to a higher level of unpopularity there than in the West Bank.

Moreover, while the large majority of Palestinians in the Gaza Strip consider Israel the primary source of this current and new Nakba, criticisms against Hamas have become more and more prevalent since 7 October. As Mahmoud Mushtaha argues, in an article in *+972* in August 2024,

> as the war has dragged on, displays of public opposition to or criticism of Hamas have grown among Palestinians in Gaza. Many accuse Hamas of failing to anticipate the ferocity of Israel's response to the 7 October attacks, and hold the group partially accountable for the dire consequences they are now facing.

In response, Hamas has not hesitated to repress individuals, raising criticisms against the party and its actions in the past few months.

Mushtaha adds, however, that 'despite widespread anger toward the Hamas leadership, Gazans do not hold the young resistance fighters themselves accountable, recognising that they are also part of the population who were coerced into the war'.

At the same time, there is a trend toward the diminution of public support in the West Bank and the Gaza Strip for the 7 October attack by Hamas. While the latest poll at the time of writing still shows a majority of 54 per cent in support, this is a decrease from

67 per cent in June 2024, and 71 per cent in March 2024, according to the PSR. This diminution in the support came from both the West Bank and Gaza Strip, where it stood, in the end of September 2024 poll, at 64 per cent in the West Bank, a decrease of nine percentage points, and 39 per cent in the Gaza Strip, compared to 57 per cent three months prior, a decrease of 18 percentage points. In March 2024, 71 per cent of Gazans stated that Hamas' decision was 'correct'. At the same time, expectations that Hamas would win the war have also continuously decreased. According to the PSR's poll of September 2024:

> Half of the public expects Hamas to win, compared to 67 per cent three months ago and 64 per cent six months ago. It is worth noting, as the figure below shows, that fewer Gazans, at just 28 per cent today, expect Hamas to win compared to the results three and six months ago, when those percentages stood at 48 per cent and 56 per cent, respectively. Hamas's expectation of victory has also dropped significantly in the West Bank, where today it stands at only 65 per cent compared to 79 per cent three months ago. It is also worth noting that while 4 per cent in the West Bank expect Israel to win the current war, a quarter of Gazans expect Israel to win.

More generally, most of the indicators of the poll related to Hamas' popularity declined since the beginning of 2024, although they remain relatively high. Indeed, 58 per cent of the public interviewed at the end of September 2024 (73 per cent in the West Bank and 36 per cent in the Gaza Strip) said they preferred the return of Hamas after the end of the war to other options, while satisfaction with Hamas still was at 61 per cent. In comparison, 71 per cent of the West Bankers and 46 per cent of Gazans said they prefered to see Hamas remaining in control in the Gaza Strip in May 2024.

Moreover, following the conclusion of the ceasefire in the Gaza Strip, Hamas has been able to re-establish some form of relative security, to restrict looting, and to begin restoring basic services in some regions. While Hamas' capabilities, both in terms of armament and human capacities, have been largely destroyed during the Israeli genocidal war, the Palestinian Islamic movement remains deeply rooted in the Gaza Strip, politically, socially and militarily. For instance, in a recent interview for *Reuters* after the ceasefire entered into effect, Ismail Al-Thawabta, director of the Hamas-run Gaza government media office stated that the Hamas-run administration continued to function, with 18,000 employees working daily to provide services to the local population, while Hamas has likely continued to recruit thousands of new fighters to its military wing.

Any assessment of Hamas' 'victory' following the conclusion of the ceasefire should be nuanced, to say the least. The ceasefire deal did not put an end to the deadly blockade on the Gaza Strip and allowed for the Israeli occupation army to consolidate its military occupation of the Gaza Strip. Indeed, the deal permitted Israeli control of a crucial strip of land along Gaza's border with Egypt, along with the Netzarim Corridor, an occupation zone constructed by Tel Aviv to divide the Gaza Strip into a northern and southern region, alongside an extension of Israel's military domination over a wider 'buffer zone' which is achieved through the destruction of Palestinian houses and the displacement of populations along Gaza's eastern and northern borders with Israel. This situation suffocates even further the small territory of the Gaza Strip and is in addition to the unprecedented level of destruction and ruins caused by the Israeli genocidal war against the Gaza Strip. According to a UN report, the reconstruction of the Gaza Strip could take 350 years if the blockade remains in place.

Another significant question is the relative weight of the internal and external, military and political wings of Hamas' developments. The political weight of the Gaza Strip's wing within Hamas has been increasingly dominant within the movement's internal structures compared to the West Bank and the diaspora wings, starting slowly with Hamas' sole control of the Gaza Strip in 2007, passing through the regional uprisings in the 2010s, and finally materialising in the election of Ismail Haniyeh as head of the bureau's political movement in 2017 after the end of the mandate of Khaled Meshaal (1996–2017).

The assassination of Sinwar, after Haniyeh and longtime leader of al-Qassam Brigades Muhmmad Deif, and continuous destruction of the Gaza Strip could potentially change this balance of forces towards the diaspora wing in the future. This said, for the current period, the dominant force in the party likely remains the Gaza wing. Indeed, since the assassination of Yayha Sinwar, his younger brother Muhammad Sinwar has been the shadowy leader of the al-Qassam Brigades in the Gaza Strip, while Khalil Hayya, who hails from the Gaza Strip and who has been designated as the group's new leader in Gaza, has been the main figure involved in negotiating the ceasefire. All these personalities enjoy good relations with Iran.

## Political strategy and regional alliances

Hamas has been able to position itself once again as the leading actor on the Palestinian political scene, further marginalising the already weak PA, with the 7 October military operation. Its main objectives were to challenge the status quo both on a national and regional level, which were both threatening the Palestinians' future. First, the actions aimed at responding to the continuous violations of human rights by the Israeli apartheid state, the siege in Gaza, attacks in the West Bank and expansion of settlements, attacks on al-Aqsa Mosque in Jerusalem, and so on. Second, at the regional level the 7 October operation temporarily suspended the process of normalisation between some Arab states and Israel. Hamas' attack on Israel on 7th October, and Israel's response to it, have had the effect of undermining the process of normalisation initiated by Donald Trump and carried over by Joe Biden, ensuring that the occupation cannot be ignored on the road to smoothing out formerly hostile relations within the region. Soon after war erupted, the Kingdom of Saudi Arabia responded by temporarily halting all progress on bilateral agreements between itself and Israel. During the ceasefire, Riyadh indicated that it is open to resuming talks.

Hamas' calculations regarding the 'day after' 7 October have, however, been demonstrated to have been largely misguided. The party was likely betting on a popular uprising in the occupied West Bank and a large participation of its regional allies of the so-called 'axis of resistance'. This has been limited, at most. In the West Bank, the Israeli occupation intensified its repressive campaigns and violent practices against the Palestinians with the aim of dissuading Palestinians from opening up a second front. As explained by the Palestinian Journalist Qassam Muaddi, writing in *Mondoweiss*,

> In the first two months after 7 October, Israel doubled the already existing Palestinian prison population, at one point reaching over 10,000 prisoners... The scope of arrests also increased, widening to include Palestinians from all walks of life, including many who are not politically active. Many of the arrestees are community leaders, journalists, and civil society activists with little to no tenuous ties to politics. Inside the prisons, human rights reports and testimonies of released Palestinians all revealed unprecedented levels of humiliation, abuse, and torture, effectively extending the genocide of Palestinians to Palestinian prisoners in Israeli custody.

Regarding Iran, Hamas' main regional ally, its strategic aims, particularly since 7 October, have been to improve its political standing in the region so as to be in the best position for future negotiation with the US, and to guarantee its political and security interests. Similarly, Hezbollah exercised restraint against continuous and violent Israeli attacks and bombings throughout the Lebanese territory and not limited to the border regions, evidenced by its avoidance of attacks on Israeli cities or civilians. Israeli military operations killed nearly 600 Hezbollah fighters in Lebanon and Syria between October 2023 and September 2024, including many senior officers.

Israel's war against Lebanon since mid-September 2024, with the support of the United States, challenged Hezbollah's plan to prevent a full military confrontation with the Israeli occupation army. Israeli intelligence first exploded thousands of communications devices used by Hezbollah members, both civilians and soldiers, which killed nearly 40 people and wounded several thousands, upon which its Air Force initiated a massive bombing campaign that also assassinated the party's senior military and political leaders including Secretary-General Hassan Nasrallah. It also killed several thousands civilians and forcibly displaced over a million Lebanese citizens. The Israeli occupation army subsequently commenced a ground invasion of a strip of territories in the south of Lebanon.

Israel's occupation army has therefore been able to pursue with full force its genocidal war in the Gaza Strip, while expanding its military and brutal repressive actions in the West Bank, as well as launching a war against Lebanon, occupying further territories in Syria after the fall of the Assad regime, and continuously bombing the region.

Hamas' calculations were based on a political strategy that did not necessarily differ from that of other Palestinian political parties. According to its 2017 charter and official statements from its leadership, Hamas seeks political alliances with the region's ruling classes and their regimes to support their political and military battles against Israel, so as to potentially reach a brokered settlement based on a two state solution.

Based on this perspective, Hamas leaders have cultivated alliances with Qatar and Turkey in recent years, as well as with the Islamic Republic of Iran, its main political, financial and military supporter. Iran's yearly direct assistance to the party has been estimated to be around $75 million.

The conclusion of the US-brokered Abraham Accords in the summer of 2020, and the further normalisation of Israeli relations with Arab states, as well as the rapprochement between Turkey and Israel, only increased Hamas' fears and concerns of a liquidation of the Palestinian issue and strengthened the party's crucial alliance with Iran – and therefore Hezbollah.

The leadership changes within Hamas' political movement have also had an impact on its regional alliances, most directly the recent elevation of figures drawn from its military wing to higher positions within the organisation. While the relationship with Iran has certainly been maintained on a political and military level over the last decade (despite disagreements about the Syrian uprising), the replacement of Khaled Meshaal with Ismael Haniyeh as Hamas' leader in 2017 opened the door to closer relations between Hamas, Hezbollah, and Iran. Meshaal had made attempts during his rule to steer Hamas away from Iran and Hezbollah in favour of improved relations with Turkey, Qatar, and even Saudi Arabia, a move opposed by the al-Qassam Brigades' leadership. Haniyeh's ascension, combined with the nomination of al-Qassam founder Sheikh Saleh al-Arouri as deputy head of Hamas' political bureau, put a decisive end to any such shift, and Yahya Sinwar as the leader of Hamas in the Gaza Strip only consolidated the alliance with Iran.

At the same time, Hamas has been attempting to improve its relations with other Gulf monarchies, most importantly the Saudi Kingdom, but with more difficulty. In the beginning of 2021, following the reconciliation between Qatar, Saudi Arabia, and the United Arab Emirates, Hamas leader Ismail Haniyeh praised Saudi King Salman bin Abdul-Aziz al-Saud's and Crown Prince Mohammed bin Salman's (MBS's) efforts to resolve the Gulf crisis and achieve reconciliation. In 2023, senior Hamas leaders visited Saudi Arabia for the first time since 2015, while the Saudi Kingdom started releasing, during the same period, the sixty-eight Palestinians and Jordanians arrested in 2019 and accused of having links to an unidentified 'terrorist organisation'. This included, a few months before Hamas' visit to Saudi Arabia in October 2022, the release of a former representative of Hamas, Mohammed al-Khudari, eighty-four, and his son, Hani al-Khudari, who had been held in detention for more than three years. Both were subsequently deported to Jordan.

The evolution of the situation between Saudi Arabia and Hamas was connected to the rapprochement between Tehran and Riyadh, which is ongoing. The temporary suspension of the normalisation process between Saudi Arabia and Israel following the Israeli genocidal war on the Gaza Strip also reinforced cooperation between the two. This normalisation process was an outcome of Saudi Arabia's evolving strategy of regional foreign policy. The confrontational and aggressive foreign policy adopted by MBS, symbolised by the deadly war initiated against Yemen in 2015 and the maximum pressure put on Iran and its allies in the region, has been a failure. This policy turned out to be too politically costly and damaging to the Saudi Kingdom's project of reforming the economy. Riyadh has therefore tried to establish more cordial relations with its neighbours and more generally seek a form of authoritarian stability in the region. Finally, the reorientation of Saudi foreign policy is principally linked to the need for the kingdom to concentrate on economic reforms and the Saudi Vision 2030 objectives.

The aftermath of 7 October has seen a show of rhetorical support by Gulf monarchies and Turkey to the Palestinians, and condemnations of Israeli war. However, regional states remained relatively passive in practical terms in the face of Palestinian suffering during the Israeli occupation army's genocidal war against the Gaza Strip. Leaders of Arab and Muslim countries at a joint summit of the Arab League and the Organisation of Islamic Cooperation (OIC) on 11 November 2023 in the Saudi capital did condemn the 'barbaric' actions of the Israeli occupying forces in the Gaza Strip, but refrained from issuing punitive economic and political measures. No Arab regimes have broken their peace agreements with Israel, while Egyptian authorities, which have collaborated with Israel in the blockade of Gaza since 2007, have not attempted to break the blockade and alleviate the famine in Gaza. In addition, Egypt started to build, in early 2024, a walled enclosure and cleared more than six square miles of land in its North Sinai province. This was intended to 'park' Palestinians if a large number of them were expelled from the Gaza Strip towards Egypt by Israel's occupation army. This enclosure is surrounded by concrete walls and far from any Egyptian settlements.

Although the now toppled Syrian regime through Bashar al-Assad rhetorically declared solidarity with the Palestinians, it showed neither an interest in nor the capacity to directly participate in a response to the Israeli war on the Gaza Strip, despite also suffering constant Israeli attacks even before 7 October. This was in line with the Syrian regime's policy since 1974 of trying to avoid any significant and direct confrontation with Israel. Further, condemnation by Syrian officials of the Israeli war would not lead to any form of military or political support for Hamas. There would be no strengthening of relations between the two actors, no return to the pre-2011 set-up, which was cut after Hamas refused to support the Syrian regime in its murderous repression of the Syrian uprising. While the Syrian regime restored ties with Hamas in summer 2022, that took place through Hezbollah mediation, and relations between Syria and Hamas remained mainly governed through interests structured by and connected to Iran and Hezbollah. Moreover, Damascus continued to label Hamas as "traitorous" and ordered the arrest of individuals connected to the group, even after the reconciliation between both actors. Following the fall of Assad's regime, documents revealed ongoing operations to target anyone with ties to the Palestinian Islamic movement, according to the pan-Arab Al-Quds Al-Arabi. It remains to be seen whether Hamas will establish better relations with the new Syrian government.

On their side, Saudi Arabia, as well as the United Arab Emirates (UAE), played an important role in helping Israel Occupation Forces neutralise the Iranian 'attack' in April 2024 by sharing information with the US and Israel. The Saudi monarchy also authorised US Air Force tanker planes to remain in their airspace to support US and allied patrols during the operation. Moreover, any show of sympathy on social media or in public to Hamas in the Saudi Kingdom has been severely repressed.

Turkey, despite Recep Tayyip Erdogan's criticism of Israel and a government-imposed trade ban on Israel since May 2024, maintains close economic ties with the country. According to data released by the Turkish Exporters' Assembly (TIM), Turkish businesses appear to be bypassing the trade ban by routing exports through Palestinian Authority customs: there was a 423 per cent increase in exports to Palestine during the first eight months of 2024, with exports in

August alone surging by over 1,150 per cent, climbing from $10 million last year to $127 million, as revealed in *Turkish Minute*. Trade between both countries has also been ongoing through third countries like Greece, as revealed by Ragip Soylu in *Middle East Eye* on 4 September. In addition, Turkey and Israel also found common ground during Azerbaijan's military aggression against Armenian-controlled Nagorno-Karabakh, populated primarily by Armenians. Israeli and Turkish drones, as well as support from both countries' intelligence services, proved essential to Azerbaijan's victory over the Armenian armed forces. More than 100,000 Armenians, nearly the entire current population of 120,000, have been forced to flee Nagorno-Karabakh and become refugees.

☭

## Conclusion – Hamas repeating old mistakes

Hamas has been trying to balance its relations with these different actors. On one side, its relations with Iran, alongside Hezbollah, has been crucial to provide Hamas with military assistance including weapons and training, in addition to important financial funding. Hamas, however, has never been and is not a simple puppet of Iran. It has its own autonomy in relation to Tehran.

On the other side, Hamas wants to maintain its close relations with Turkey and Qatar, which are considered key intermediaries to reach the USA and European states, and important locations for their political activities and to raise money through donation campaigns for the movement and charitable institutions affiliated with the movement in the Palestinian territories. Hamas also wants to develop more cordial relations with Gulf monarchies, particularly Saudi Arabia, and other Arab countries, including Jordan and Egypt.

Hamas will likely continue to seek the support of both as a strategy to strengthen its position against Israel and in its attempts to arrive at a two-state solution.

However, rather than advance the struggle, these regimes restrict their support for the cause to areas where it advances their own regional interests and betray it when it does not. The reluctance of Iran and Hezbollah to react and launch a more intense military response to the Israeli war of October 2023 against the Palestinians in order to preserve their own political and geopolitical interests demonstrates this. Iranian leaders have repeatedly reiterated their unwillingness to extend the current war to the entire region. Rather than a full-scale military engagement of Hezbollah in Lebanon against Israel, they preferred that Hezbollah serve as a 'pressure front' against Tel Aviv, as expressed by the late secretary general of Hezbollah, Hassan Nasrallah. Iran did not want its crown jewel, Hezbollah, to be weakened.

After the escalation of violence of the Israeli occupation army against Lebanon in mid-September 2024 and attacks on Hezbollah's infrastructures and leadership, the Lebanese party's main and most urgent priority was first of all to protect its internal structures and its chain of command, including by filling the vacuum at the top by electing a new secretary-general and replacing its political and military leadership, all of whom were assassinated by the Israeli occupation army. This was also part of its attempt to maintain and protect its military capabilities, including long-range missiles and rockets, against Israeli attacks and offensives. Persisting with the strategy of 'unity of the fronts' became more and more difficult to defend in the face of mounting losses and destruction.

This shift in priorities partly explained the rhetorical evolution of Hezbollah regarding its objective since October 7. Hezbollah officials stated after the assassination of Hassan Nasrallah that their priority was to end the Israeli aggression against Lebanon and to support a cease-fire regardless of the status of the fighting in Gaza. Similarly, during his tour in the Gulf, Iranian foreign minister Abbas Araghchi confirmed the separation between the Lebanese and Gaza fronts, saying 'there must be a cease-fire in Gaza and Lebanon, but the idea that stopping the fighting in Lebanon is a necessity and a priority is also correct'.

A ceasefire was eventually concluded on 27 November 2024, between Hezbollah and Israel. The ceasefire agreement provided for a sixty-day period (until the end of January 2025) for the Israeli army to withdraw from South Lebanon and Hezbollah fighters north of the Litani River, while the Lebanese army and UN peacekeepers were to deploy in these regions. The ceasefire, however, did not prevent the Israeli army from continuing to carry out strikes and incursions and delay the withdrawal from villages in the South, destroying infrastructure, bombing and killing civilians. These actions served as a message to Hezbollah that Israel will continue its actions despite the end of the war to prevent the Lebanese movement from reconstituting its military capacities in these areas. In addition, there are still significant doubts that Israeli occupation forces will withdraw from south Lebanon at the time agreed in the ceasefire, at the end of January 2025. Meanwhile, Iran's geopolitical objective is not to liberate the Palestinians but to use these groups as leverage, particularly in its relations with the United States. Iran's reluctance to react and launch a more intense military response to the Israeli war against the Palestinians in order to preserve its own political and geopolitical interests is proof of this. Moreover, Iran in the past has not hesitated to reduce the funding for Hamas when their interests did not coincide: Tehran had diminished significantly its financial assistance to Hamas after the eruption of the uprising in Syria in 2011 and the Palestinian movement's refusal to support the Syrian regime's murderous repression against Syrian protesters.

On the other side, Qatar, Turkey, Saudi Arabia and other Gulf and Arab states are very much connected to US imperialism and will not challenge this relation for the sake of the Palestinians. Doha welcomes the largest US military bases in the Middle East, with more than 10,000 US personnel at Qatar's Al-Udeid Air Base, home to the Forward Headquarters of US CENTCOM and USAF Central Command's 379th Air Expeditionary Wing, while the emirate was designated by the Biden administration in 2022 as a 'major non-NATO Ally of the United States'. Moreover, Saudi Arabia is ready to pursue the normalisation process with Israel if Washington accedes to Saudi Arabia's demand of a 'mega deal', including a US security umbrella like Israel's and aid for the development of a civil nuclear program. The advancement of the normalisation process between Israel and Arab countries, particularly Gulf monarchies, is an important objective of the US government to consolidate their interests in the region, including in its rivalry with China.

Hamas, like the majority of dominant Palestinian political parties, seeks political alliances with the region's ruling classes and their regimes to support its political and military struggle against Israel. This is, however, a recipe for defeat, as past experiences with Fatah and PLO have shown. Hamas collaborates with these regimes and advocates non-intervention in their political affairs, even as these regimes oppress their own popular classes and the Palestinians within their borders. In addition, these regimes are often entrenched in the US capitalist and imperialist system and / or enjoy good relations with other imperialist forces such as China or Russia, while only seeing the Palestinian issue as a cause to instrumentalise for their own political and geopolitical interests. At worst, they both directly repress Palestinian movements and crack down on any form of solidarity with Palestine seen as a direct threat to their own power.

This said, Hamas can't be compared with the Palestinian Authority (PA) and its policies. The peace process reduced the PA to ruling over a bantustan entirely under Israeli control and occupation. The US and Israel supported the PA, which controlled Palestinians in the West Bank as well as Gaza (before the latter was taken over by Hamas in 2007). The PA has been acting as a police force for Washington and Tel Aviv's interests. The latest example is the violent repressive campaign led by PA security forces against Palestinian armed groups, particularly militants affiliated with the 'Jenin Battalion', in the Jenin refugee camp in the occupied West Bank that began in December 2024. This came after a particularly bloody year of Israeli repression against the refugee camp, which suffered nearly eighty Israeli raids during 2024, killing at least 220 people, according to the Palestinian Ministry of Health. This unprecedented repressive campaign by the PA of course serves the Israeli security agenda and seeks to demonstrate its usefulness and role in the Palestinian Occupied Territories to the US administration under President Trump. And after the PA and the armed factions in the Jenin refugee camp finally concluded an agreement, the Israeli occupation army launched a large-scale military operation against the camp.

While recognising the difficulties of the Palestinian situation characterised by a genocidal war, apartheid, colonisation, ongoing occupation, fragmentation both territorially and at the level of its population, etc., and while supporting the principle of the right of resistance, it must be understood that Hamas and other Palestinian political parties' current policies and regional alliances do not create the conditions for, nor a trajectory towards, the liberation of Palestinians. Palestinians need allies in order to free themselves from the State of Israel, which is a major economic and military power far superior to the Palestinians, but they will not find them among the existing regimes in the region. Moreover, the Israeli economy is not dependent on the Palestinian labour force, which does not play a key role in its capital accumulation process, unlike, for example, during Apartheid in South Africa. Historically, the primary goal of Israel and its settler-colonial project is not to exploit Palestinians and depend on their labour force, but to to see them disappear.

In this context, it is necessary to consider the Palestinian and regional popular classes as the central social forces capable of creating the conditions required to envisage a strategy of liberation. A large majority of the regional popular classes identify with the struggle of the Palestinians, and therefore see their own battle for democracy and equality as bound up with its victory. That is why there is a dialectical relationship between the struggles; when Palestinians fight it triggers the regional movement for liberation, and the regional movement feeds back into the struggle in occupied Palestine. Their united revolt has the power to transform the entire region, toppling regimes, expelling imperialist powers, ending both these forces' support for the State of Israel and weakening it in the process. Far-right minister Avigdor Lieberman recognised the danger that regional popular uprisings posed to Israel in 2011 when he said the Egyptian revolution that toppled Hosni Mubarak and opened the door to a period of democratic renewal in the country was a greater threat to Israel than Iran.

On an international level, the most important task for those outside the region is to win the left, unions, progressive groups, and movements to support the campaign for Boycott Divestment and Sanctions against Israel and make the latter completely *persona non grata* at all levels. Forcing this on institutions and corporations in the imperialist powers, especially the US and European states, will help block their support for Israel and other despotic regimes and weaken their hold in the region.

Palestine has become a political compass and the worldwide massive mobilisations in favour of its liberation have created the conditions for the potential structuring of a progressive pole within our societies – the fruit of the growing awareness that a victory for the Palestinian cause would be a success for our camp, opposed to the destructive impulses of neoliberal capitalism and the rise of fascism.

BARNABY RAINE

# What Do People Panic About When They Panic About Anti-Semitism?

'We have become the Gaza of Europe.'
– Geert Wilders, Amsterdam, 8 November 2024

We know that in so many words – 'terror', 'peace', 'hate', 'safety' – *redefinition* and *redescription* are key tools in the colonial arsenal[*]. Not just 'anti-Semitism' but also 'Jews' are words subject to that process now. And if Palestine is a site of crystallisation for a global emancipatory politics for many millions in solidarity movements around the world, I want to offer some preliminary suggestions about why an idea of 'Israel' is a similar site of crystallisation for the politics of empire.

---

[*] This text originated as a talk delivered at the conference, 'The Struggle for Palestine and the Architectures of Settler Colonialism', hosted by Forensic Architecture at Goldsmiths University, May 2024. Concentrating on Britain and Europe, this essay was written before Donald Trump's assault on higher education - including threatening to pull $400million of federal funding from Columbia University - repackaged an old McCarthyite bid to secure cultural hegemony under the newer pretext of protecting Jews. My thanks to beloved friends and comrades from as far as Eritrea, Iran and Leeds who have thought with me about diaspora.

## Getting the questions right

Why the panic across the West today about Jews? The question might seem to be: various groups suffer racial discrimination, why does the ruling class proclaim sympathy for Jews more than others? In Britain, when the Board of Deputies of British Jews proposes the adoption of the International Holocaust Remembrance Alliance (IHRA) definition of anti-Semitism, the Conservative Party says 'yes' and great pressure is put on the Labour Party until they do the same, along with countless institutions from local government to universities. When the Muslim Council of Britain (MCB) tries the same strategy, their proposed definition of Islamophobia is rubbished after, importantly, the police worry openly that adopting it would interfere in police work. The Conservative and Labour Parties both share coffee with the Board of Deputies but boycott the MCB. This predicament is sometimes discussed today as a dreaded 'hierarchy of racisms'. That language presupposes that *we all agree racism is bad*, so that critique ought to illuminate and to explain the different levels of hostile attention paid by power to different prejudiced views. This will not do. Shifting from what Arun Kundnani has recently called the 'liberal' to the 'radical' conception of racism, from seeing racism as a psychology of the ignorant to seeing it as (also) a structure of material power, we might ask instead: why does the state racialise Muslims as security threats, migrants as economic threats, black men as criminal threats, but Jews as subjects for its protection, along ostensibly passionate anti-racist lines discovered and aggressively championed in this one case only? Protecting Jews is now a prominent claim deployed against leftwing politics, often in defence of overt bigots on the right, in Britain, France, Germany, the United States, Chile and elsewhere. What explains that ostensibly sympathetic construction of Jews by racist forces?

Two bad answers prevail today, which are in turn philo-Semitic and anti-Semitic, and are not mutually exclusive. The philo-Semitism explanation holds that the ruling class genuinely like Jews more than they like Muslims, which only begs the question. This gap has to be explained historically. Why did we move in Britain from a position where the monarch was a friend of Hitler in 1936 to one where the monarch lobbies the BBC to demand they refer to Palestinian resistance fighters as terrorists, in support of a campaign launched by the Board of Deputies? There is today a New Anti-Anti-Semitism where defenders of 'Christian civilisation' – a phrase invented to send chills down Jewish spines, since we killed their god – now talk instead of 'Judeo-Christian civilisation'. Even if the change of opinion is genuine, why now?

Here we come to the second bad answer, the anti-Semitic one: the rightwing media maligns every other minority in Britain but celebrates Jews because Jews control it. It is worth stressing that a softer version of this claim ('surely the wildly different treatment meted out to Jews is a product simply of Jews being wealthier and better connected to power than other minorities') is, as Barbara and Karen Fields say of racism in a different case, intuitive. In the absence of a theory capable of explaining why power claims to like x group, the simplest answer is that x group holds power.

Consider a better question. What do people panic about when they panic about Jews? In formulating the question this way, treating debates about minorities as *also* sites where the society works through its other problems, two influences stand out.

First: Fanon in *Black Skin, White Masks* treats different racisms as projections of different anxieties. A sexually aggressive patriarchy reads black men as voracious threats to women, Fanon says, and a capitalist society reads greed as the property of Jews. Racism projects facts about the society onto a debased Other who concentrates all that we dislike in ourselves, a kind of inversion of Feuerbach on gods as idealised projections. Indeed, in 1843 Marx already approached debates about Jewish emancipation by asking what broad social and political work was being done by images of 'the Jews' in those debates (to endless misinterpretation since). Like Marx and Fanon, we might ask: what content gets projected onto the two fantasies 'anti-Semite' and 'Jew' in the New Anti-Anti-Semitism?

Secondly: in the richest intellectual tradition bequeathed to Marxism in Britain, Cultural Studies, *moral panics* are deflected expressions of real anxieties at a moment of epochal transition. Moral panics work by fixing responsibility for the dislocations experienced during epochal transitions onto outsiders who are themselves changed by the transition. Reading symptoms as causes, Mods and rockers are imagined *causing* the decline of deference in 1950s Britain rather than being produced by it (in Cohen, *Folk Devils and Moral Panics*), and black unemployment and crime is thought to cause the crisis of Fordist stabilities rather than being produced by it (in Hall et al., *Policing the Crisis*). Extending Fanon, the question here is not just what projections are involved in the moral panic but also what processes of social change are narrated in it. In one of the great insights of *Policing the Crisis*, moral panics work to constitute hegemonic blocs to smooth epochal transitions. On my reading, the moral panic about anti-Semitism narrates crises of postcolonial neoliberalism through anxious images of the wretched of the earth, a spectre now redescribed as anti-Semitic, the better to cohere alliances against it.

In the remainder of this essay, I will sketch hypotheses about three things: first, the psychic and social needs answered by the New Anti-Anti-Semitism, second, the troubling theory of anti-Semitism implied by it, and third: what alternative starting points for a different anti-anti-Semitism could look like, through some thoughts on diaspora and identity.

## 1.

The New Anti-Anti-Semitism offers an explanatory framework for addressing connected economic, geopolitical and demographic angsts.

First, the economic, in the long crisis of neoliberal technocracy since 2008 and the return of anti-elitist politics in various forms. An image of anti-Semitism as the unique prejudice that punches up, imagining Rothschild bankers controlling the world, sees the Labour MP Siobhan McDonagh warn that anti-capitalism is intrinsically anti-Semitic. This is the old claim about a 'socialism of fools', deployed now to cast suspicion on socialism in toto. A nebulous 'populism', spanning left and right and everywhere but the technocratic centre, often sees anti-Semitism soon invoked. Anti-Semites see politics as 'a battle between the virtuous masses and a nefarious, corrupt elite', says the *Guardian* columnist Jonathan Freedland. Lest we be in any doubt about how widely the anti-Semitic rot spreads, Freedland clarifies that 'plenty of Jews have themselves internalised it – including no less than Karl Marx.' Internalising the anti-Semitic picture of power as Jewish, this view defends power by recoding hostility to elites as racist. It reads anti-Semites as something like Nietzsche's revolt of the lambs against the birds of prey. Following Foucault's provocative link between genealogies of 'class struggle' and 'race struggle', this reading discredits the former by redescribing it as the latter. This makes anti-anti-Semitism a convenient anti-politics, a compelling way for those who mourn Peter Mair's 'void' of 1990s consensus to experience and to express their angst about the return of antagonism by associating it with spectres everyone agrees are frightening – like Kristallnacht. This image of Jew-baiting forgets why Trotsky was once as important as Rothschild to anti-Semitism, and why a liberal billionaire (George Soros) now occupies much rightwing attention for his supposed border-spanning attempts to bring down the West. It is an image that misses the conservative core of anti-Semitism, on which more later. But the image of anti-Semitism as a brand of radical politics does its work in communicating a particular feeling of unease or panic.

Second, capital lives in national and imperial shells. We might trace a line from Ronald Storrs, Britain's colonial governor of Jerusalem, favouring a Zionist state in the 1920s as a 'little Jewish Ulster' to police Britain's regional interests; to 1956, when Britain and France launched their neo-colonial invasion of Egypt from the Zionist state; to today, and the IHRA banning as anti-Semitic the diagnosis of that settler-colonial state as racist, mobilising the memory of the Holocaust by appending a pre-existing text to the name International Holocaust Remembrance Alliance. Here we see the use of proclaimed anti-anti-Semitism, claims to protect Jews, as a direct tool of colonial power: imperial, then settler-colonial. Its effect is to discredit anti-colonial politics. In David Baddiel's telling argument, the left disgraces its anti-racism when it fails to defend Jews *on the terms demanded by the IHRA*, which means defending a racist state. While the philo-Nazi Freedom Party in Austria calls for bans on kosher slaughter, they happily adopt the IHRA, pleased at the chance to attack the colonised. Meanwhile, consistent anti-colonialism is tarred with insinuations (or worse) of racism.

By consequence, the New Anti-Anti-Semitism legitimates colonial power by depicting the colonised as unenlightened savages (racists). It is a logic of projection: when the Palestinian writer Mohammed El-Kurd misspoke at a rally – missing out the word 'not' in 'We must not normalise massacres' – he was accused of genocidal intent precisely at the moment that he was naming and opposing a live genocide. Colonial power knows only violence. It reads the colonised as incurably violent in order to defend its violent repression of them. Palestinians are recast as racists when they object to their racist colonisation, and anti-colonial politics in general – sympathy with the West's victims at a moment of fear and decline for the West – is recast as racist by positioning Jews as the canary in the coalmine for the impending collapse of that civilisation. Tony Blair warns that Jeremy Corbyn is, of course, an anti-Semite, because his 'anti-West' worldview demands it. While Liz Truss threatens 'ten years to save the West', the New Anti-Anti-Semitism offers a vernacular at once anxious and proud for communicating the peripheralisation of the old imperial core within the world system. The spectre of global South solidarity with Palestine works to vindicate an old claim, that the West's rising Others are savages. The British state commissions a former head of Labour Friends of Israel, John Woodcock, to write a report calling to ban both Palestine Action and Just Stop Oil, repressing nonviolent civil disobedience where it challenges the colonial and ecological violence that constitute this civilisation. When Palestine Action responds that he palpably represents the Israel lobby, he says that is evidence they are anti-Semitic and should be banned. The colonised and their supporters are savages. In the post-Holocaust, postcolonial, post-Civil Rights order, racialised savagery is a harder claim to make so it is today recovered, in a moment of ironic genius, by accusing the savages *of racism*. That meets our strange times, when racist power endures while everyone claims to be anti-racist. Accusing racial Others of racism is thereby thinkable as a strategy for defining the un-Enlightened savage, which is a relief to those looking for ways of narrating the crisis of the West, and a view of anti-Semitism as prejudice against power and against a Western ally makes it perfect to those ends.

Capital's imperial shells are defended ideologically through racialised framings of social conflicts. That brings us to the third, more local anxiety.

While I was canvassing near a barracks during the 2019 election, a veteran in union jack tattoos opened the door to tell me he would never vote for Jeremy Corbyn. Corbyn, he said, loves IRA terrorists and hates Jews. What image of 'Jews' was involved for him here? Why was it intuitively compelling to him that someone disloyal to British imperialism in Ireland would also hate Jews? Over the last year, far-right counter-protestors have on several occasions targeted Palestine marches, talking of great replacement theory: a conspiracy theory originally oriented around Jews, here used nominally to defend Jews from replacement by Muslims. These anxieties appear too in the mainstream of the civilisation. The former immigration minister Robert Jenrick, seeking the Tory leadership by opining on television that multiculturalism has failed, was asked to evidence the claim. He pointed to the Palestine marches in London. Jews, he said, were now at risk because of multiculturalism – because of migrants and their children and grandchildren, whom he accused of 'clearly not sharing British values'.

An image of Jews is therefore mobilised, as a vulnerable group threatened by the savage hordes, to defend both colonial and *metropolitan racial* hierarchies by redescribing the dominant power in those hierarchies as protective over the vulnerable. That presentation works to legitimate horror at class politics and anti-colonial politics in the twin crises of neoliberalism and American unipolarity. It also offers a frame for narrating the ascendant theme of right-wing politics. The New Anti-Anti-Semitism is a subset of that more general anti-migrant politics which increasingly provides the core purpose of the right in the global North, such that *this* anti-anti-Semitism ambivalently self-presents as anti-racism but in truth it now constitutes an important element of European racism.

These last two dynamics, the global and the local scales, were united in November 2024 in the Netherlands. When far-right Israeli football hooligans ripped down Palestinian flags and shouted genocidal abuse on the streets of Amsterdam, they were confronted furiously by locals. Not only the Zionist state but European governments, too, reacted with horror at Arab immigrants disturbing European serenity through their barbarian inhospitality to genocidal guests. Amsterdam's mayor, nominally of the Green Left, said the Israeli fans had been victims of a 'pogrom'. A Sky News report clarifying the responsibility of the Israeli fans was quickly deleted and replaced with one depicting them as victims: the logic of the panic is like a wave that engulfs, insisting on its significations of the world. The mayor awkwardly retracted her pogrom comment. But Geert Wilders, the far-right leader fresh from topping the polls in the last Dutch election, quickly called for the deportation of 'Moroccans'. He said: 'Muslims hunted Jews on the streets of Amsterdam.' Then, crucially, he said this dynamic was at work in Gaza too; he claimed the Netherlands was now Gaza. Imperial alliances, colonial hierarchies and metropolitan prejudices are all today defended by a binary between a protected minority – whose protection legitimates Western power – on one hand, and on the other hand a horde of brutes eager to tear chunks out of that vulnerable group. In Amsterdam's city council, only those commonly termed the 'migrant parties' spoke out against the pogrom framing; this is a harbinger of the politics to come, of its new dividing lines with immigrants cast as radical political subjects, threats to white society and its Jews.

This emerges from a familiar strategy, wherein powerful actors legitimate their power by painting it as protective over vulnerable people. The word patriarch ostensibly denotes the protection of women and children by men whose violence is described as necessary to ward off threats; in fact, that position and the structure of male violence it governs constitutes the threat. In America's

Jim Crow South, lynchings frequently followed rape charges, with racial power justifying its violence as necessary to protect vulnerable white women from aggressive black men. Jews are treated in the New Anti-Anti-Semitism like white women in that American experience. A particular fantasy of our vulnerability is necessary to the defence of racial power. In Europe today, Islamophobia is sometimes wrapped up in LGBT advocacy – a strategy pioneered by the far-right former Marxist Pim Fortuyn in the Netherlands, and now reaching Britain, too, with the Prevent agenda enforcing 'British values' on the rest of us, starting in the school classroom, preaching LGBT equality to Muslim students as a test of their integration: supposing improbably that homophobia is not a 'British value'. Racism is thereby constructed as an Enlightened necessity to police a backward and homophobic Other. Finally, Sai Englert has shown in Spectre how a logic just like the one I am describing was used by the French state in Algeria to present Jews as its protected minority who would be harmed if Algerians won their freedom: again, an 'anti-racist' racism requiring a protected minority for its legitimation.

The protected minority can kill and maim and taunt the savages endlessly and still be depicted as the victim, since the structure of racialisation codes victim status on the basis of one's perceived essence, not one's acts. The coding assumes the language of essentialism. But in truth, it is not our fictitious racial essence but our usefulness to power that dictates our racialisation. Eastern Europeans were 'stealing British jobs' two decades ago, but now Putin bombs them and so British ministers find it convenient to invite Ukrainian families into their spare bedrooms. Likewise, the apparent whitening of Jews, such that we become worthy of protection, really represents our deployment as an alibi for three angsts (economic, geopolitical, demographic) of white society. Jews are human shields for the other agendas of imperial power. We are a double shield, in fact. We are thrown into the line of fire to defend Western civilisation in Asia, and then thrown into the line of fire all over the world by the settler state's explicit and constant insistence that it represents world Jewry. That insistence does precisely what human shielding always does: it says, 'you want to attack me. I think I'll be safer and look nobler if I strap *him* to me and encourage you to attack him instead.' Jews may often participate enthusiastically in it, but as a wider politics the New Anti-Anti-Semitism is not really about keeping Jews safe, any more than the moral panic about supposed 'Muslim paedo gangs' is really about protecting children. Other hungers are satiated by the panic. Racialising Western power defends Jews only contingently, only insofar as we play the role it wants of us; hence secular leftwingers and Hasidim, two groups that usually imagine they have little in common, both sometimes find themselves outside the offer of protection and are read through old-fashioned anti-Semitism instead, since both offer awkward reminders of Jewish worlds before and beyond embourgeoisement and Zionism. These are Jews who slip, to use Judith Butler's metaphor for gender, in enacting the scripts assigned to us. If the offer of protection can be revoked from those who fail to play their assigned role, then the real story here is not just a whitening one.

Shifting from a theory of racism to one of racialisation means registering *both* that logics of racialisation shift, *and* that they use complex racial codings to launder and to divide us in ways not limited to open hatred. Hence the importance of treating this category, the protected minority, critically rather than credulously.

I have suggested so far that the first great achievement of the New Anti-Anti-Semitism is in offering a discourse for answering three anxieties of power at once, along class, imperial and locally racial lines. The contemporary anti-Semitism panic narrates conjoined economic, geopolitical and identitarian anxieties as the Washington consensus falters, fixing some of the dizzying dislocations produced in that crisis onto a neat image: the anti-Semite adorned in a keffiyeh, who can be imagined as the image of the crisis so that the crisis can be expressed in terms consistent with the ideology of the crisis-ridden racial and class order. Explicitly in the statements of Robert Jenrick and Geert Wilders, the keffiyeh stands for the horrors at the gates, which would run free if the West fell. In the USA, the Anti-Defamation League rushes to the defence of

Elon Musk's Roman salute (nothing to see here from the far-right white South African; just a chance similarity to a Sieg Heil) while their Director states explicitly that the keffiyeh is the contemporary swastika. I am suggesting there is a logic to this madness. This is a *moral* panic because it expresses social crises as moral breakdown; the reactionary temporality of moral panic is always the catastrophe of degeneration and lost innocence, where our problems are caused by a moral stain affecting part of the civilisation, a moral failing in some of its populations. In this case, the Enlightened civility of the West since 1945 is broken by invading hordes from overseas, who *bring back the worst of ourselves, the bastards, after we had done so well to cleanse ourselves*! The moral idiom views political life as a contest between good and bad people. This is how Europe sees anti-Semitism today, in self-righteous tones that performatively reproduce the shedding of Holocaust guilt by passing that parcel of guilt to the barbarians. The novelty since the 2010s has been the growth of proclaimed anti-anti-Semitism from a local, Zionist function to a general one, in the opposition to leftwing and anti-imperialist politics across the global North. A particular view of anti-Semitism works alongside shifts in Jews' geopolitical and class locations, all coming together in a moment of crisis for Western imperial hegemony, neoliberal technocracy and South to North migration flows to form a complex conjuncture in which attacks on emancipatory politics frequently take on the alibi of protecting Jews. This was the dynamic with Corbyn in Britain and it is now repeated aggressively against Mélenchon in France, who is depicted (including by the Nazi-descended far-right) as the voice of the banlieues against the Jews.

We turn now to a brief overview of the theory of anti-Semitism that sustains this panic. We begin with the Holocaust, which presents a more awkward case for the New Anti-Anti-Semitism than it cares to admit, and so we find the repressed in this discourse, its two symptomatic silences.

## 2.

Diagnoses of a 'New Anti-Semitism' began in the late 1960s, proliferating in the 1970s primarily as a strategy for countering allegations of racism levelled at the Zionist state. As Tony Lerman has shown in his *Whatever Happened to Antisemitism?* the 1975 United Nations General Assembly vote (made possible by newly independent, formerly colonised states) to designate Zionism as a form of racism was a crucial event in mobilising a campaign, in which the State of Israel was thus directly invested, to counter prevalent leftwing and anti-colonial renditions of anti-fascism and anti-racism. More broadly, today's New Anti-Anti-Semitism first emerged against the backdrop of Cold War attempts to reckon with the facts of the Holocaust, the actuality of anti-colonial revolution and the shifting class and geopolitical position of Jews in the West amid embourgeoisement and Zionism, such that claims to defend Jews became thinkable even as the racialising logics underpinning the Holocaust remained active in the West and globally. This history matters in our changed present, laying the groundwork for an understanding of anti-Semitism that removes Western civilisation from the ambit of critique.

In the Cold War, 'anti-totalitarianism' offered Western civilisation a desperately needed alternative to Soviet anti-fascism and to Adorno: 'those who do not wish to speak of capitalism must remain silent about fascism.' In depicting an apolitical tyrannical impulse common on extremes of left and right, anti-totalitarianism fit with a picture of anti-Semitism as 'the oldest hatred', the nasty and rebellious poison in common souls that explained the Nazi genocide. As a reading of the Holocaust this required great historical distortion, and not only in passing over the millions of non-Jewish victims. Contrast the presently hegemonic story of the Holocaust as the product of a singular and eternal hatred for Jews with Père Lachaise in Paris, the cemetery where memorials to the dead of the camps appear alongside the graves of French Communists and Vietnamese anti-colonial leaders. They all stand in the shadow of the Mur des Federées, where the leaders of the Paris Commune were lined up and shot. Those Holocaust memorials were built in the

1950s, when a section of popular common sense still treated the Holocaust as a grotesque instance of Western civilisation. That is how Aimé Césaire, George Padmore and other anti-colonial figures read Nazism in its moment, and it is what permitted a Nazi police chief to round up the Jews of Paris and then shoot down Algerians protesting in the same city after 1945. Far from the anti-colonial left, Hannah Arendt's classic account treated centuries of Christian power targeting Jews enabling, in modernity and with the rise of the nation state and race science, the reimagining of religious Others as racial and national Others, such that anti-Semitism is a tool in the arsenal of conservative power.

Recent historical scholarship offers many resources for extending the point: Isabel Hull's work on links between perpetrators of the Herero and Nama genocides and the Holocaust; Mark Mazower's stress on the British Empire as Hitler's conscious model; James Whitman's reconstruction of Jim Crow laws in America shaping Nazi racial laws; Robert Gerwarth's history of the post-1918 moment of anti-Semitism across Central and Eastern Europe as the racialised rendition of anti-Communism (hence Isaac Deutscher's comment that when the Freikorps murdered Rosa Luxemburg and Karl Liebknecht and threw their bodies into a canal, 'Hohenzollern Germany celebrated its last victory and Nazi Germany celebrated its first'). In all of this, we find resources for an account of the Holocaust as the progeny of this civilisation rather than a revolt against it by untrammelled subaltern rage – to say nothing of Gramsci's treatment of fascism as the politics of hegemonic blocs against proletarian revolution, or Frankfurt School accounts of factories of death as the end point of the instrumental rationality of bourgeois society.

But in liberal anti-racism, with its focus on *attitudes* whose wrongness is unaffected by the social power of the bigot, anti-Semitism is instead a raving bigotry, a jealous loathing of Jewish success. Holocaust education means guarding against everyday prejudice (hence the American classroom experiment where children learn not to discriminate on the basis of eye colour), and so identifying prejudiced individuals means completing a trajectory of historical progress in the vanquishing of racism: all the better if those bigots are relatively powerless demographics you didn't like anyway. There was an anti-elitist claim in Nazism, an ambivalent discursive relationship to class just as to modernity. But this is an account of anti-Semitism that cuts it from its social role and its two most central associated commitments in Nazism: to anti-communism and to European nationalism. Such is the ground zero for a more general project in eliding the conservative function of anti-Semitic politics, its bid to purify the social order of a supposedly alien virus.

Closely entangled with conservatism, there is a second central feature of the Nazi genocide strikingly absent from contemporary thinking about anti-Semitism. An erudite Marxist account, from Moishe Postone, offers a useful example. Postone concentrates on the personalising of power involved in anti-Semites targeting Rothschild or Soros rather than capital itself. That risks reading all politics from Bernie Sanders to Occupy as anti-Semitism, since they talk of nefarious agents, and since this account misses the importance of racialisation: anti-Semitism reading power struggles as racial struggles. The anti-Semitic claim is that Jews distort the world by virtue of our racial essence, loyal intrinsically to others with that essence and seeking to persecute those racially unlike us. Even though the prevalent codings of Jews might have changed so much that they no longer imagine us as Semites, contemporary Jewophobia still imagines powerful Jews distorting the social world in order to serve racially cohered Jewish interests. The racial imaginary defines the line between anti-colonial opposition to Zionism and hatred of Jews; the fight against anti-Semitism is a fight against imagining the world as ultimately determined by race. For this very reason, race is nowhere in dominant accounts of anti-Semitism today.

Bringing racialisation back into our account of Jewophobia reveals some of its contemporary motors. The racialising view of politics that fuels Jewophobia is aggressively encouraged by the post-9/11 politics of the War on Terror (where fundamental conflict was back after the end of History, not as social conflict over social power but as cultural and racial conflict: burgers facing off against burqas). That racialising view of politics is then directly encouraged by the hegemonic view of Jewophobia, the New Anti-Anti-Semitism. One could scarcely find a sharper example than a Zionist activist, Gideon Falter, approaching a pro-Palestine march full of Jews and agreeing with the police that he is not safe there *as a Jew*; or Leeds University, where the Jewish chaplain travels to commit war crimes in Gaza and then the Jewish Society sees its building defaced; or the state covering up the Holocaust Memorial in Hyde Park before Palestine marchers travel past, implying that we would deface it; or the Metropolitan Police seeking to ban a major national demonstration for Gaza from assembling outside BBC headquarters, because a synagogue is nearby, then arresting the head steward of the demonstration and interviewing Jeremy Corbyn and John McDonnell under police caution. The New Anti-Anti-Semitism reinscribes the existing Jewophobic frame that reads social conflicts as conflicts between the world and the Jews, and it does so quite consciously in order to bolster its case for the necessity of the Zionist state and crackdowns on Muslims in the West, among other causes. This agenda impedes the work of confronting and displacing anti-Semitic attitudes, including where they claim to speak for the colonised and the exploited. It prefers to muddy than to clear the water between anti-Semitism and emancipatory politics, boosting the former by association to help tar the latter.

These two silences, conservatism and race, fundamentally impede the New Anti-Anti-Semitism's account of the phenomenon it claims to describe and oppose. The 'New' in the supposed 'New Anti-Semitism' is partly an attempt to evade conservatism by suggesting a prejudice transferred from Junker aristocrats to Arab fedayeen, repositioning anti-Semitism as a radical assault on Western civilisation. But the enduring power of Jewophobia at the end of History is its ability to code social conflicts that generate an experience of powerlessness in racial terms, which suggests answers other than the unthinkable, impossible work of comprehensive social transformation. This is a conservative discourse for racialising the experience of powerlessness by imagining that social power is hoarded by a group of essential outsiders, a view which militates against a politics of social transformation. Jewophobia either treats the problems of capitalism or imperialism as a racial cancer to be removed while leaving the broader social order intact; or else it makes the intractability of racial conflict the basis for a deep pessimism, suggesting social transformation is impossible in the face of an omnipotent conspiracy of Jews. As I suggested in *Salvage 6*, this pessimistic implication might be crucial to understanding Jewophobia's contemporary attraction. When more bullish rightwing figures who reach many millions on social media begin to challenge Israeli violence, ideological purveyors of anti-wokeism (Candace Owens) and masculinity (Dan Bilzerian), blaming the Jews and Jewishness is part and parcel of their bid to isolate Israel as a violent phenomenon alien to the wider civilisation they defend.

A triumvirate of events – 1989, 9/11, 2008 – now combine to demand a politics of the economy and of civilisational crisis amid the apparent impossibility of emancipation and the negotiation of social antagonism through cultural and racial fields. The same triumvirate is experienced by the defenders of Western, capitalist power as the crisis of their recently triumphant world order, and they seek stories for narrating that crisis in terms that make them feel good (or let them enjoy their pain) amid the aggressively restated centrality of Arabs as objects of contemporary imperial violence since 2001. Thus the conditions are today present for two, co-dependent panics about Jews amid the slow end of the West: overt Jewophobia, and a moral panic that claims to be about said Jewophobia but really satisfies other hungers. The left missteps by assuming the moral panic overstates the prevalence of Jewophobia, which is like homophobia in its ubiquity; the panic does not exaggerate but misreads that prejudice, to nefarious ends. People dislike Jews, mistrust Jews and conjure imaginary Jews all the time, and the New Anti-Anti-Semitism is worse than useless as an instrument for understanding and opposing that reality. In the New Anti-Anti-Semitism, Jewophobia's entanglement in racialisation and its conservatism have to be elided to produce an Anti-Anti-Semitism in the conservative defence of racist power. But these two elements are crucial to designating the specificity of Jewophobic thinking and combatting it.

The theory of anti-Semitism that sustains the New Anti-Anti-Semitism is a thin one oriented around four things: a liberal, attitudinal reading of racism as prejudice and ignorance; the punching up claim for the uniqueness of anti-Semitism; internalising the anti-Semitic image of Jewish power; and the eclipse of race and racialisation in the account of anti-Semitism. Together, these four build an image of society as constituted by powerful Jews facing off against idiots and bigots who froth at the mouth in the face of power and so hate Jews. This hampers the work of specifying and tackling the conservative and racialising ideological pressures sustaining Jewophobia, since the goal of the discourse is less the defence of Jews than the defence of Western civilisation.

## 3.

The sharp irony is that the New Anti-Anti-Semitism constructs 'anti-Semites' as it once constructed 'Jews'. Jews were named as Semites by the German publisher Wilhelm Marr in 1870. Hence in Edward Said's high moment of Orientalism, Jews were racially identified with Arabs ('Turks' and 'Moors' were also common terms for Jews) as people liminal to Europe, lurking at its physical or metaphorical borders. Jews were not cast in the same role as Africans or native Americans, people (to Kant and Hegel) without history, with space read as time so that their spatial distance from Europe figured them as analogous to Europe's distant, primaeval past. Rather, Jews were located within Europe's pores, in its cities and ghettos. Jews were – as Isaac Deutscher said of us, and as CLR James said of Caribbean immigrants in Britain – here but not of here, connected to others like them across borders and overseas, with loyalties other than to the particular flag and monarch under whom they might happen to live, a dangerous fifth column. At their most radical, shorn of ties to nation, these rootless people might tear down that whole world of nations. This is the 'Semitism' that anti-Semites identified, and which is worth recovering and defending. This is how Hitler spoke of Jews in *Mein Kampf*, where centuries of stable local and national economy were broken by a race whose transnational status saw them benefit from the weakness and dissolution of nation states and empires. In 1920, Winston Churchill put the point forcefully when he wrote that anti-Semitism was appropriate against bad 'international Jews' – naming Trotsky and Rosa Luxemburg – but, through Zionism, Jews could become allies and policemen in the order of Western civilisation instead.

So, we might wonder, who carries this treatment today, the anti-Semitism of old and the radical possibilities of Semitism? In 1974 Huey Newton celebrated black internationalism in just these terms in his classic essay on 'Intercommunalism', championing a people without loyalty to the American state that kidnapped them, seeing in that existence outside national belonging the possible subjective basis for radical politicisation. Paul Gilroy ended *The Black Atlantic* by noting this parallel between blacks and Jews, people of hybrid border-defying identities. More recently, is this not exactly how Robert Jenrick spoke of the Palestine protestors? A frightening fifth column, not loyal to 'British values' but to transnational communities of the colonised instead: communities fashioned and refashioned by histories of domination and uprootedness. In the streets for Palestine, today's hated Semites are found. They are the children and grandchildren of Asia and Africa and Ireland and the Caribbean. In the multiracial city, they meet and forge new traditions. These diasporas terrify because they threaten to destabilise existing identities; this has long been the fear animated by the rootless cosmopolitan Jew, shuffling from place to place and making revolutions there, turning all that is solid into air.

Reflecting on the tragedy of Zionism as a negation of the diasporic standpoint, Stuart Hall celebrated that standpoint as the enemy of all 'identity politics', since 'no identities survive the diasporic process intact and unchanged, or maintain their connections with their past undisturbed.' The late nineteenth and early twentieth century image of the Jew-as-Semite was a pure diasporic image: diasporic everywhere, unable to point to a map and comfort ourselves with thoughts of home, where we were not the Other. Semitism, then, might name forms of identity and of politics that celebrate that experience, making new homes in places we share with others.

Hall's words also involve a claim about a relationship between identity and time. Diasporic communities are always in a process of becoming. Radical politics entails a giddy openness to that which destabilises. And though all the violence of the world can make forms of conservatism preferable instead, Semitism says that path is an illusion. We have nothing really to go back to, and the communities we build now – communities that others terrorise – are always processes in motion. For those of us who are diasporic, community cannot stably name a fixed or a pure ideal. It is notable, then, that Zionists frequently claim the language of indigeneity in Palestine quite differently from some diasporic protagonists of the Palestinian liberation struggle. Rightwing Zionists summon a distant history to claim an exclusive relationship to the land, denoting the purity of an essential subject, whereas the call to liberate that piece of the world from processes of colonial domination is uttered by the colonised but often in the knowledge, as Ghassan Kanafani's *Returning to Haifa* long ago dramatised, that nothing in the future will be the same as the past.

This embrace of fungibility is not to denigrate and certainly not to cast aside traditions. It is to cherish the traditions that develop when one stands outside the order of land and then nation state, including the emancipatory universalist hope born at the edges of that exclusion: that the world should be turned upside down until nobody is a preyed upon Other. In Jewish Messianism, the yearning for a totally different future is built into identity in the present. We pray three times a day for that rupture, where the lion will lie down with the lamb. Semitic revolutionaries ask: what futures might we envisage, we who have never been national insiders anywhere, never wanted to be? What visions emerge out of the mess and the beauty that we all inhabit, but which none of us claims to own? Jewish anarchists, socialists and Communists have sometimes been good at posing that question, as have many other itinerant revolutionaries with different skins and different faiths. This is why the Jewish anti-Zionism that says, "I'm not Israeli, I'm a good Brit/

Frenchman/American!" was always at some level the bourgeois kind. Nostalgia means the longing for a home; Marx's Semitism was nostalgic for the future, which is the only homeland Semites have. Rightwing politicians in Britain who talk today of 'British values' and then proceed to praise Jews do so precisely because they imagine anti-Semites as Semites[†].

These are confusing contortions. The discursive problematic *Western anti-Semitism* emerged to police anxieties including the instability of identities, and since those anxieties have not gone away, the discourse remains: it is occluded, though, by a switch to constructing Jews as protected minorities, so that not Jews but supposedly those who attack Jews become the enemy, redescribed in the same way as Jews once were. For our part, Jews are redescribed by the panic away from being liminal outsiders to whiteness and are imagined instead as the purest exemplars of whiteness.

The result is an anti-anti-Semitism that still seeks to negate Semitism. When the State of Israel says, as in Netanyahu's 2024 address to the US Congress, that it acts in defence of Western civilisation, it insists on a recategorisation, a redescription of Jews. Its destructive effect has been comprehensive. It has uprooted, dispossessed, expropriated, ghettoised, beseiged and bombed the Palestinian people to such a point of desperate violence that one strip of Palestine has been turned to scorched earth. What of those it claimed to protect? Zionism aided in obliterating in a few short years a vast and storied Arab Jewish civilisation, as Avi Shlaim's recent memoir confirms with a calm fury. Zionism built a safe space for Jews where Jews are less safe than anywhere else in the world – and Zionism has made Jews less safe all over the world. That balance sheet ought to give us pause in defining Zionism on its own terms, as a strategy for Jewish safety; its rise is incomprehensible outside the context of imperial sponsorship, and its imperial

---

[†] This point has wider geographical scope. When a major American publisher commissions a book titled Why the Left Left the Jews, arguing that 'identity politics' have replaced 'labor politics' and that sea of minority struggles should be rejected as a threat to Jews, we are through a kind of looking glass: Jews were once imagined by such rightwingers as the harbingers of newfangled minority struggles displacing the majoritarian, bread-and-butter demands of real workers rooted in the eternal national soil.

sponsors hoped to protect their own investments (real and figurative) by the use of the Jews. Zionists need not be naive about this. Embracing the tragic orientation, Zionism looks at a mountain of Jewish corpses and says of Western civilisation, 'if you can't beat it, join it'.

We all lose from racialisation by reactionary power, just as we all do from patriarchy. These are hierarchies that make us less than we could be, that fix us into roles useful only in the reproduction of hierarchy. Revolutionaries want, romantically, to free all of us from all those roles. The revolutionary Semitic conclusion now, seeing Jews cast as human shields for the civilisation of the gas chamber, is that the victory of the Palestinian resistance and the end of Western civilisation offer the only, slim hope for utterly breaking a structure of racialisation that today suffocates Jews under a mountain of praise. The New Anti-Anti-Semitism is a discourse that conflates Jews everywhere with genocide in order to shield the latter, appended to a Western project for materially transforming Jewish life: to make us their bulldogs. As Yahya Sinwar told an interviewer in 2018: 'They (the Jewish people) were people like Freud, Einstein, Kafka. Experts of maths and philosophy. Now they are experts of drones, of extrajudicial executions.' He should know. The Semitic, the diasporic point is not that we want to go back entirely to being whatever we imagine we were before. We want the freedom to become something new, in the creative refashioning of traditions that nourish us and in dialogue with the different people among whom we live as equals. We want to shape our identities under the impulse of a shared and heterogenous freedom, whose culture is that creation which flourishes where everyone controls everything. Racialisation by power, contrastingly, is a kind of division of labour with roles as miserable as they are necessary to keep empires afloat and to keep us from one another. It produces violent cultures.

Like love, radical politics rearranges us. The global solidarity movement resurgent since October 7, 2023 has involved the untangling and remaking of diasporic community, as some Jews exit Zionism and find our people instead among others resisting racialisation. I want to finish with a great twentieth century novel of oppression and revolution relevant, I think, to us now: Mikhail Sholokhov's *And Quiet Flows the Don*.

It is a saga of the Cossacks and it begins in imperial, Tsarist Russia on the eve of the First World War. All I ever heard about Cossacks growing up was of their brutality and terror. These were armed bands who attacked Jewish life across Russia's Pale of Settlement. I knew nothing about their background; I knew only that my family's encounter with them may eventually have forced some to leave their homes and come to Britain. It was never demanded of me that I knew, still less that I showed sufficient sympathy for, the stories of the Cossacks who murdered my people. Nobody ever asked me to prove my regret for their suffering before earning the right to speak about mine. Of course, racism is the name for the difference between that experience and the experience of the Palestinian people today.

Who were the Cossacks? Many were runaway serfs. They had fled a condition of agricultural slavery and the Tsar permitted them to live free so long as they did his dirty work, including fighting his wars and carrying out pogroms to scapegoat Jews for social problems. My ancestors encountered Cossacks as murderers, and they were right to, but Cossacks were not themselves possessed of much power. They were tied into a repressive function, mercenaries for the Tsar, as the guarantee of their measure of safety from him. This is not to deny Cossack responsibility for massacres. In Sholokhov's prose, Cossacks are hit by the Russian Revolution. The Bolsheviks make them an offer: abandon the Tsar and take a leap into freedom, without the guarantees of imperial power behind you but without its whip too – it was only ever really protecting you from itself, it was the real cause of the violence in your world. Very few Cossacks took up the offer, but there was at least one regiment in the Bolshevik Red Army, fighting the forces of the old power, led by Cossacks. They abandoned the safety of a home they had furnished, a form of life that was theirs. That was no easy or smooth thing; it was like the end of one lifetime and the start of the next. In refusing to be the Tsar's protected minority, they refused to be his tools for the violent subjugation of others. In so doing, they freed themselves.

GHALYA SAADAWI

# Against History: Art, Culture, and Business-as-Usual under the Gazan Genocide

The Israeli mass killing in Gaza has been unrelenting. More than 70,000 tons of bombs dropped. At the time of writing, the death count is 46,584; an underestimate given that in June 2024 it was estimated that 200,000 Palestinians had been murdered since 7 October 2023. Tens, if not hundreds, of thousands more maimed, crushed under rubble for days, family registries decimated, suffering unthinkable illnesses and deaths in the shattered husks that serve as hospitals. A completion of the Nakba, which, as Rabeah Eghbarieh has demonstrated, is no longer an event of the past but a foundational and recurring condition of Palestine; a legal concept.

At the time of editing, Israel is incinerating housing blocks in Beirut, detonating entire villages and groves across the South and the Bekaa valley as it attempts to invade, thinking it can accumulate more land, or at best create a demilitarised zone for itself, whilst attempting to eviscerate Hezbollah's resistance fighters, cadres and caches. The currently fascist-led Zionist entity, alongside the US, is not mowing the lawn but continuing the arc of its version of the War on Terror and a new Middle East.

As before, this unfolds with the complicity of a subdued Arab bourgeoisie and Arab States, with the support of a new Gulf petroclass, emboldened by the recent Abraham Accords. We witness the entire Western militarised, liberal order close ranks in defence of capital, allying itself to a neo-fascist Zionism. This is abetted by a White House funnelling billions to Israel, and rolling out fascist agitators and tanks on student encampments: a 'colonialism turned inward' as Aimé Césaire would put it. Various parties, parliaments and institutions mobilise the twisted International Holocaust Remembrance Alliance (IHRA) definition of antisemitism to pretend to endorse an older anti-antisemitism, and repress and criminalise dissent with amped policing, surveillance, court hearings. The legacy of Germany's un-de-Nazified anti-antisemitism, relentlessly, in every military, social and cultural form, perversely supports Israel; the UK's sham two-party system has tightened its genocidal ranks on the question of Palestine, partaking in US-Israeli militarism as it has done since the Iraq war, and revamping its counterterrorism machine, while both pummel Yemen, and threaten Iran.

Since the start of the genocide in Gaza, hundreds, if not thousands, of art and cultural centres and universities have doxxed, silenced, fired, threatened, or expelled writers, students, artists, scholars and doctors. An insufferable stream of hasbara fills Western mainstream press and is reiterated in sync by politicians and university boards, in museums and art magazines. Pro-Palestine protest, including displaying the Palestine flag or keffiyeh, is banned in Germany and France; Palestine activists are interrogated, on trial, or serving jail time for direct action, or inane instagram posts. The demonstrations of a nascent antiwar movement are called 'hate marches' in the UK. TikTok faces hearings and an outright US ban (in part over its proliferous Palestine hashtags).

The Western cultural establishment has demonstrated a consistent complicity with a ruling order bent on the continued destruction of Palestinian life, people, and infrastructure. Art and educational institutions (especially in Germany and the US) have closed ranks in their commitment to ensuring that culture and the ruling class are in tow, propelling the punishment and revocation of hundreds of speakers, events, talks, fellowships to scholars, and going so far as to threaten deportation and travel bans for those who show alignment with Palestinian liberation. Not to mention the deafening silence of the rest. In a dangerous relativism, as we see below (albeit expectedly in a German context), art and culture spaces have even pitted other struggles such as those in Sudan, or the Congo against that of Palestine. Vaster and more pernicious than first perceived, the repression has taken its most mediatised version through the spectacle of police clampdowns on hundreds of anti-war, pro-Palestine encampments across US universities – the largest student protest encampments since the 1960s.

The social order has cracked open for many to see. The struggle against this late-stage imperial capitalism, as embodied in the Zionist state and its allies, has erupted across various social arenas (notwithstanding the resistance fronts themselves), as politics and economy can be said to enter culture as a site of contradiction and struggle. The cultural superstructure particularly writ, could once more become a site where critique as praxis can function in opposition to financial interest and total war, forging a historical movement from and within the event.

Hundreds of thousands have demonstrated across European cities and campuses. University students across Europe and the US have studied investment portfolios and organised en-masse for divestment from arms and from Israel. New albeit small alliances commit to institutional boycott – Strike Germany, Strike Outset, and Writers Against the War in Gaza (WAWOG) – and have formed platforms for direct action as well as pushed for vast endorsement for the implementation of Boycott Divestment and Sanctions (BDS) and the Palestinian Campaign for the Academic and Cultural Boycott of Israel (PACBI). Writers have publicly withdrawn from PEN America for proceeding with business-as-usual over its refusal to support Palestinian writers, while some have have declined the German DAAD Artists-in-Berlin programme following the Strike

Germany call and the cancellation of scholar Nancy Fraser in Cologne for her support of the Israeli boycott. Thousands of writers have signed statements committing to a boycott of Israeli publishing – similarly in academia and law. We have witnessed thousands of individual resignations and boycotts of film festivals and art exhibitions; new progressive journalism platforms; student and academic led research and reports that follow-the-money on institutional investments, such as Coalition for Palestine and Scientists Against Genocide at MIT; weapons factories organising in Britain by Workers For a Free Palestine and other groups, not to mention dockworkers from Sweden to Italy and Greece refusing to load arms shipments to Israel. The list is longer.

Palestinian liberation has once again erupted as cause and symptom in the nexus of struggles against capitalism and neo-colonialism. Lined-up against liberation are both financial capitalism and the emerging forces of late fascism who – in Europe, the US, and Hindu nationalist form – thrive inside the very economic and political structures of undecolonised 'democracy'.

The economic tides of the last decades – financialisation, debt-austerity, poverty, stagflation – we are seeing another spectre looming; the spectre of war. A new sort of class war and antifascist war intersecting in the calls for a global intifada where Palestine becomes the universal name of emancipatory struggle, potentiating transversal alliances from Palestine resistance to land and climate struggles, from Dakota and Congo to Ecuador, from unions on Amazon's packing floor, platform driver strikes, to Stop Cop City. Social contradictions come to the fore in a profound manner. A historical feeling, a historical consciousness – we have been here, but it's so new – are we equipped? – has set upon us.

Tractor-like historical change, delicate, momentous. In various eruptions, political organising has returned to the streets and beyond, as ruling confluences are being pushed back against in stronger measure. Much seems to hang on it, against liberal and fascist elites, labour, housing, and new social movements; between the imperial war machine and armed resistance, grassroots antiracist and anti-extractivist movements, to revitalised political Left forms. The legacies and the future of anticolonial, communist and communising conjunctions are at stake. Justice as struggle seems to return to a scene it left only as lull, or through revisionist coercion.

☭

**Be grateful for what we give you**
Under a crisis of legitimacy for a genocidal consensus and its counter-insurrectionary injunctions, contemporary art has demonstrated some sinister instances of art's twisted autonomy. An underhanded line splits those inclined to strike and boycott as a decisive measure of solidarity with Palestine from the others whose fears and calculations eat their dissent. *e-flux* Criticism – one of the streams associated with wealthy entrepreneur and filmmaker Anton Vidokle's art advertising and publishing project, e-flux – ran an editorial in late 2024 titled 'Biting the Hand' (minimally crude given the current use of starvation as tool of war in Gaza), paternalistically seeking to protect from criticism those not inclined 'to bite the hand that feeds them': those for whom art making and exhibiting comprises their livelihood, allegedly complicating their capacity to take dissension very far.

> This [support of boycott, strike, or withdrawal] is amplified by a tendency to dismiss any artist who bites the hand but accepts the food as guilty of hypocrisy. One obvious problem with this is that artists still have to eat, and the insistence that they should forego the opportunity to reach a public is another form of silencing [...] this attitude seems to presume the existence of a space perfectly insulated from the structural injustices of society, within which artists might present their work with an immaculate conscience.

In attempting to turn this debate into one of moral relativism from which no one can emerge but the struggling artist, seemingly, those in need of protection are not those summarily dismissed and marginalised for rebelling against the genocide in Gaza, but those artists and their ilk who accede to business-as-usual to maintain the status quo. In a crude inversion, they claim that this itself – the pressure to oppose, protest, and withdraw labour in the form of strike – is a form of silencing those who prefer expedient quietism within the circuits of art and capital. They should remain 'free to choose' unsolidarity. Here, free choice in an economy of so-called free exchange takes over commitments to a struggle that far supersedes art. Using the tried and failed trope of 'artists need to eat', the editorial summarily resounds with the union-busting moral imperatives of bosses execrating those who believe in strike action, and in this case support the successful BDS movement. The anonymous editorial opines that boycotts threaten to abandon art and culture institutions to incipient fascism:

> It is hard to find many shows in New York speaking on behalf of that large part of the American population that will shortly vote for an aspiring dictator, yet it is to their credit that the curators of the current Whitney Biennial have elected to foreground artists representing causes vulnerable to the dismal eventuality of his election[...] the problem is that withdrawing from the public arena cedes it to others, and that there is no guarantee of getting it back.

The pacifying piece thus asks artists and those who work in culture to ignore calls to escalate and boycott institutions complicit in genocide via their economic and political dealings, because they must first look after their own labour as an allegedly isolated, ahistorical social relation, as mere livelihood! They must confine dissent to that which does 'not descend into disorder' (per Biden) lest their boycott hand the space of art to fascists; and instead use art to 'smuggle' a narrative amenable for contemporary art to express dissent: 'An alternative is to continue to participate in public spaces while highlighting the dissonance, using the opportunity to broadcast whatever opinions it is possible to smuggle into them'.

Artists need to eat. As does everyone else. Invoking this in the context of forced starvation in Gaza, is an insult to the art that purports to show itself in the name of avoiding starvation, and in the name of the others they claim will be under fascist tyranny in the US (how, in this climate, artists making art will prevent this is unclear). Moreover, the disdain for those who vote for the 'dictator' flies in the face of any class and historical analysis that seeks to understand the conditions that produced the right-leaning, reactionary moment we inhabit. Optimistically, perhaps forcing a choice between (good) genocide Democrats and (bad) fascist Republicans (as per the e-flux symptom) pursued the other way, via its own deep contradictions, could bring about the needed radical change that overruns the false choice once and for all.

As Hannah Black, Tobi Haslett and Ciaran Finlayson reminded us some years ago in their argument for the boycott of the Whitney Biennial – renamed the tear gas biennial due to the economic holdings of CEO William Kanders:

> This argument (artists need to eat) flies in the face of history and turns the very notions of strike and boycott on their heads – as if they were marks of luxury, rather than acts of struggle. Although in some cases made in good faith, this view promotes the reactionary fiction that marginalised or working-class people are the passive recipients of political activity as opposed to its main driver.

Within the field of contemporary art, in conversations between artists, in op-eds, inane art reviews, art academia, including profitable platforms like *e-flux*, there has not been a dearth of talk that artists are living precariously. This precarity – not one analysed in terms of surplus populations, immanent characteristics of accumulation, decades of financialisation, or the ills of piece work and wage work – has positioned artists as presumed sources of critique and subversion. This anti-aesthetic trope of the bohemian artist with severed ties to patronage leads to an aversion toward structure and professionalisation as signifiers of commerce that are said to exist within contemporary or immaterial modes of production.

Artists (but not those who work for a wage inside the art establishment?) must *not* be *forced* to engage in forms of dissent (since they are dissent?) such as strike and boycott, particularly those of boycotting art institutions and art shows where their art is made, consumed and circulated, even if (or these days, *because*) these are found to have donors and heads of boards fully imbricated in various forms of police repression, the prison complex, tear gas manufacturing, right-wing think tanks, even Likud affiliations and outright support for Israeli genocide. Labour is contradictorily avowed (precarious culture workers) and disavowed (no to labour strikes and boycotts). Accordingly, then, artists are never really workers, nor analysed as belonging to the working class. Simultaneously, thereby, the working class is not only not the main driver of history, but also its driver if it is alleged to vote for a Republican dictator. It is thus both scapegoated and judged in need of paternalism and protection when artists are concerned, thus repudiating entire class struggles' historical forms of organising. Positions like *e-flux*'s are thus uncritically anti-historical. The fact that artists and others who work inside institutions have political alliances and class positions that set them on a path of struggle precisely because they understand who is affected by it, including those communities where art finds and shows itself – seem to run amiss.

Black, Haslett and Finlayson reminded us in 2018 that tear gas manufacturer Warren Kanders sat on the board of the Whitney Museum of American Art, making ample donations to a biennial concerned with disenfranchised communities, while also sitting at the head of Safariland – which, while producing tear gas, also 'does a brisk trade supplying batons, handcuffs, holsters, and body armor to police and security forces including the IDF and the NYPD' to police the neighbourhoods where said art is displayed and consumed. A contradiction that could not but come to a crisis point.

The sorts of positions like those in *e-flux*'s editorial, with a stretch, recall the reactionary tendency to mis-assign the cause of systemic distress caused by economic and social policy over decades – the crisis of neoliberalism reaped in the present – to outsiders, migrants, refugees, or to the Left rather than to the beneficiaries of this systemic disaster. Against history, it presumes that the solution lies with the individual and the individuated, or within the narratives conjured by the artist. How can this not remind us of the Benjaminian critique that communism politicises art, in contradistinction to the aestheticisation of politics?

It is worth recapitulating it: Benjamin warned that fascism reorganises the now proletarianised masses, explicitly giving them the right to express themselves while preserving property relations of domination, which those same masses sought to abolish:

> The masses have a right to change property relations; Fascism seeks to give them an expression while preserving property. The logical result of Fascism is the introduction of aesthetics into political life.

In other words, even as liberalism holds that expression is better than no so-called freedom of expression (they have not understood the fascist inversion of their own dictum because they are not dialecticians), we must still contend with the form of that expression and its political valences. Efforts to render politics aesthetic, or, aestheticising politics, culminates in war, or, at best, fascist agitation. Benjamin's formula for the fascist aesthetic was: 'war and war only can set a goal for mass movements on the largest scale while respecting the traditional property system'.

Quoting F T Marinetti's 1920's futurist manifesto, he reminds us:

> War is beautiful because it combines the gunfire, the cannonades, the cease-fire, the scents, and the stench of putrefaction into a symphony. War is beautiful because it creates new architecture.

More on point for our present, Marinetti rallies for a new aesthetic order wherein politics lies at the service of aesthetics:

> Poets and artists of Futurism! ... remember these principles of an aesthetics of war so that your struggle for

> a new literature and a new graphic art ... may be illumined by them!

Art for its sake becomes, for Benjamin, the culmination and consummation of man for himself, satiated by the artistic scene of a war, where self-alienation had 'reached such a degree that it can experience its own destruction as an aesthetic pleasure of the first order. This is the situation of politics, in which Fascism is rendered aesthetic. Communism responds by politicising art'.

☭

## Art Value Infrastructure

We know from Marxist cultural analyses if not baseline historical materialism, as well as from some meticulous readers of the edifices of capitalist totality, that social structure and the superstructure that composes, say, culture, art, education, law, is in dialectical – and sometimes contradictory – relation with the historical and particular moment of production it finds itself in. For vast social and political transformation, these have to be taken into account in the totality of relations under capitalism. If this superstructure, as it were, both serves and reproduces the ruling class order in various ways, it is as much a practical location for contradiction and antagonism that help overturn that order.

Terry Eagleton obliquely claims that

> since the material production that gives birth to culture is racked by conflict, bits of this culture tend to be used from time to time to legitimate the social order that strives to contain or resolve the conflict, and this is known as ideology

– an allusion to the dialectics of base and superstructure. At certain historical junctures when certain contradictory economic conditions and revolutionary forces come to a head, creating contingency in what had been seen as deterministic history, the site of culture appears as one of the grounds for political and economic critique, if not outright struggle.

The story of art's autonomy, originally grounded in the unique conditions of the late eighteenth century, coincides, in some accounts, with the dependence of modern culture on the surplus generated by labour for capital. As art assimilated under capitalism, it led to conditions in which art's contradictory dependence and independence was the basis for the critique of and struggle against capitalist commodification: caught between autonomy and social forces (or heteronomy), it became a source of both capital valorisation and negative critique.

The notion of art's disinterestedness – which today may paradoxically appear as renditions of contemporary art as critical virtue because it understands itself as market and institution-opposed – has its roots in a Kantian aesthetics that divorced art from labour, or production. Not dismissing it entirely, the prescient and inimitable late Marxist theorist Marina Vishmidt clarifies, 'modernist aesthetics generates notions of the freedom of subjectivity. This is a subjectivity rooted in the unconditioned or 'disinterested' nature of aesthetic experience and not in labour or production.'

Vishmidt has reminded us how early Italian feminist theorists of social reproduction, amongst others, enabled us to extend the view that any arena of life is both a site of capital valorisation and simultaneous struggle (say, for wages), coinciding with the adequate critique of conditions of production and reproduction. Eventually, in modern art uselessness *and* usefulness too came to function, not always symmetrically, in line with use and exchange, creating and succumbing to abstractions that have real consequences. This uselessness – this alleged standing outside – can, but not in an overdetermined way, forget that it is underpinned by violent infrastructures, or, invertedly, mistake itself for being critically useful (against history) because it forgets that it is otherwise bound by history.

It has been the object of much speculation whether the art existing as part of contemporary art (artworks, institutions, discourse, transnational commodity flows, etc.), and where the latter sits within the cultural field, could produce any critique at all, much less one beyond the legacy of art as institutional critique, and moreover, if it could deploy its infrastructural imbrications within the political-economic and social order.

There may not be shortage of cynicism among those who work in the art establishment still attached to what became the institution of institutional critique, as Andrea Fraser might put it, towards (although not directed at) what Vishmidt has theorised, but did not have time to fully develop, as infrastructural critique: practices and artistic engagements that consider infrastructure, the determined capital flows, costs, and value that it generates, and speculatively, artist risks and wagers. Those that run counter to the defunct and now stylised negations of traditional institutional critique, stipulate either that art cannot really exist outside the institution, is the institution, or that the institution is bad and that artists need to be freed from it. The unheeding of mainstream contemporary art in looking at infrastructure tout court – of art and of capital – belies an obfuscated class struggle and prefers to maintain itself on the basis of an attitudinal 'we are not surprised'. Its timbre being that radical institutional considerations are naïve and counterproductive; reform institutions by making more art, more content, more affirmative representation inside them. Moreover, it cynically misreads the call to boycott (with its historical heritage of the strike), claiming (per *e-flux*) that it is in effect the precise opposite of what it is: a retreat from the world! 'It is not only misguided, but counterproductive: to insist that art retreat entirely from the complexities and contradictions of the world would seem to condemn it to irrelevance.' This should be inverted to say that it is indeed irrelevance that looms large, if not already actualised, if (contemporary) art does not study, foreground, speculate, and even leverage its aesthetic and non-artistic valorisation mechanisms.

As Vishmidt has reminded us, the more art has become an asset class and a 'laundromat for hegemonic values' the more it shrinks art's contradiction between its self-reference and the horizon of emancipated social relations – its negative critique. Key for the idea of infrastructure in art is not content but as Vishmidt says:

'how the art is inscribed into circuits of valoration', even if not necessarily value producing in itself (like other forms of labour), and thus is not about finding the 'value behind a certain form of art but to ask instead why is it now that in our society value (also) takes the form of art.'

Art does not stand outside the mode of production that is capitalism. And if, in the broader anti-capitalist, anti-imperialist struggle, a version of contemporary art is chiselled away, this will be part of the tectonic shifts that will shatter its postmodern particularisms, historicism, institutional 'criticality', and its style of styles that it prides itself on presenting as universal, against the pale of history.

If that version of art is to be abolished (by being made irrelevant, discredited, or dismantled) under social revolution, it is because, like other social divisions in the capitalist totality, it has served to reproduce that denial of totality, of history, of labour, of 'multiple determinations' in one manner through its own disavowals. Or, as Trotsky reminded us (contra Marx) in 1938:

> Art can neither escape the crisis nor partition itself off. Art cannot save itself. It will rot away inevitably – as Grecian art rotted beneath the ruins of a culture founded on slavery – unless present-day society is able to rebuild itself. This task is essentially revolutionary in character.

Or, at the very least, 'art must make its own way by its own means.' The bourgeois structure of feeling exemplified in editorials such as the ones by *e-flux* but also across art in the latest round of business-as-usual under genocide, have already countlessly been demolished, including in the tear gas biennial critique cited above. And yet they return. They seem more and more intent to have you keep your head down and work to make a living in an unlivable economy, while your dissent and critique are registered on the level of your (tepidly political) artistic content, or historically remote modernisms, because we may well now finally be in the true absence of the referent qua postmodernity, as Suhail Malik has remarked. And because they think that infrastructure analyses of and as art – with serious formal implications – within the broader economy is an old problem; that post-history has no resolution except, tautologically, using art to make art about the world modelled after its own image. Otherwise, you are told, you threaten with obsolescence the value of art as an alleged platform of social engagement, as though art itself as mediation, was not full of contradictions to be enunciated and confronted. Or, as Anna Kornbluh argues in her critique of immediacy as the style of too late capitalism: it is as though art was not in fact already mediated and mediation, rather, used here as a conduit to engage in some sort of immediate (or ideologically transparent) aesthetics and politics. In other words, once again: use that public space afforded you to *communicate* your grievances (as if mediation was translucent) within the confines of the styles afforded you by a history not yours that you nonetheless repeat. This is what Adorno and Horkeimer call a 'system of non-culture, to which one might even concede a certain "unity of style" if it really made any sense to speak of stylised barbarity.' Symbolisms, reruns, identities, all manner of stories will be allowed within the so-called safe space of free speech, as well as the enjoyment of the political subject matter of destitution that you may, or may not, manage to bring into the space of art (depending more recently on how pro-Palestinian and anti-genocide you are), which is nonetheless the same site from which you garner value for being virtuous and for being critical. And yet, we remind them, even their good social engagement qua art – the commodification process of observing art as social practice – can also become a derivative device in the form of the Social Impact Bond. Adorno and Horkheimer remark, in *The Culture Industry*:

> A style might be called artificial which is imposed from without on the refractory impulses of a form. But in the culture industry every element of the subject matter has its origin in the same apparatus as that jargon whose stamp it bears.

Subject matter garners exchange value. Museums, galleries and art institutes, publicly funded or not, are happy to debate anything in indeterminate ways (except Palestine liberation, for now) from climate catastrophe to mid-century anti-colonial movements, so long as, for the most part, the confines of the product don't spill into the infrastructure that makes it possible, creates value, or speculates on art's capacity for negative critique. The fantasy being that this kind of art in itself (and not for itself?) is a form of immediacy (immediate experience regardless of the types of contemporary art, which trumps the mediation of the money / exchange / commodity form). Or, a kind of disavowed mediation; it already holds the outside in it, is its own mediation. While it is a mediation for, by and as capital.

The artistic and non-artistic are dialectically entwined (akin to the very historiography of art's autonomy and heteronomy). Their separation now under the guise of the opposite – make socially-engaged art about whatever you want within the art establishment, publishing houses or production houses, on decolonisation, world-making, nationalism, archaeology, oil extraction, but don't boycott, or bring attention to labour, or financial investments for those same reasons – would render art as it emerges today, irrelevant. Not the inverse.

If art as it stands – here mostly so-called contemporary art as a vast arena of the culture establishment – is already irrelevant (as a barometer of social transformation, say), Suhail Malik's position in these older debates has been that art needs to exit contemporary art, in its valorising, critical virtue. So that contemporary art holds traction (for Tirdad Zolghadr) as it only symbolically claims to do, it must leverage its knots, bolts, and labour to do so, where curation and art could become both work and organising, as they remake art in ways that mediate the very alienation the former begs to transform, or at least to mediate. In the many contestations of institutional critique, it was said to have turned its own conceptual critique of the scaffolding of art into a thing repeated enough to congeal into a reified style, removed from the scene of its birth, and the conditions of its making. An important contestation by

Malik claims that saying 'no' inside art institutions is an affirmation of contemporary art's critical virtue and the fiction of the artist's total freedom (as an absolute right), where 'the critical virtue of contemporary art manifests the affirmative negation of institutionalisation required by the civic virtue of rights' (think of the radical 'rights' being evoked as the new right-wing Republicans eviscerate institutions). These *affirmative negations* should turn into a loud, vociferous 'no', like that of the institutionalised ape who had gained language in *Rise of the Planet of the Apes*, one that in fact affirms through negation the institutions that one wants to see come into existence, to build, to destroy, from which the determinacy of critique and praxis can emerge, and whose function is not solely to self-valorise value. Wedded to this point comes serious reflection around the ways art and society, the artistic and the non-artistic actually mesh; how to work in coincidence with, or through the destruction of, institutions for a wider struggle. Avoiding words like 'smuggling', and not even beginning to refer to tokenising diversity and equality, these invitations focus more on how to force what exists to bring about what does not yet exist, and to formalise this in practice internal to the places of work, relations, art forms, contracts, and so on.

### Solidarity

Between 2017 and 2020, there was a wave of Black Lives Matter acknowledgements on art institution websites and #MeToo ricochets in the form of signposting campaigns such as the open letter: 'We are not surprised.' Given the complicit silence over the genocide in Palestine, let's face it, the former's ultimate horizons were vague gesturing, some more quotas, and looking politically good. When the struggle became concrete on the streets, as we witnessed in the 2020 riots, the ruling classes in the US, the liberal base and establishment, went on to nearly claim that no riots had taken place across the cities where intense protests had occurred, weaponising what suited them from that insurrectionary moment. It seemed that many years later those same organisations and individuals were not surprised enough that Israel and its US-Euro allies were committing mass death, ethnic cleansing and starvation, to proclaim their solidarity, because this time they understood that proclaiming was taking historical action their property relations could not afford, gaining traction in a time where statements of allegiance became speech acts of commitment. The silence was deafening and humorous. Solidarity appeared conveniently as dinner table sympathy because no identification with shared struggle seemed possible without concrete risk.

I've inquired elsewhere about the way class composition presents itself in contemporary art, the ways 'cultural workers' claiming they are workers sits repellently with those who see that curators, dealers, heads of museums, and artists who lubricate the global flows of capital can hardly nudge themselves into this made up strata (although they can certainly leverage their positions), and that the question of labour in art, and its status as a (non) commodity, is still unresolved. Today, perhaps since masks have fallen off, solidarity indeed has come to mean praxis. The desired replacement by immaterial and mental labour does not resolve, or dissolve, the problem of the violence of abstraction (real abstraction). Rather, the crisis of labour and wage, life and exchange, under late capitalism is still very much at stake.

Where do we place the cultural establishment's tendency to incriminate boycott, strike, and maintain business-as-usual not only under genocide made possible by their patrons in Europe and the United States, but also in relation to the latest waves of labour organising across the world since 2019? Over the last few years and into the Covid-19 pandemic, after the drawn-out aftermath of financial collapse, the bailout of banks, the crises of production/debt, the further intensification of austerity and rise of right-wing populism, strikes, riots, social movements, as well as labour organising, have been on the rise – the inheritors of the coming of age of the Occupy movements and the redrawing of communisation lines among Leftist activist and theory circles. An uncanny grammar. These new waves across the global north for one, from nurses, doctors, university unions, and *gilets jaunes*, to Amazon, Google and platform delivery workers (today the Palestine movement trying to engage directly with arms factory workers), had some effect in the art field. Art handlers and museum workers organised to form unions in various US cities; interns circulated spreadsheets detailing their working hours and major discrepancies in pay; various US and UK museum workers and artists banded to end museum investment in fossil fuel, the prison complex, tear gas, dire labour practices, and beyond (e.g. Liberate Tate, Gas Art, Strike MoMA, preceded by Gulf Labour Artist Coalition and G.U.L.F); artists and researchers followed-the-money on museum board members evidently finding imbrications in all manner of ruling elite filth, such as the spyware Pegasus owned by then Serpentine CEO Yana Peel's husband, and links to the Netenyahus and the Israeli Occupation Forces by the likes of the Gertlers and their funding patronage outfit, Outset – to name but two.

Since the Gazan genocide began, a recent activist call was Strike Outset (the art fund, Outset is run by the Gertlers who are close with the Netanyahus, and are apparently implicated in right wing think-tanks in the apartheid state of Israel), coming at the heels of Strike Germany launched by writers and artists asking to unequivocally boycott German cultural and academic institutions for their now farcical, perverted and total support of Israel against the Palestinians. Strike Germany also came with a clear set of demands against the IHRA definition of antisemitism (and the anti-BDS motions both voted on in the Bundestag) asking scholars, writers and artists to decline all invitations and withdraw their labour from German institutions.

The BDS movement and PACBI were conceived prior to the second intifada and have now returned with force, as the powers against them work across parliaments to pass outlaw motions. The attempts at banning and shaming, if not criminalising the premise of boycott, including in the fields of art and education (now we see more clearly the extent of universities' military research and support of genocide in Israel and the US), had been pre-emptive before October 7, aimed at undermining the movement's concrete effects against Zionist profit and reputation. Today, this contributes to the fat financing poured into doxxing students at Harvard, and the aggressive clampdowns on hundreds of university encampments across Europe, the UK and the US, as the correlation between state, police, million-dollar educational endowments and billionaire boards is all too evident. Organising to divest from weapons and block arms shipments to Israel (including by dock and factory workers) can become successful politically and also exposes the logistical nature of capital as targetable because indeed (also) premised on what Charmaine Chua would call circulation as a mode of production. Boycott and divestment are chokepoints. Blockades and boycotts *are* effective. As they are also contained inside the so-called field of culture.

The dominant stance across contemporary and culture art (as we witness through editorials, vast silences, firings, censoring and lately the pitting of African and Afro-Deutsche causes against those of Palestine, as happened at a decolonial Berlin event at the Haus der Kulturen der Welt (HKW)) has conveniently perceived the strike and boycott as in themselves another form of repression. As Ciaran Finlayson reminds us, if we forget art's dialectical autonomy, its uselessness *and* its being subtended by an infrastructure that is itself subtended by the violence of both wage and slave labour, then we are doing bad politics and bad art. This liberal establishment politics indicates the drive to un-read the gravity of this historical moment as an intensification of past-present economic conditions, and a propitious one for movements, labour organising, and a communist politics bent on changing those conditions. And that bad politics and art, broadly writ, which mistakes art's dialectical condition, propagates a self-image as non-contradictory and critical only on the scale of its discourse – an irony in today's neo-McCarthyist era. Together these two bad sides progress to remake the very status quo of art that, at best, valorises the value of either socially good art, or only indeterminate poetics ungrounded from histories of form, and plays a key role in intensifying the conditions where art value is the site of inscription in networks of value production for capital by and large.

Art, like other sites of circulation, consumption, and reproduction, could be a site of struggle and a site where the liberal political consensus can recompose itself. As such, asking the question what is to be done? through, as we understand it, an infrastructural critique in art that can find form to speculation/speculating on inherent contradictions, as we understand Vishmidt to have meant, *and* through organising (boycotts, strikes, divestments, plans for new formations, methods to abolish), is a concrete social question. Because then we also speculate on art and the institution as imbricated in broader struggles and movements against the violent manifestation and abstraction of infrastructure (per Vishmidt). The clash between a self-perception of art as social engagement cum critical poetics, and the obfuscated struggle with capital infrastructure and logistics is clear to see. Anyone who cuts off that confrontation serves the liberal ruling consensus, and is politically naive and cynical. In the end, all this but affirms that this conjuncture must end; 'the necessary prerequisite to the creation of a new world and a new life'.

ANDREAS MALM

# The Politics of Life

In early November 2024, something historic happened in Spain.

The story starts with the violence of climate change. We all saw the scenes of sudden apocalyptic inundation in Valencia: the streets turned into roaring rivers, the people floating away, the piles of automobile carcasses. More than two hundred people died in the disaster. Then, on 9 November, more than 100,000 locals marched through Valencia in protest against the authorities, and the most enraged bloc clashed with the police. This was the first climate change riot in the global North, the first time an episode of destruction fuelled by fossil fuel combustion directly precipitated militant confrontations in the streets – the first time, but not the last.

Protesters accused the authorities of having killed the flood victims. There is substance to this allegation, because the first thing the coalition of the right and the far-right did when it came to power in Valencia last year was to close down an emergency response unit, formed by the previous red-green coalition to coordinate relief efforts in the event of a flood or heatwave, or other extreme weather event. The climate denialist right considered that a waste of money.

There will be more protests of this nature: against governments that fail to protect their citizens against the blows from climate breakdown.

But at some point, such protests must also make the leap to a higher level: the next riots, in a country like Spain, should target Repsol, the Spanish oil and gas giant, one of the world's most aggressive investors in fossil fuels. Because renewables generate so little profit, Repsol continues to pour capital back into the expanded reproduction of oil and gas fields around the globe. As long as companies like Repsol remain in business, disasters of the kind we saw in Valencia *will* multiply – this is an immutable iron law. It follows that as long as protests stay on the frontline of adaptation, as long as they do not also cross over into the field of mitigation, we are destined to experience ever-worsening catastrophe. As Wim Carton and I argue in our forthcoming book, *The Long Heat: Climate Politics When It's Too Late*, challenging the dominant classes for maladaptation as we saw in Valencia is henceforth an inevitable part of our struggle, but there can be no fair and just and meaningful adaptation if fossil fuel combustion does not stop. No cities, however well-governed, will be safe from inundation if the likes of Repsol keep pumping oil and gas out of the ground. No shields will be strong enough to withstand the ever-stronger blows from business-as-usual.

For that necessary hope, we must shift our gaze from Valencia to Colombia. For the first time in its history, Colombia has a left-wing government. The country has long been utterly dependent on producing and exporting fossil fuels, which account for more than half of its exports. Colombia is the third largest producer of such fuels in Latin America. When Gustavo Petro ran for president in 2022, he posited what he called a 'politics of life' against the prevailing 'politics of death': he promised to end all exploration for fossil fuels if he won, and in the two years of his presidency, not a single new exploration deal has been signed for any of the three fossil fuels.

Oil and gas production can be sustained only if new fields are located and opened, once the old have been depleted; if drilling is banned, the business will naturally come to an end; and so now Colombia is on track to terminate oil and gas extraction *in its entirety* sometime during the next decade, possibly as early as 2031.

After Petro won the presidency, he took direct control of the state-owned oil company, appointed his campaign manager as its CEO and instructed it to *turn down* offers of deals with foreign partners (most recently: Occidental Petroleum, one of the most aggressive oil and gas corporations in the US) *even if* such deals promised massive profits. The CEO of Occidental replied by denouncing Petro as 'anti-oil, anti-gas, anti-fracking and anti-United States', as if these were slurs. Coal is going the same way: open-pit mining is slated for shutdown.

None of this is happening because there is no more oil and gas and coal left in the ground: all of it is happening because Colombia is governed by people determined to leave them in the ground untouched. As Petro has said, there is a weapon of mass destruction in the Colombian subsoil.

We should be clear about just how exceptional this is. No other fossil-fuel producing country in the world has a government of anything like this mindset; no one else is actively trying to phase out the fuels of death and destruction and liquidate primitive fossil capital; none is ruled by a president – a former guerilla fighter – who reads contemporary Marxist theory and is himself working on 'a book that will explore whether capitalism can address the climate crisis.' In a recent profile in *Time*, Petro said of addressing the climate crisis: 'If capitalism *cannot*, because it lacks planning capacity, then humanity will overcome capitalism on a global scale because the alternative is that humanity will die with capitalism.' The president of a significant fossil-fuel producing country uttering words such as these is not a situation we are spoiled with often, and so we should appreciate it all the more.

This is not a matter of Petro alone: at least as important is the Minister of the Environment, Susana Muhamad. She recently unveiled a public investment plan worth $40 billion to get the transition going. Like so many other countries in the global South,

Colombia has enormous potentials for producing solar and wind that remain untapped; the plan is to massively expand their production. Colombia is now on track to generate all its electricity by renewable means – going further, it aims to export such electricity. Muhamed and Petro want to shift from sending fossil fuels around the world to dispatching electricity from solar and wind through a pan-American grid. This, of course, is the essence of an energy transition: shutting down fossil fuels and *replacing* them with fully scaled-up solar and wind.

Colombia demonstrates that such a transition is possible, it is eminently feasible, and the obstacles to it are not technological but political. What determines whether such a transition takes place or not is exclusively the political balance of forces. This balance seems nowhere and never to be to our advantage, and in Colombia itself, powerful forces are stacked against the transitional project. Against that backdrop, the Colombian experiment is a model of what should be done. It is a model of the kind of heterodox ecological Leninism some of us on the left have wanted for years. A mass uprising on the streets – the revolt of 2019–20, with its mixture of student rallies, indigenous protests, workers' strikes and militant confrontations with the police – was converted into an electoral campaign that won control over part of the state apparatus and targeted fossil capitalists as enemies of subaltern life.

Colombia is also a model of the contradictions such a project encounters. The country is facing a foreign investment strike. It has a deep state at one with the dominant class, both working to obstruct the Marxists in nominal charge at every step. The opposition has made strides recently, in parliament and elsewhere. Some promises remain unfulfilled: the expansion of wind-power has not been sufficiently enforced, for example. Perhaps most importantly, Colombia illustrates not only the impossibility of socialism – ecological or otherwise – in one country, but also the futility of attempts at energy transition in one country. The uniqueness of the Colombian experiment is its greatest weakness: all other major energy producers in Latin America – Brazil, Venezuela, Guyana, Mexico – are throwing themselves into the global frenzy for fossil fuels and accelerating production as fast as possible, even if governed by parties and presidents nominally of the left. As long as this remains the case, as long as Colombia is an isolated anomaly, there will be no progress, and Colombia itself is likely to slide back into business-as-usual. The left might then struggle to justify forgoing fossil profits as the planet heats regardless, while the right targets electoral gains by opposing climate action pursued alone. Such is the prisoners' dilemma of our time. Capital and the nation form are twin obstacles to a politics of life, now as in Lenin's 1914.

Nonetheless, we are so starved of positive examples, we are so unfamiliar with the living experience of a left seizing power that we should savour even the evanescent taste of it. We should talk about the Colombian experiment, learn more about it, see what could be done to internationalise it, because the politics of death and destruction rules supreme in this world. The darkness is nearly total, and so we should cherish even the smallest sparks of light.

The darkness is nowhere as concentrated as in Palestine. One is here tempted to see it as more than a coincidence that the foremost attempt at a politics of life, on the other side of the world, is spearheaded by a Palestinian woman: Colombian Environment Minister Susana Muhamad is of Palestinian descent. It is certainly not a coincidence that the Colombian government has also pursued a consistent policy of boycott: on 1 May, Petro announced the termination of all diplomatic ties with the Zionist entity. In August, he banned all export of coal to that state. Before this decree, Colombia was the number one supplier of coal to the occupation: now it sends nothing. Keep the coal in the ground, and start by not selling anything to the state of Israel – this is the politics of life in the twenty-first century. Netanyahu consequently denounced Petro as an 'antisemitic supporter of Hamas', while actually existing Hamas published another of its brilliant statements praising Colombia as a model for the rest of the world to follow. 'We call on all countries to sever the relations with this fascist entity and to work by all means to boycott, isolate, impose sanctions on it, and prosecute its leaders', said Hamas – as with the transition, an option that can be pursued. What everyone knows *is* to be done *can* be done.

On the ground in Palestine, the political situation is qualitatively different from the one in Colombia, or anywhere else, because the forces of destruction are unleashed in Palestine without any inhibitions, with an intensity that consummates the unity of genocide and ecocide: a systematic shattering and levelling of *all possibilities for life* in Gaza, and beyond. But Palestine is exceptional only because it crystallises the general forces in motion in this world. Among other spectres, Palestine prefigures the endpoint of global warming: a world with nothing left but ashes and smoking rubble. This is already the case from Jabaliya to Rafah, but it will also ultimately be the case on Earth as a whole, if the politics of death is not defeated and the forces of destruction are not themselves destroyed.

It is a serious political imperative, then, to pay tribute to the resistance: to those who cherish life sufficiently to confront the forces of destruction, treating a politics of life not as the thin pacifism that declaims violence now and *to hell with the consequences*. Rather, resistance entails understanding the struggles required now to hand life and freedom to those who come after us.

We leftists can start with the left. We should talk much more about the Jabha Shabbiye li-Tahrir Falastin, the Popular Front for the Liberation of Palestine, because at this point of intense destruction, the PFLP is present and puts up resistance to the best of its ability. This is not a left in government – this is a left that fights from the position of the most extreme powerlessness and exposure to the most overwhelmingly powerful forces of destruction, and precisely for this reason it deserves special respect and appreciation. When in early November 2024, the occupation carried out a sweep of abductions in the West Bank and Lebanon, the mission specifically targeted the Front and arrested more than 60 of its militants – an index of the threat it is perceived to pose.

The Front has offered martyrs on every Palestinian frontline of Toufan al-Aqsa. Consider the following tiny sample of examples. Abed Tahani, a comrade of the Front, journalist, founder of the independent media network *Taqadomy* ('Progressive') was killed in Jabaliya alongside his brother Abdelfattah, fighter in the Abu Ali Mustafa Brigades, ten days after October 7. As the Front wrote in a tribute to Abed Tahani: 'Abed banged on the walls of the tank, as did Gaza's resistance on October 7'. That phrase banging on the walls of the tank is a reference to Ghassan Kanafani's *Men in the Sun*. I have argued previously in *Salvage* that this image paints the most striking picture of resistance in a world on fire.

Suleiman Abdul Karim al-Ahmed, a field commander of the Abu Ali Mustafa Brigades on the northern battlefield, was martyred a year after October 7 on the border with Palestine while resisting the invasion of Lebanon. Mohammed Abdel Aaal, head of security for the Front, a novelist, organiser, military operative, was assassinated in Beirut in autumn 2024. He was singled out for his role in building cells of the Abu Ali Mustafa Brigades in the West Bank – when I visited Beirut in April, his brother Marwan, leader of the PFLP in Beirut, could still receive me openly in party offices in *mukhayam* Mar Elias; he has since been forced underground but he sent out a communique mourning his martyred brother:

> The heart gets lost in the chaos of war. Even the evening news for the whole family is about war – the destruction of homes, missile strikes, the levelling of neighbourhoods, the burning of refugee tents. We cannot remove war from our lives. We didn't learn its arts; rather, it imposes itself on our daily lives and teaches us its lessons, so that we may survive erasure and extermination, and remain alive for the name that Palestine deserves.

Continuing the resistance against all this destruction is now an affirmation of the very possibility of life itself. Abdaljawad Omar, who has become a major interpreter of the resistance in this moment and who appears in this issue of *Salvage*, recently captured the point in an interview with *Jewish Currents*: 'resistance is less about achieving a specific endpoint and more about affirming a presence, a refusal to be erased'.

We should pay tribute, then, to the comrades of the Front who have given their lives in this resistance; but none of its martyrs – as the Front itself would be the first to recognise – have come close to the epic heroism of Yahiya Sinwar, Abu Ibrahim, the leader of the politburo, who did not keep the captives as human shields; who did not hide behind civilians; who refused the offer of safe passage to exile; whom the enemy could never find – but who found the enemy.

He donned a military vest and a keffiyeh and took up position in a house in Rafah. He threw two hand grenades against the soldiers of the genocidal occupation; making them run for their lives; making them shell the house from a distance and send in a drone like cowards. You have seen the pictures: Yahiya Sinwar, again, as after the war in 2021, sitting like the king of rubble in a chair, only now with one of his hands blown off, and when the drone comes closer, he throws a stick at it – all around him, rubble as far as the eye can see, everything pulverised by the machinery of death and destruction: and yet there he is, resisting, even when it is too late, even after everything is lost, banging on the walls of the tank.

This is the spirit we will need in the years ahead: in the second Trump presidency and in the coming decades of catastrophe.

JULES GILL-PETERSON & SOPHIE LEWIS

# The Politics of Childhood: A Conversation

*The following is a lightly edited transcript of the* Salvage *panel at the Socialism conference in Chicago in 2023. Jules Gill-Peterson and Sophie Lewis were interviewed by* Salvage *Editor-in-Chief Rosie Warren.*

**Rosie Warren**
Many people have noted that the Right (in the US in particular, but also elsewhere) is focused on attacking reproductive rights and bodily autonomy; seeking to criminalise both abortion and gender-affirming healthcare. It's obvious to many people now that we need to coordinate a defence around questions of bodily autonomy, reproductive justice and self-determination.

Today I'd like to talk about one aspect of the present cluster-fuck, which is the way that children are the focus of reactionary politics right now. We see this in the attacks on Drag Queen Story Hour, in the criminalisation of parents who affirm their trans kids' genders, the attacks on gender-affirming educators using children's preferred pronouns, and in the moral panics around puberty blockers and around gender-affirming healthcare in general.

It's interesting to me as someone from Britain that what we've seen in Britain has been more of a moral panic on behalf of cis women – or, as the TERFs insist on calling us, adult human females (which I think is relevant to this conversation) – mobilising feminism and accusing trans women of a range of perversions. And one notable result of that is that in Britain the folk devils are trans people themselves, almost always trans women, and the people who are being 'protected' are 'adult human females'. Children have almost been an afterthought.

In the US, it seems like it's the opposite. It's gender affirming parents, educators, healthcare professionals – themselves not usually trans – who are most often positioned as responsible for corrupting the children, as well as drag queens, who are also not necessarily (or even usually) trans in the contemporary sense. I'm not drawing a hard distinction here, of course. Both schools and healthcare professionals are increasingly being accused of colluding with and encouraging children's 'fantasies' in Britain. And, of course, trans people are accused of the same perversions in the US. But the dominant, the most vocal, moral panic seems to be of a slightly different character, so there's a really interesting difference to be explored in how these two related but different moral panics have developed.

So, my first question is: how do we make sense of all of this? I want to start here in part because it reveals that the mobilisation of the protection of children is not in some way inevitable. It's not necessarily how this moral panic had to play out, even though it might sometimes seem that way. So why has it been focused on children? And why is the protection of children such a powerful rhetorical move in the US public sphere?

## Sophie Lewis

I find this question of specifically why the child is at the centre of the moral panic in the US right now – and why it's mainly, by contrast, the predatory adult 'unwoman' in the discourse on TERF

Island aka the UK – quite perplexing. Does the non-cissexual child represent the most eloquent symbol of a felt demographic threat to the American empire's secure future, while the British specter of the non-cissexual woman lurking in the ladies' toilets represents something more directly related to the xenophobic border animus expressed in Brexit?

Several different things come to mind. Why, for example, is it that the US is the only country in the world that still hasn't ratified the UN Convention on the Rights of the Child? There's something about the figure of the child in contemporary American discourse that suggests a need to look into the deep history of parental rights, *qua* property rights, in relation to settler colonialism and chattel slavery. After all, the child in the US is a piece of quasi-property. Perhaps, then, the slogan 'Save the Children' has to be understood as a defence of a particular racial regime of private property. Recall how this phrase animated the homophobic campaign spearheaded by Anita Bryant in the 80s, and then, more recently, was the rallying cry of QAnon. The basic structure of the sex panic *qua* counterinsurgency echoes again and again across the twentieth century. Every time, it draws on nativist fears about the dilution of citizenship, white birth rates, and uncertainty about the stable reproduction of an 'American' future.

Still, I wonder if the differences between the US and Britain in this respect – namely, end-of-Empire melancholy and nostalgia – might be more superficial than they appear. The trans panic after all seems to be ricocheting back and forth across the Pond, gaining strength every time it makes the crossing. I know Jules has written brilliantly about the transformation of QAnon into a thing one could call TAnon (where the 'T' stands for transgender, and the conspiracy focuses specifically on the 'transing' of children, 'white slavery' style). That phenomenon is both highly reminiscent of late nineteenth century moral panics about an imaginary spate of child abductions into sex trafficking and, again, thoroughly transatlantic, just like those much older panics, I think.

There has certainly been a ping-ponging back and forth between the UK and the US when it comes to reactionary feminisms more generally: for instance, TERFism came from fringe eco-radical and ex-Catholic feminist theologians in the US in the early '70s, but was then incubated, institutionalised and made hegemonic in the UK, prior to making an unwelcome comeback in America in recent years. If there are outward 'trans panic' formatting differences between the two shores to be explained, I'd (again) mainly just want to repeat that this particular settler colony, the US, has a very specific history of criminalising Black childhood and disqualifying blackness from the rubric of childhood. Meanwhile, as we know, some classes of adults – think Brett Kavanaugh – enjoy a prolonged condition of privileged childhood in the indulgent eyes of the courts, whenever they behave delinquently. I'm not an expert in Critical Childhood Studies, but I'd guess this is a culture where we are especially used to worrying about the self-'emancipation' of certain kinds of unruly children, and about the risk of contamination of all children's minds by the 'wrong' kind of children's political visions. In any case, I think you're right to pose this question as a way of reminding us that none of this is inevitable. Jules, what do you think about Rosie's question?

## Jules Gill-Peterson

I mean, it occurs to me that another way of describing that ping-ponging you are talking about is through the relationships or bridges between contrasting terms. 'Women and children' isn't just a trope or an old fashioned phrase for no reason, right? One of the ways we might draw the contrast [between them] is by understanding their relationship as pivotal. And one of the broader commonalities between anti-abortion and anti-trans political movements is that they're actually, broadly very popular. There are liberal articulations of them and there are far right articulations of them. There are left-wing articulations of them. There are secular formations and there are openly evangelical or Catholic ones. And in some ways the question of solidarity is about learning to see those series of connections and understand what they mean for organising or out organising this strange-bedfellows-world we're living in, where you have not even *that* right wing feminists aligning themselves with, say, white supremacist groups in various settler colonies. There are an array of alliances here.

But think a little bit about the child here: the formation of the kind of child around whom you can have a moral panic is really, historically speaking, a product of largely the late nineteenth century. It's a very Victorian kind of child. And that's something that I understand to be a truly Anglo-American, largely a British and American, invention that has since been exported in different forms and imposed in various ways throughout the world. There's a lot of intimacy and entanglement here in ways that are both alarming and upsetting. And so there are very short term explanations positing that QAnon really explains a lot about the United States, even though having moral panics around children is one of the oldest political playbooks in this country. Whereas the UK version has always seemed, at a distance, to be much more about white bourgeois women's function as the gatekeepers of world empire. You know, a role they might have enjoyed much more literally in the nineteenth and early twentieth century, but one that has incredible symbolic resonance.

There's so many ways to imagine what the phrase 'women and children' might mean. And so maybe one I'll just throw out is, for example, for trans women in the United States the practical, political, moral impossibility of having recognised relationships to young trans people that are relationships of solidarity or political co-organisation. It's not that it doesn't happen, but it feels largely impossible to do in any way that would be public or known. And that to me is a really interesting dilemma of 'women and children'. Further, we can think a lot about the contrast between the sort of public sphere dilemma of that versus, say, the wealth of Black, trans, political infrastructure throughout the United States where women and young people already live in relationships of solidarity, mutual aid and political co-organisation. That just looks like I put more dishes on our proverbial buffet table, but now we have a lot to eat.

**Rosie Warren**
Yes, I think we'll come back to a lot of those dishes. Thanks, Jules. As you touched on, obviously part of what's at play here is a particular idea of children and of childhood, which imagines children to be both incapable of self-knowledge that contradicts their parents' ideas of them, and without the agency to judge, to make decisions or accurately articulate themselves and their self-image such that they must be encouraged, groomed, forced, tricked or misled into seeking recognition and healthcare that affirms a different gender than the one that was assigned to them. I feel like this idea of children is so well hegemonised, so deeply embedded, in modern society that a lot of the time we can't even really see it happening. And I wonder, Jules, if you could talk about the way that that is an extremely historically specific idea about children. If you could talk a little bit about the history of that particular idea of childhood, when it came into being, how it was first and subsequently mobilised.

**Jules Gill-Peterson**
Sophie mentioned earlier, a key motif, which is children as a quasi-form of property – and I really mean quasi because the history of treating people, *actual* people as *actual* property comes into play here and I wouldn't want to flatten the difference. Nevertheless, if you want to make all of those series of ascribed differences real, that children are unknowing, incompetent, innocent, incapable, unreasonable, closer to the state of nature – if you're Jean Jacques Rousseau. All of those ideas become a manifest problem in the industrial era because, of course, children are leaving the household economy either to work, as Dickens gave us: suffering in all sorts of ways that both sentimentalised and *problematised* those really serious issues. And at the same time, the movement for the abolition of slavery is scoring a series of successes. And so, in the case of the United States, which is the version I know the best, we sort of emerge in the chaos and the white supremacist backlash of Reconstruction, asking questions that are at once legal, economic and literal.

The United States was founded on a very clear distinction between some people being people and some people being things or property. Now you're getting to this era where, you know, the widespread recognition that children should be working and should be in school is brushing up against the intense project of trying to maintain racial domination as close to the modality of legal slavery as possible. And so it's really in that kind of maelstrom that you get the production, on the one side, of the kind of Victorian, innocent child we all recognise. A white child with exaggerated big eyes who's completely helpless and really cute and not capable of doing anything and doesn't know anything. And, my goodness, we wouldn't want *that* kid to be cleaning chimneys! *That* kid should be in grade school! And then, also, families will learn to love that child in place of expecting that child to bring in wages or to do a bunch of labour in the home to sustain the family unit. So you get a sentimental economy replacing a formal economy, and the production of that child who is protectable but also incompetent and undeserving of civil rights, as they are being articulated after the Civil War. That child can only be produced if you produce its foil, right? In the US, the foil of that child is the Black child, and historians have really convincingly dug into the ways in which Black children aren't really seen as children anymore, come the Victorian era.

You can look at the formation of the juvenile justice system. You've got the first juvenile courts at the very end of the 19th century – the first one is in Chicago. I mean, these things are ghastly nonsense, right? It's a really *lovely* court where when you go to it, you have no procedural rights, you don't have a right to an attorney, you don't necessarily get a list of all the charges or evidence brought against you. You can be hauled in for anything, right? You could be arrested and sent to a juvenile judge because you are causing a ruckus at home. Or because you were just loitering on the street or running around or whatever. And these judges could basically come up with any sentence they want, because they're acting like parents. They'll send you away to a reform school or something like that, often until you're twenty-one. And that's a terrible contraction of the economic and political agency of white, innocent, protectable children that we punished under this regime.

But right from the very beginning, historians have found that those things, juvenile courts, essentially are interfacing with the advent of Black Codes, after the Reconstruction Era. Black children are arrested at far disproportionate rates, both in the urban North and in the Deep South, and these courts are essentially leasing them out – not essentially – they're *literally* leasing them out into *de facto* conditions of enslavement. And so you can see that sort of sharp distinction, which also shows up culturally. Robin Bernstein's book *Racial Innocence* talks about this.

You can see the distinction between Victorian white girls learning to play with white dolls and care for them and love them and actually learning – and there's lots of material culture and archives around this – to treat Black dolls violently and learning to see them as unfeeling and inhuman. And learning that if you punch a Black doll, it doesn't really hurt it. And so there's this whole cultural modality that comes into play, where creating a protectable, innocent child is not really a great deal for those children who are classified under that rubric. But it also creates some of the most dehumanising, violent corollaries.

And we could talk about the openly genocidal project of forced schooling of Indigenous children, kidnapped on purpose from their communities, wrenched away, put into schools, and intentionally abused on a mass scale to destroy not just Indigenous culture but Indigenous polities as well, by breaking down their reproduction from generation to generation. This larger project has to do with industrialisation. It has to do with the problem of children working – and creating the sort of alternative child to that, unsurprisingly, requires creating a series of disposable children. And that might help us understand why, in order to protect some children from the abuse of adolescent transition, we have to intentionally abuse trans children. Pretty extremely. Those sorts of contradictions are quite symptomatic of this regime of Victorian childhoods.

**Rosie Warren**
Thanks, Jules. That's very useful to thread those together. I want to get into a little more of the difficulty of navigating some of this stuff in the present moment. Because part of the problem is that – even with all of that very real historical construction – part of

the reason that appeals to protect the children are so seductive is because children *are* physically fragile, right? They are easily physically overpowered and can be forced to do things in a much easier way than most adults can. They're really little and they trust people very easily. That does seem to be true, even if there's also a historical construction of children in an exaggerated way. And it's also the case that emotionally, mentally, there are certain developmental milestones. Which means that the judgements and thoughts of children are at least different from those of adults, even if we might not want to say that they're less. They lack sufficient knowledge or understanding of certain situations to adequately assess danger. That seems pretty uncontroversial to say about all children. They are vulnerable, they cry out for protection.

But they're also vulnerable because they're legally entirely dependent on adults. They don't have the means to acquire food, to acquire shelter without any adult assistance – it's illegal for them to work – and they don't get to make any choices for themselves. They're entirely at the mercy of adults until they are themselves deemed to be adults by whatever state they're living under. Thinking about this conversation, I tried to come up with a list of the things that I think *specifically* children need to be protected from, as opposed to things everybody needs to be protected from, like war, starvation, homelessness, unwanted sexual contact and violence and so on. And I realised that the specific things that we might want to protect children from are actually mostly things that shouldn't exist, right? Like credit cards, weapons and busy roads. We've created a dangerous situation for children, but they're not natural things that children are incapable of dealing with, they're the worst inventions of capitalism.

So my question is: how do we balance? Children do have agency and they should have their agency acknowledged and they should be respected when they tell us that they are someone else than who we think them to be – I feel that very deeply. How do we balance that with also thinking about the actual vulnerability, physical or otherwise, of children when we're thinking about the politics of childhood? How do we think about the kernel of truth of innocence and protection versus children as kind of political and agential people? Sophie, maybe you could start us off with that one.

**Sophie Lewis**
There's a lot of emotion vested in the idea that childhood is in some way a constructed category. It's almost universal to feel a strong objection to something like that. *What are you academics talking about, children exist!* There's no disputing that we as a species are young and small before we are less young and small. Children do exist! But the questions Rosie has just asked are fantastic ways of putting us back in touch with our most utopian horizons and our fundamental goals as anti-capitalists, as communists, as people struggling for the abolition of the present state of things. Because as she began to show, there's nothing that we would want for the children that we would not want for ourselves. Thinking about what children are owed, what we owe to children, as it were, is a great way of thinking about what we owe ourselves and each other.

The boundaries between these things don't really exist in any stable way. Liat Ben-Moshe, earlier at this conference, was talking about infantilisation as it applies within the institutionalisation of disability. There is the assumption that certain sorts of disabled people require care similar to the care imposed on many children, ie, a certain kind of desexualising custodial care – except forever, in this case, and with no possibility of graduating into an integration into society, into community. What if we think about infantilisation in dialogue with disability liberation? I think it becomes easier, if we do, to see the false binaries, the false choices, the false oppositions that are posed in the context of care, such as: institutionality or the private nuclear, heteropatriarchal household? The authority of carceral care in an institutional setting, or the authority of the proprietary parent? Neither please!

But that's also an easy thing to say given that we often don't concretely have another obvious option, as individuals struggling to survive in the interstices of a deeply brutalising, individualising, atomising mode of reproduction. What is harder to grapple with is the possibility that 'the children' really do need to be understood in fairly theoretically informed ways, by all of us, as indeed, yes, *constructs* that are there, in part, to keep class society going. Childhood is a temporal category that helps naturalise the "work society" and manufactures mass acceptance of waged labour. It is widely imagined as the time when we do not labour to produce surplus value, and serves thus as a way of buying us off, making it seem inevitable that we must then graduate into the rest of our lives, meaning lives that we – most of us – must give away in work. This is why I talk about the family as a technology of work, because of the sense in which it is – specifically because it is the children who require us to go to work before they are themselves required to grow up to go to work and have children of their own in turn who will require them to keep going to work – an immense naturalisation of work.

Children in the real world are not simply the reason adults want to go to work and have to go to work, however. They are often carers themselves, besides being (if they are lucky) cared-for. We would do well to remind ourselves: children often have abortions, children often have sex. Children can get married at any age in many states within this Christian-nationalism saturated settler colony, even if they are not legally allowed to have sex outside of marriage. These sorts of things really expose the core logic of reproductivity- and fertility-protecting nativism at the root of the politics of childhood.

To try to return back to the point: how do we think and talk about care and autonomy, vulnerability and responsibility, with, not just in reference to, children? This is the conversation I want to have here. The current state of play feels like a gridlock, like a terrifying terrain of fear and individuation. It's almost socially impossible in many settings to speak with children if you're not vested with the authority and authorisation to do so, an authorisation that has to be either kinship, or medical, or school-related, or carceral (the police are always allowed).

Again: when we think about caring for children, what is it that we think they need that we think we do not need? What do children remind us, inconveniently, that we owe to each other? I suggested in *Full Surrogacy Now* that we are all the makers of one another.

And the task of communism, I really believe, is to learn to act like it; to organise infrastructure as though we really are each other's harvest, for better and for worse. And that's a desegregating horizon when it comes to this category of children, as much as it is (in the context of disability that I was referring to before) an horizon of de-institutionalisation, a radical upending of categories such as insanity and sanity, and independent and dependent, and adult and other.

**Rosie Warren**
Thanks, Sophie. Jules, did you want to come in and add to that? Respond? Disagree?

**Jules Gill-Peterson**
I wanted to underline something you're saying, Sophie. I loved what you were saying at the end about what we might call a project of desegregating the difference – the ostensible differences – between children and adults that have served to naturalise so many systems of domination. And I like to think of it as the principle of superintendence that some people – whether through a fantasy of nature or some circumstance – deserve to be deprived of, in some cases, minimum degrees of self-determination in favour of being lorded over by others who implicitly or explicitly deem themselves superior. The concept of the child we've been talking about in some sense facilitates that principle, which is absolutely bedrock to the capitalist political economy, but also – not to be too professorial – the history of Western political thought and the formation of the state. I mean it's the actual bedrock principle of the settler project that you would arrive and not simply endeavour to replace people already living there but also appoint yourself their superintendents. And, not surprisingly, the most relevant body of case law in the United States for the mistreatment and the legal alibi for the United States and its modern containment of an attack on Indigenous sovereignty is treating Indigenous polities as 'domestic dependent nations'. As if they were the children of the United States living within it.

So, to me, part of this question is words like 'care'. I mean, maybe the only place there's a shade of interesting friction for me is that I'm so intensely anti-utopian. I tend to be not very good at offering political programs or infrastructure for that reason, but it comes from a kind of deep pessimism about how difficult the critical project is up front. I'll use the metaphor of unlearning, but I don't just mean that in an educational or scholastic sense. It can be a matter of collective organising. But really, how? How can we even first unlearn, destroy if you like? There will be harmful coercive modes of care. Custodial relationships, superintendents that are not only the stuff that makes the world work, but unfortunately the very psychodramas of our family, youth, kinship structures, relationships, the so-called private sphere as well. And to me [unlearning those] feels like a really important project at a moment when there's such over drafting of child moral tenets.

To take abortion and trans issues as examples, many of the initial responses have just been embarrassing. And they have also been kind of haughty: 'look at these stupid fascists! All they want to do is ensure that pregnancies are carried to term and then they just abandon children, end of story.' A moral superiority affect or aesthetic. There's a really difficult but quite crucial and immediate task of figuring out what it would entail to smash some of these structures both at their massive scale and then in the micro scale.

The one other thing to say that's only half true is that ostensibly all adults were previously children, and that's sort of true and not true if we want to be really careful about it. But in any case, there's something that I find disruptive about the dismissal of teenagers and of young people's particularly political actions in this moment. The vitriolic disavowal of young people's organising against gun violence. Just utter, utter ridicule of young people. Also, young people's mobilisation around the climate crisis is just treated as if it were the most ridiculous thing that has ever happened, right?

And similarly, the idea of the social contagion of being transgender is premised on the idea that young people are foolish and are susceptible to one another's whims. Therefore we don't have to care at all about what they want or say about themselves. Those are some starting places for that unlearning process and also the terrain on which to build relationships of solidarity with young people who are already busy doing things that are, frankly, informed.

**Rosie Warren**
Yeah, I think, maybe unconsciously, one of the reasons I wanted to bring the two of you together is that you, Jules, sit in this kind of pessimistic camp and Sophie's kind of a perennial utopian. And I'm maybe some odd mix: a utopian pessimist.

**Sophie Lewis**
Well, let me just come back on the utopian super briefly, because I will stand up for it as a decolonial heuristic and as a method. There are at least two quite different histories of utopianisms, or so I have been taught by the comrades in utopian studies. Yes, one of them is colonial to the core, flowing from, e.g., Thomas More's desire to map the ideal society. But there are also utopianisms of cyborg decolonisation that are more about making the road while, or by, walking. One option, if you don't like the idea of utopianism, is to espouse Frederick Jameson's formulation: the anti-anti-utopian. It is imperative to oppose anti-utopianism. If we wish to denaturalise capitalist work, capitalist subjectivity, the givens of the social reproduction of labour, the idea of capitalist kinship, colonial kinship, etcetera, we absolutely need to denaturalise the given. I would say that that gesture, which has nothing to do with writing recipes for the cook shops of the future, is the core of a critical utopianism we cannot afford to abandon. It's about having the courage to mount a fundamental 'no' to the shibboleths of the liberal individual, despite not knowing exactly who else we might collectively become.

**Rosie Warren**
Utopian whether you like it or not, Jules. I do want to touch on with you, Sophie, something that Jules was talking about. I know that you've been doing a lot of thinking and research about the history of children's liberation as a concept, as a movement. The description of a course that you have taught on Children's Liberation says:

not so long ago, radical movements in America around Black Power, crip or disability liberation, domestic violence, sexuality, transgender freedom and socialism all related to children, to some extent, as political actors in their own right.

Why did the horizon of children's liberation largely vanish from the left? I wonder if you could tell us a bit about the history of children's liberation and what happened to it as a movement. When and why did feminists and queer people want to liberate children, and why don't they anymore?

**Sophie Lewis**
Many people don't know that kids' lib, or youth liberation, or children's liberation – whatever you want to call it – was a completely common category in the so-called red decade of the Long Sixties. Whether it's Ros Baxandall or Linda Gordon's women's liberation collectives or the Boston Gay Liberation Front or the Third World Gay and Lesbian caucuses, everyone was talking about cooperative childcare and radical nurseries, projects that often came with extremely ambitious agendas of unmaking, for example, even the common sense that children by default only have two parents. Leftists were truly trying to get a national network of nurseries and co-ops off the ground in which the quasi property status of the child would be troubled and a sense of genuine responsibility from all to all would be incubated. There were men's childcare centres and free schools. There was discussion of children's liberation in Mad and Crip power circles, and the concept of liberating oppressed childhood was also being theorised in the milieu of Black Power – the Black Panthers for example were frequently thinking about the revolutionary task of forming new humans from infancy onward, not to mention what is due in the meantime to comrades who are not yet adults. There's also an interesting history of Youth Liberation that is led by children themselves. For instance in Ann Arbor. This was a project that was supported by the White Panthers and by the Human Rights Party, and featured a fifteen-year-old running for

the Michigan school board in the early seventies, but being denied on the grounds that she was too young. There followed a national litigation of the rationale for excluding someone from their own school board on the basis of their age.

Anyway. Why did all of this agitation against 'adult supremacy' die out in the eighties? I'd love to hear your perspectives on that, Jules. I tend to reach for the explanation that the ruling classes crushed the utopian energies of the sixties and the seventies into dust and that an extremely sophisticated and cunning counter-revolutionary project simply won out, and became dominant. The left simply was defeated, I believe – but then we compounded that defeat by erasing or ridiculing our own most utopian desires and demands. Suddenly there was a whole ecology of counter-revolutionary institutions, organisations and myths installed to wipe our own movement memory clear.

One very effective counterinsurgent strategy was the Right's paedophilia smear against queer and feminist allies of children. That's something that the left never really strategised an effective or courageous united response to. Back then it was 'queers lurking behind ice cream vans and gender-bending feminists in daycare centres are polluting, contaminating, harming, scheming, infecting the children'. In the twenty-first century it's substantially a replay with a transgender twist. We've been here before. But, indeed, we were there in the 1910s and 1920s when 'white slavery' undergirded a reactionary international. Entire purpose built organisations sprang up to prevent the despoliation of white girls by a fictional nation-threatening menace. We should be talking about this history, in my opinion, and more importantly, figuring out how to break the cycle whereby leftists and feminists and queers split with one another in the face of the Right's divide-and-conquer virtuosity with the bludgeoning figure of the Child.

### Jules Gill-Peterson
Maybe one other thing we could chew on together is the history of political economy and shifts in the labour market. The entry of

women into the labour force in the global north on mass also created, among other things, the crisis in social reproduction, the child care crisis. But also the domestication of certain minimal planks of youth movements: lowering the voting age in the US in the 1970s; kids have actually some civil rights at trial for the first time. There are a series of liberal modernisation initiatives that I suspect had, whether they were designed to or not, the effect of depoliticising a lot of the antagonisms erupting in the 1960s as generational conflict – this is a kind of compliment to just the brute crushing of the seventies.

**Rosie Warren**
Thanks, Jules. Thanks to both of you. I'm sorry we ran a little over our time, but can you really blame me?

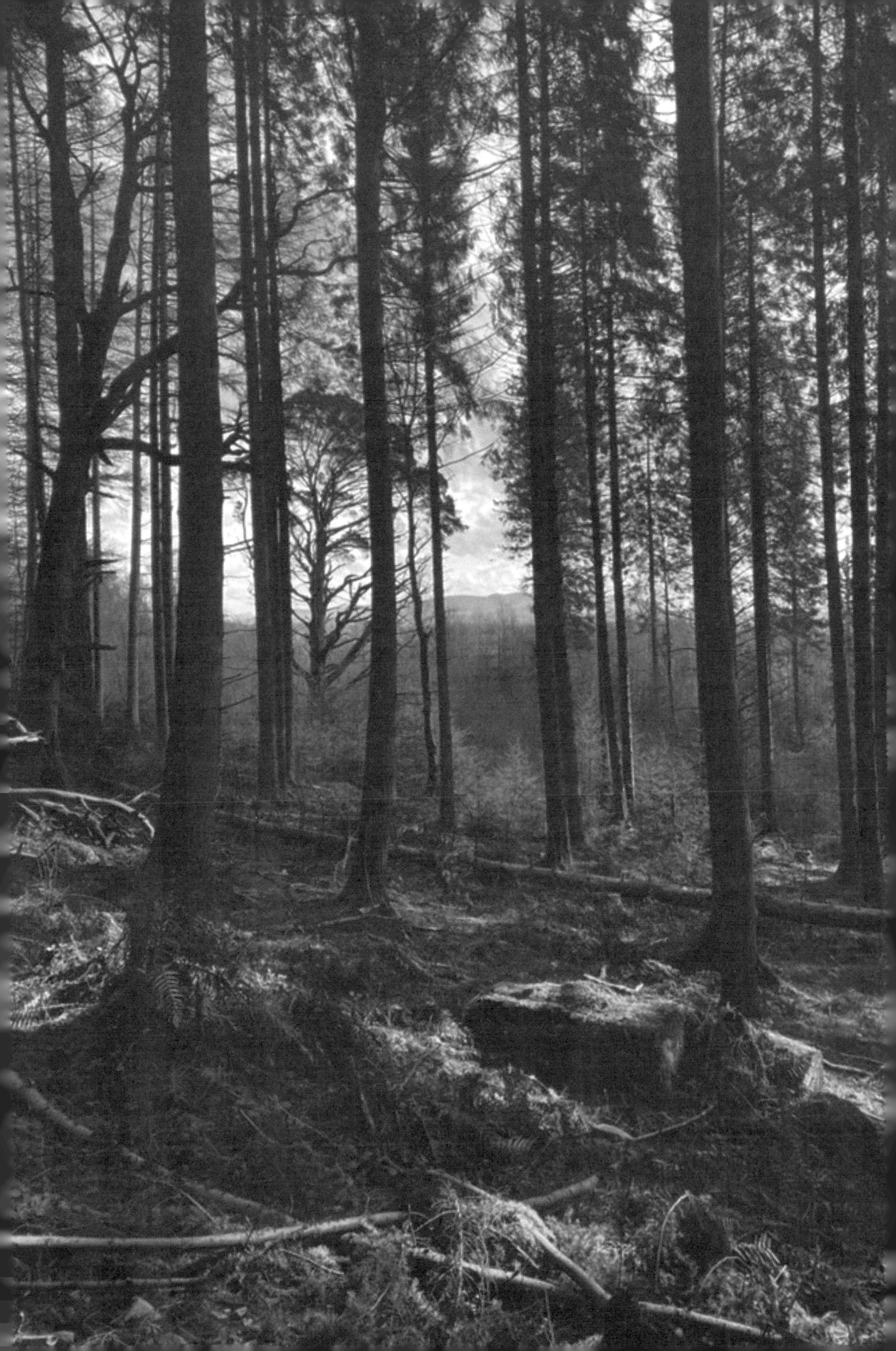

REBEKAH DISKI

# The Full Force of the Law: Protest and Repression on a Scorched Earth

At 3:45am on 17 October, 2022, a lone car approached the Dartford Crossing from the north and slowed to a standstill at the middle of the bridge. Two men, wearing backpacks, waterproofs and woolly hats, got out of the car and jumped over a hip-high fence between the road and the bridge towers. The taller man clipped his climbing harness to the bridge while his partner, checking for oncoming vehicles, ran across the three empty lanes and did the same on the other side. Both men then swung onto the suspension cables, secured their ropes, and slowly shuffled up to a height of sixty metres.

After a three-hour ascent, they left the relative stability of the cables and hung in mid-air, throwing each other a network of lines with which to secure themselves and the load they had carried up. The man on the eastern side of the bridge took a bundle out of his backpack, passed it by 'washing line' to his partner and they jointly hoisted a banner. At first the message was partly obscured by a stubborn piece of masking tape, but the wind rushed in to dislodge it and the canvas unfurled to read 'JUST STOP OIL'. At midday, having fastened the banner to the bridge's central towers, the men finally climbed into the hammocks they had brought and waited for the helicopter camera crews to arrive.

A little more than a year later, I visited HMP Highpoint, where Marcus Decker and Morgan Trowland were serving what were then the UK's longest ever sentences for peaceful climate protest at two years and seven months and three years, respectively. I had met Marcus before he went to prison and knew he was committed to the cause: he had been arrested several times and frequently spent the night in his hammock to protect trees condemned by insurance claims or property developments. But he had never tried anything like this. This time, he said, 'it felt like a really serious thing'. When I recognised Marcus in the news reports from the Dartford Crossing, his serene face framed by outraged headlines, my first thought was how brave this was; my second was, will it make a difference?

The Dartford Crossing action was part of an escalation by Extinction Rebellion (XR) offshoots Just Stop Oil (JSO) and Insulate Britain to recapture the momentum lost during the pandemic lockdowns and to keep climate change on a political agenda preoccupied with economic recovery. Covid-19 briefly created conditions in which both the global cooperation and popular support required to avert ecological cataclysm might have been built. Concerted state action, public education and behaviour change, the flourishing of mutual aid, the (fleeting) appreciation of socially important work and, tragically, the experience of mass death: all apt lessons for a world facing the existential threats of climate and ecological breakdown. Lessons that challenge the sacred logic of capital augmentation and lessons that therefore remain unlearned.

As hopeful calls to 'build back better' receded and the oppressive machinery of business as usual cranked back into action, there was a surge of popular protest. JSO's civil disobedience coincided with the sudden appearance of thousands-strong Black Lives Matter demonstrations after the police murder of George Floyd, and an increase in labour militancy responding to the egregious treatment of workers during the pandemic. The government answered with a legislative backlash comprising the Police, Crime, Sentencing and Courts (PCSC) Act 2022, the Public Order Act 2023 and the Minimum Service Levels Act 2023.

Marcus and Morgan were charged with public nuisance under the PCSC Act. They expected a custodial sentence, but their heavy-handed treatment took them, and many others, by surprise. Denied bail, they joined record numbers languishing in overcrowded prisons. After seven months on remand, they were found guilty by a jury in Basildon, a short drive from the Dartford Crossing. On the morning of the sentencing, JSO lawyers were optimistic that the time already served would suffice, asking Marcus: 'should we get you out of here today?'

Instead, he was moved to Highpoint in Suffolk. At the visitors' centre, I emptied my pockets and queued in the waning afternoon sun with a group of mothers, partners, and children, waiting to be patted down and inspected by a sniffer dog. Marcus sat at a low plastic table, immediately recognisable by his long dark hair, beard, and grin. Each table bore a laminated list of rules, starting with 'no excessive or prolonged physical contact'. Marcus was upbeat, having heard about the acquittal of the 'HSBC 9', a group of nine XR protestors that broke the bank's windows to protest its fossil fuel investments. He reflected that the jury in inner-London Southwark was likely to be more sympathetic than his jury in Tory Basildon, but the choice of target was surely significant too.

The Dartford Crossing action partially closed a major artery around London for forty hours, causing an average delay of six minutes and six seconds per driver, according to the judgement, albeit considerably longer for some. Judge Shane Collery KC explained the unprecedented sentences to the defendants: 'You have to be punished both for the chaos you caused and to deter others from seeking to copy you in the next protest.' Marcus said the sentence 'felt like an extreme breakdown of democracy ... You can only be accountable if dissent is allowed, and silencing that dissent makes the world a little bit darker.'

The pair's appeal was blocked by a panel that included environmental lawyer Justine Thornton who happens to be married to Ed Miliband, now Secretary of State for Energy Security and Net Zero. Marcus was released in February 2024 but is now on immigration bail: a German citizen previously with leave to remain, he is appealing a deportation order which would separate him from his partner and her children. He wears an electronic ankle tag that requires charging for ninety minutes a day, during which time he is attached to a wall socket. After a spate of acquittals by sympathetic juries, judges have made some forms of evidence – like the small matter of the earth-boiling effects of our fossil-based economy – inadmissible. In July 2024, five JSO activists were tried for conspiracy to cause a public nuisance that blocked the M25. Four of the five defended themselves, repeatedly ignoring instructions not to mention the climate and ultimately being dragged by police from the courtroom. The jury took just a day to unanimously find them guilty. Roger Hallam, one of the defendants and co-founder of XR and JSO, was sentenced to five years; the others received four years (these were recently reduced slightly on appeal). Michel Forst, the UN special rapporteur on environmental defenders, attended the trial, calling the result 'a very dangerous precedent, not just for environmental protest but any form of peaceful protest'.

Instigated by an ailing government in the throes of a legitimacy crisis, these developments have been clapped along by a right-wing media branding protestors as 'eco-loons' and 'fanatics'. Grasping for the nationalist truncheon usually reserved for racialised others, the *Daily Mail* called Marcus and Morgan (originally from New Zealand) part of 'JSO's Foreign Legion'. Class identity is more plausibly weaponised, with the tabloid press relishing in the double-barrelled names and private education of some climate activists and the *Spectator* declaring 'eco-loonyism ... an upper-middle-class rite of passage'. Journalists, many with their own double-barrels and elite schooling, indulge in a kind of fetishisation of the humble commuter against whom they gleefully cast these spoilt activists.

This to-and-fro between state, courtroom and media reinforces an upside-down common sense, in which blocking a road or spraying a building is extreme, while burning a planet is not. Those who cannot rouse themselves over the loss of entire species were suddenly incensed by the threat of JSO's cornflour paint to rare lichens in a recent action at Stonehenge. The monument, secured in concrete since 1964 and cherished by hippies, neo-pagans and counter-cultural fellow travellers, was immediately reclaimed as a nationalist symbol desecrated by the 'eco-mob'. The lichens themselves will of course frazzle in the heat of global warming. Sunak and Starmer raced to condemn the group with a vigour they could not muster for the Israeli perpetrators of genocide in Gaza. Starmer, so squeamish about the prospect of an ICC arrest warrant for Benjamin Netanyahu, declared that JSO should 'feel the full force of the law'. David Lammy scolded both climate and Palestine solidarity activists that he favoured 'change through power, not protest', but anyone hoping that a Labour government would break with Tory authoritarianism has been roundly disabused.

A week into the new Labour government, Youth Demand, a JSO offshoot focusing on Palestine, chalked next to the cenotaph the staggering number (180,000) that the *Lancet* estimates could be the real death toll in Gaza. The veterans minister condemned the action as 'abhorrent': a war memorial was no place to remind us of the unjust death in our midst. The gradual red-pilling of the mainstream climate movement has prompted promising cross-fertilisation with struggles against other capital-authored injustices. The state has observed this exchange with alarm: John Woodcock, the government's 'extremism tzar' warns that protest launched from the 'far-left subculture' is a threat to democracy, as if such action was not itself a symptom of democratic desiccation. Insisting on the inalienable rights of councils to invest in fossil fuels and of arms manufacturers to equip a genocidal army, Woodcock demands that lawmakers 'reject the idea that there are causes so important the end justifies the illegal means'.

The extremism discourse used to denigrate those who challenge the status quo inevitably spills back onto the street. Climate protestors have been hauled out of roads and rammed with cars. A video of someone shooting fireworks at Marcus and Morgan as they dangled in the dark above the Thames went viral: the comment sections were full of calls to 'shoot them down'. After far-right former Home Secretary Suella Braverman described pro-Palestine protests as 'hate marches', a retinue of genocide apologists lined up to declare central London a no-go zone for Jews on demonstration days. Meanwhile, those expressing solidarity with Palestinians – many of us Jews ourselves – have endured racist and antisemitic abuse and physical intimidation from a deranged alliance of Zionist and white nationalist counter-protestors.

What now? How should we turn the renewed energy of the Palestinian solidarity movement, the osmosis between struggles and the outrage at ruling-class repression into a sustained answer to the crises of late capitalism? Cracks have already appeared: on Gaza, these have been all too gradual, but the mass mobilisations undoubtedly shifted UK policy, precipitating (qualified) calls for a ceasefire and undermining Labour's sandcastle majority in the 2024 election. The climate protests of 2018-2020 inarguably heightened public awareness and forced a political response; Labour has pledged to end North Sea oil and gas licensing – JSO's original demand.

The radical flank of the climate movement continues to court arrest with disruptive and spectacular actions, adhering to the logic that Suffragettes and civil rights activists were unpopular in their time. As Marcus remarks, 'no one needs to like Just Stop Oil'. But neither JSO nor its mainstream counterparts have achieved the scale or regularity of mass participation that we have seen for Gaza. This surely reflects the sheer horror of livestreamed atrocity, the visibility and brazenness of its perpetrators, and the palpable complicity of our own leaders. A pro-Palestinian activist using an ongoing genocide to defend their actions against an Israeli arms manufacturer is, in this moment, more viscerally sympathetic than a climate activist pointing to the floods in Pakistan while they block the M25 (although both defences are now legally inadmissible).

Marcus insists that the motorway is a key site of harm, although he accepts that the disruption is felt by people driving to work, hospital appointments and funerals – the subject of many a talk show phone-in. In *How to Blow up a Pipeline*, Andreas Malm exhorts the climate movement to substitute what he sees as self-defeating actions of public inconvenience for sabotage of corporate property. Marcus points out that in April 2022 JSO did target fossil fuel infrastructure over several weeks that saw protestors occupy oil terminals, lock themselves to tankers and drill into tyres. Despite leading to hundreds of arrests, the action was relatively under-reported.

Perhaps more instructive, for those considering Malm's manifesto, is the response of a state in lockstep with oil interests: high court injunctions swiftly banned protest at key nodes in the oil distribution network and actions such as 'locking on' were promptly transposed into new offences. Confronted with the mind-boggling intransigence of those barrelling towards mass extinction, the moral rationale of Malm's call to arms is clear, but the suggestion that such action would compel states to urgently decarbonise seems less assured. The escalation of protest tactics would be met with further repression: intensified surveillance, longer prison sentences, limits to legal defence.

As I spoke to Marcus about his inventive strategies to escape the twenty-three hours a day that most prisoners spend in their cells – his work on the gardening team; a choir project; voluntary attendance at religious services – it was clear that his was not the typical prison experience. Nonetheless, the monotony of confinement, the proximity to violence, and the helplessness in the face of fellow prisoners' crises were hard to bear. The separation from his partner, and now the prospect of deportation, have taken a toll on his family. With judges now zealously meting out multi-year sentences, how many others will pay this price?

Alongside, and often in service to, the formidable foe of fossil capital, the Left must confront an ascendant far-right. Co-opting the real and increasingly pervasive experience of insecurity and atomisation, it scoffs at the supposed 'degrowth austerity' of climate action and invokes a threat to such degraded symbols of liberty as the fossil-fuelled commute. It casts the convivial struggles for racial, Palestinian and trans justice against traditional national values. Mobilising this decade's preferred discursive mode

– the culture war – it promises to restore past privileges predicated on race and citizenship. Neutralising the revanchist appeal of the far-right requires taking popular understandings seriously. Street movements are crucial, but they are not enough, and their momentum will wane without deeper modes of organisation. Incipient collaboration across movements is heartening, but these must be reinforced by activity at the workplace and community level. Given the urgency of the crises, the need to organise 'in and against the state' seems inescapable. In the years ahead, we can expect the full heft of the fossil machine to be thrown at these struggles and the alliances that are surely needed to take it on. The exact constellation of strategies is not yet clear, but the future depends on us working it out.

NICK DYER-WITHEFORD

# Biocommunism

Biocommunism emerges from the catastrophes now inflicted throughout the *bios*, the realm of life itself, by capital. It calls for new disaster relief systems, opening borders to climate refugees, the expropriation of capital from crisis-critical industries, the rationing of consumption, the mobilisation of emergency labour, and ecological and economic planning.

Biocommunism affirms the potential of a new, plenitudinous mode of species reproduction drawing on clean, renewable and socially-distributed solar energy and other renewable sources. But this will only be created under emergency conditions of disaster, rescue, repair and restoration, as a massive operation of 'salvage.' This will require both the mobilisation of resources only presently commanded through the state apparatus, *and* new forms of autonomous organisation and mutual aid. Battles are now fought out on already-catastrophised ground, and demand more extreme remedial measures than envisaged in many eco-socialist versions of a Green New Deal or other preventative plans.

'Biocommunism' disputes the hyphen of eco-socialism. The hyphen, while bringing the ecological and social together in left thought, also continues to conceptually separates them. This obscures the profound imbrications of the social and the natural so apparent in the current polycrisis, where, for example, imperial geopolitics spawn wars that create energy crises that shift the dynamic of climate crisis, and those ecological dynamics then rebound as the catalyst of further social conflicts. Biopower, biopolitics and biocommunism are terms proper to a moment in this unified field where 'ecological' and 'governmental' processes relentlessly loop in mutual reconfiguration.

Marx often used the terms 'socialism' and 'communism' interchangeably. But, since Lenin, it has generally been held that 'socialism' refers to an initial stage of human emancipation, where liberation must contend with poverty, material shortages, and other residues of capitalism, while 'communism' designates a later or higher phase where, with the forces of production freed from archaic restraints, society can be organised according to the principle of 'from each according to their abilities, to each according to their needs'.

It may be objected that what is described here as biocommunism, including mention of essential labour, rationing of resources and even ecological limits to growth, is really an account of socialism. However, in an age of extinctions – both human extinctions of other species, and risks of human auto-extinction – the relation of socialism and communism should be rethought. Socialism could be understood as a phase in which an emancipatory project depends on a progressive amassing of the capacity to mobilise human populations and environmental resources for production. Communism – or biocommunism – might then be a moment at which, for still-anthropocentric reasons of self-preservation, biopower is subjected to a social limitation to avoid eradicating the ecological 'web of life' in which humanity is enmeshed. This would be a point at which 'to each according to their need' is re-interpreted by the recognition that human need includes, materially and psychologically, the need for flourishing non-human species and populations of plankton, fungi, insects, frogs and other entities upward along the evolutionary scale.

In capitalism, where resource allocations continues to be stratified by intersecting forces of class, gender and racialisation, the restraint or reduction of productive powers, repudiating growth to diminish ecological destruction, would be tantamount to reactionary consolidation of established pyramids of exploitation and dispossession. The only way in which a self-diminution of human interspecies ascendancy could be socially tolerable is if it were accompanied by a razing of differential intra-human allocations of wealth and well-being. That is why biocommunism must be a project both equalitarian and ecological, a double subversion of capitalism sufficient to revive a name striking fear in the current order; 'commie' – or rather, 'biocommie.'

## Vital Systems

As capitalism's own forces of production turn against it, biocommunist organisation starts at the point of destruction, ensuring the safety of populations struck by disasters, fast and slow: pandemic outbreaks; fires, floods, super-storms, droughts and heatwaves whose frequency indexes global warming; what Jairus Groves terms the 'savage ecology' of war. The multiplication of these terrifying events, and consequent collapse-threatening pressures on hospitals, medical aid and burial services, food and water supply, transportation, energy grids and communication networks, signals the failure of the existing social order. Rescue and protection of the endangered becomes a touchstone of any successor system.

Stephen Collier and Andrew Lakoff describe how in advanced capitalism there is an apparatus of 'vital systems' used for the 'government of emergencies.' It comprises centralised and specialised organisations (e.g., the United States Federal Emergency Management Administration or Centre for Disease Control), and regional and municipal agencies of rescue, policing, hospitalisation, medical care, shelter and sustenance of displaced populations and reconstruction of damaged areas. These institutions were created to manage risks arising from within the capitalist modernity they defend, as a biopolitical tool-kit to control civil disorders, suppress diseases of urban poverty and in preparations for war.

In the era of neoliberalism, however, such crisis services have been undermined by the accumulative logic of the very order they protect. Austerity cut-backs and just-in-time logistics have depleted or dismantled supply depots, dissolved organisational centres, privatised and outsourced operations. Increasing threadbare 'vital systems' are tightly geared to protection of property and the circulation of capital. They are shot through with authoritarianism and discrimination, manifesting in racialised policing of storm-struck cities and repeated failures to protect low-income communities. Emergency relief problems of capacity and inequity festering for decades are now about to be intensified by global polycrisis.

This lack of preparedness was demonstrated by Covid-19. Confronting a long-predicted zoonotic pathogen crisis, liberal democracies oscillated between the dual priorities of preserving social reproduction (shutdown) and continuing capitalist accumulation (business as usual), and were beset by institutional incoherencies and material shortages. Decades of underfunding, deregulation and privatisation of health care systems intensified the pandemic chokepoint of intensive care services, whose collapse could only be forestalled by broad restrictions on public behaviour.

Although in the wealthiest nations relatively generous unemployment benefits were available for some workers, elsewhere employees had to fight for 'quarantine' wages, while designated 'frontline' workers had to toil on, sometimes without basic sick leave provisions. These real governmental failures were avidly exploited by the far right, mis-representing a scene of disarrayed disciplinarity as a sinister, seamless conspiracy of elite control. Neo-fascists seized on Gorgio Agamben's portrayal of lockdowns and vaccine mandates as totalitarian biopolitics to repudiate any broad social solidarity, promoting ideologies of individual sovereignty and/or race war.

The task of biocommunism is not to ratify such occult theories, but rather, criticising the insufficiencies of capital's disaster relief, to build new vital systems. Biocommunist disaster relief is a politics of care. It would make major social investments to deal with epidemiological, meteorological and military disasters, ranging from distributed vaccine manufacture capacities to urban cooling centres to evacuation and shelter provisions, with special focus on the most vulnerable social strata. It would normalise replacement income for livelihoods lost to disaster, rebuilding of destroyed homes, and reconstruction of disrupted communities, including trauma treatment, relocation and retraining for disaster victims. It would prepare cadres of communicators who could, across class, gender and racialised social divisions, convey the rationale for emergency measures and relay criticism and counter-proposals from varied social groups to planners.

None of this would prevent disaster relief from being painful and contentious. However, in contrast to the seething social toxicity stirred by capital's partial efforts, it would foster communal solidarity. Nor should vital care systems be purely state-led. Mutual aid practices that emerge in catastrophes inspire anarchist and autonomist concepts of 'disaster communism,' which the Out of the Woods collective describes as 'a seizing of the means of social reproduction.' Recent instances include Occupy Wall Street relief operations after Hurricane Sandy, community movements after Mexican earthquakes, and volunteer Covid-19 pandemic activism in Milan. It is impractically romantic to imagine mutual aid could currently replace state-based vital systems for marshalling technologies, supplies, personnel, and expertise. But the reorganisation of such services to combines state provision and self-organisation is a real possibility. In this respect practices of popular mobilisation in face of natural disaster, still alive in Cuba as an offshoot of revolutionary war tradition, should be revived within biocommunism, now as part of populations' struggles against capitalocene calamity.

## De-Bordering

Issues of migration and refuge are central to biocommunism. Poverty, ecological devastation, war and oppression today displace millions. Globally, populations least responsible for carbon emissions, and most vulnerable in terms of poverty, frail infrastructures and insufficient public services, are subjected to the most serious climate cataclysms. Flight tends to local routes, from one poor and disadvantaged country to another, but also presses towards the rich world, across the Mediterranean, the US–Mexico border and other frontiers where migrants face exclusion, detention, deportation, criminalisation, abandonment and death.

Biocommunism embraces the necessity of a new politics of movement. This paper does not adjudicate debates between advocates of 'open borders' – relaxing state regulation on migration – and 'no frontiers' – aiming for the abolition of states tout court. But it does affirm a broad 'de-bordering' orientation, understanding that this process may require several stages and components to building the infrastructures, policies and practices to transform flows of movement and settlement. Thomas Nail categorises these under the headings of 'sanctuary' – refusing cooperation with (or dismantling) state agencies seeking to arrest and deport migrants; 'solidarity' – providing access to medicine, housing, learning and communication; and 'status' – recognition as a full member of a new community.

But biocommunism is not just expansion of liberal immigration programs. Rather, it recognises the proletarian nature of global migration. Thus 'sanctuary' will become governmental protection of migrants from racist persecution, human trafficking, workplace exploitation, and slave labour. Solidarity will encompass the original meaning of the term as *labour* solidarity, systematically connecting and integrating migrants with unions and worker organisations, combatting the way capital benefits so powerfully from division and insecurity in the workforce, while 'status' would comprehend new rights of livelihood for all detached from a competitive wage market discussed later in this paper.

Migrancy is geopolitical issue involving out-flow as well as in-flow. Joseph Nevins makes the case for 'migration as reparations,' whereby populations deprived of the 'right to stay' in home regions wracked by destructive colonialisms and climate change gain a 'right to move' and participate in the remittance economy. This is a compelling argument. But it carries the implicit dangers of treating out-migration regions as sacrifice-zones fated to become uninhabitable. Biocommunism therefore defends the right to stay as well as the right to move. This requires more than just large scale international subsidies for mitigation and adaption measures in the regions of climate change's most severe effect. Military interventions causing migrant flight, such as those in Afghanistan, Iraq, Libya, must be ended, as should the extractive ventures of multinational capital creating ecological and social chaos in the global South. All these steps need to be set within a framework of long-term planning for the steady equalisation of global. living standards.

De-bordering is difficult, not just because of practical problems of reorganising vast planetary population flows, but because of racism. The European and North American response to Ukrainian refugees from Russian invasion demonstrates the humanitarian generosity that migration can inspire, but also, in its contrast to treatment of refugees from other parts of the world, and in occasions of glaring discrimination against Ukrainians of colour, how selective that benevolence can be. Migration is the chosen field on which 'fossil fascism', as Andreas Malm and the Zetkin Collective dub it, will fight in the era of global warming, setting against it notions of nationalist eco-sustainability. Yet the costs and dangers of perpetual fortification against migration, the labour shortages of zones with ageing populations and low birthrates, the intensification of internal climate-migration, not to mention every impulse of human-kindness ultimately tell against the far right. Biocommunism dissolves borders and redefines sovereignty for a nomadic global worker.

## Emergency Expropriation

Socialised ownership of the means of production is a basic tenet of communism. Its importance heightens amidst interweaving disasters. But in a variation on classic Marxist thought, while expropriation is today sometimes vital to expand production, it can also be necessary to shut production down. Two campaigns by movements for global equality and ecological protection indicate this dual case for expropriation of crisis-critical capitalism.

The first is the 'no profit from pandemic' campaign for eliminating the intellectual property rights of big pharma. Rapid development of Covid-19 vaccines by companies such as Pfizer and Moderna, achieved at record speed in the United States, the European Union and Britain, was an outcome of state-capital cooperation. Governments partnered with drugmakers, pouring in billions of dollars to procure raw materials, finance clinical trials and retrofit factories. Billions more were committed to buy the finished product. But this success created stark global inequities in availability – vaccine apartheid. This global inequality allowed Covid-19 to continue spreading and increased the likelihood of vaccine-resistant variants. India and South Africa advanced an initiative to temporarily suspend intellectual property rules for Covid-19 vaccines and other coronavirus-related medical equipment, waiving patents to allow more countries to manufacture Covid-19 doses. Mounting worldwide pressure forced the US to shift from opposition to partial support, making some short-term patent waivers, but leaving the full scope of vaccination segregation untouched. This and scores of other examples of unevenly researched and distributed medical drugs make the case for moving their control from private hands to new global-public institutions.

The second example is the 'Leave It In the Ground' campaign against carbon capital. Ending global boiling demands drastic reduction in fossil fuel use. Full use of known reserves would (absent massive and, at the moment, speculative, techno-fixes) drive atmospheric $CO_2$ concentrations to extreme heights. Therefore one thrust of radical ecological movements is conversion of fossil capital enterprises to public utilities – to shut them down. Thus, Holly Jean Buck's program for 'ending things' includes a five-step fossil fuel phaseout, moving through moratoria on prospecting, subsidy withdrawal, capping and ramp-down of production and 'nationalisation to exit.' As a major share of global oil production is undertaken by state owned companies, such as Saudi Aramco. biocommunist socialisation therefore cannot be conceived simply as nationalisation. It would be a deeper de-commodification, replacing management cadres and reorienting enterprises away from the world market, and towards goals of eliminating carbon emissions, ensuring a just-transition for fossil industry workers (a process crucial to disarm opposition) and converting facilities to the production of publicly owned and controlled carbon capture technologies.

These two cases illustrate the double-sided case – expansionary, for vaccines, terminative, for fossil fuels – for counter-catastrophic capital expropriation. There are many other examples. For example, inseparable from discussion of energy extraction is that of governance of electrical grids, in which private and public utility companies with entrenched attachments to carbon capital vie with unregulated green capitalism whose freebooting avarice threatens to make clean energy transition massively costly for working-class households. Adjacent to operation of the grid itself is the nexus of platform capitalism, its importance highlighted both by the logistical demands of pandemic crisis, and the destructive effects of social media mis- and dis-information, spurring parallel discussions about the public expansion of basic digital services and of reducing the flows of mis or dis-information fostered micro-targeted advertising).

Stressing the 'expropriative' aspect of biocommunism qualifies a term now widely used in discussion of collective resource control: 'commons.' The concept of the common is central to any communism – how could it not be? It has been crucial to developing models of communal ownership more varied and inventive than bureaucratised nationalisation: trusts, cooperatives, open-source production and peer-to-peer networks. But 'commonist' discourse can suggest a supersession of capital by a sheer proliferation of commons – say, creation of open-source software or establishment of worker cooperatives. As these example suggest, capitalism can accommodate a multiplication of commons, foster their initiation and certainly reap their fruits. Coexistence of commons and capital is feasible, but nearly always to the latter's advantage. Commons move towards communism only when they diminish capital. That is why, in the face of intensifying climate disasters, new disease outbreaks, blackouts, power failures and information wars it is important to emphasise not just developing new forms of communal production but also abolishing privatised ownership of key industries.

☭

## Ration and Provision

In the age of catastrophe, the obverse of socialised production is rationed consumption. Rationing is not a topic favoured by Marxisms; confidence in expanding forces of production steers away from the topic. Even eco-socialists, rightly critical of corporations shifting responsibility for climate disaster to individual eco-footprints, fight shy of rationing discourse. Yet in polycrisis, rationing repeatedly rears its head, either as immediate response to shortages of oil, gas or food caused by wartime disruptions and corporate opportunism, or, in a longer-term horizon, as an emergency fallback if carbon taxes, carbon trading and other market mechanisms fail to halt global warming.

Biocommunism must therefore revisit the ration question, in both ecological and equalitarian aspects. While the topic summons the binary trope of 'despotic state versus free market,' it also prompts recognition of markets as systems of rationing by price. Focusing on use- rather than exchange- values, rationing foregrounds the material effects of capitalism's patterns of production and consumption on bodies and ecosystems with specific metabolic limits and tipping points, rather than endorsing illusions of infinite fungibility implicit in monetary general equivalence.

Stan Cox's *Any Way You Slice It: The Past, Present and Future of Rationing* shows that: i) the ration was basic to many pre-capitalist societies; b) socialist societies have used rationing as a means of social equalisation; c) within capitalism, non-market rationing is regularly deployed to allocate necessities such as food, fuel, or water when escalating inequities threaten social order. In authoritarian regimes, (e.g., contemporary Egypt), a food ration for the poor, coexisting with markets for the better-off, stabilises vertiginous inequalities – unless the ration is reduced, an occasion for riots. But in crisis situations comprehensive rationing of food and other supplies has not only enjoyed broad support, but also modelled wider social equalisation, as Britain's war time rationing prefiguration of a welfare state.

The ruling class's major contribution to ecological crisis is its control of investment in production, but consumption is an aspect of this larger situation. Carbon emissions rise with wealth, peaking for a billionaire class with multiple mansions, giant yachts and private jets. Rationing of specific ecologically damaging goods, such as airline flights, would restrain consumption in ways that both reduce ecological destruction and inequalities in access to material resources. Broader quotas would have more pronounced effects. In their *Half Earth Socialism* Troy Vitesse and Drew Pendergrass propose a '2,000-watt society', with per-person limits to energy use requiring 'severe cuts in the rich world while allowing growth in poor countries'. Buck points out that in 2016 a Shell Global report proposed a 'decent quality of life' requires 100 gigajoules of energy per person per year. Noting that the USA consume 300 gigajoules of energy per person per year, while Europe and China use 150 and 100 respectively, it proposed (conveniently for Shell) doubling global energy production, but also equalising use levels around the planet, a 'radical proposition' that Buck observes, 'far to the left' of mainstream Western environmentalism.

Rationing should be reconceived as not just limit but guarantee, prohibition but also promise, security as well as scarcity. The long-running debate about Universal Basic Income is in its way a discussion about a ration, albeit one that confirms the norm of commodity exchange. More promising is the Universal Basic Services proposition, in which all members of a community receive unconditional access to some mix of shelter, sustenance, health care, education, and legal aid. However, this proposal too is conceived as a subordinate, palliative addition to a market system – a dole of use-values.

A potential reversal of this logic is George Monbiot's 'public luxury, private sufficiency' principle. This envisages major social investment in urban environments, public services, collective housing projects and mass transport systems, combined with rotated chances for everyone to occasionally enjoy extraordinary holidays and cultural events, alongside modest, ecologically sustainable levels of personal consumption. Monbiot shrinks from calling for decapitation of capital, sticking to a familiar green trope of 'neither communism nor capitalism' – yet his model actually implies dislodging for-profit accumulation from its direction of everyday life, organising society around universal provision of a limited but assured and equalitarian basket of goods. As capitalist poly-crisis renders markets chaotic, exacerbates social inequalities and accelerates ecological devastation, such biocommunist guarantee may become increasingly attractive.

☭

## Essential Workers

Biocommunism will not be a post-work utopia but rather a radical recomposition of labour. Covid-19 showed how rapid such recomposition can be. Jobs were suspended or relocated, with or without recompense; governments recruited and redirected workers into designated sectors; for millions, home transformed to workspace; for millions others, a hazardous mobility accelerated; unwaged, gendered social reproduction labour was highlighted; frontline workers in previously despised low wage sectors or public services loudly praised, (though largely without improvement in the conditions of their toils. As Sandro Mezzadra has observed, a central figure became 'the essential worker' – labour, ranging from hospital staff to supermarket workers to cybersecurity personnel, governmentally required to toil through crisis.

Under current conditions, 'essential work' legitimises continued exploitation of labour indispensable for commodity production and circulation – forced labour. But it is worth thinking what form it could take in a system whose prime directive was the social and ecological well-being of its population. Writing of climate emergency, Cory Doctorow observes:

> Remediating climate change will involve unimaginably labor-intensive tasks, like relocating every coastal city in the world kilometers inland, building high-speed rail links to replace aviation links, caring for hundreds of millions of traumatised, displaced people, and treating runaway zoonotic and insect borne pandemics. . . . Every person whose job is obsolete because of automation will have ten jobs waiting for them, for the entire foreseeable future.

To this list can be added emergency firefighters, mass tree planters, rewilding land clearers, solar panel installers, housing insulators, coders of climate-sensing software , gigafactory workers, and many more – a belated fulfilment of plans for 'a million climate jobs' or a Green New Deal, but unfortunately now instantiated not in forward-looking crisis anticipation but under increasingly chaotic conditions of biospheric deterioration.

In capital, much truly essential work will, because unprofitable, not be considered 'essential' at all. It will remain undone as habitats degrade. Public order will be maintained by threadbare state agencies. More lucrative developments in protected housing for the rich, geotechnologies and corporate-designed urban reconstruction will spur a growing commercial or private-public climate adaptation and mitigation sector. Essential work will be exploitative, with core teams of technical expertise surrounded by a penumbras of precarious labour, shielding enterprises from financially volatile conditions but providing workers only minimal protections from mounting environmental risk. Biocommunism, however, will socialise essential labour. Catastrophe remediating work–running vital security systems, constructing and operating refugia and sanctuaries, operating communal utilities, maintaining childcare and schooling providing universal rations and services, and in planning of all the above--will understood as both a necessity and a communal responsibility.

In 2016 Fredric Jameson controversially proposed a socialist utopia based on a 'universal army of labour.' All capable persons would perform publicly crucial tasks for four hours a day (or an equivalent period calculated weekly, monthly, annually) as a condition of citizenship. Outside of this period, people's time would be their own. All those fulfilling this obligation, and all those excused for reasons of health, or domestic care, would receive their equal share of social wealth and services. Jameson's 'army' proposal shocked left anti-statists and anti-militarists. But his 'army' is clearly intended to conduct tasks across the entire economy, auto-dissolving its military vocation. And while the thought of state mobilisation may reasonably trigger nightmares of totalitarian control, it is worth imagining other possible instantiations.

We can envisage polycrisis pressures producing an enlarged version of the 'government job guarantee' attached to some versions of Green New Deal, as an employment opportunity and perhaps as social obligation. The execution of 'essential work' can be conceived not as authoritarian control but as a process rich in contradiction, contention, and social ferment. Its decision-making should be understood not as top-down command, but rather in terms of mission-oriented tasks, in which execution of broad objectives is devolved to on-the-scene units, and alternative implementations debated and worked out.

Biocommunist essential workers will have their own work-team organisations, combining features of both worker cooperatives and unions with voice on issues of public provisions, worker health and safety, task assignment and execution. These will be engaged in projects, such as greening cities, or localisation of food supply, for communities of which they may themselves be a part, and whose survival and flourishing will be an object of pride. These communities too will have their own councils and assemblies, which can both contest work-teams' decisions and practices and collaborate with them to make interventions and adjustments at higher levels of the project.

Seen in this light, Jameson's universal army, with its half day dedicated to labour in the realm of necessity and half liberated for realm of freedom, comes to resemble the mix of anarchism and central planning imagined in Ursula Le Guin's sci-fi depiction of the communised planet Anarres. The essential worker becomes 'essential' not only in protecting vital social and species functions but also as a crucial agent in collective planning, to which we now turn.

☭

## Bio-Planning

Foucault's concept of biopolitics is associated with his idea of governmentality – that is to say, government conceived not solely as state power but in a more capillary form, enacted through a range of institutions and organisations with varying relations to and degrees of autonomy from the centralised apparatuses of rulership, combining – in Deleuzian terms – both molar and molecular components, or, in Foucault's own language, a 'mesh of power.' The political valency of this 'mesh' is ambivalent. It has the potential to be a creeping, insidious and implacable disciplinary mechanism, all the more deadly to the degree that is diffuse and decentralised But there is an inverse concept, where the disaggregated and distributed nature of power becomes the occasion to reverse or oscillate the directions of its biopolitical flows from heights to depths, peripheries to centres, hubs to spokes, persistently reconfiguring the architecture of power.

Replacing profit with planning is core to any society beyond capital. The last decade has seen a striking revival in left discussion of planning processes, with emphasis both on the possibilities of distributed, rather than centralised planning, and on ecological planning. In biocommunism, the unions of emergency workers and the councils of environmental proletarians, and other communal organisations become interlocutors of state planning agencies so that proposals from above engage with counter-planning critique and counterproposal from below. In this way, planning is a function diffused out and away from the organs of a centralised state into a wider, democratised process – what Marx and Engels in *The Communist Manifesto* refer to 'vast association.' When populations cease to be the object of biopower, but become its subject a 'biopolitics from below,' a powerful, protagonistic biocommunism, becomes possible.

Biocommunism would be system steering between a ceiling of environmental sustainability and a floor of equalised social development. The conceptual basis for such planning exists in 'boundary models' presented by green authors such as Kate Raworth advocating for a zone of 'fair and just' social development between ecological overshoot and economic shortfall. The problem with such programs is, however, their chronic refusal to confront the incompatibility between its goals and capital's accumulative drive. In practice, boundary modelling has been repeatedly hijacked by corporate green-washers to legitimise ongoing economic extraction, preserving the 'growth' imperative. Biocommunist planning would be a counter-version, weaponised to fight through to the abolition of capital.

Biocommunism would therefore be a system without a compulsion to economic growth, capable of both expansion and contraction of humanities material throughputs; as Alessandra Mularoni and I put it elsewhere, this

> would likely mean less of some things and more of others: degrowing carbon industries to termination; growing renewable energy sources; degrowing high-intensity consumption in the Global North while improving living standards in the Global South; more bandwidth for planning global energy flows, less for planetary selfie-tsunami.

Biocommunism would not discount possible technological solutions to the climate emergency and other ecological crises, but also recognise such fixes are not going to arrive in time to prevent the need for deep civilisational changes. Biocommunism reworks both the 'relations' and 'forces' of production, subordinating the pro- and anti-tech question to the double imperatives of ecological vitality and social equalisation

Biocommunist planning need not necessarily supply the highly variegated complex consumerism of advanced capitalist economies. Although digital, networked and algorithmic planning hold out possibilities for solving historically intractable 'calculation problems' presented by such economies, it should not be presumed that such a consumption-driven society would be the biocommunist *summum bonum*. A mode of production beyond capital could have different goals, trading off high consumerism for free time, environmental plenitude, social solidarity and species-survival. This essay has suggested that ecological and equalitarian principles favour provision of a common 'basket of goods,' and observance of 'public luxury and private sufficiency' principles, perhaps with a subordinated market sector supplying a reduced range of consumer items. To the degree that social consensus is forged around such common goals, calculation problems are simplified. Struggle towards such an end is truly radical but may also come to seem pragmatic in the midst of the vast market breakdowns in which capital initiates its own spontaneous, barbaric degrowth.

DAISY LAFARGE

# The Sick Rose

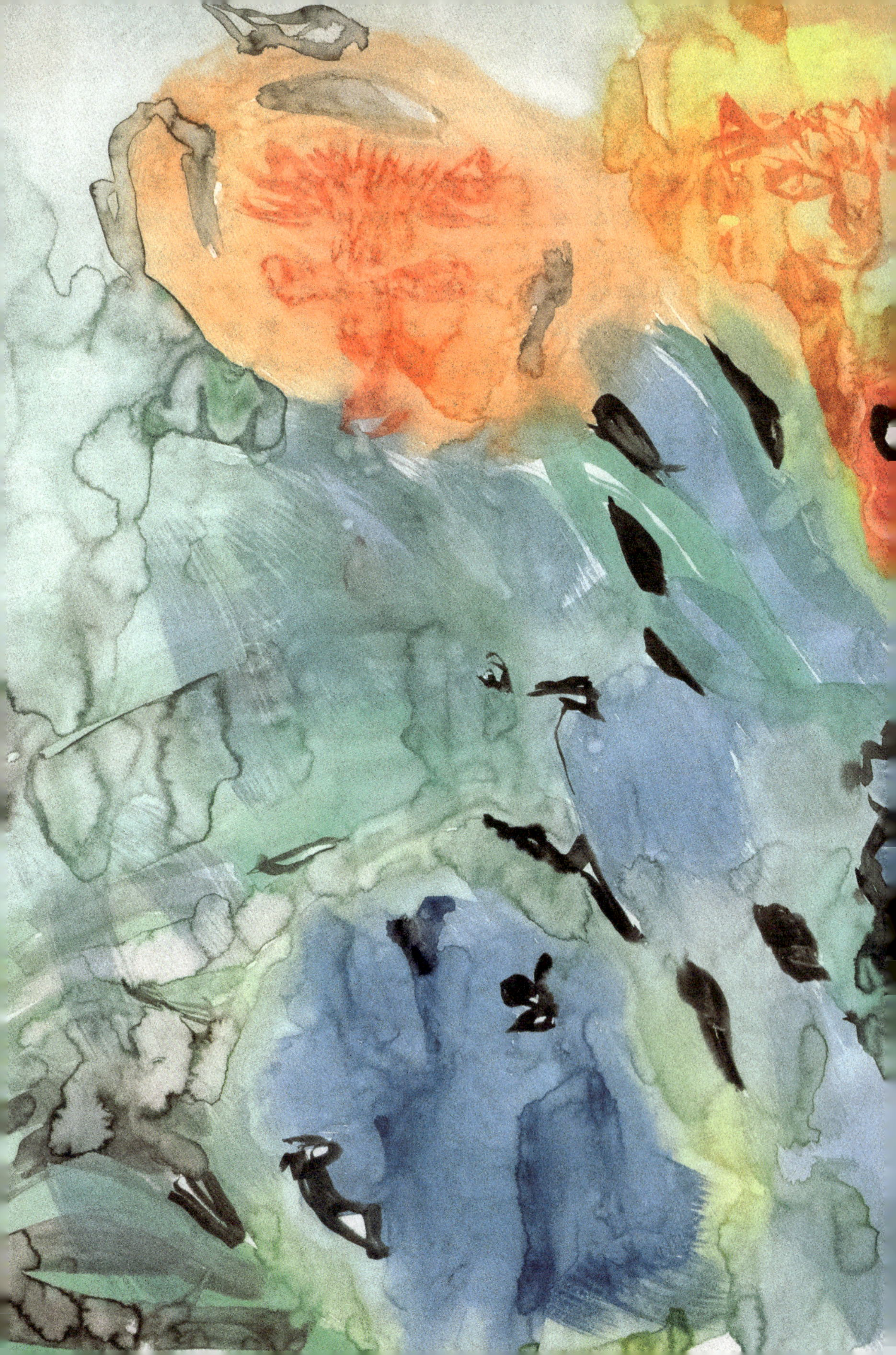

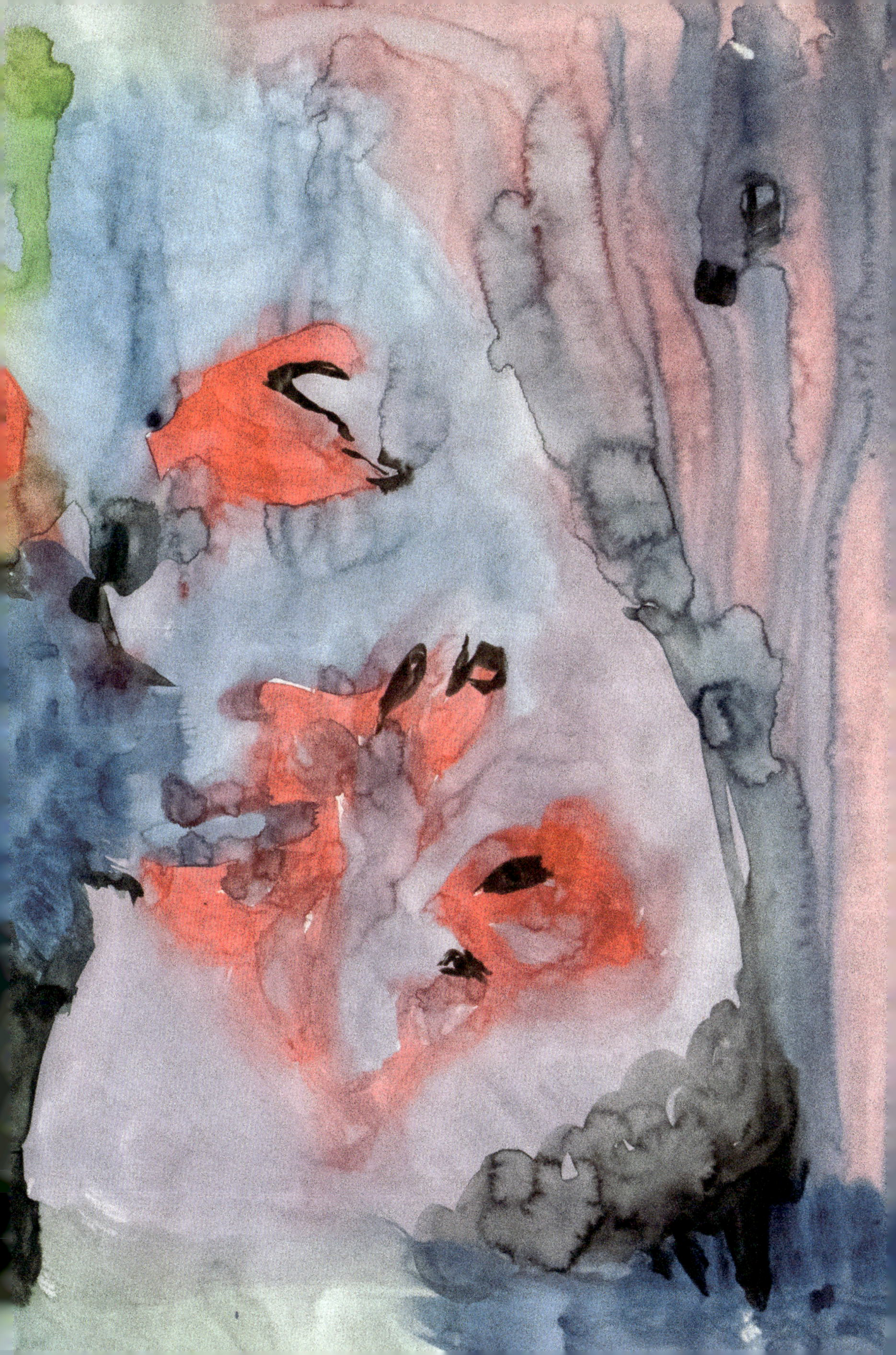

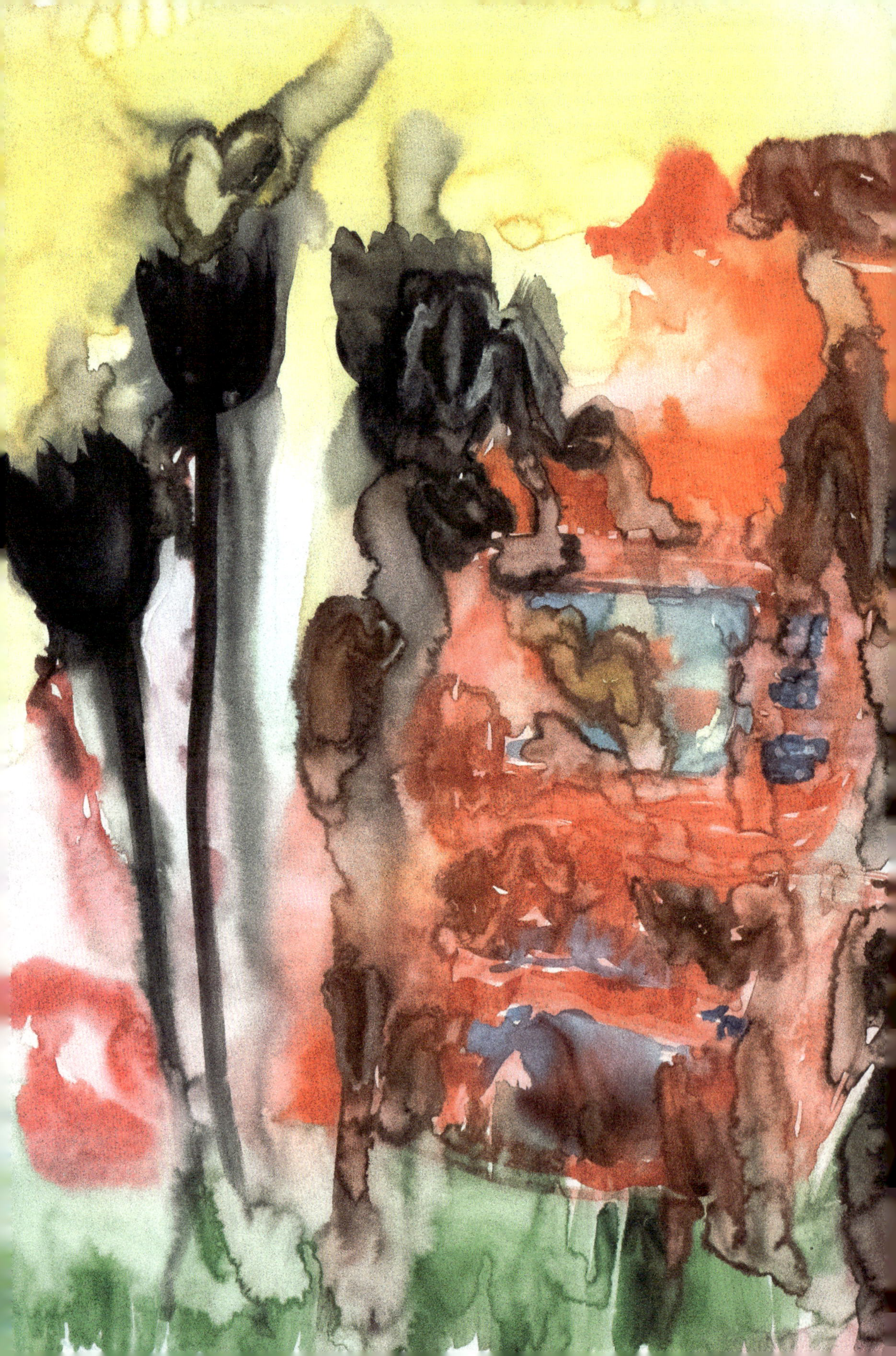

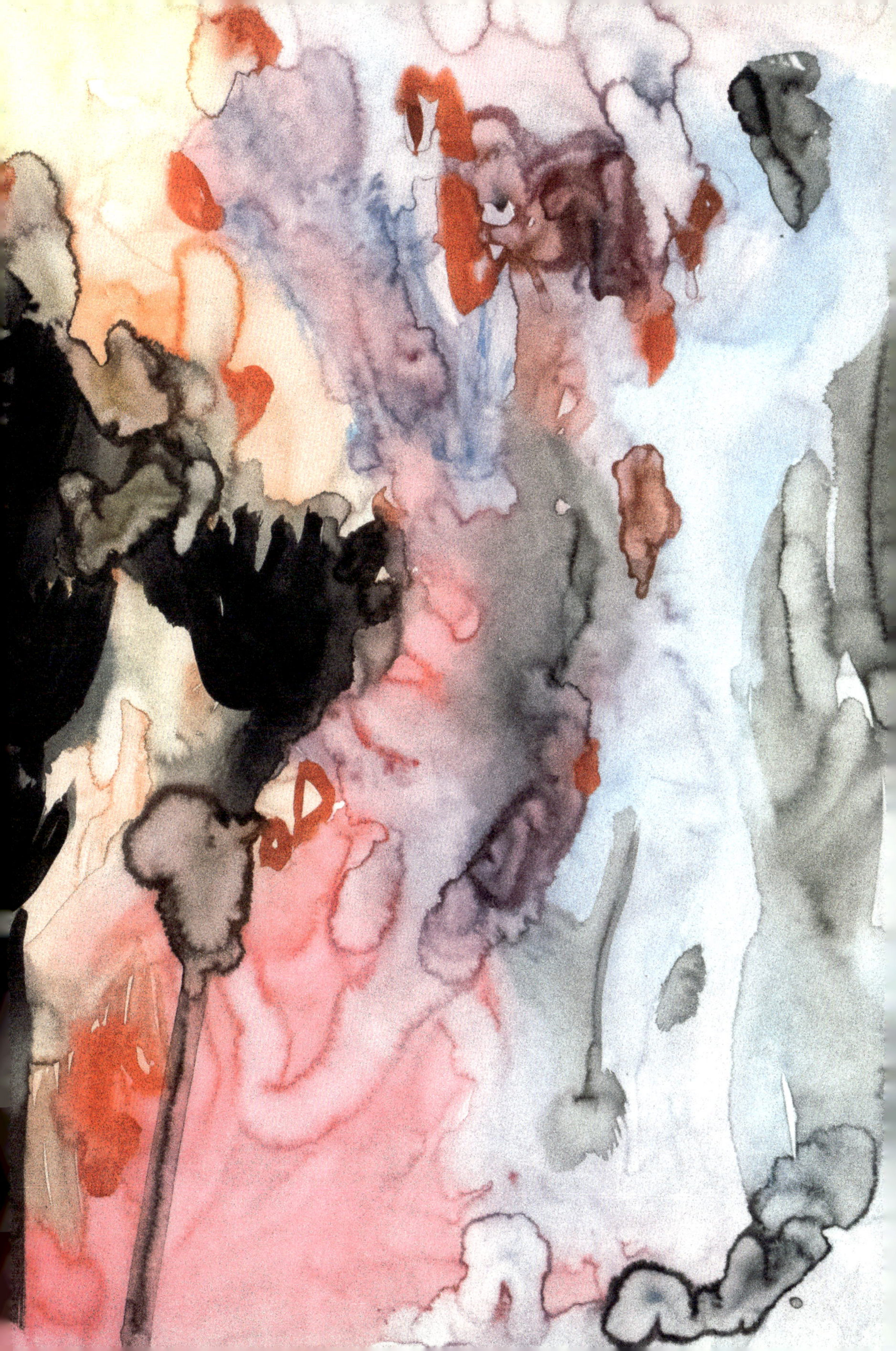

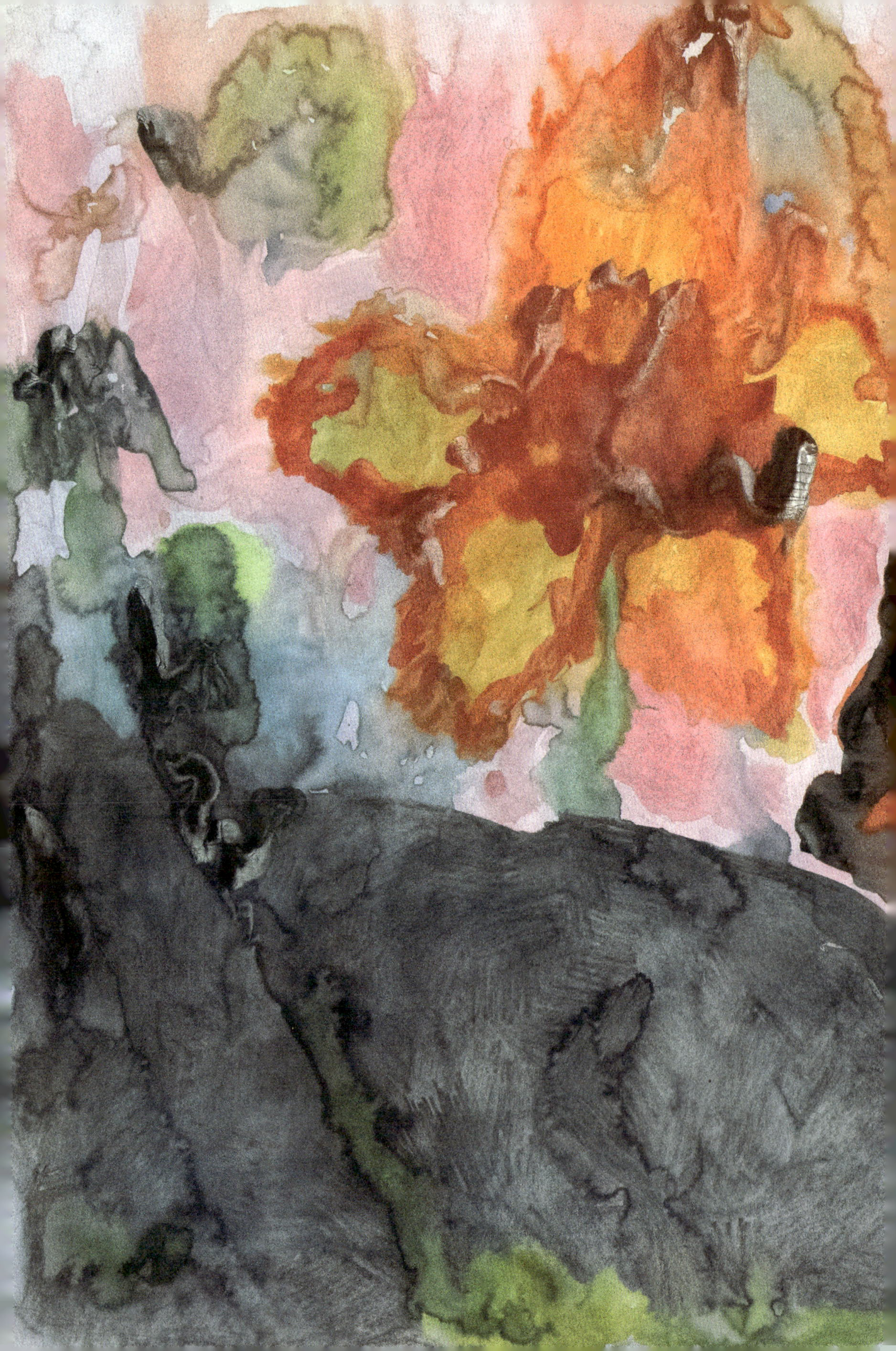

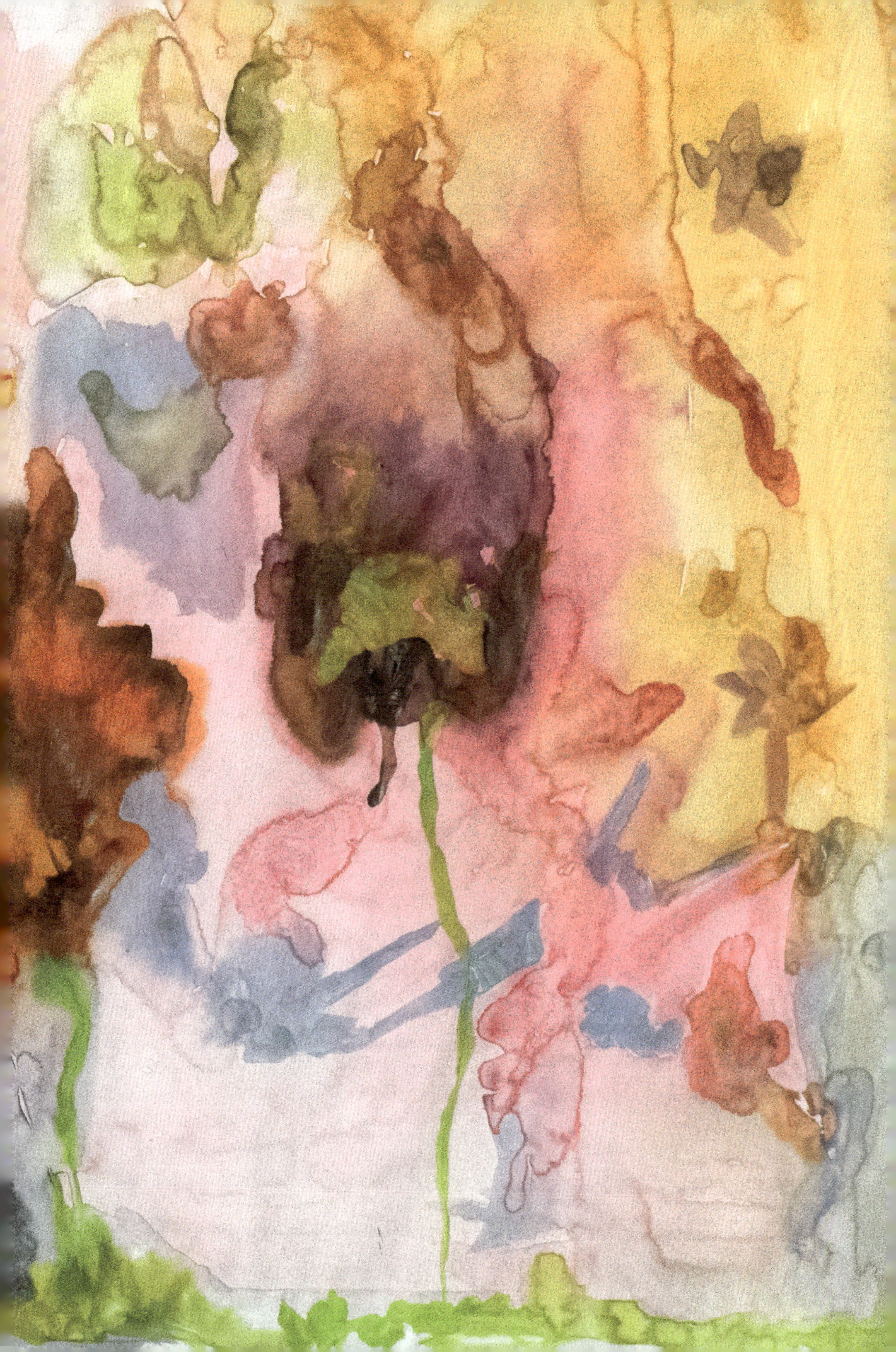

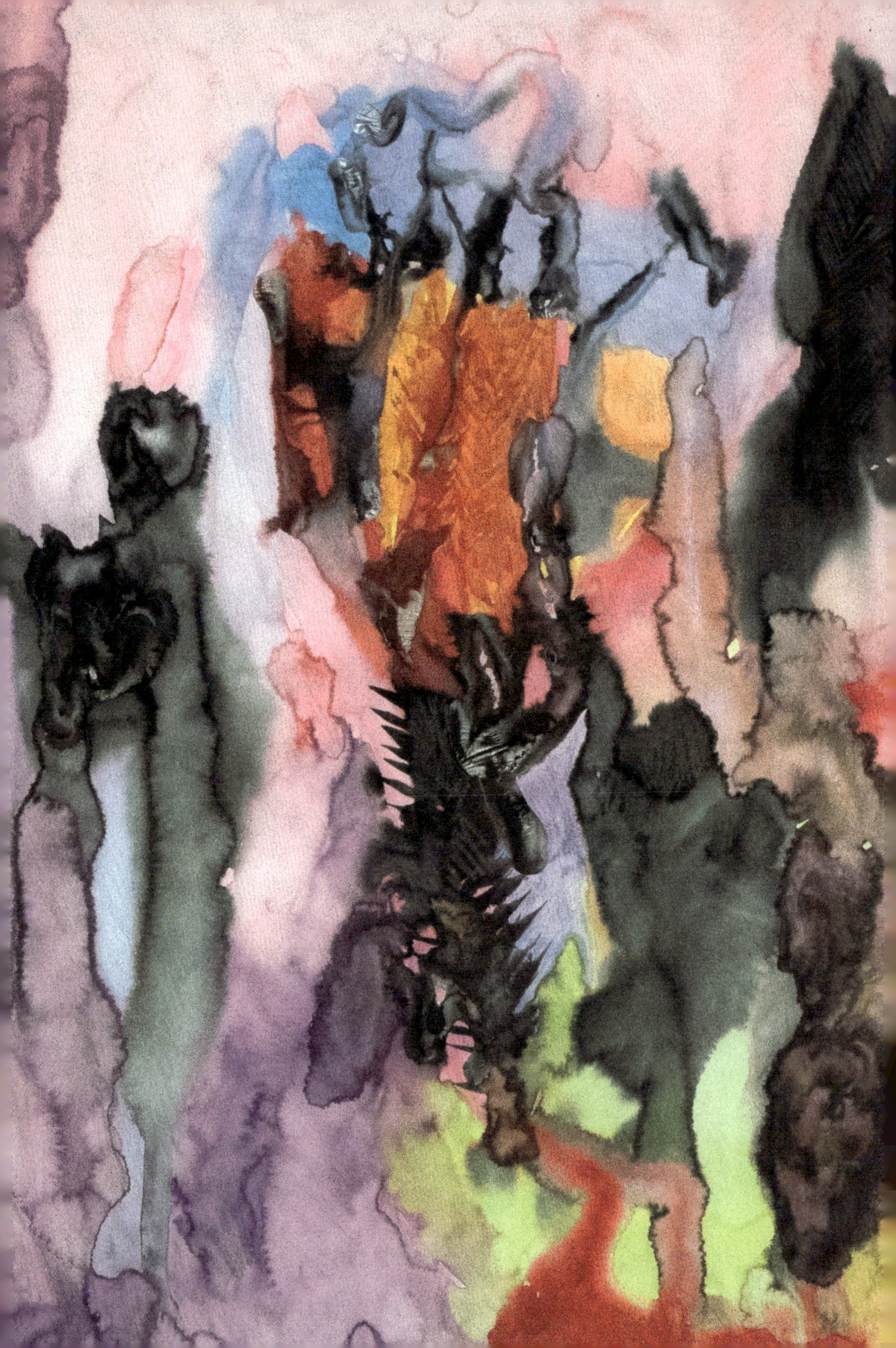

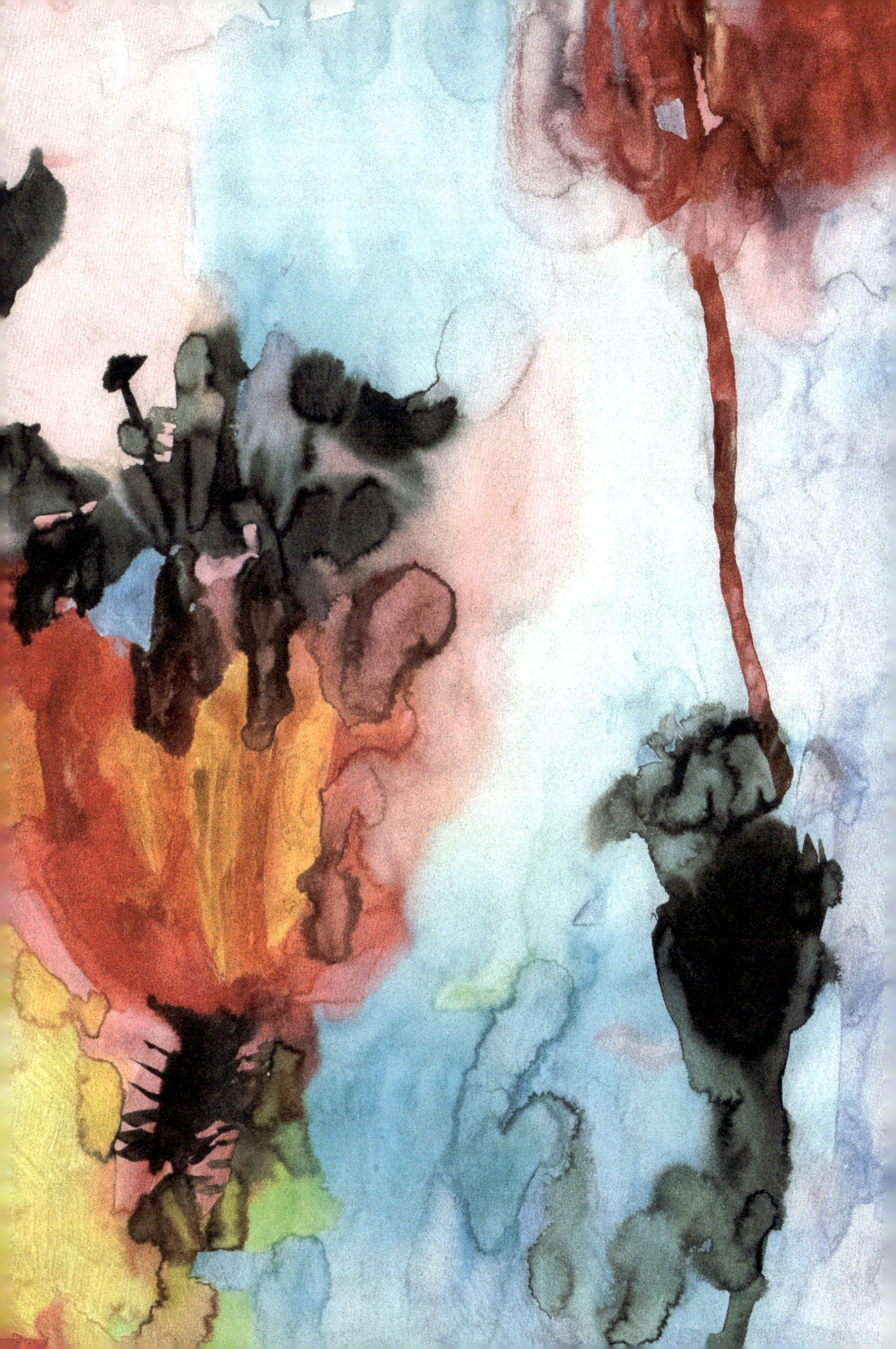

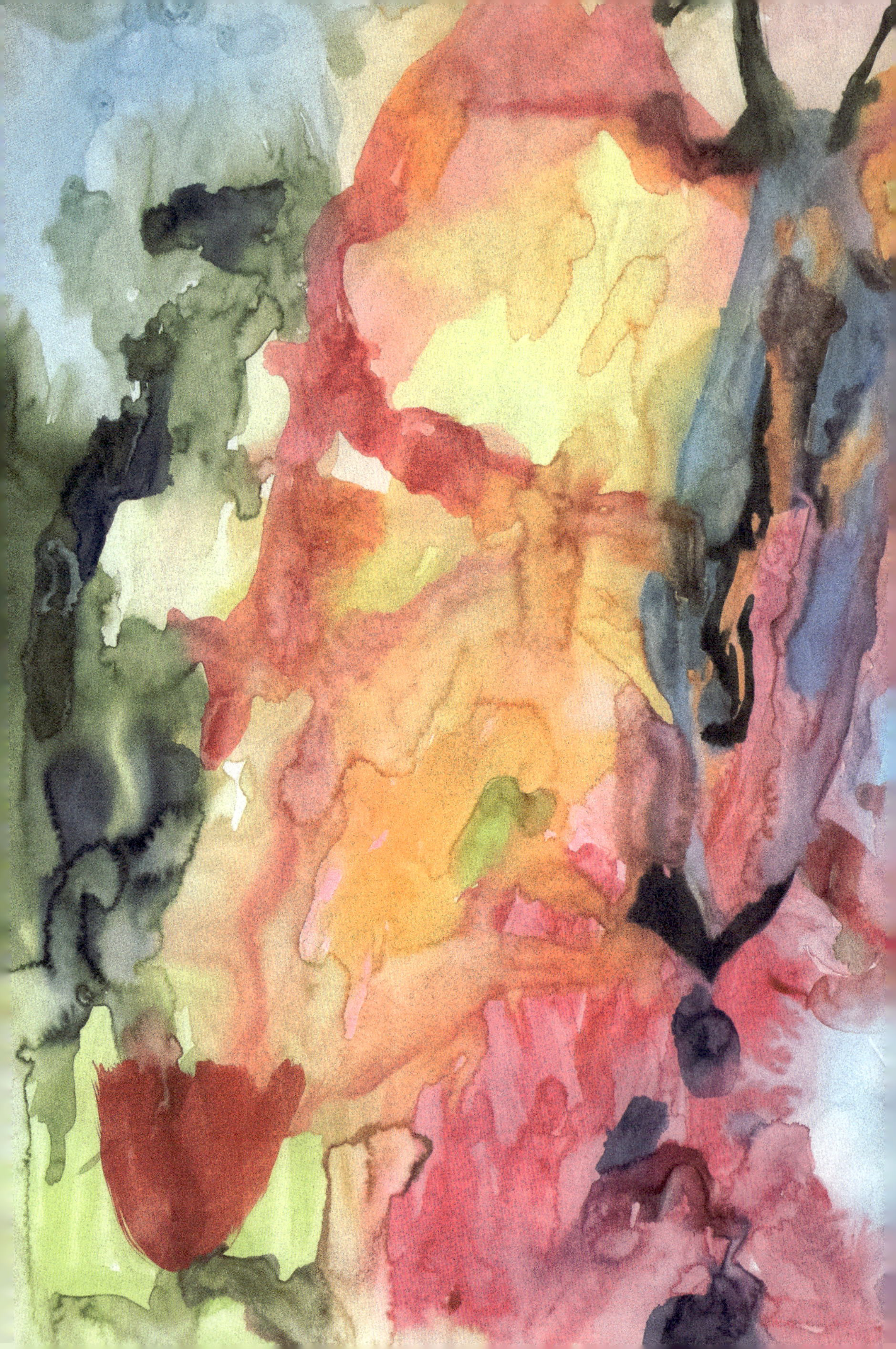

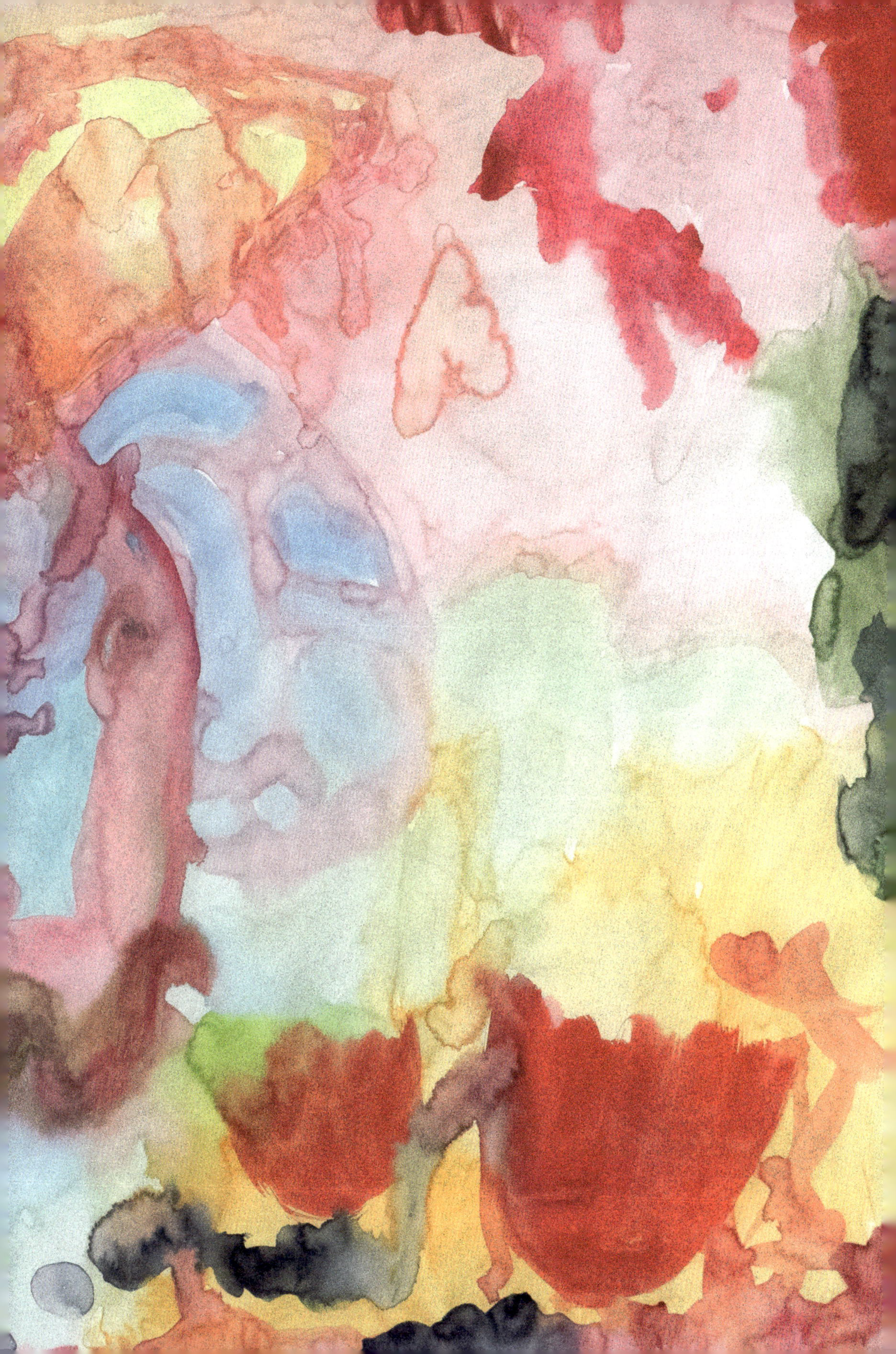

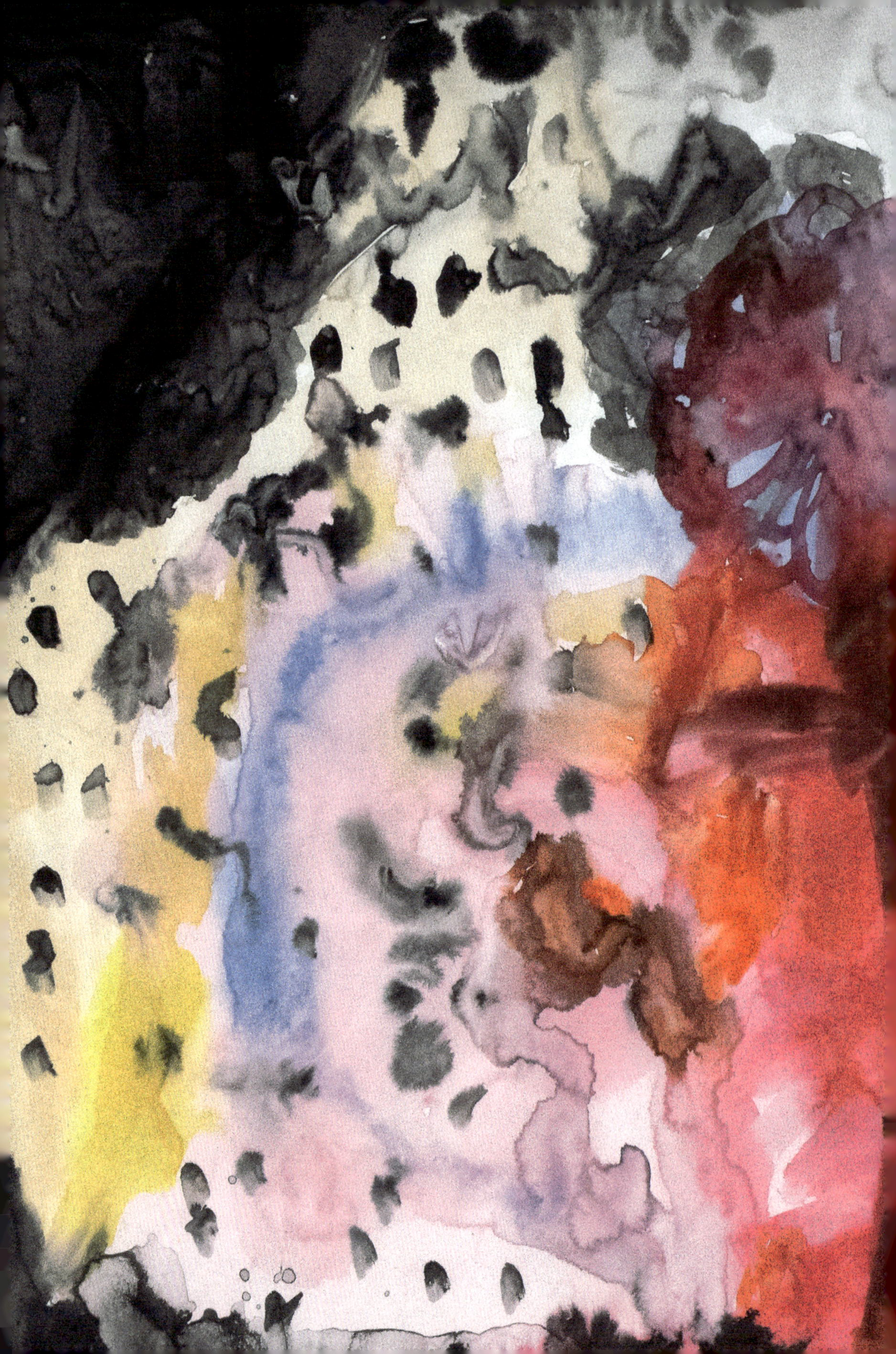

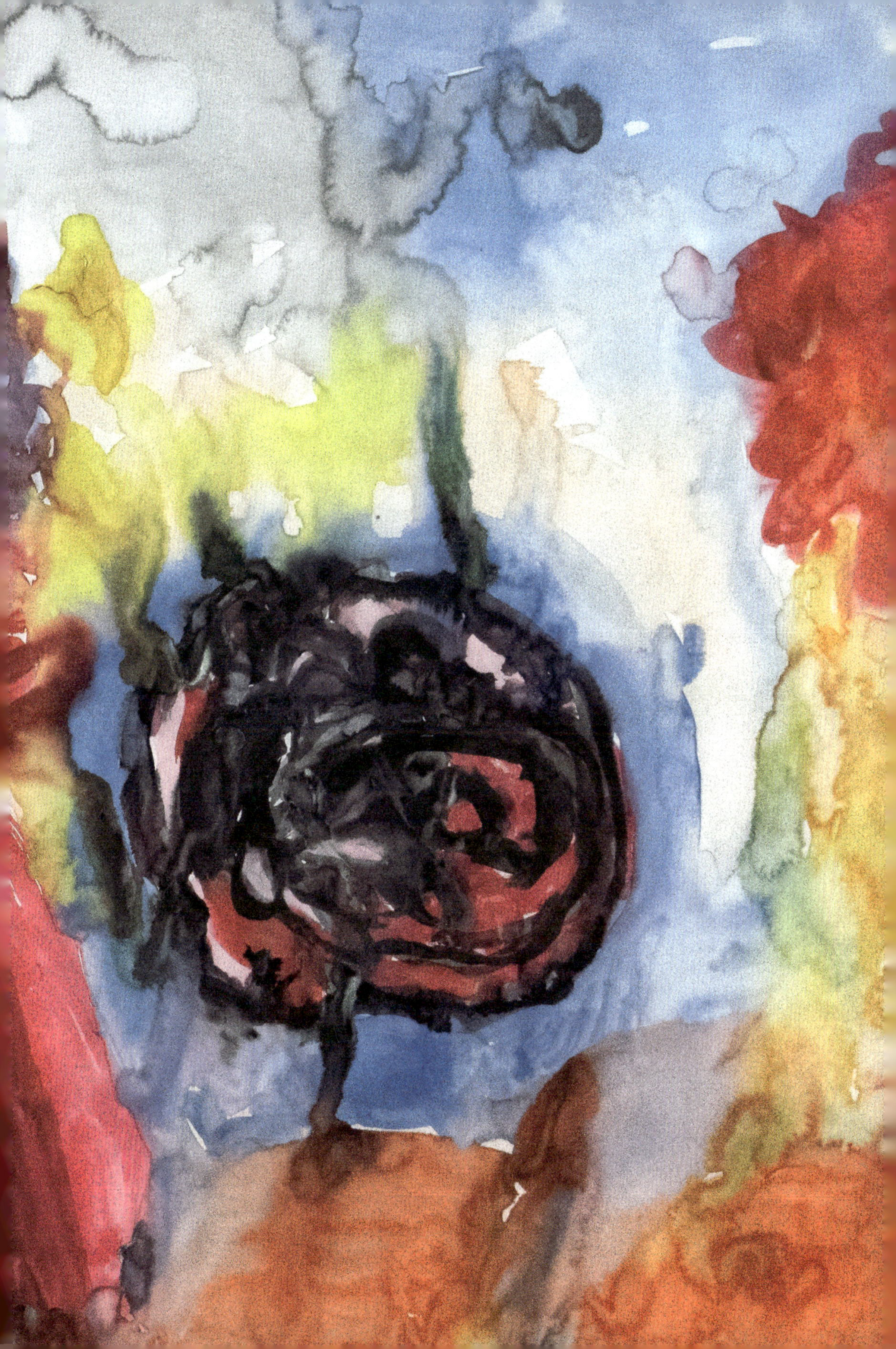

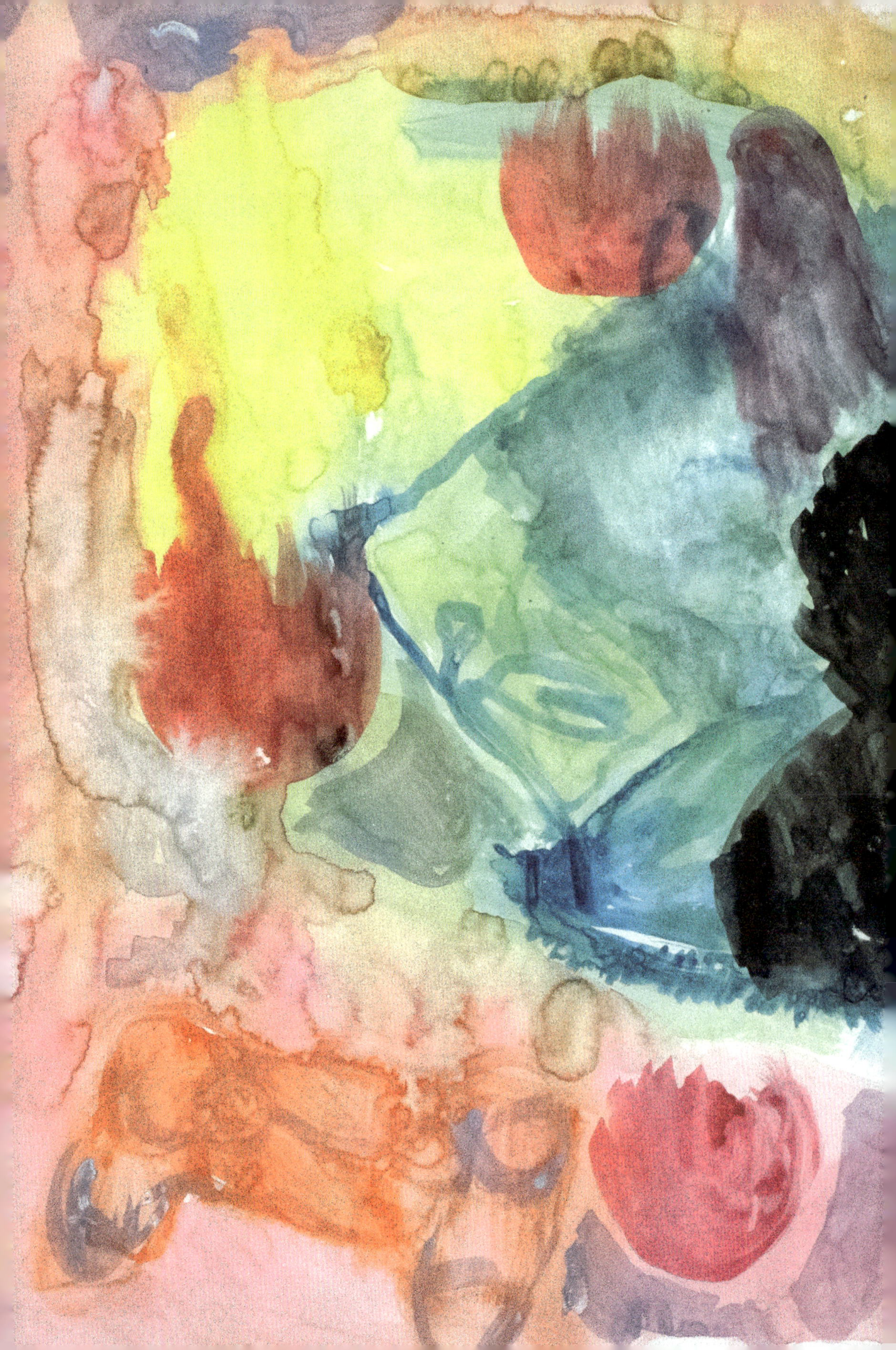

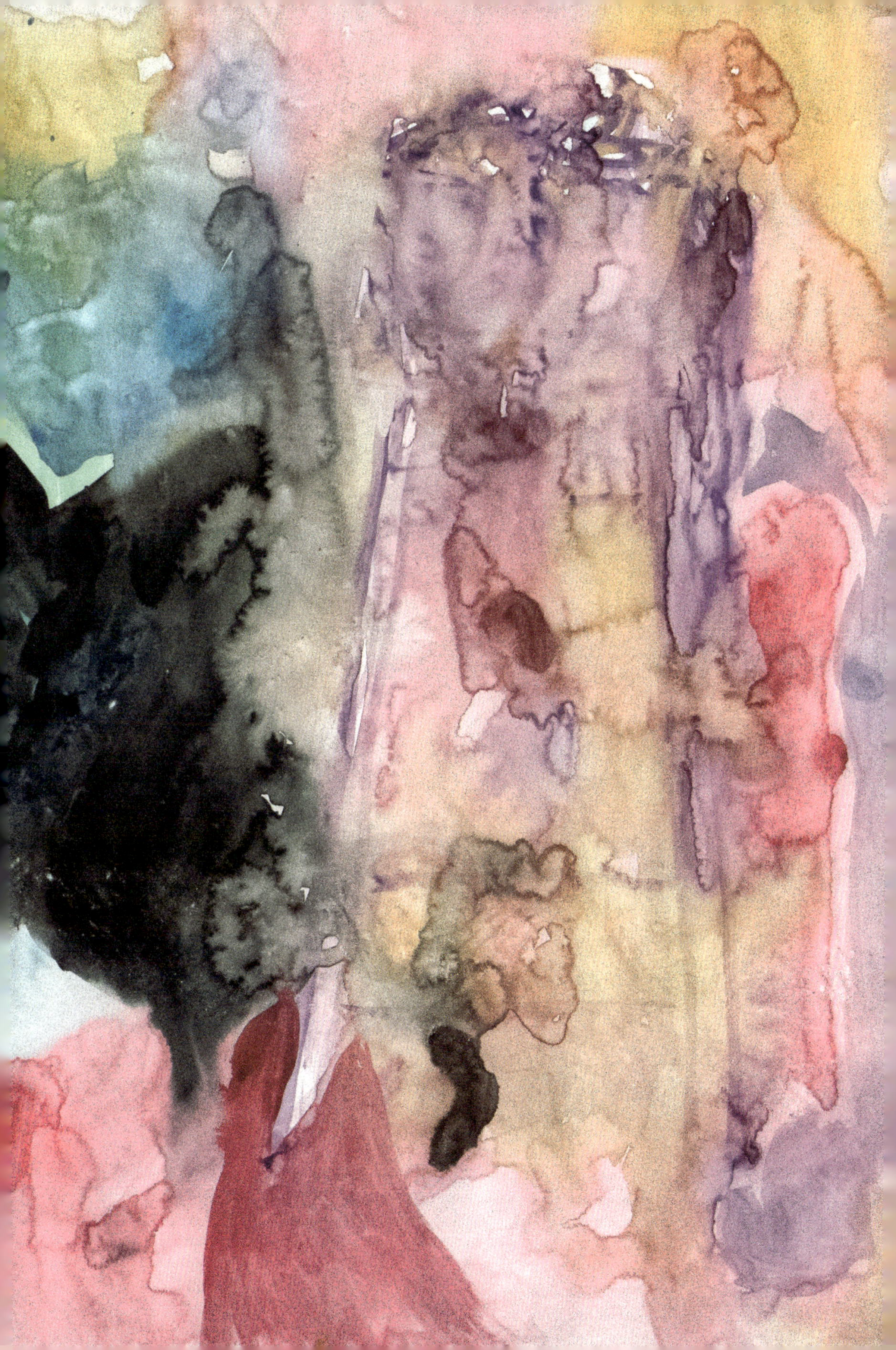

Titles

*Birthday*

*Black Tulips*

*Sick Garden (I)*

*Sick Garden (III)*

*The Invisible Worm*

*The Sick Rose*

*Your Pain Is As Unique As You Are*


 *The Sick Rose* presents a series of seven paintings made in 2024, and takes its title from William Blake's 1794 poem of the same name. Fragments of domestic objects and pet portraits bloom into sick gardens and become swamped in recurring motifs of roses and insectile forms. The paintings are affixed with remnants of kinesiology tape used to support and compress unstable joints, and watercolour functions as a medium of pleasure, immediacy and minimal physical strain. Made during episodes of severe chronic pain, remote NHS chronic pain sessions and in phone queues and conversations with Social Security Scotland, the paintings came into existence as a way to steal something back from time spent trying to access unreliable and punitive forms of disability support. They are also an attempt to coexist with volatile physical and psychic states and to refigure pain as the 'dark secret love' of Blake's poem.

DUNCAN THOMAS

# Kind of Blue: A Short History of Tory Decline

With the Conservative Party having collapsed to an all-time low of just 121 seats in 2024's general election, following fourteen years in which they were both in office and at each other's throats, it is easy to forget that this is – by some distance – the world's oldest and most successful example of an elite political project operating under the twin pressures of mass democracy and capitalist modernity. Each of these pressures were, from their inception, feared as existential threats to the Party's survival. Yet, these threats were not merely navigated but provided the very grounds on which the Conservatives have flourished.

Indeed, the Party's grip on power only tightened with the relative decline of its agrarian and aristocratic base. Between the 1832 and 1884 Reform Acts, marking the first period of modern parliamentary history under limited if gradually broadening franchise, the Conservatives were in power for just fifteen of fifty-two years, or around 28 per cent of the time. With the expansion of the electorate to include the majority of adult males, the Party subsequently held office for eighteen of the next thirty-two years, or 54 per cent of the time. Between the granting of universal male and partial female suffrage in 1918 and the progressive extension of voting rights to the present day, they governed for seventy-three of 105 years, fully 70 per cent of the time. While late nineteenth- and twentieth-century Britain saw the achievement of formal liberal democracy, the height of the welfare state, and the country's only general strike, it was also undeniably a 'long Conservative century', to use the phrase of Tory historian and commentator Anthony Seldon. Such has been the Party's hold on power that it can, with some plausibility, claim many of what are traditionally seen as Britain's major achievements as its own: early industrial dominance, imperial grandeur, victory in two world wars, even the lion's share of the post-war boom were all won under the guidance of the Conservatives, binding the identity of both nation and state to that of the party which ruled them.

How, then, has the 'natural party of government' fallen into an apparently permanent crisis? What has degraded a lineage of once consummate state managers and political operators into, to borrow Dominic Cummings' description of the Johnson cabinet, a parade of 'fuck pigs and morons'? In trying to explain why the Party finds itself in its current impasse, bereft of any real sense of collective purpose, ideologically exhausted, and electorally wounded, I will not offer a detailed account of their previous fourteen years in power, recount Westminster manoeuvrings or focus extensively on individual ministers and administrations. Similarly, given that this article was written in the immediate aftermath of the 2024 general election, whatever has happened to the Party in the months since will necessarily be absent from whatever analysis I can offer. Instead, I want to understand how the current state of the Conservatives reflects transformations in the foundations of their historic power.

Specifically, I contend that the Party's disarray – witnessed since at least the Brexit referendum of 2016, but arguably dating back to the ousting of Thatcher in 1990 – results from three major dynamics that have seriously undermined their traditional modes of political practice: the recalibration of capital–state relations under contemporary capitalism; ruling class and elite recomposition; and changes in the broader class structure and everyday life.

There is an irony here, for the tendencies I sketch below were all largely instigated by the Conservatives, particularly the Thatcher governments, as a response to the crisis of post-war capitalism – although many elements naturally predated the 1980s and have since been enthusiastically developed and accelerated by Labour administrations as well as Tory ones. All can be broadly related to neoliberalism as a term encapsulating changes to the economy, society, and culture since the 1980s. While much of what I argue below is well known, these changes are generally seen as a problem for the left (in both its reformist and revolutionary variants) and a straightforward victory for the right. However, as I hope to show, a number of unintended consequences of the Thatcherite settlement have also undermined the Conservatives as a broad right force, to the point that the Party's very survival is now commonly talked of as being under threat. While actual extinction is unlikely to materialise, the Party has been undeniably reshaped by its long period of crisis and recomposition, making it quite different to the organisation which has dominated British politics for most of the last two centuries.

☭

## State and capital in neoliberal Britain
As the post-war settlement unravelled amidst economic crisis and social unrest, Margaret Thatcher came to power in 1979 aiming to fundamentally transform British capitalism. While the tactics she employed were more contingent and improvised than often assumed, more than once bringing her close to defeat, there is no doubting either the fact or scale of her success. Disarming opponents and destroying organised labour as a significant political force, she set the agenda for every subsequent government, including the current Starmer administration. This success, however, came at a price, with shifting relations between capital and state undermining not only reformist social democracy, but the political autonomy upon which Tory statecraft itself has historically depended.

The tendencies causing this erosion are well known, as the financialisation and internationalisation characteristic of neoliberalism globally have diminished the power of states everywhere to exercise political control over the economy. Such tendencies, however, are particularly pronounced within Britain, pointing to the vanguardist role the country played in the dismantling of mid-century Keynesianism. The Royal Economic Society estimates that when Thatcher came to power in 1979 manufacturing accounted for 28 per cent of GDP; today, the Office for National Statistics places it at just 9 per cent, far below that of most international competitors. Conversely, finance has exploded from just 2 per cent of GDP in the 1950s to around 30 per cent today when accounting for directly related services in accountancy, law, consultancy, and IT, making it the single biggest sector in terms of output. While triggered by Thatcher's policies, this rebalancing – or at least, its scale – was never the goal of her governments. Rather, they hoped that opening industry to private capital and market competition would restore the country's status as the 'workshop of the world' after two decades of pronounced underperformance. The de-industrialisation that occurred in place of this intended revival was driven not by ministerial intent but by the re-assertion of long-standing structural features of the British economy as the post-war interlude came to an end. Barring a short period in the mid-twentieth century, the low productivity which had vexed governments since the early 1960s – and continues to do so today – had been present since the late 1800s, as British industry traditionally relied on colonial super-exploitation and imperial monopolies rather than technological innovation to maintain its advantage in the face of rising international competition. This orientation towards the world market had likewise produced an oversized financial sector as far back as the 1600s, as new forms of incorporated capital, shareholdings, and investment spurred mercantile conquest, commodity exchange, and financialised models of popular slave ownership. As Britain's industrial decline accelerated through the 1980s and with capital becoming increasingly mobile, the City of London came to represent the country's most obvious source of comparative advantage.

It was therefore logical that the Thatcher governments would come to embrace and promote the financial sector as a means of defending Britain's international position within a rapidly changing global economy.

However, while emerging from the inheritance of an imperial past, the mode of Britain's financially driven integration into global capitalism has shifted. At the height of empire, the City exported capital across the globe. Now, it largely attracts it from abroad: from under 4 per cent in 1981, foreign ownership of assets on the London stock exchange had risen to 40 per cent by 2010. By 2014, for the first time in history, the value of these assets outweighed that of the foreign investments made by British capitalists. Capital inflows, foreign direct investment (FDI), and international mergers and takeovers are all, similarly, far higher than in most other advanced economies. This pivot towards finance, particularly following the 'Big Bang' reforms of 1986, also had the unintended but significant effect of exposing uncompetitive national industries to foreign takeover. In 1979, overseas ownership of UK firms was just 3.6 per cent, an all-time low, but by the end of the century, as David Edgerton writes in *The Rise and Fall of the British Nation*, the country was unique among core capitalist economies in having 'no approximation to a national major car firm, chemical firm, electrical engineering or electronic firm operating on its territory'. Not only has the state relinquished direct control of key strategic economic sectors to private capital, but ownership of those sectors themselves is now held disproportionately by international companies and investors who have little tying them to Britain *per se*. Similarly, while the City remains, as it always has been, a system for the appropriation of globally produced surplus value, the rise in foreign ownership of assets and the declining importance of Britain itself within international capital circuits means that, as finance capital has become increasingly dominant, its mode of accumulation has also been decoupled from any imperative towards broader national economic development.

This has serious implications for state managers. Some of these are well known, others less so. On the one hand, the dominance of finance over other sectors within the power bloc (to the degree that industrial capital itself is now heavily financialised), coupled with the transnational integration and mobility of capital, binds states ever closer to a mode of accumulation centred on asset trading, share-price valuation, and non-productive speculation. This encourages chronic short-termism, in which the immediate need for profit maximisation and other time-scales associated specifically with finance capital override any longer-term developmental strategy and divert investment from productive ends. Share valuation and investor confidence, which in reality express nothing more than a belief that financial assets can be traded for immediate profit, come to represent overall economic health. In Britain, this is partly expressed at the state level by measures such as the abandonment of capital controls, the delegation of interest-rates to an independent Bank of England, and the submission of spending plans to technocratic bodies such as the Office for Budgetary Responsibility, all of which depoliticise economic governance by placing it beyond the bounds of democratic debate or even rival elite strategies.

This tendency represents the *strength of capital* under neoliberalism via its *power over the state*. This, however, is not the only dynamic at play. Equally important is the contemporary *weakness of capitalism* as a regime of accumulation, which produces a parallel *dependency on the state* as a final and increasingly direct guarantor of private profit. For, whatever claims may be made, neoliberalism has not in fact seen the withdrawal of states from economic affairs, nor even a real reduction in public spending as a proportion of GDP. Rather, it has recalibrated the state's mode of economic intervention in the context of what the *Financial Times* calls a global 'secular stagnation', now spanning several decades. Within Britain, this has seen persistently low growth, declining productivity, and chronic underinvestment from both the state and private capital. Searching for reliable and attractive profits in an overall depressed environment, the latter is increasingly drawn to risky speculative bubbles, cross-investment between enormous capital management firms now controlling many trillions of dollars in funds, warfare and its preparation, and the seizure of privatised state assets.

Only the state is able to bailout firms considered 'too big to fail', inject enormous *qualities* of liquidity into depressed financial markets via 'quantitative easing', or prosecute major international conflicts. It is only under the express direction of successive governments that welfare and public spending have become increasingly direct means of subsidising capital. For example, prior to Thatcher, around 80 per cent of state spending on housing was used to actually build houses. Now 85 per cent goes on housing benefit, a 'welfare' payment which serves to prop up private landlords, construction firms, and speculators by maintaining otherwise unsustainably inflated property prices. Crucial public infrastructure is now funded through eye-wateringly expensive Private Finance Initiatives, which the Institute for Government estimates will cost the public around three times the capital value of the schools, prisons, hospitals and other assets built under such contracts. Privatisation of critical natural monopolies in energy, communications, transport, and service provision offers lucrative and virtually (in some cases, contractually) guaranteed profit streams.

The general shift in state financing from public and corporate taxation to financialised debt, as detailed by Wolfgang Streeck in *Buying Time*, provides a vast and uniquely reliable source of value extraction for global capital. All of these avenues, and many more besides, are structural features of neoliberalism which express not only the relative weakness of the state vis-a-vis capital, but the chronic need of private capital for enormous, publicly backed income streams that are at least somewhat insulated from market turbulence. These fixes stave off collapse for both state expenditure and private profit, and yet all deepen tendencies towards capital's productive decay. Quantitative easing, for example, did not encourage productive investment, but merely channeled huge economic resources into hoarding and speculative bubbles, while burdening the state with levels of debt that further mitigated against any change of course.

Often presented as a straightforward victory for capital, it is important to understand the resulting capital–state relations as expressing the contradictory but mutually reinforcing tendencies of the latter's simultaneous *power over* and *dependency on* the former. Taken together, these dynamics have radically narrowed the strategic options available to state managers, reducing their 'relative autonomy' from capital and diminishing their ability to resist immediate, factional demands in the interests of the health of capitalism as a whole. This is not simply because states are dominated by capital, but because the ultimate imperative of sustaining accumulation in the context of neoliberalism's failure to restore the profitability of productive investment pushes them towards short-term fixes and away from long-term strategic economic management.

For the Tories, this has undermined what Andrew Gamble, in *The Conservative Nation*, terms their historic 'flexibility and political common sense derived from [the party's]s relative independence from the dominant sections of property', originating from its aristocratic constitution within an increasingly industrial society. Nigel Harris, in *Competition and the Corporate Society*, likewise saw the Conservative Party as possessing a 'facility for disentangling itself from temporary association with any one group' within changing economic circumstances. As the needs of financialised capital have become hegemonic, the strategic field and hence the Party's flexibility has diminished. A sign of this eroded political independence is both the Party's imposition of austerity as a response to the 2007-8 crash and its subsequent failure to change course, despite repeated proclamations that it intended to do so. From George Osborne's vision for a 'Northern Powerhouse', to Theresa May's pledge that 'austerity is over', to Boris Johnson's post-Brexit agenda to 'level up' and rebalance the economy: disingenuousness and plain incompetence aside, the binding of government policy to a course of action rhetorically disavowed by a series of administrations speaks to an inability to move against factional interests within the ruling bloc, even if such a move may be a more likely road to both economic revival and renewed political support.

This was not always the case: from the assault on its own aristocratic roots with the 1846 repeal of the Corn Laws, to the imposition of Keynesian managerialism on private capital, to Thatcher's own assault on the outdated 'gentlemanly capitalism' of traditional City finance, the Conservatives have historically known when particular sections of the elite need to be sacrificed in the interests of capital as a whole. Tellingly, the only real pushback against the policies pursued by the Tories between 2010 and 2024 did not come from state managers committed to long-term economic re-orientation, nor from non-financial sectors of the ruling bloc, nor even from oppositional social movements, but from the markets themselves in response to Liz Truss' disastrous 'fiscal event'. On paper a neoliberal dream (and effusively praised as such in the Tory press), her unfunded tax cuts and plans for even greater financial deregulation led to runs on the pound, soaring inflation, and spiralling government borrowing costs, as investors and bondholders lost confidence in the British state's ability to service its debt. Granted, this is not simply a political failing but speaks to a general problem for capitalism at its present stage of development: unlike previous eras of crisis or stagnation, there are no obviously ascendant dynamics ready to restructure the world economy along new lines as, for instance, neoliberalism did to post-war capitalism in the 1970s and 1980s with its global expansion of production and pivot towards finance. As previous instances of the Conservatives' evolution have signalled transformations within the structure of capitalism itself, so too does their post-Thatcherite stasis reflect the lack of any truly paradigmatic change in the period since 2008.

This inability to change course also meant the state was ill-equipped to respond to the two defining events of the Conservatives' time in power: Brexit and the Covid-19 pandemic. While the former was suboptimal for capitalism as a whole, the gutting of technical and administrative expertise in the civil service since Thatcher also left the state unable to provide serious impact reports or strategic guidance to capital in the new environment. Habituated to the outsourcing of trade negotiations to Brussels, it also conspicuously lacked legal, diplomatic, financial, and economic competence vis-à-vis the European bloc. Meanwhile, the lack of both a national bourgeoisie and strong industrial sector, combined with the state's inability to pivot towards radical strategic interventionism, meant that the structural conditions necessary for a 'successful' Brexit in capitalist terms were absent. The pandemic, similarly, demonstrated the path-dependency and critical failure of the British state model. While the scale of its economic intervention was huge, this did not mark 'the end of neoliberalism' as was claimed in some quarters. What we saw was not a return to Keynesian principles, but a doubling down on the existing model of capital–state relations. This was shown partly through the reliance on subcontracting to deliver critical services and infrastructure, guaranteeing profits to corporations in logistics, pharmaceuticals, construction, and other sectors – an inefficient and expensive mode of provision, even before accounting for the tens of billions of pounds lost to waste, fraud, misappropriation, and non-delivery. In similar terms, social provision was directed through channels that carefully preserved existing relations: furlough was not an individual grant, but a subsidy to business handled through corporate payroll; no restrictions to lay-offs were implemented and no union involvement required in job retention schemes; quantitative easing, low-interest loans, and direct grants provided liquidity to financial and corporate sectors; and strictly temporary rent protections and mortgage holidays maintained the value of housing assets without fundamentally changing the status of tenants or making home ownership more accessible. Overall, as Robert Knox and David Whyte observe in *Vaccinating Capitalism*, the response to Covid-19 was 'a system of life support for profit-making corporations ... Crucially, the effect was to keep the corporate sector intact without the state infringing on its economic decision-making power'. The death toll and broader social impact aptly demonstrate the inability of this approach to actually deliver policy and preserve life.

In more discrete areas, too, the post-Thatcherite state now infringes upon the Conservatives' ability to make good on their promises. Not just social provision, but the repressive apparatus central to the traditional party of 'law and order' is now feeling the squeeze of diminished funding and capacity. Nearly 450,000 people await trial in an overwhelmed court system; prisons are running at up to 170 per cent capacity, with fewer than 100 empty cells across the whole of England and Wales at the time of writing. Meanwhile, £10 billion was committed to the theatre of Rwanda deportations, but an administrative backlog means that 166,000 asylum applications cannot be processed and, consequently, those making them cannot be removed from the UK. While increasingly reliant upon authoritarian, racist, and chauvinistic rhetorics, and ostensibly passing legislation to put this into force, at the institutional level the Conservatives presided over a sprawling dysfunction which damaged the state's capacity to enact the will of the executive across a number of policy areas traditionally central to the Tory agenda. Besides ministerial incompetence, bureaucratic lethargy, or the need to focus resources on Brexit and the pandemic, these issues are partly due to finances being increasingly diverted to the subsidy of private capital in ways previously outlined, as well as expensive and inefficient models of outsourced service provision undermining the state's capacity to perform a variety of basic tasks.

In this context, Thatcher's famous refrain of 'there is no alternative' takes on new salience. Once a victory cry over vanquished opponents, it now encapsulates the self-inflicted dead-end of Tory statecraft. With the increasing entanglement of capital and state, driven by the former's simultaneous power over and dependency on the latter, the Party has lost a critical degree of strategic independence which has historically made it ideally suited to the role of state manager. As the institutions of state have become more directly involved with supporting profits in a degenerate mode of accumulation, their capacity to balance between factions of the ruling bloc and set long-term strategic pathways for development has become attenuated. This is a problem for all parties, but perhaps particularly for one whose identity and modes of political practice are so closely bound to the history of the state itself within capitalist development.

## Elite recomposition and the reproduction of the ruling class

Within these macro-trends, the post-Thatcherite period has also seen significant sociological change among the upper layers of British society. Historically, the role of the Party has been to identify ascendant elite factions and metabolise them into the power structure in such a way as to preserve the whole by gradually changing the nature of its constituent parts. This has been the case since at least the mid-1800s, when the Party first cast off its original and specific identification with landed property to become, by the end of the century, the preferred political representatives of a unified aristocratic and bourgeois bloc in a way unimaginable across much of continental Europe. From that time on, whatever other changes may have occurred and whatever internal divisions may have existed, the Conservatives have generally stood for the whole of elite society. From this perspective, the Thatcherite leap from small and large national businesses to international capital followed the traditional Tory pattern, as existing alignments with declining sectors were set aside to reorient the Party towards those on the rise. However, just as the internationalisation and financialisation of capital have degraded state autonomy at the level of political economy, similar dynamics at the level of sociology have eroded the collective identity and corporate solidarity of the British ruling class itself. With this development, the Party has lost its traditional anchorage within a nationally specific class faction and, as a result, its character has changed in a number of important and historically novel ways.

In his 1991 study *Who Rules Britain?*, John Scott documented how the British elite had evolved over time while maintaining its internal cohesion. Up to the 1980s, dense patterns of mutually interlocking directorships and corporate shareholdings produced a high degree of national economic coordination, overseen by a distinct and closely connected social group. In the time since, this has given way to more disarticulated and internally fragmented structures at the national level, driven by the larger economic developments sketched in the previous section. The impact of this shift has not just been economic, but social, as layers of provincial capitalists who once provided a countrywide bedrock of Tory support have been all but destroyed. Ferdinand Mount, surveying local Conservative Associations in the mid-1960s, hailed

> the support of every local business owner worth his salt. There they were ... with waistcoats and watch chains: wool merchants in Bradford, steel men in Swansea, carpet makers in Kidderminster, fireworks manufacturers in Halifax.

This local bourgeoisie has now been replaced in regional economies by large, international employers, upon whom entire towns and their surrounding areas are now often totally dependent. Nissan, Ford, Airbus, Amazon, Tata Steel, and many more: heavily subsidised by the state, but with a purely instrumental and contingent relationship to both the Conservatives and Britain as a whole – poor substitutes for the organic, multi-generational connections of their waistcoat-clad predecessors. While small and medium capital still constitutes a significant social layer and makes up the clear majority of all businesses, they are no longer as tightly bound to the Tories as they once were, with significant proportions switching allegiances to the series of Eurosceptic Faragist parties or, indeed, to Starmer's aggressively pro-business Labour Party. The supply chains into which contemporary SMEs are most likely to be inserted are, similarly, themselves articulated by global economic patterns and are ultimately dependent on large international capital – a different economic, cultural, and ideological arrangement from when a national bourgeoisie was sustained by an Empire managed by the state and its habitual Tory rulers.

The evolving composition of the Sunday Times Rich List (STRL) further highlights shifts in the make-up of the ruling class proper. The first edition, in 1989, was dominated by aristocratic families and established British business owners; top spot, fittingly, was held by Queen Elizabeth II. By the early twenty-first century, it was populated largely by international capitalists; and, by 2015, the Queen was no longer in the top 300. A 2022 STRL survey carried out by the University of Warwick found that over a quarter of billionaires with significant British interests were foreign nationals, another quarter were 'non-doms', one in seven lived abroad in tax havens, and around half of those resident here had equally important foreign investments. Speaking to the BBC to mark the List's twenty-fifth anniversary, the compiler, Philip Beresford, attributed its transformation explicitly to Thatcher, commenting on how her economic policies had shifted the balance away from inherited wealth towards the 'self-made' international nouveau riche.

Alongside this recomposition 'from above' has run a similar process of erosion 'from below', as significant upwardly mobile sections of the petit bourgeoisie and lower middle-classes have gained new power, wealth, and status, particularly through the expansion and diversification of finance. While boosting the power of the City, Thatcher also recognised that its stuffiness, traditional structures, and 'old boys' elite networks were ill suited to capturing market share in a new financial landscape characterised by digital information flows, accelerated trading, and innovation in forms of assets, securities, and credit provision. As Alexander Gallas documents in The Thatcherite Offensive, this entailed the dismantling of the 'gentlemanly capitalism' of the old City, with historic family firms and personal networks replaced by more cut-throat international (particularly American) companies and traders, along with an influx of British professionals from more modest class backgrounds. The impression made by this new blood on London's traditional elite is captured by Stephen Hoare's memoir and history of the city's exclusive club scene, *Palaces of Power*, which recounts how many hallowed membership institutions were morally scandalised yet saved from financial ruin by the coarse manners and new money of the venture capitalists, hedge fund managers, and floor traders brought into the sector after the 'Big Bang' of 1986. Among this new generation was one Nigel Farage, who assumed his future lay at university or in the military until he heard of free-wheeling young traders making good in the City. Resolving to become one of them as quickly as possible, he joined the London Metal Exchange as a broker; his subsequent career neatly illustrates how disruptive sections of this new elite, embodying the aggressive and cavalier tendencies of finance in their attempts to reorient Britain's geopolitical stance, have since become for the Conservative establishment.

A further marker of elite transformation is the declining importance of private education. In *Classes and Cultures*, Ross McKibbin recounts that in the 1950s 95 per cent of male children from families earning over £1000 were privately educated. In *Tory Nation*, Samuel Earl estimates that today 'only' 60 per cent of children from families earning over £300,000 follow the same route – a stark educational divide and continuing marker of privilege, to be sure, but significantly below historic levels. Scott's study similarly shows that over three quarters of the post-war business elite attended fee-paying schools and that the same was true for a significant majority of directors of financial firms up until the 1980s. Now, this applies to just 34 per cent of FTSE 350 CEOs, with 43 per cent of these and 51 per cent of the STRL educated abroad. Similar dynamics are observable across state institutions, as shown by studies carried out by the Sutton Trust and Social Mobility Commission. In 1971, nine tenths of top generals and admirals were privately schooled; in 2019, the proportion was less than half. The rates of top civil servants likewise fell from 90 per cent after the Second World War to 59 per cent in 2019; ambassadors and diplomats from over 80 per cent in the 1980s to 52 per cent by recent estimates. Overall, these reports estimate that just 39 per cent of the British elite across politics, business, law, the media, and other key sectors are privately educated, although the distribution and pace of the decline is uneven and somewhat accentuated by the rise of Premier League footballers, largely from working-class backgrounds, into the ranks of extreme wealth. While still hugely disproportionate to the 7 per cent of the general population enjoying such educational privilege, the trajectory is clearly and significantly downwards. Simultaneously, private schools themselves are drawing from more diverse layers, with even Eton no longer such a family affair. Whereas 60 per cent of students had alumni parents in 1960, this is now true for just 20 per cent. Similarly, around a third of pupils at top fee-paying schools are foreign nationals, leading the headmaster of

King's College to warn that they were becoming 'finishing schools for the children of oligarchs' in an interview with the *Guardian*.

As the locus of ruling class integration has increasingly shifted to the transnational level, the role of Britain's elite schools has likewise evolved: they are no longer an exclusive mechanism for the specific reproduction of the British elite per se, but more of a networking opportunity for the global rich. This has diminished their centrality in providing successive generations of the British ruling class with an almost universally shared experience of formative socialisation, important not just for instilling cultural assumptions of their own inherited superiority over the masses, but for maintaining social cohesion and class continuity at the elite level. While the ruling class obviously still exists and pursues its interests with considerable force both in Britain and globally, it is questionable now the degree to which it retains its traditional sociological cohesion at the national level. The exceptional historical continuity of the British ruling class, which provided the Conservatives with an enviable social foundation and recruitment ground across the transition to capitalist modernity, has thus been significantly attenuated. While direct and specific conclusions are difficult to draw, it seems reasonable to infer that elite groups in Britain today may be less likely than their forebears to perceive themselves as a unified social body possessing distinctive, collective, and cross-generational aims, embodied in a national state, to which individual interests and ambitions can be subordinated.

As with all previous periods of elite recomposition, these tendencies are closely reflected within the Conservative Party. Between 1925 and 1955, 94 per cent of Tory ministers were privately educated; Thatcher's first cabinet, at 91 per cent, showed no great departure, and neither did the wider parliamentary Party at 73 per cent. As with the broader elite, the Conservatives were also characterised by exceptionally close familial ties, leading to them being popularly known as 'the cousinhood' until the mid-twentieth century. From the first modern Conservative leader, Robert Peel, in 1830, to Alec Douglas-Home in 1965, three quarters of all Conservative leaders were either the sons or sons-in-law of prominent Tory politicians; since then, none have been. More broadly, according to Earl, up to the 1930s around a third of their MPs could be placed on the same family tree, and even by 1960 there were still 19 different members of the Cecil family (or, to give them their noble title, the Salisburies) in parliament. In this way, the Tory Party embodied and guaranteed a core tenet of conservatism as a political creed: the need for and desirability of the preservation of a specific ruling caste, the socio-genetic reproduction of which passed the qualities and skills for leadership from generation to generation. The durability of this ethos is shown by the cognitive dissonance experienced by members of the traditional elite at Thatcher's assent: the daughter of a shopkeeper, she was widely (and, apparently, falsely) rumoured to be the illegitimate granddaughter of the aristocrat Harry Cust, who allegedly had an affair with her grandmother when she worked as his maid. Only by ascribing blue blood to the Iron Lady could the upper circles of the Party make sense of Thatcher's obvious leadership qualities – although this did not stop her foreign secretary, Lord Carrington, from describing her as a 'fucking stupid, petit-bourgeois woman' to cabinet colleagues.

However, while the modest backgrounds of Thatcher, Major, and Heath before made them outliers at the time, their rise foreshadowed genuine party transformation. David Cameron and Boris Johnson may have recently returned the Party to Old Etonian leadership, but, overall, this tendency has been greatly diluted. Tim Bale's recent study, *The Conservative Party after Brexit*, shows that, among recent cabinets, the proportion of ministers with private school backgrounds has ranged from around 65 per cent under Sunak and Truss – still very high, but well below any other period – to as low as 30 per cent under Theresa May. At one point, there were only ten Etonians in the whole of parliament; following the 2024 election, according to a Sutton Trust survey of the backgrounds of parliamentarians, under half of all Tory MPs were privately educated. This relative decline of the privately educated is also seen in the comparative rarity of large landowners (such as Lord Salisbury) and major industrialists (such as Andrew Bonar Law) rising to positions of prominence, with this decline mirrored by the rise of the lower-middle classes. According to Erzsébet Bukodi's *The Changing Class and Educational Composition of the UK Political Elite Since 1945*, individuals from families of small employers and the self-employed made up a fifth of the Party leadership between 2010 and 2021 – a significant *over-representation* of the middle classes and petit bourgeoisie compared to the population as a whole. The ascent of Thatcher thereby accelerated dynamics initiated by postwar efforts to provide routes for intra-Party mobility, producing what dissident Tory Geoffrey Wheatcroft describes in *Bloody Panico!* as a 'class war' between patrician aristocrats and a politically active lower-middle class, who first took over the constituency associations before moving into the parliamentary Party itself. The displacement of the more conciliatory post-war generation of Butler and MacMillan (whose family press, fittingly, had published the works of Keynes and who embodied the Party's reconciliation with post-war capitalism) over the course of Thatcher's time in power by these newer, lower-middle-class layers without experience of managing large national firms or negotiating with union leadership itself arguably contributed to the Party's pivot to a more aggressive, confrontational stance towards organised labour during the 1980s.

Simultaneously, the centre of gravity in the Party has shifted increasingly towards finance, which as a highly internationalised sector has also heavily contributed to increasing the remarkable and very possibly unparalleled ethnic diversity of recent Tory frontbenches. David Cameron, Theresa May and Rishi Sunak all had backgrounds in the sector, with the newly elected Kemi Badenoch linked by her financier husband, along with all but one of the Tory chancellors since 2010 – with the single exception, George Osborne, joining Blackrock soon after leaving office. This lop-sided integration is also evident in MPs' post- or para-parliamentary careers; as destruction loomed in the 2024 election, a swathe of high-profile Conservative MPs announced their resignations, with many moving onto extremely lucrative positions in finance, investment capital, hedge funds, and corporate lobbying – precisely those sectors most likely to prioritise short-term profit maximisation over long-term developmental strategy. While Tory parliamentarians have always been intimately connected to private business, this is no longer generally as 'captains of industry' or through experience in any particular productive sector. While John Ross' *Thatcher and Friends* shows that 70 per cent of Thatcher's first cabinet served as directors and executives, collectively holding positions on the boards of 473 companies, MPs now largely hold such posts in an honorary capacity, presumably granted in return for the connections they can offer to state institutions rather than their professional experience or technical competence.

The cumulative effect of these changes has been to gradually alter the nature and role of the Conservative Party. It now functions less as a collective means for defending the historic power of a specific national class and more as a vehicle for individuals to secure their own advancement within a more fluid elite class structure. Together with the economic changes outlined previously, this further mitigates against strategic thinking and long-term statecraft because, increasingly, *there is no all-encompassing, collective goal*. Instead, in a party famed (albeit only partially deservedly) for its outward shows of unity, the tendency is towards open factionalism and high-level churn: while, in the post-war period, ministers commonly served for three to five years, between 1974 and 2023, the average tenure was 2.1 years, far lower than most other major democracies, with the longest periods in office occurring under New Labour. Between 2019 and the end of the last Conservative government, it had fallen to just eight months, although this number is somewhat skewed by the Truss interlude. At one point, medics reportedly stopped asking concussion victims who the Prime Minister was, as such knowledge had ceased to be a reliable indicator of mental capacity. While a multitude of factors lie behind this degradation, it nonetheless speaks to a party that has lost its collective purpose, commands little visible loyalty from its most prominent members, and serves largely as a kind of high-level internship on the pathway to vast personal riches in the private sector or even a personal place within the ruling class proper, no matter how undistinguished one's performance in government has been.

As the corporate solidarity of the British ruling class has waned, so the Conservative Party has become estranged from its historic purpose and, therefore, from its distinctive modes of political practice that lent it an unparalleled sense of permanency and continuity both in material terms and within the national imagination. Thatcherism, and neoliberalism more broadly, have been highly successful class offensives in terms of the upward redistribution of wealth and insulation of economic power from democratic pressures. However, it has also seen the erosion of the British ruling class as a distinctive social body and, with it, the loss of an elite ethos in which state service carried significant prestige and essential purpose. By monopolising state institutions, primarily through the vehicle of the Conservative Party, the British aristocracy was able to defend its social position even as it ceased to be the most important economic faction. Careful management of the state and even personal sacrifice in its service – for example, through the once common front-line military service – were therefore central to ruling class reproduction. As that sociological basis has dissolved, the Conservative Party has come to embody another set of moral values, more traditionally associated with the middle classes, not only in its outward ideological pronouncements but in its internal constitution and character: individualism, personal advancement, and fratricidal competition. Conservative commentators are aware of this process, with the likes of Roger Scruton and Peregrine Worsthorne mourning the passing of the nation's aristocracy as bearers of unique moral purpose and political acumen. We need not share their supplicancy to recognise that their lament points to a real social process, through which the once distinctive nature of the Conservative Party has been significantly eroded.

## Losing the base
While ultimately rooted in the elite, the Conservative Party obviously requires much broader support in order to govern. It has achieved this by managing processes of democratisation in such a

way as to ensure ruling class preservation, possibly with a greater degree of success than anywhere else in the western world. Historically, the Party has won the votes of around a third of workers, particularly the more affluent layers or those concentrated in small workplaces and provincial settings; in short, those sections of the working class most insulated from the appeal of socialism. The real mass base of the Party, however, has been middle class, encompassing property owners and professionals, farmers and landlords, small capital and the petit bourgeoisie. The attraction of these constituencies towards Conservatism is explained by their shared anxieties. Intermediary social positions render whatever advantage they have gained within the class structure vulnerable to both larger concentrations of capital and proletarian agitation. This status produces paranoia and the perception of precarity, and hence a proclivity towards ideologies that promise to reinforce the existing order (or restore an idealised lost one) by identifying and eliminating threats from both 'above' and 'below'. Playing into these anxieties has historically allowed the Conservative Party to represent itself as not just an elite project, but one that speaks for 'the people', stands up for 'common sense', and defends the middle classes as the moral backbone of the nation. Far from a recent innovation, this 'populism' is an essential component of Tory tradition, endlessly recycled and recalibrated as social anxieties are reproduced by the turbulence of capitalist development.

When Thatcher reconstructed popular Conservatism by peeling off layers of affluent workers and pitching for the petit bourgeoisie and small business owners, this was in no way a departure from the Party's historic methods for gaining mass support. Just as, in the mid-1980s, the lower-middle class was mobilised against the miners' strike, so too in 1926 the petit bourgeoisie had provided the majority of strikebreakers. Thatcher, far more than the Labour Party at the time, was attentive to underlying changes in the class structure inculcated by the very model of post-war capitalism she was about to destroy. Better-off workers, anxious to defend their advance towards the middle class in the face of economic crisis and social unrest; small capital, squeezed out by big national corporations and hostile to union power under Keynesianism; a wider distribution of prosperity during the boom years, creating a 'consumer society' less bound to collectivist cultures and non-commercial recreation: this provided a social base that Thatcher rightly sensed was ready to be radicalised, mobilised, and incorporated into her bloc. This was largely achieved through what Stuart Hall famously termed 'authoritarian populism', in which free-market capitalism was combined with a 'law and order' appeal that cast industrial militants and racialised outsiders as the enemies of social peace. Ideology was bolstered by material benefits specifically targeted at these groups, most notably 'Right to Buy' and the sale of shares in privatised state companies, which together created a new mass layer of homeowners and individual investors whose interests were aligned with rising asset prices and falling inflation.

This has formed the core of the Conservative vote ever since. For some time, however, it has been clear that this base faces a crisis of reproduction. While, in each of Thatcher's three election victories, more people aged eighteen to thirty-five voted for the Tories than for any other party – often by wide margins – by the 2024 election the age at which someone is more likely to vote Conservative over Labour had risen to sixty-three: precisely the age someone would now be had they first voted for Thatcher as an eighteen-year-old in 1979. In a very literal sense, the Party's support base simply *has not changed or renewed* in nearly half a century. Expansion beyond this core is of course possible and has at times been achieved, but only in an unstable fashion reliant upon conjunctural factors, as shown by the growth of the Party's vote in 2019 and its subsequent recession in 2024. As Phil Burton-Cartledge argues in *The Party's Over*, a key reason why Tory voters are not being replaced at a sufficient rate is that younger generations are increasingly struggling to get on the housing ladder, meaning that the conservatising effects of home ownership are delayed. This presents a serious dilemma to the Conservatives, as any move to address the housing crisis risks crashing the asset values of existing mortgage owners and outright owners, including the cohort of pensioners who make up an increasingly large proportion of the Party's supporters and rely on housing wealth to fund their social care or provide meaningful inheritance to their children. The same could be said for the other major material offer of the Thatcher years: 'shareholder democracy' or 'popular capitalism'. While initial waves of privatisation swelled the number of individual shareholders from 7 per cent to 25 per cent of the population between 1979 and 1991, a recent article in the *Economic History Review* shows that by the start of the twentieth century this had fallen back to just 2.5 per cent, as ownership was once again centralised and concentrated in fewer hands. And unlike in 1979, there is no source of readily available wealth equivalent to the national industries or North Sea oil that can be easily diverted through targeted redistribution to the lower middle-classes to cohere popular support, nor a booming sector on the scale of the City in the 1980s that can provide an avenue for upward mobility and class recomposition in terms favourable to the Conservatives.

If the Party's base is locked into a declinist dynamic, the wider political landscape is increasingly volatile. This is partly due to conjunctural reasons, most obviously Brexit. But gone are the days when future voting behaviour could be reliably read as that of the past: according to the British Electoral Survey, half of all voters switched party at least once across the 2010, 2015, and 2017 elections. In 2024, the Conservatives lost 47 per cent of their 2019 voters. Beyond the specifics of individual leaders, manifesto promises, or immediate issues, the growing tendency for voters to switch parties – or, indeed, simply not vote at all – is related to changes in the underlying class structure and associated developments in political identities and socio-cultural habits and norms. Again, these changes are clearly related to neoliberalism in general and Thatcherism in particular, but they are generally regarded as posing problems for the left. The destruction of the labour movement was a key Thatcherite objective, and one that was largely achieved, with figures provided by the Trades Union Congress showing that trade union membership has fallen from 13 million in the 1970s to under 7 million today within a much larger workforce. Industrial employment has similarly collapsed, from around 30 per cent of all jobs pre-Thatcher to just 8 per cent now according to the Resolution Foundation. Along with the direct political defeat of organised labour, this has also meant the destruction of a distinctive working-class *habitus*, as associational life, collective institutions, and identifiably proletarian leisure practices have faded.

As the relatively defined class blocs and lifeworlds of the mid-twentieth century have diminished, the class structure has exhibited a growing complexity. In particular, there has been a proliferation of intermediate, petty managerial positions, such that over three million people now work in lower technical and supervisory roles: store managers of Tesco outlets, overseers in warehouses, call centre supervisors. While often barely better off than their subordinates in material terms, the social positions and supervisory responsibilities of these groups differentiate them from the working class proper. A second major development has been a huge growth in self-employment, as recently discussed by Dan Evans in *A Nation of Shopkeeper*. Under Thatcher, this category grew by 68 per cent, far outstripping any other major economy in terms of proportionate increase. From 8 per cent of the workforce in 1975 to almost 15 per cent today, this peaked at over 5 million people pre-Covid-19 – almost matching the numbers employed in the entire public sector. Of all those registering as self-employed, only 2 per cent employ others, down from around half in the 1970s. For Evans, this means that the majority of the self-employed now fit the classic definition of the petit bourgeoisie, owning their own means of production but not employing wage labour. Evans argues that at its lower end, typified by 'gig economy' delivery drivers and other highly exploited platform workers, this class occupies a 'grey zone' between the petit-bourgeoisie and the proletariat, due in large part to the individualised subjectivity promoted by these labour practices; others, such as Jamie Woodcock and Callum Cant, view them as a significant new working class layer. More important than technical classifications, however, is a recognition that, despite some examples of gig workers successfully challenging platforms through collective action and unionisation, the platforms themselves are clearly designed in ways intended to mitigate against such outcomes. And, by and large, they succeed. For Evans, the gig economy enforces intra-worker competition, individuates work practices, and promotes entrepreneurial modes of action that are both function to capital accumulation and extend traditionally petit bourgeois norms of labour and socialisation to much wider sections of the population, complicating the widespread notion that the 'Red Wall' seats that flipped from Labour to Conservative and back again between 2019 and 2024 can be identified as straightforwardly 'working class'. Beyond those working for platforms like Deliveroo, TaskRabbit, and Amazon Flex, the solo self-employed comprise personal trainers, hairdressers, taxi drivers, and tradesmen, along with creative professionals, consultants, and a myriad of other freelancers who range from the impoverished to the very highly remunerated. The growing heterogeneity of self-employment further complicates the class structure and the production of political and social identities. Studies of gig workers highlight, on the one hand, widespread support for unionisation, minimum standards of pay, and protection from dismissal and discrimination – that is, the classic demands of waged labourers. On the other, they find the proliferation of individualised, 'entrepreneurial' tendencies as a way to improve their conditions: upgrading the 'means of production', no matter how meagre (a better car, a motorised bike); rigging platforms to allow them to take on more work (and thus depriving other workers, with whom they compete, of 'gigs'); informally sub-contracting work to younger family members or friends (in a manner analogous to traditional self-employed tradesmen). If this creates a large layer of voters who are theoretically 'up for grabs' by whoever can most effectively appeal to their diverse and contradictory interests at any particular time, it also disarticulates the coherent social blocs upon which all parties have traditionally relied.

The Conservatives' struggles in constructing a durable new popular bloc are heightened by the virtual disappearance of one very particular expression of associational life that has withered since its post-war height: the Conservative Party itself as a mass organisation, as detailed in studies such as Martin Pugh's *The Tories and the People* and *Angels in Marble* by Robert McKenzie and Allan Silver. As the franchise expanded (largely through Tory legislation), new voters had to be managed and won over to the Party's cause. Particularly following the 1867 expansion, the Conservatives either founded new local membership organisations or formally incorporated pre-existing ones into the central party structure. By 1880, there had developed a complex party structure reaching large swathes of the population, with the Conservative Registration Association, Conservative Club, Conservatives Working Men's Club, Primrose League and Orange Lodges all likely to be present to some degree in both rural and urban constituencies. The real strength of these associations, which each had different relations to the central Party, during the nineteenth century is difficult to measure, and the leadership was always careful to withhold any actual power from those organisations aimed specifically at workers, often offering free membership to avoid any actually enforceable demands for influence over policy. Nonetheless, by the end of the century there were around 300 working men's clubs, with some cities such as Liverpool boasting several thousand members. Similarly, the arm's-length Primrose League, founded to promote conservative values through family-friendly social activities, could boast 1.5 million members, and was unrivalled by any other party machine anywhere in the world. In *Tory Nation*, Earl recounts how the events it organised featured 'a mixed bag of entertainers, including flying trapeze artists, clowns, minstrel shows, trick bicycle riders, jugglers, ventriloquists, marionettes, and brass bands.' Responding to the 1945 election defeat, the Party added a million new members in just eight months, reaching a peak of nearly three million in 1952. As Tim Bale documents in *Footsoldiers*, his study of contemporary party memberships, by 2019 this had fallen to just 190,000, a decline of 95 per cent. Kemi Badenoch was elected leader by just over half of 95,000 member votes on a turnout of around 73 per cent, indicating a total current membership of only 130,000.

In *The Conservative Century*, Anthony Seldon and Stuart Bell discuss the previous centrality of the Party to many aspects of social life, recounting how in many rural areas and smaller towns it often provided the major outlet for leisure activities, networking, and match-making for young singles. The networks of cheap pubs, village fairs, and variety shows also created organic forms of mediation and connection between the Party leadership and ordinary members, as well as a means through which to attract local businessmen and other notables to bolster the Conservatives' support among small capital. As individualism, consumerism, and modern leisure practices have spread, the cultural institutions of Conservatism have suffered just as much as those of the trade unions and popular socialism: the lifeworld of mass Toryism is now a relic of the past. This does not, of course, mean that conservative social values have or will disappear or even necessarily recede. It does, however, suggest that the Party is less able to bind these values to a broader political agenda that can both win mass appeal and be centrally controlled. Worse, as that membership has receded to a hardcore rump more and more out of step with the population as a whole, the Party has clung to it with increasing desperation, empowering a rank and file with the final say over electing the Party leader. This has consistently saddled the (relatively speaking) more moderate parliamentary Party with leaders reflecting (authentically or otherwise) the views and priorities of a more extreme membership, simultaneously boosting the importance and visibility of backbench groups promoting similar agendas as they jostle for prominence. The effects were clearly seen in the parliamentary impasse over Brexit and the profile of the likes of the European Research Group. Ironically, William Hague, who first granted members a say over the leader, now sees returning to a model of purely parliamentary selection as being essential for taking back control of the Party's future direction. In last year's leadership election, the farce of the relatively centrist James Cleverly's supporters inadvertently sabotaging their own candidate by switching votes to Robert Jenrick in a botched attempt to keep Badenoch off the final ballot shows how one of the Party's traditional great fears has been realised: control by a vulgar rank and file that it must court, but ultimately detests.

The decline of the Thatcherite bloc, reworking of the class structure, and destruction of the mass party – alongside the erosion of important aspects of state capacity discussed earlier – mean that the Tories are unable to reliably capitalise on the social anxieties their policies have produced. Again, this is exemplified most clearly by Brexit – both the wedge issue through which the Party secured its only convincing parliamentary majority in over twenty years and the source of a historic split in the right-wing vote which threatens their long-term electoral prospects. While Reform, with 14 per cent of the vote in 2024, did not substantially improve upon UKIP's 13 per cent in 2015, the series of Faragist parties pose a persistent challenge to the Tories' right, of a significance and scale that they have rarely if ever had to contend with. The appearance of this revolt on the right is related to all the major dynamics discussed thus far. Neoliberal patterns of accumulation and changing modes of state intervention have produced wider inequalities between London and the British regions than exist between East and West Germany or North and South Italy, with those areas most weakly integrated into the contemporary economy most likely to support Brexit and, at best, feel ambivalent towards a party so closely associated with a state that has largely abandoned them. Splits in the ruling bloc and the Party's loss of collective discipline opened the way for minority factions of finance capital to ally with personally ambitious figures within the Tory leadership to reorient British capitalism away from Europe and towards the more lightly regulated American model, in a way that was dysfunctional for accumulation as a whole but served factional agendas well. And the withering of the party structure and consequent loss of popular socio-cultural identification saw hitherto impeccably loyal constituencies jump ship: a quarter of small business owners voted UKIP in the 2014 European elections, around 20 per cent of Conservative members view big business as exploitative of the common people, and a majority of the rank and file stated that they wished to see Brexit through even if it meant the destruction of the Tory Party itself. In the 2019 European elections, they were as good as their word, with 60 per cent of Tory members voting for the Brexit Party and only 20 per cent for their own. And, while it remains to be seen whether the Reform vote share is a staging post to bigger things or a high watermark, there are signs that Farage's pop-up parties are beginning to achieve something that the Conservatives have singularly failed to do: win sections of the youth, particularly young men, over to right-wing politics. Combined with their close relationship with the newly re-elected Donald Trump and links to a number of extremely wealthy international donors, as well as Farage's ability to tap into a burgeoning right-wing alt-media, this suggests that the challenge from Reform is indeed set to become more significant over the course of this parliamentary term.

The rise of the Faragist right points to a number of historic fractures in the Conservative bloc: between rival sections of large capital, which the Party can no longer effectively unify behind its leadership, and between large and small capital, testing the alliance the Party has historically formed between big business and middle class reaction. As these contradictions intensify, the temptation will be to continue to veer to the right. But this threatens to further accelerate and radicalise a populist dynamic, seen most clearly in Brexit, that the Party no longer has the means to control. Even if electorally successful, recent years have shown that governing in such terms threatens to bring the Party into conflict with the state institutions and sections of business with which it has historically been so closely identified. But going in the other direction by returning to a more socially liberal tenor offers no guarantees either, at least as long as the Faragist guerilla challenge continues. Here, the arithmetic is of little help: the recent election saw 19 per cent of 2019 Tory voters defect to Reform, with precisely the same number splitting in the opposite direction to Labour, the Liberal Democrats, and Greens. After dominating the first 150 years of mass democracy in Britain through its unparalleled ability to integrate competing ruling class factions and agendas behind its domination of state power, the constituent parts of Conservatism are coming apart at the seams: globe-trotting, free-market liberal capitalism and little-England Toryism; centralised authority and provincial appeal; open elitism and populist agitation; ideologies of state, nation, and individualism. Whether these elements do in fact split in formal terms is open to question and still appears unlikely.

It does seem, however, that they can no longer be as easily articulated into an effective whole in the manner that they have been for most of the Party's modern history.

## Conclusions

Does all this mean that the Conservatives are bound for extinction, or, less dramatically, that their immediate and mid-term electoral prospects are bleak? Not necessarily. In electoral terms, as mentioned, there are serious problems with renewing their vote base. However, the Labour Party has its own set of challenges, reflected most obviously in its committed lack of ambition and victory through a series of marginal wins amidst depressed turn-out. After 2019, commentators widely predicted a 'decade of Boris'; Starmer's 'ten-year plan' could easily go the same way as disillusionment sets in. If that were to happen, the likelihood of a return to power of an even more populist or authoritarian incarnation of the Conservatives – perhaps even in coalition with Reform – cannot be ruled out. As chaotic as the Tories seem and as far as they have fallen, *any* determined ideological attack that succeeds in appealing to a significant section of the discontented electorate has the potential to seriously threaten a Labour administration that bases its entire pitch on mere (and as yet unproven) technocratic competence.

But the increasingly wild swings of electoral politics should not detract from the longer-term dynamics I have tried to sketch above. The Conservative Party may return to power sooner than some think. But it is unlikely to show the same levels of stability and statecraft that have hitherto marked its history. Times of rule may return and may even, such as, from 2010 to 2024, be relatively extended; but they are unlikely to show the same level of purpose or strategic intent as prior periods of domination. The transformations of state, capital, and class since the 1980s, authored in Britain largely by the Tories themselves, have eroded much of what made the Party distinct in the intervening years. What, beyond a general social and public degeneracy, have the Conservatives achieved over the last fourteen years? Their record will surely not bear historic comparison with earlier lengthy spells in office: propped up by an electoral system designed to protect them, the Party had nowhere to hide, its decomposition as publicly evident as that of a corpse in a gibbet. As with previous periods of evolution and crisis within the Party, given their exceptionally close association with the state and the ruling classes, their present crisis reflects and encapsulates certain features of contemporary capitalism: its persistent exhibition of a 'perma-crisis', its evacuation of democratic society, its production of social volatility and dissolution of traditional lifeworlds.

This is, of course, part of an evolving international field. The shift from Keynesianism to neoliberalism did not, of course, represent a replacement of 'national' by 'international' (far less, 'good, democratic' by 'bad, elitist') capitalism, but a shift in global regimes of accumulation and Britain's place within them. Much of the Conservatives' traditional claim to wisdom, competency, and strategic statecraft was made far easier by the enormous resources captured by empire, and later generated by the unprecedented and seemingly unrepeatable post-war boom. The degeneracy of Britain's natural party of government is not, therefore, simply an issue of personnel or even of its broader sociological composition, but a reflection of an ongoing relative national decline which makes it immeasurably more difficult to chart a long-term path or disguise fundamentally elite politics with cheap imperial imports or hand-outs skimmed from a once dominant international position. As the traditionally pre-eminent party declines, ruling class factions become more difficult to bind into a stable bloc and political space opens on all sides to competitors. The left may rightly find pleasure, amusement, and vindication in the Conservatives' electoral decimation. But their crisis will not necessarily be to our advantage. Instead, as long as the Party remains locked into a radicalising dynamic with its rump base, which it can no longer control, it is likely to destabilise the entire political field, creating a void on the right that both Labour and Reform will attempt to capture for themselves and feeding a dynamic that may see us alternate between periods of technocratic liberalism and middle-class reaction. This bifurcation ultimately reflects increasingly sharp splits within the ruling class itself, as different factions adopt either aggressive or defensive orientations towards the states and global institutions of the existing order within the context of rising international competition, impending climate crisis, and mass migration. As satisfying as it may be to see the Tories suffer, whether their crisis provides any cause for triumphant optimism remains a very different question.

HAN DEE

# Trieste: Where Mad Minds Can Fly

The morning sun is already high and hot as we enter the grounds of San Giovanni Park, the former asylum in Italy's north-eastern city Trieste, through Europe's largest rose garden – 3000 varieties in mid to full bloom, hot-pinks and blood-reds, lemons, peaches and creams. 'A multitude in place of economic and moral servitude', our guide Pantxo Ramas suggests, motioning towards the old pavilions ahead of us, where interned patients were forced to work for free in the name of 'ergotherapy' before the old regime was dismantled in the 1970s. The gardens, initiated in 2009 by Franco Rotelli (by then the director of Trieste's Healthcare System), were intended for staff and service users to 'touch the earth and water the roses' while 'changing things'. Today they are maintained by a social cooperative and offer a gathering point for all kinds of visitors, like the group of young service users we will meet later, who meet weekly to garden, socialise, and discuss the history and politics of this place.

'Beauty is truth, truth is beauty', reads a banner hanging along the walkway, drawing me towards the tall perimeter wall which once imprisoned over 1300 locals. I lean against the rough stone for a while, taking it all in. The group I'm with, an international network of researchers, practitioners, survivors, and activists, are among thousands to have travelled to this epicentre of Italy's movement for Democratic Psychiatry, which led to the definitive closure of the country's asylums. The last one shut in 1999. At the movement's height in the 1970s and 1980s, health workers, trade unionists, artists, students, leftists, feminists, housing campaigners, ravers, musicians and various public figures and intellectuals, flocked to participate in this simultaneous destruction of an old and hated institution while inventing new forms of care rooted in the life of the city. Now recognised by the World Health Organisation (WHO) as one of the most advanced public mental healthcare services in the world, people continue to come, in my case carrying a curiosity that lies very close to home.

In 1971, the year San Giovanni's new medical director Franco Basaglia arrived at the asylum with an agenda to overturn it, my uncle was embarking on what would turn out to be a thirty-year stretch under a hospital order in England's high-security psychiatric system. Family visits to see him in Broadmoor, the most notorious of these 'hospitals', brought my first encounters with carceral institutions and a whole world of suffering that I was too young to understand but would soon become familiar with. Decades later, Rotelli's acknowledgement that 'using language to enter into madness is like using a tape measure to measure a liquid' has already warmed me to the humanism at the heart of this project to revolutionise how mental suffering is understood and treated. The gardens bring home to me its affinity with Ruth Wilson Gilmore's 'abolition geography': the 'premise that freedom is a place' where 'we figure out how to combine people, and land'. For Rotelli, the beauty of a collectively tended garden was to serve as 'the cypher of what is possible, of what has not become true in that true life that we wanted to live, for us, for the loonies, suffering brothers and sisters with whom we have done a long walk'.

### It all began with a no

In Britain, the Italian movement is often associated with the 'anti-psychiatry' movement – R. D. Laing, David Cooper, Thomas Szasz and Erving Goffman, among others – whose scathing attacks on powerful institutions captured the popular mood in the 1960s and 1970s. There were indeed generative encounters between the Italian and

British movement, although Basaglia rejected the term anti-psychiatry, describing its 'great success' as deriving 'from the ideological more than the practical view'. In this acknowledgement of success, Basaglia also identified the danger of caricature when it comes to flattening the variety of critiques and experiments that emerged in the UK, and were, in turn, part of an international movement operating in divergent contexts, notably France, Brazil and Algeria where anti-fascist and national liberation struggles were central.

Today in Britain, the post-WW2 asylum closures are often associated with neglectful 'community care' policies which have been accompanied since the early 1990s, by rising rates of compulsory detentions and the imposition of 'community treatment orders'. Similar associations can arise in relation to Italy's headline grabbing 'Law 180'- which ordered the closure of asylums while introducing a raft of equally significant but less well publicised measures: the integration of mental health treatment into a newly established national health service; removal of 'dangerousness' as a basis for detention (something that remains at the heart of UK mental health law); and emphasis on voluntary, community-based treatment with strict limits on the use of compulsion. Limited knowledge of these constructive aspects of Italy's reform movement is compounded by the unavailability of Basaglia's key works in English, including the collectively written *L'Istituzione Negata* (The Institution Denied, 1968). Changes in mental health provision have also impacted unevenly across the country's twenty regions, and everywhere the hopes of those early days have suffered from the ravages of neoliberalism, successive economic and political crises, and gains by far-right parties and fascist groups.

For Basaglia and the broader 'Democratic Psychiatry diaspora' – a term coined by John Foot in *The Man Who Closed the Asylums* to capture a campaign that involved many different actors across numerous cities – the asylums' 'destruction' was only the beginning. Necessary to release those designated 'mad' from the death of social exclusion in order that they might re-enter life in the city and create alternative forms of care as part of a 'radical change in social relations'. Shaped by Italy's intense labour struggles, Democratic Psychiatry was distinctively class oriented in its analysis of mental suffering and assertion of the liberatory potential of 'loonies' as part of a working class invested in social solidarity. 'We cannot understand what disease is as long as the primary needs of men are not met', Basaglia argued. This is captured beautifully in *Fit to be Untied*, produced by the Italian film collective 11 Marzo Cinematografic, when a worker reflects on his experience of labouring alongside people previously institutionalised as 'subnormal': 'they taught us something we had lost, our humanity, how to love'. Above all, Democratic Psychiatry was about practice, or the 'practically true' as Basaglia would say – invoking Sartre – pursuing an art of the possible by working through the contradictions of everyday life.

It is true that Italy's movement 'all began with a no', as Franca Ongaro – Basaglia's long-time collaborator, who penned most of his written work alongside her own – put it. Arriving at Gorizia asylum, about thirty miles north of Trieste, in 1962 for his first medical directorship, Basaglia was hit with a 'terrible smell of death', the 'symbolic smell of shit' which took him 'straight back to the war' and the Venetian prison he had been incarcerated in for chalking up anti-fascist slogans at his university. That night he refused to sign the usual order for restraining patients. 'Violence [is] exercised by those who hold the knife on the side of the handle', Basaglia wrote, 'against those who are hopelessly dominated'. Basaglia had broken out of prison in 1945 in an uprising of prisoners and guards which drove the Nazis out of Venice. He had seen hope in the most miserable of places and knew which side he was on.

Gorizia's asylum, like the town, was deeply marked by war and empire: built under the Hasburg monarchy, destroyed during the First World War and divided by the iron curtain after the Second. Among those detained were Hungarians, Slovens, Austrians, concentration camp survivors and others who were deemed 'unreturnable'. 'At the border between life and death, between normality and non-normality', suggest two members of *Radio Fragola* Gorizia Guillermo and Alessandro, when we meet them at their small studio in 'Area 174' – formerly the asylum mortuary nestling right on the boundary with Slovenia. 'This is the house of the crow' Guillermo says pointing upwards at the sky where imposing, blue-black birds make a regular appearance, 'they're known as *kavkaž*'. We later realise the correct translation is jackdaw, but looking out to the flimsy wire fence, just a few metres away from where tanks once patrolled, and back over the sweeping vegetation surrounding what is now Gorizia's twenty-four-hour mental health walk-in centre (MHC), it's hard not to think of Kafka's outcast crows doing the impossible: trespassing forbidden territories.

When we are guided into the main building by Marco, the MHC's clinical psychologist, we are greeted by a member of the centre's archiving team with descriptions of the asylum's 'shocking' conditions before Basaglia: grey uniforms, patients tied to beds – toilet

holes dug into the
mattresses for those immobilised,
locked cells, and the smell. These conditions were standard across
Italy's asylums then governed by a 1904 law which authorised the
detention of anyone 'affected by mental illness' considered 'dangerous
to themselves or to others', or the cause of 'public scandal'. The violences
described are familiar to me. I already know about the tactic of wrapping
a patient's head in a wet

sheet (sometimes covered in urine) and tightening round the neck to cause unconsciousness – 'throttling out' as my uncle recalls it from Broadmoor and Rampton Hospital. And that deathly smell he could not escape during his first months in Broadmoor's admission block, an 'uncomfortable' and 'fearful' smell.

## The Institution Negated

Basaglia, like many other critical voices of the time, identified the sickness' in front of him as induced by the institution, and drew on his knowledge of the 'therapeutic commnunity' at Dingleton Hospital in Scotland

and Institutional Psychotherapy in France to begin the work of 'negating' it. Interviews with patients in *L'Istitutzione Negata* capture some of these experiences: Marghertia, Daisy and Carla (a holocaust survivor), tearing nets and padlocks from the beds that had imprisoned them, removing leather binds and straightjackets and entering the grounds untied for the first time, having previously been bound to trees and benches; Andrea, president of the daily assemblies, 'begging' people who were 'frightened after being closed for so many years', to 'open their mouths' and participate in this new democracy; Furio, editor of the new patient magazine *Il Picchio* (The Woodpecker), who had found daily life 'tortuous' after being interned for attempting suicide, joyfully joining others to pull down the asylum walls.

It was a complex, messy and at times violent process. Many staff, some fascist sympathisers, resisted the changes. Patients who had endured years of subjection and institutionalisation were afraid and still looked for permission or authorisation to act. There remained problems of paternalism. Pent up rage. Chronicity induced by years of internment and inhumane treatment. The stakes were high. In 1968, Milena Kristianic was killed by her husband after he was released into the community. While the state pursued criminal charges against Basaglia, patients, staff and volunteers in the asylum sought ways of making sense of what had taken place – considering their responsibility for these events and taking steps to relate to those patients who remained less engaged. A different sort of accounting for a terrible harm that those of us pursuing responses outside of carceral systems still grapple with today.

Influenced by various thinkers and political currents, including Gramsci, Sartre, Primo Levi, Surrealism, aspects of Maoism, autonomist Marxism, phenomenology and Robert Castel, Basaglia and the asylum's larger *équipe* of staff, sought to go beyond models of a therapeutic community that functioned like 'a micro-society', 'reduced to an internal perfectionism' and 'unable to effect outside'. It was not only the asylum that was being critiqued, but institutional treatments of human suffering that 'emptied' madness of

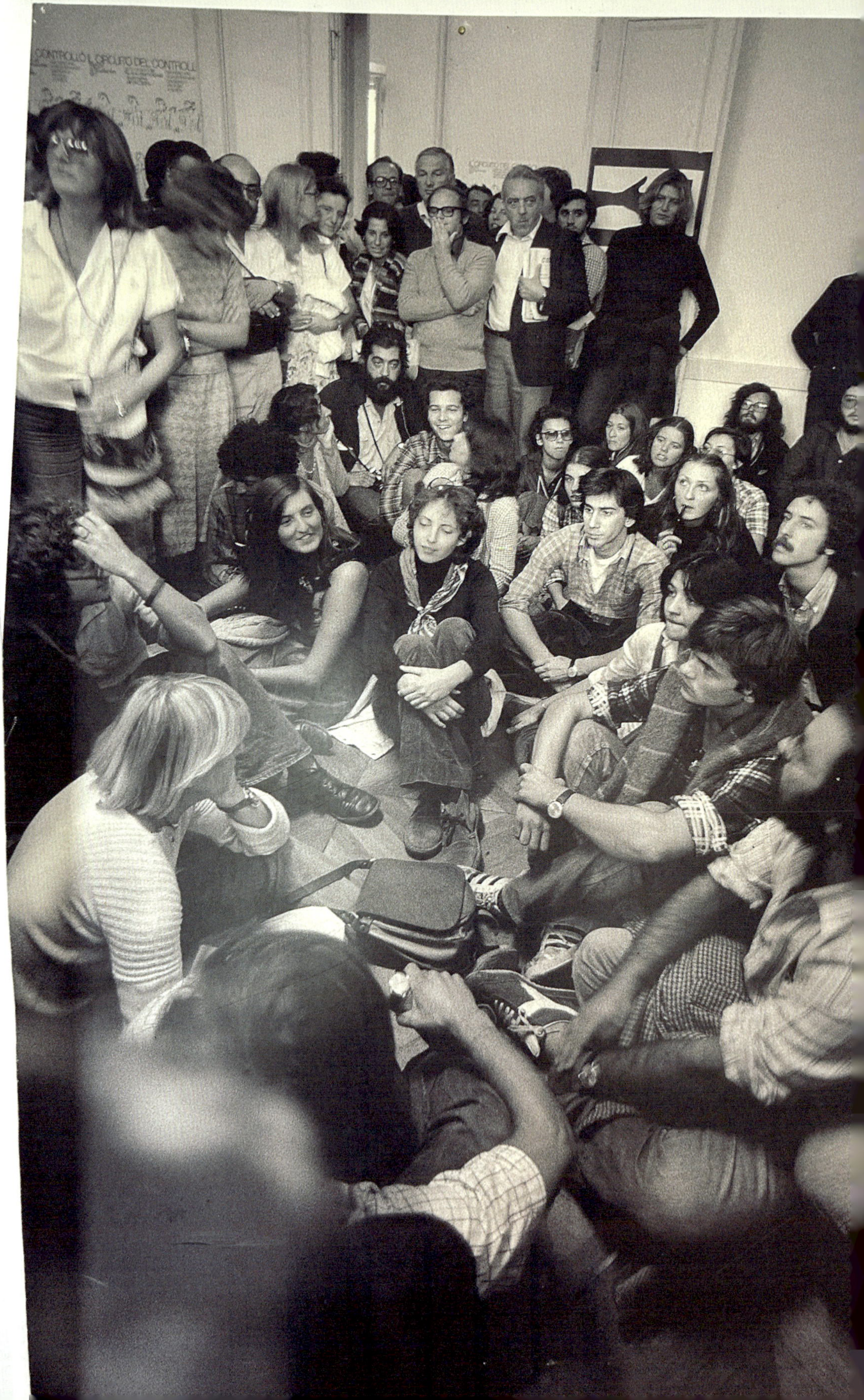

its social content; severing its relationship with 'a system of production that organises the masses ... reduced to so many bodies deprived of subjectivity.'

The struggle to understand and alleviate human suffering therefore could not be confined to a psychiatric practice conceived as a discrete branch of medicine requiring technical improvements. It had to be located within the political sphere. Not only because social conditions – poverty, housing or workplace stress, social isolation and oppression – drive mental distress but because survival inside a globally violent system involves forms of suffering that are so entangled with our social fabric that they can only truly become knowable, and perhaps transformed, as part of a struggle to overturn it.

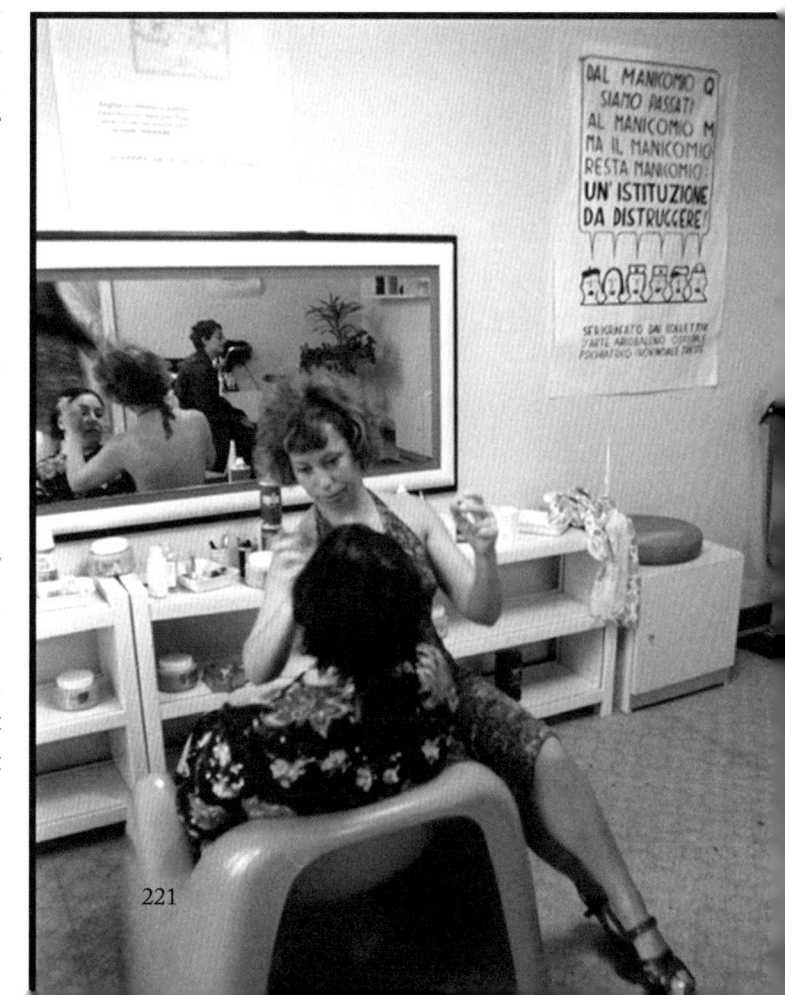

'New forms of research and new therapeutic structures' were required (Basaglia), existing hierarchies between 'technicians' and patients needed to be upended, and both needed to join the 'struggle for health in the factories, the workplaces, homes *and* the hospital' (Ongaro). This emphasis on patients' *political* agency with daily assemblies serving not simply as forums for democratising institutional life but as spaces for self-organisation and realisation, was of course part of a larger wave of protest sweeping Italy most visible in student-worker occupations and assemblies. Gorizia, the town, however, remained 'absent from the whole experience' and it was this that Basaglia set out to change in Trieste.

☭

## Peacetime Crimes

By the time Basaglia arrived in Trieste in 1971, he was part of a movement of challenge and experimentation across Italy and carried the support of the province's governing majority to act on conditions that were causing public scandal. During the Second World War it was one of many European cities to host concentration camps, and the only one in Italy with a crematorium. Thousands had been deported to death camps and up to 5000 Jews and political prisoners had been murdered on site. Lying on bordered lands, the people of Gorizia and Trieste had been traumatised by successive imperialist conflicts. Trieste's large refugee population, targeted by fascist organisation, also helped to make it a place where affinities between different communities could emerge.

Walking through the main grounds of San Giovanni Park past the hubbub of the café and social centre *Il poste dell fragole* and along the old living quarters – pavilions now bright yellow with bold red slogans painted on the walls such as 'Freedom is Therapeutic' – I stop at a steel sculpture. A winged figure emerges from a cage overlooking a long boulevard, part of the original layout of 'The Magnificent Psychiatric Hospital' opened in 1908, where guards in long black steely buttoned coats and peak caps used to stand watch. It's called 'The Dive'. To fly or fall?

Just below, the Mental Health Department (MHD) coordinates services for the regions of Trieste and Gorizia from a pavilion previously used to detain patients labelled *sudici* (dirty) or *paralitici* (with disabilities). Pantxo has a friend who was interned at St Giovanni and remembers the nurses calling it 'the pavilion of the *cagoni* – literally the 'shitters' – his friend was just seven when they threatened to send him there as punishment.

The department's location is intentional, harking back to the early days of San Giovanni's 'negation', when the most degrading blocks were closed or repurposed. A wall poster designed for the patient magazine *847* in 1974 indicates the closures of Block C and P (for the 'agitated' and 'semi-agitated') with a large X. Block P was later used as an art space called Laboratory P, while women in Block C were moved to supported flats in the administration block. This was part of a larger reorganisation of residents into five open communities grouped according to people's connection with the city – where they had lived or worked – rather than their perceived 'dangerousness'. The poster is one in a series of graphics displaying San Giovanni's transformation: from the 'total institution' in 1908, to 'the institution negated' in 1971, the 'institution invented' in 1979 and finally 'the city that heals' in 1996. Together they capture the central strategy pursued by Basaglia's team of embedding an 'ecology of care' into Trieste's urban space (described in detail by Pantxo in *Caring Ecologies*, 2019).

In *Peacetime Crimes*, written in 1974, Basaglia and Ongaro sought a 'higher level of clarity and struggle' to challenge 'the logic of capital' as it was imposed not only on healthcare but 'every institution' forced to function like 'a productive organism'. Instead of being geared towards the valorisation of labour, the organisation of health and society needed to start from the 'value of [human beings]' where 'health and normality cannot be the norm because the human condition is that of being healthy and ill together, normal and simultaneously abnormal'. It strikes me that this understanding of health as part of a broader strategy of collectivising social reproduction and its expansive view of class struggle shares an affinity with social reproduction theory. Given the spread of insurgent struggles into so many aspects of society encompassing workplaces and universities, the street, housing, health, abortion rights and a strong feminist movement, this is perhaps not surprising, but is in stark contrast to the relative marginalisation of mental health as a political issue on the UK left.

It was a huge undertaking and, fifty years on, San Giovanni Park still vibrates with the history of unmaking the old asylum while inventing new ways to care. Black and white photos throughout the buildings show the emergence of everyday life where torture and terror once resided: eating, chatting around a table, smiling, reading newspapers, making art, drinking tea, recording a radio programme, playing draughts, meeting, debating. Ugo Guarino's sculptures, assembled from bits of old asylum furniture thrown out and smashed up, occupy corners like hauntings from the past. There was 'nothing left, just the walls', the former head nurse Graziella Tiselli recalls in Erika Rossi's film *Trieste Racconta Basaglia*. One netted bed seems to have survived, now displayed on an outdoor balcony, and our hosts at the MHD, Claudia and Elisabetta, have to remind us that the spacious, sunny rooms we walk through once served as patient dormitories or living rooms where people would be caged in all day.

I squint and think of my uncle's descriptions of being locked in Broadmoor's dorms overnight, 'packed like sardines' in beds 'inches apart', no plumbed toilet, night terrors, threats. Or the women in the adjacent blocks to him, forced to piss and shit in buckets in the day rooms. 'It was not a lovely atmosphere', he says.

☭

## To obey is no longer a virtue

One of the slogans daubed on the pavilion walls above the wreckage of dismantled beds implores, 'Dear women, to obey is no longer a virtue'. In another photo, people crowd round in debate, one among thousands of assemblies and perpetual discussions which 'gave dignity to words', a nurse observes in *Trieste Racconta Basaglia*, where silence and compliance had ruled. These words would lead to the establishment of Italy's first social cooperative in December 1972, Cooperativa Lavoratori Uniti (CLU – United Workers Cooperative) after patients who had kept the asylum running in the kitchens and gardens, cleaning and shovelling coal for cigarettes and minor 'privileges', demanded wages and recognition as workers. Since the 1904 legislation excluded them from any citizen rights, these demands were initially refused until rising agitation and strike action forced an intervention by the provincial council which approved their demands by resolution. And so, the wretched made history.

In former Pavilion M, now host to *Lister Sartoria Sociale* (a tailoring cooperative), I come across a 1975 poster advertising an excursion over Trieste which saw 100+ patients fly over the Friuli Venezia Giulia area, their journey celebrated by the Association of Partigiani (veterans of the WWII resistance) who threw a party, celebrating with a live band and dancing to *Bella Ciao* in the Communist Party's association premises.

Just down the corridor I meet Diego Porporati, one of the resident artists who offers to draw my portrait, shapeshifting me into a horse with his pen – a homage, I realise, to Marco Cavallo, the life-size paper mâché horse made by patients in 1973 during two months of art making and storytelling. Named after the asylum's laundry horse (one of the few 'residents' able to leave the

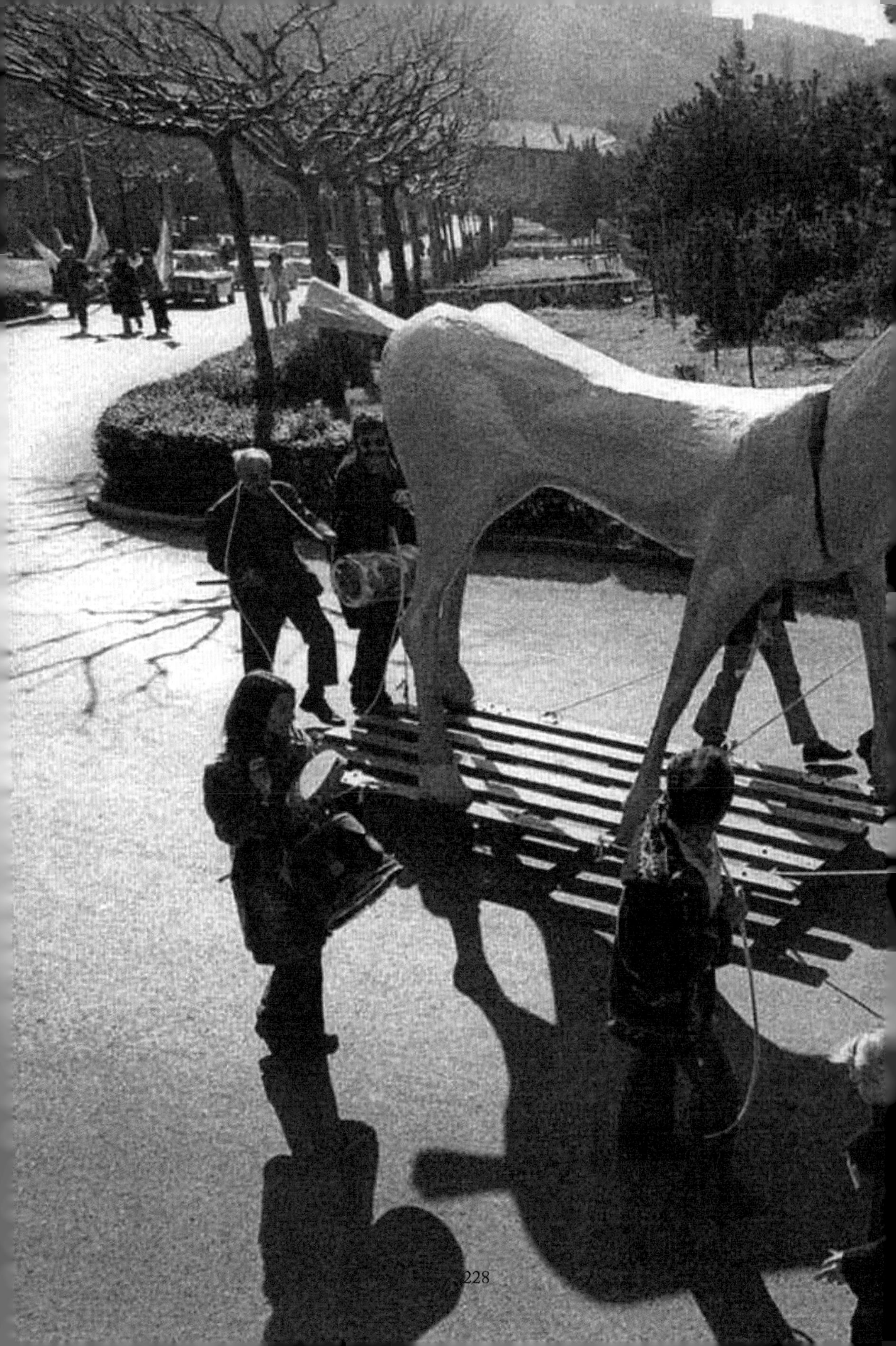

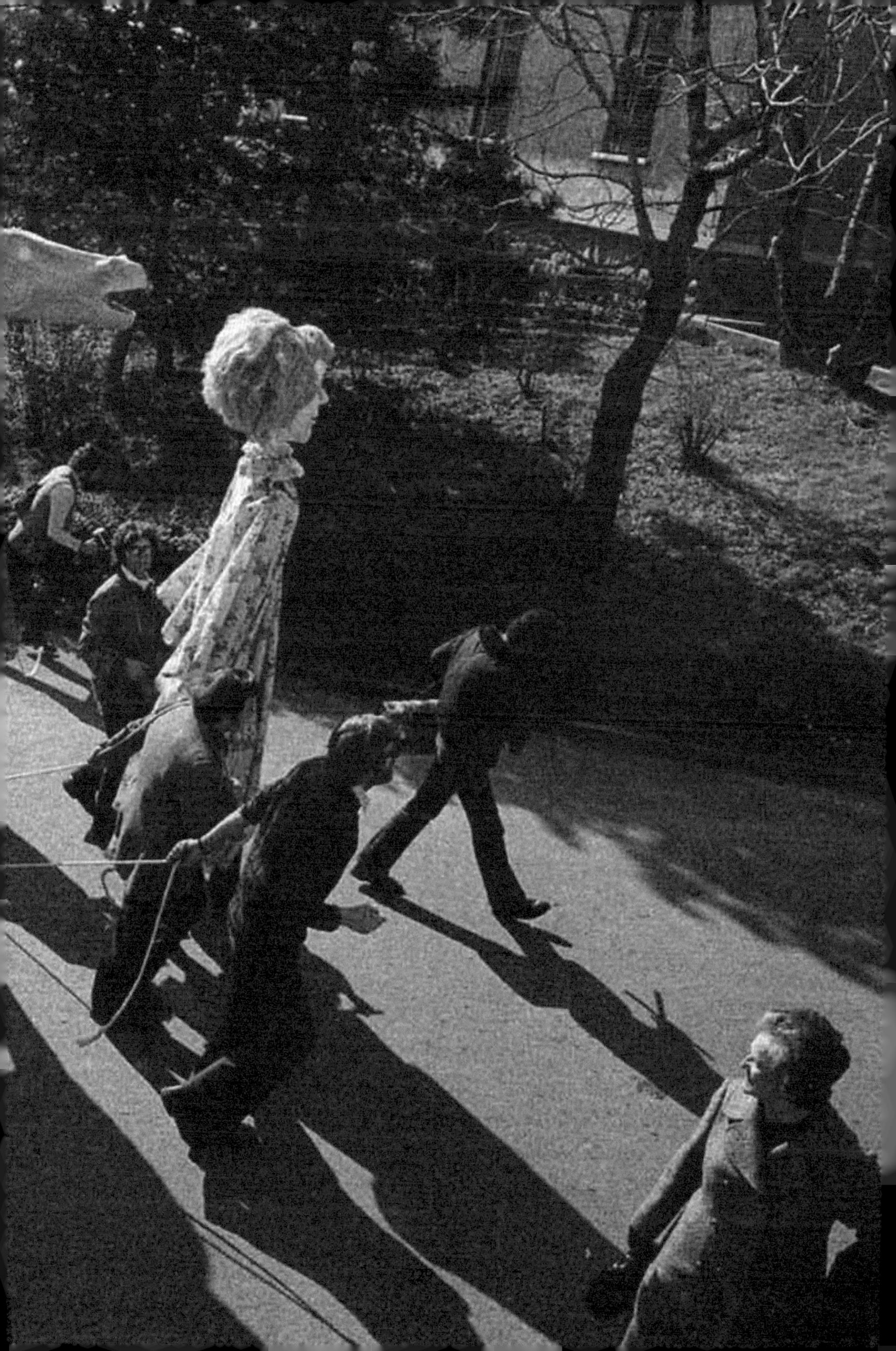

grounds until he was slaughtered) and painted a bright sky-blue, Cavallo turned fable when he was symbolically broken out of the asylum and marched into the city to join a local festival with several hundred patients, nurses, artists and volunteers in a joyous carnival of the mad.

In the context of a politically polarised debate about mental illness and 'dangerousness', spectacle and propaganda mattered. But these initiatives were also part of a 'medicine' that was concerned with attending to the multiplicity of people's needs and desires, energising collective yearnings as part of a radical project for social change and finding imaginative ways of bringing people together. In preparation for the flight, the air-craft crew worked one day for free visiting patients to discuss their curiosity and fears. Marching with Cavallo, striking nurses raised demands about workers' and patients' treatment and conditions.

Basaglia had said the system makes the patients and nurses sick, but this sort of unity was not a given. He formed an *équipe* at San Giovanni out of newly qualified medical students, doctors and volunteers – those who were less likely to be contaminated by prevailing medical cultures. (Block C had been closed with the help of volunteers – conscientious objectors – who chose to help at San Giovanni as their penalty for refusing military service). But change needed the nurses who, numbering 350+, were the majority. 'Many were glad to be no longer victimised', Giovanna Battaglia, a nurse interviewed by *Asylum* magazine, explains referencing the 'rigid hierarchy system', but were 'strongly opposed to being stripped of their own power'. There was also significant resistance from locals, stoked by different political and business interests, along with the media, which seized on a small number of serious and tragic cases. A former patient who killed his parents. A woman who after being denied hospitalisation killed her son. Another former patient who died of neglect in his family home.

Such deaths understandably provoke concerns about the capacity of a social movement to look out for vulnerable people. The proximity of mental suffering to deathly feelings and suicidality is pressure enough against taking risks. So I was moved to discover *Stories from the Asylum* in San Giovanni's documentation centre, edited by a member of Basaglia's *équipe*, Peppe Dell'Acqua, which evidences a remarkable attention to detail in the work undertaken to help individuals access liveable lives. These included Elda who had been diagnosed with 'schizophrenia' during the Second World War while assisting partisans in need of safe passage to fight the

Nazi occupation. Having been hospitalised for good in 1960, she was found in 1971 without teeth, like many patients subjected to ECT or beatings, sitting under tables, eating with her hands, and unable to take visits. By 1973 Elda was participating in art classes, enjoying spending her newly discovered war pension on clothes and personal effects, making sense of shifting geo-politics (is fascism over? is Russia capitalist?), and was ultimately offered a home by a woman living in the city. It was in removing the psychiatric screen from those interned, Dell'Acqua argued, that 'unsolved problems' were revealed, and it was in seeking to address them that solutions were sought in the city.

## An Ecology of Care

By 1975, 646 patients remained resident in San Giovanni, 403 of whom were 'guests' – no longer under a compulsory order or considered in need of treatment, but with nowhere to go. Between 1975-7, six mental health centres were established across different districts in Trieste, each evolving to serve as an access point for care, medication and therapeutic support, meals, community, social activities including cinema, art, a library, and short-term overnight accommodation. These centres would become a key node in an infrastructure of care concerned with cultivating collaborative relationships between doctors, nurses, 'patient' and 'citizen' and advocating an acceptance of illness and madness as part of life – 'up close no one is normal', Basaglia would say. An 'availability service' was established in the general hospital to act as an 'emergency aid station' for people in crisis, thus averting many from being sent to the asylum's admission ward which remained open until Law 180 took effect. With the final closure of the asylum, the aid station formed the basis of a Psychiatric Emergency Unit in the General Hospital (*Servizio Psichiatrico di Diagnosi e Cura SPDC*) that is operational today, just seven beds to replace 1300. These facilities connected mental health with the general health system, while social housing, cooperatives and a broader network of associations and local solidarities served as the tissue for this emergent ecology.

Affordable housing was scarce in the city. The search for solutions – individual residences, supported housing and group homes – led to an occupation in 1978 of Case del Marinaio (Sailors House) to secure a space 'for 200/300 patients who have not yet left San Giovanni but also a very large segment of the Trieste population'. The action agitated for the introduction of a social wage. This broader struggle to address people's need for a secure income was at the heart of Ongaro's 1980s campaign to achieve legal recognition of social cooperatives. Passed in 1991, Law 381 conferred benefits and funding to cooperatives employing 30+ per cent of workers with a 'disability'.

Today these enterprises employ around 500 people across Trieste, providing employment designed to be supportive and flexible around people's lives be they dealing with illness, addiction, a history of imprisonment, child-care responsibilities, or other forms of marginalisation. The cooperatives are critical to the city's mental health infrastructure and practice, Pantxo says, serving as the basis of a network of service users who, beyond nurses, psychologists and social workers, support the 'sociality of others'. I think of my first encounters at Gorizia MHC, of the workers tending flowers at an entrance once dominated by the old water tower, the receptionists who greet people when they first arrive looking for help, and others who visit people in supported housing, convene groups and social activities.

Pino Rosati, who helped establish *Lister* as a social cooperative in the wake of the 2010 economic crash, shows me how he uses the work of upcycling waste objects (especially umbrellas frequently destroyed by the strong winds known as 'the bora') to create bags, kites, rain capes and more, as a metaphor for the wider system. 'We give what we have taken. We look for equilibrium, we don't want to produce a surplus' he says softly between short breaths. 'Like a patchwork, we sew parts of society, young and old, working in the kindergartens and the prisons. This is not only about ecology but transformation'. Pino, who arrived at San Giovanni in 1983 conveys the precarious nature of the work. 'We have eight workers, but it isn't easy. We are hidden in the wood like a fairy tale. We are always in a struggle, a search, a battle. At night when the things we make are moved out of the corridor, the asylum comes back'.\*

## At night the asylum comes back

These problems speak to the systemic contradictions this project occupies. 'Fanon was able to choose revolution' Basaglia wrote, after his resignation from a hospital post in Algeria to join the anti-colonial resistance. 'Our situation is that we are forced to live through the contradictions of a system which creates us, managing an institution we deny/negate'. Pantxo defines this approach as a 'counter practice of welfare', 'acting through the hierarchies of institutional health care to disrupt the institutional logic' – neoliberal or social democratic, entrepreneurial or paternalistic. If the space for configuring care along these lines has narrowed, some practices have endured and even advanced. The MHD has resisted privatisation which has seen so much parasitic activity by companies; ensuring no private facilities are funded by public money with a quarter of their income preserved for service users' 'personal budgets', used to support individuals to access their needs directly.

Another initiative is the Habitat Microareas established in 2004 to encourage cooperation between health, housing, and social services (the ASUGI Healthcare District, Regional Housing Authority – ATER – and Trieste Welfare Services) in collaboration

---

\* Pino sadly died on July 14 2024, not long after we had left Trieste

with residents. There are now seventeen catchment areas covering around 19,000 inhabitants in total, 'like an octopus that reaches into the social fabric' Christiana, our guide, suggests, organised in a way to encourage the co-creation of care by empowering residents to make use of the state resources to meet their needs. She takes our group to the smallest project involving 190 residents where Antonella, the neighbourhood 'concierge' greets us. Antonella lives on the estate in accommodation provided by ATER and ASUGI, supported by a 'work bursary' as part of her health budget, and is paid to maintain the central hub, a one bed flat with a garden which functions as an open meeting point for workers and residents to meet, share meals, discuss care needs and plan activities. These include a programme for children (no doubt welcome to the high number of single parents), and a peer-support and consciousness-raising group for women.

Christiana shares an example of the co-production of care made possible, narrating the story of a local woman in her eighties whose son was hospitalised following a stroke, leaving her without support. An 'extended family conference' with staff, neighbours, friends, and family members was called to discuss solutions that would avoid her being placed in a home or leave her nearest relative carrying sole responsibility for care. A plan was developed, and a health budget organised to support her to remain living independently with the company and support of others. 'We are always criticised for being too social and not clinical enough' Claudia and Elisabetta say, but in their view 'needs are rights'.

The centring of rights is evident in the ongoing commitment to an 'open door', no restraint policy, which means that there are no locked doors across the service and a commitment to not using restraint on patients by medical staff, regardless of the circumstances. During our visit to Gorizia's MHC, I notice a reproduction of an Ugo Guarino cartoon in the office depicting footprints charting people's flight from a cage. What, I ask Marco, would he say to those in the UK, who insist on the need for these physical measures, at least in 'emergency situations'. 'You talk', he says. 'You negotiate, you stay with the person, you go with them. If they go to the mountain you go, if they go to the sea, if they go to the bar, to their home, you go'. 'You can do it one way' (he imitates a perfunctory conversation): 'How are you? Good? And the medicine? Good ok then.' 'But', he continues, 'that way you won't get to build a relationship.' To do that you have to go beyond the small talk and be prepared to 'emotionally expose yourself'.

I realise there are limits to this. Before visiting Trieste, I had workshopped the questions I would bring with my uncle. Having found our quite different encounters with the UK mental health system frightening and disturbing, we both know that it is not for me to judge people's experiences from the outside. There are however some markers. Can people in Italy refuse medication in all circumstances? Can they be sectioned? The answer to the latter is yes. Compulsory orders can be made. They are limited to seven days and must be authorised, with the support of two doctors, by the city mayor rather than a judge. This places the decision at least nominally within a sphere of public accountability. Since these restrictions were introduced, compulsory admissions in Italy have more than halved, from 20,000 in 1978 to less than 9,000. This is in stark contrast to the UK, which since the late 1980s has seen what *Modernising the MHA 2018* describes as an 'inexorable rise in detentions', with the Care Quality Commission identifying 'too many abusive and closed cultures' in mental health' in its 2022-3 annual report. I've experienced just how far the threat of a section can poison your capacity to access help when it is desperately needed, even if it is far more likely you will be ignored, put on a waiting list, given an IAPT referral, maybe CBT, or a drug prescription. Unless, that is, you are racialised or suffer from a form of distress that bears the brunt of societal discrimination. Trieste's service users also talk about avoiding compulsory orders only by agreeing to take medication. Practitioners may seek to negotiate with the state, but neither they nor those deemed sanctionable can escape its disciplinary functions.

This is most apparent where mental health intersects with the police and criminal justice system. When Law 180 ordered the closure of asylums, it did not include Ospedali Psichatrici Giudiziari's (OPGs) used to detain people convicted of criminal offences and deemed to be mentally ill. This is just one example of how an intact state remains empowered to redraw the line between those considered deserving of freedom and those not. After a sustained campaign and facing international condemnation, Law 81 (2014) finally mandated Italy's regions to replace OPGs with Residential facilities for Security Measures (REMS) to provide care to people judged to be dangerous and in need of psychiatric treatment. It is stipulated that these must be used as a last resort, located in the same region where the person lives, based on a mandatory personal care plan in forty-five days, with no restraint, and for no longer than the maximum penalty for that crime. Having seen my uncle serve thirty years in the UK for an offence bearing a maximum criminal penalty of five, I know how significant these measures are.

The numbers held in these institutions is around 600 across Italy, 40 per cent less than those detained in OPGs at the time of closure, with just two 'guests' detained at Trieste's facility (six across the Friuli-Venezia Giulia region). When we arrive at the facility I notice that the external wall is not sealed, we hear about the ways in which a routine is first established with new arrivals through negotiation and request, walk around the surrounding gardens where activities are opened up to the local community, and view several spare rooms used to accommodate the family and friends of those detained when they visit. These are all progressive measures.

However it is impossible not to feel the tension between an ethics centred on 'freedom', which emphasises the protagonism of people experiencing mental distress, and the limits imposed on residents' mobility, as well as their use of space and time, even if indirectly. Staff may only be able to advise residents not to breach the boundaries of the facility, but if they do so the police will arrest them. As Alessandro N, who coordinates the team in this service, is keen to point out (referencing Basaglia), 'The sentence of the asylum implied and implies the rewriting of psychiatric knowledge ... In the same way the condemnation and the overcoming of the OPG, must lead to the rewriting of the judicial knowledge, because in this case the judiciary was and still is, the strong technical power'.

Unfortunately, that rewriting has not taken place. And this lack of change has occurred in parallel with a 42 per cent increase in Italy's prison population between 1991 and 2022, with almost a third now classed as 'foreign residents' despite composing just 8 per cent of wider society. There are also people stuck in prison unable to get into a REMS.

## The cypher of what is possible

On the final day of our visit, we gather with Trieste's service users and staff for an object exchange. Different generations and experiences fill the room as we place our chosen artefacts on red cloth laid out in the middle of the room. Guillermo has brought a tiny machinic device, a gift from Diego who used to make these constructions in the outdoors 'to cure sickness in society' until their increasing scale led to police visits. He is 'a technician of the imagination' Guillermo says, 'and helped me into radio'. Carlotta has brought a toilet roll which 'saved her' during a hard time in hospital, when one day feeling its rough texture she was inspired to start making art out of it.

I have brought my uncle's words, his experiences at Broadmoor typed out in Italian and accompanied by photographs of a seclusion cell, a corridor, a day room and the admission block. Broadmoor, I tell them, was one of the inspirations for Italy's early asylums and shares similarities with San Giovanni in the bad old days. They read the words. Guillermo is visibly shocked and wonders aloud about the different fates of patients between the two institutions. I tell him I've been thinking the same. What if my uncle had been in San Giovanni instead of Broadmoor in 1972? What if Basaglia had turned up in Reading instead of Trieste? I don't share my fabulation, featuring Marco Cavallo's festival of the mad arriving at Broadmoor's gates, dancing with trumpets as I stand trembling, diminished and alone, waiting for the long walk of locks and keys. Still, the recognition of different histories of pain between us is like a balm.

Before I leave Trieste, I take one more walk around the rose garden. I can't put my finger on the feelings – wanting to weep and laugh at the same time. I think of Gargi Bhattacharyya's *We the Heartbroken*: 'There can be no remaking of the world without ways to allow for our collective sorrow'. Tentatively I allow my sadness to swell as the sweet smells of Italy's warm summer air lift me.

Black and white photos by Emilio Tremolada apart from p.228–9 by Claudio-Ernè and p.227 by Tiziano Neppi. All other photos by Han Dee. Interviews conducted with Rachel Wilson.

Thanks to Pantxo Ramas for introducing me and our team to Trieste's history and services, and to all the wonderful people involved in the work who hosted, greeted and gave their time.

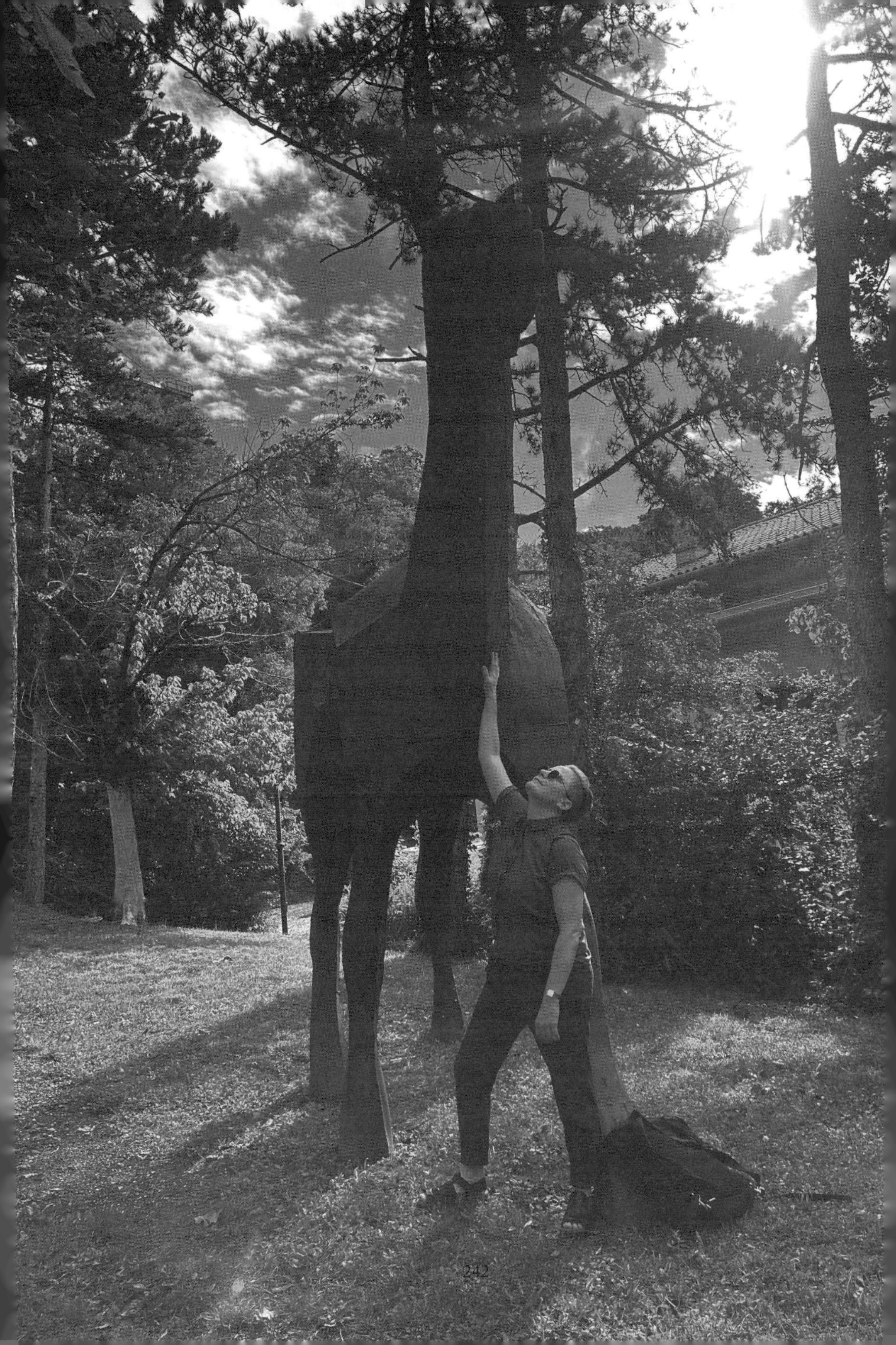

# LA FESTA DI MARCO CAVALLO

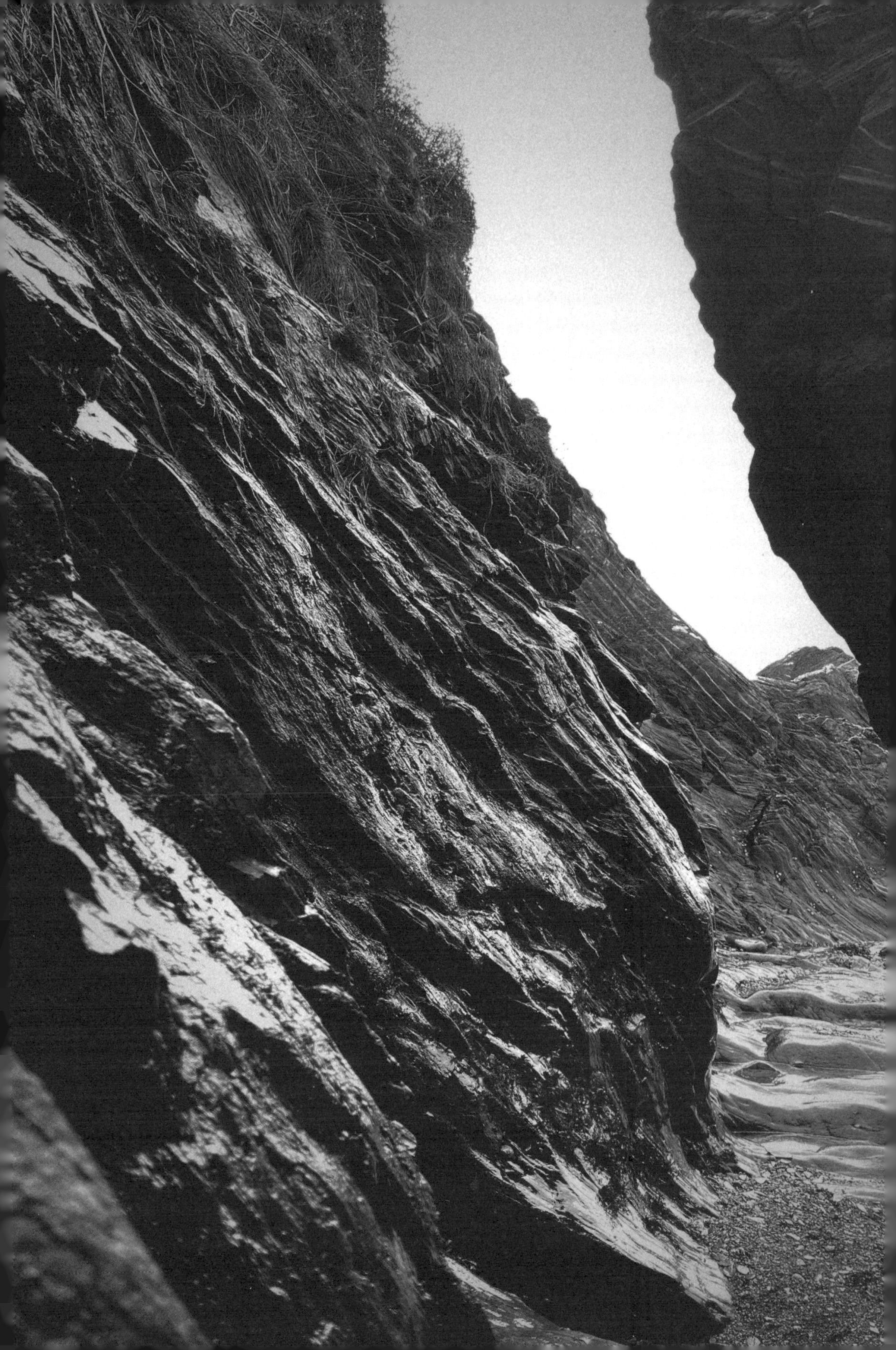

JONAS MARVIN

# The Medical Law of Accumulation: Putting the Sick on the Line

Turning down Dividy Road and onto the Bentilee housing estate in a rural corner of Stoke-on-Trent, I am struck by two images. First, an unavoidable eyesore – a house adorned with a Trump 2024 flag – is followed by three houses each receiving visits from three individual health professionals. Then, amid a sea of semi-detached 'sunhouses' sits the Bentilee District Centre Project: its health centre gushing with people walking in and out. Once the largest council estate in Europe, Bentilee provides us a snapshot of class decomposition in Britain's rustbelt regions.

This place was once home to miners, unionised workers and nodes of the labour movement. Ruth Wilson Gilmore has long insisted that our times are captured by a term from Peter Drucker's 1990s management manuals, 'organised abandonment,' where companies profit like Gordon Gekko did in *Wall Street*, by consciously destroying lifeworlds. Britain's rustbelt has faced a kind of disorganised abandonment. In the absence of social democratic state planning and with the breakdown of the neoliberal social contract, the dominance of global financial and rentier capital over the operations of British capitalism has debilitated the nation state's capacity to reproduce conditions for accumulation, leaving vast swathes of the urban and bodily space of the contemporary proletarian to rot. Bentilee is the poorest place in Stoke: workers earn £10,000 less every year than those in Stoke's richest areas. Unlike other parts of the city, Bentilee is not dominated by private home ownership. Bentilee's history and spatial makeup are unique in many respects, but in two key ways it is indicative of a developing picture of Britain. The bulk of its working residents are employed in care, health, and 'elementary occupations' and they suffer a lower life expectancy and poorer health than their counterparts across the city. The work of caring for sick and broken bodies becomes more and more dominant – as Gabriel Winant's *The Next Shift* has recently tracked in the American case – while those doing the work are often the same people whose sickness and exhaustion feeds the growing industry. A person's place in the nation's hierarchy of class power can be read increasingly through the lens of health outcomes, which tell a story about where you live and what job you do.

Marxists might imagine this is nothing new, and nothing remarkable; since at least Engels's Condition of the Working Class in England we have been familiar with furious protest at the ways that capital accumulation attacks our health. But some updating is in order too. In *Capital*, Marx seems to treat the sick as a fixed category. It is a surprising step. Chapter twenty-five, Marx's famous 'General Law of Capital Accumulation', narrates a cycle of attracting and repelling workers to and from the labour market amid fluctuations in capital's needs, which produces inequalities and stratifications among proletarians through the constitution of an industrial reserve army of unemployed workers. That cycle influences how much workers earn; how much power they have; their life prospects. The different moments of the cycle shape how dependent a worker is on an employer, but also the relationship of states to workers and workers to other workers – generating divisions, forms of sectionalism and cultures of recrimination between workers who find themselves competing against one another. Marx relates the cycle to the state of the population-at-large. Refusing the Malthusian 'law of population', Marx thus related the health, wealth and general conditions of life of the population less to eternal and biophysical laws than to cycles of capital accumulation. These cycles exercise some determination over what Beatrice Adler-Bolton and Artie Vierkant describe as the 'worker/surplus binary', the social categorisation of who is and is not 'deserving' of dignity and life. But Marx deposited the sick as the 'dead weight of the industrial reserve army': one impotent cohort in a sea of pauperism.

That view seems today to jar with his insistence that we treat the character of populations as transient and subject to the laws of capital accumulation. Sometimes, capital's impositions on populations have circular effects on accumulation. The sick and ill appear today as a substantively large fraction of the population, which ruling classes are desperate to force back into the labour market. The ills of austerity, labour degradation, neoliberalism's psychic wounds and the spread of social pathologies have come back to haunt capital, and so it now calls for solutions through the regulation of our health. In Britain today, it is possible to diagnose a new capitalist biopolitics, a central feature of Keir Starmer's project in governmentality. Intensifying rhythms of capitalist exploitation and domination have not only weakened proletarian power and the ability to organise; they have also inhibited accumulation by pushing workers into the reserve army when capital needs them at work. That coexistence of weakened workers and anxious employers has been a long time in the making. Part of the wider productivity puzzle, and playing a role too in panics about low-wage migration, the nightmare of the sick proletarian looms larger after Covid-19. Tracing the emergence of that angst is one way of telling the story of Britain's changing regimes of accumulation since 1945, casting fresh light on the structures of feeling we face now and their political possibilities. The wider question posed here is the one long raised by culturally inflected Marxisms: what kinds of people are the working class really, and how do they get made and unmade as political subjects?

## Disassembling the Proletariat

A world ago, postwar social democracy bred several distinctive class subjects with frighteningly radical potential. The white male Fordist car worker gradually became one of the most rebellious forces of the postwar settlement and challenged wage suppression, speed-ups and employer autocracy. The South Yorkshire miner revived age-old traditions of industrial militancy and fought against the repeated and growing effort to crush proletarian lifeworlds constructed around the mines. The part-time female clothesmaker challenged her subordination as the domestic servant in the male breadwinner single-earner family model just as she also increasingly turned to uprooting forms of industrialised housework on the factory floor. The black foundry worker struggled against racist employers and exclusionary trade union bureaucracies in equal measure, while questioning conditions of segregation, wage inequality and growing obsolescence.

This assemblage of class agents was not simply invested in fighting for better conditions or higher wages. These workers fought for greater control over the shopfloor. They brought down governments, defended old proletarian lifeworlds from ruin and struggled for the right to be free as women, as black people and as human beings. Their confidence was overdetermined by numerous conditions of possibility coalescing in the mid-century. One line of domestic economic determination in that story was captured by Michał Kalecki's 1943 warning about the 'political aspects of full employment'. With the threat of the sack lacking its usual impact in the absence of mass dole queues, workers exercised a degree of power unseen outside periods of revolutionary instability.

By implication, the social democratic state administered a tense balancing act. Its ability to guarantee capitalist profitability, control worker populations and ensure the employers' right to manage was constantly challenged and jeopardised by the class subjects it bred. Exploiting this crisis in social democratic governance, Thatcherism developed a conservative critique of redistribution, trade union power and the uneven cultural awakenings of the postwar years: all in the service of disassembling these radicalising subjects. The project did not present itself to voters fully formed. The 1979 Conservative manifesto committed to revitalising Britain's industrial economy, but that was superseded by an overarching and longer-term ambition to combat inflation and disempower proletarians. Thatcher offered early pay rises to the steelworkers, but her regime then largely refused the social democratic temptation to buy out manufacturing capital and grant wage increases. Her alternative was to build a political, economic and legal architecture capable of existentially curtailing and disheveling working class organisation and power.

When unemployment hit one million in the early 1970s, that number was seen as a fundamental challenge to Edward Heath's struggling Conservative government. Less than a decade later, and against intense opposition, Thatcher was able to present three million unemployed people as a necessary evil to control the intimately connected ills of inflation and worker power. Her monetarism was the straw that broke the camel's back for the world of the white male Fordist factory worker, long under pressure from the growth of services, the decline of industry and the insurgent claims of women to bodily and social autonomy.

Shortly after Thatcher's landslide re-election in 1983, Beatrix Campbell trod Orwell's steps again to publish *Wigan Pier Revisited*. She recounted the thoughts of a male trade unionist on what he called, 'front door socialism.' His life, he said, was 'politics first, family second.' His politics of militant confrontation with power began when he 'shut the front door' and ended when he 'came home', relying upon his wife as an 'emotional sponge' throughout. The combination of manufacturing overcapacity, energy transition and class warfare spawned mass unemployment and deindustrialisation as many older manual workers became long-term social security claimants, especially in those regions hit most heavily by the decline of coal and manufacturing. Additionally, the long-term consequences of industrial injury resulted in the number of people on invalidity and sickness benefit doubling between 1980 and 1993 to two million people. The world of 'front door socialism' had been overturned, in the words of Linda McDowell, by 'redundant masculinities'.

The introduction of means-tested benefits was crucial to the decline of these class agents. They became a staple of Thatcherite statecraft, supplementing monetarism and anti-trade union legal reform in the quest to reduce workers' bargaining power. Jim Tomlinson's contribution in *A Neoliberal Age?* rightly stresses how, as Chancellor of the Exchequer, Nigel Lawson concentrated on 'the rediscovery of the enterprise culture' through the removal of any 'rigidities and distortions' in the labour market. Lawson was especially eager to reproduce American patterns by growing part-time and casual jobs in an expanding service-sector. In practice, that meant in-work benefits were a critical component of Thatcherism's attempt to transform the workforce, topping up the pay of low-wage workers in a state subsidy to employers. The spread of low-paying jobs in education, health, social care and services was accompanied by a substantive rise in state spending on welfare.

In short: while Thatcher reformed the welfare state and the social wage to contravene proletarian power, she massively increased expenditure on welfare to cope both with rising unemployment and with deliberately aided changes in the structure of employment. Thatcher's government did not simply witness Joshua Clover's 'affirmation trap' – where, to survive, proletarians must abandon the questioning of their position as workers and affirm their place as labourers dependent on a boss. She sprung the trap too. The comfortable left adage about the enduring destructive power of that moment, reproduced in David Edgerton's story of Thatcherism as a 'rulers' revolt' can sometimes overstate the agency of the Tory Right in a global transformation, but it has its kernel of truth. In the policing of growing surplus populations through workfare and means-tested benefits, our contemporary moment is inseparable from Thatcher's mission to drastically weaken proletarian power. The spread of moral panics over 'mugging' amid black deindustrialisation, so aptly recorded by Stuart Hall and his co-authors in *Policing the Crisis*, marked an attempt to articulate racialised readings of the crisis of postwar social democracy. Thatcher attentively reproduced many a theme from the pioneering monetarist and racist Enoch Powell, racialising the experience of inner-city industrial decline as a problem of disobedient foreign cultures. The Iron Lady would be proud of how these stories continue to be taken up by her heirs.

## Thatcher's Heirs

When New Labour took office in 1997, they inherited an official unemployment rate of 6.8 per cent, or just under two million. According to a comprehensive study by Christina Beatty, Stephen Fothergill, Tony Gore and Alison Herrington, real unemployment – measured to factor in the excess early retired, the excess permanently sick and those on government schemes – was almost four million. Facing that challenge, Tony Blair argued that reducing the dole queue would 'be easier' if the labour market was 'working properly'. What was needed, in the view of New Labour ideologues, was the creation of a 'low-wage sector' predicated on low-skill jobs readily accessible to those on welfare.

Although New Labour stalled the spiralling immiseration commenced by Thatcher's war on workers, their minimum wage regulations and introduction of tax credits did not reverse the trend. Instead, their commitment to subsiding low-wage employment through tax credits, workfare, obligatory training programmes, and their New Deal for Young People were all central aspects of a policy programme that sought to provide a steady supply of precarious, low-paid workers to the service sector. According to Bernhard Rieger, New Labour's rejigging of the welfare system involved a move towards a welfare state best characterised as a 'new Speenhamland' system. The original Speenhamland system, the backdrop to Karl Polanyi's *Great Transformation*, saw the payment of wages below survival levels subsidised through the Poor Laws rate system. If that sounds like a very non-neoliberal moral economy, it was in fact recreated under neoliberalism in an effort to subsidise employers, weaken worker power and stymie the problem of poverty.

Accompanying this new welfare system, a ramped up moral panic targeted 'benefit scroungers' while Blair railed against a 'sick note culture'. As Secretary of State for Work and Pensions, Alastair Darling condemned a 'something for nothing culture'. New Labour increased spending on welfare for deeply classed, non-redistributive purposes with one hand, and held up a megaphone decrying benefit claimants with the other. Blair's party introduced Anti-Social Behaviour Orders to police unemployed urban youth and attacked single mothers through a lens indebted to the war on 'welfare queens' prosecuted by the American ruling class, stressing the need for young single mothers to restrain themselves from having more children. Helen Charman's *Mother State* captures the reactionary mood at the time, wherein single mothers 'were accused of ... producing a child to extract support from the surrogate paternal state.' In this reading, a campaign of demonisation, orchestrated on both benches of the Commons, took Britain's relatively high teenage pregnancy rate and mobilised it against a section of the population deemed a sponge on welfare and a hurdle to cultivating a slick labour market. Blair's emphasis on 'strong families' as units of production, the New Deal for Lone Parents and sex education in schools were all staples in the cultivation of a reactionary environment geared towards the proliferation of amenable, obedient forms of particularly feminised wage labour.

This traditionalist assault culminated in a young employed mother on in-work benefits, Shanene Thorpe, being invited onto *BBC Newsnight* in 2012. She was monstered by Allegra Stratton, with questions including, 'Don't you think you should still be at home with your mum?', 'Do you want any more children?' and worst of all, 'Do you think you should have had your daughter?' Stratton later worked as Director of Strategic Communications for the Treasury under Rishi Sunak, and would go on to appear as the laughing face of Boris Johnson's partygate: proving herself a libertine when it comes to the powerful skirting social duties to protect the health of others.

By the time of Thorpe's public humiliation, the assault on welfare claimants had reached its peak under the Conservative-Liberal Democrat coalition. David Cameron's government combined austerity for public services with further anti-trade union legislation, the rise of zero-hours contracts and the merging of different benefits into Universal Credit in a digitised, reduced monthly form geared more heavily towards incentivising the unemployed into shit, precarious work. The government placed further conditions on all benefits, most notably through changes to disability benefits and the so-called bedroom tax. According to the Labour Force Survey, the number of people on employment contracts with no weekly minimum hours increased from less than 200,000 in 2010 to over 900,000 in 2017. The inauguration of a grossly authoritarian benefits system alongside the growth of bogus self-employment expanded Marx's 'stagnant' surplus population – that cohort of proletarians subject to a permanent state of temporary employment – while weakening the power of workers above them in the labour market hierarchy.

Despite the punitive, austerian environment created by Cameron's Tories, the paradoxical situation of increased welfare spending and deepening public resentment towards welfare claimants grew throughout the course of the early 2010s. Spending on welfare has dramatically increased since 1979, and 7 per cent of this rise took place in the short years of that cost-cutting Conservative-led administration. Today, around half of the Department for Work and Pensions (DWP) budget is spent on pensioners, signalling the state's faltering and sticking plaster response to ageing, while 11 per cent is spent on disability benefits. Contrary to the image crafted by politicians and ideologues, when welfare spending is not being invested to cope with substantive demographic changes in the population, it is being mobilised to supplement capitalist power.

### 'Don't medicalise these issues...'

This relationship between capital accumulation and demographic transition moulds the priorities of Keir Starmer's Labour Party. Committed to keeping capital's pockets full, dogmatically in hoc to the enduring 'Treasury view' that has preached fiscal restraint for at least a century, but absolutely obsessed with ramping up economic growth, Labour's front bench have become invested in the bodily capacities of British workers. In a state of affairs that preceded the Covid-19 pandemic but was exacerbated by it, the economically inactive outnumber the officially unemployed by six to one. 3.7 million workers have declared they have work-limiting health conditions. People aged sixteen to thirty-four years old are now as likely to report a work-limiting health condition as someone aged forty-five to fifty-four in the data ten years ago. Much of this increase is a product of mental ill-health. Even more profoundly, demographic ageing has contributed to 63 per cent of the actual rise in economic inactivity between 2019 and 2021. Of the 3.5 million fifty-to-sixty-nine-year-olds inactive in 2022, 45 per cent reported ill health as the main cause of their inactivity. 900,000 sixteen-to-twenty-four-year-olds are currently neither in work, education or training. The annual welfare budget currently sits at £266.1 billion, with the Institute for Fiscal Studies reporting that spending on disability and incapacity benefits for working-age individuals is likely to increase by a further 15.4 billion by 2028-29.

These figures are lit up in the Pathways to Work Commission Report published by Barnsley Council, praised and launched in Barnsley in July 2024 by Liz Kendall, the new Secretary of State at the DWP under Starmer. The choice of location is no coincidence. Britain's northern and rustbelt towns have been described with a slew of anxious monikers over the last two decades, from 'chavs' to 'left-behind' to the vaunted 'red wall'. Today these deindustrialised areas provide the nucleus for worries about a workforce that is calling in sick rather than turning up to work. This is only the latest rendition of hand-wringing about the effects of two *longue durée* processes: Britain's relative decline within world capitalism; and the move from a Fordist Keynesian geography to neoliberal uneven development. Together, these two shifts have moved places like Barnsley from an important global manufacturing town of the industrial revolution to a national periphery amid financialised growth emanating from the City of London. Worries about sick proletarians communicate that longstanding angst. The angst is national, even transnational amid the fading of American unipolarity – that is, this discourse speaks to a panic about *decay*, after a decade of stagnant living standards amid higher GDP growth rates outside the global North – and it is especially concentrated in places like Barnsley. Compellingly this discourse connects longstanding language around 'the economy' as a dying patient ('the sick man of Europe' in sloppy diagnoses of Britain's 1970s woes) to an image of its workers as sickly, feeble and fading: and in need of a big stick. The first key trick of the discourse is to imagine that the problem is rooted in individuals' failings.

In light of this, the DWP has committed to making annual cuts to sickness benefit worth £1.3 billion while retaining the Conservatives' Work Capability Assessment, which narrows eligibility for incapacity benefits and subjects 450,000 people to benefit cuts. Keir Starmer recently confirmed to rightwing rag, *The Sun*, that he did indeed have 'the balls' to cut disability benefits even further, signalling that the regime's austerian impulse is not afraid to draw upon Thatcherite framings of a 'culture of dependency' in order to punish the poor and disabled. DWP chief Liz Kendall and special advisor Alan Milburn have set upon a plan to confront the problem of long-term sickness amongst the working population. Milburn has been adamant that the long-term sick should be forced to search for work. In an interview on *The Rest Is Money* podcast, Milburn asked that we 'don't medicalise these issues ... there's a risk that it becomes an excuse culture ... You don't need a psychiatrist, maybe a talking therapy or group therapy will help'. Concretising this logic, Kendall has declared that job coaches will visit 'seriously ill' patients on mental health wards in an effort to force them back to work, with employment advisors deployed to hospital wards to give CV and interview advice. Labour has announced free health checks in workplaces (fittingly named after the Ministry of

Transport's obligatory vehicle inspections), toyed with the idea of banning high-caffeine energy drinks and disposable vapes, prohibited vape and junk food advertising to under-sixteens, and given councils powers to block new fast food outlets near schools. Health Secretary Wes Streeting has also declared that unemployed people will be given weight-loss jabs to get them back into work, claiming that 'widening waistbands are a burden on Britain'. Streeting has attracted a £280 million investment from Lilly, the world's largest pharmaceutical company, to develop new treatments to confront obesity and worklessness. A new Labour Market Advisory Board, launched by the government in September 2024, has the sole task of addressing 'the greatest employment challenge for a generation' – long-term sickness – to boost employment as the government prepares their 'Get Britain Working' White Paper to involve Kendall and Streeting. The joint participation of those two departments is meant to send a message; the goal is a healthier population *because the goal is a more hardworking population.*

All this is to identify a capitalist biopolitics. The ruling class is clearly concerned that capital accumulation is encountering limits that need to be removed, and those limits are constituted in our fungible bodies and brains. Across large parts of the world, ageing, sicker and shrinking populations are becoming the norm, constraining productivity and inhibiting economic growth. In this context, the principles of maximum economy come to the fore, creating room for greater coercion on the part of states and more disciplinarian attitudes to the growth of sick proletarians who produce tighter labour markets, the potential for increased bargaining power by those in work and higher welfare bills. This renewed attention to the proletarian body, reorganising the line between the worker and the surplus population, signals a new course of capitalist governmentality, viewing the physical state of workers as key to reviving British capitalism's fortunes.

## Repair and revolution

There are opportunities in the ether. Starmer's purge of Corbynism appeared in Opposition as an attempt to crush radicalism in the Labour Party. In office, it is also a project to undermine the policy radicalism that Corbynism was able to mobilise. According to the British Social Attitudes Survey, positive views of welfare have increased over the last ten years, with rising support for welfare spending and growing dissent from images of the undeserving poor. Similarly, the proportion of people who thought falsely claiming benefits was never justified fell from 85 per cent in 2011 to 67 per cent in 2023. With 38 per cent of Universal Credit claimants in low-paying work, it is no wonder that, according to the Office for National Statistics, street theft has risen by 40 per cent and shoplifting increased by 30 per cent over the last year. EP Thompson's notion of a 'moral economy' – which he used to describe the clash between trade liberalisation, price rises, and a consequent explosion of popular revulsion, food riots and theft in the eighteenth century – is today reappearing not in the softened form of a social contract managed by the state, but once again in its insurgent original shape from below. And we are shifting somewhat away from the cultural resentments of peak neoliberalism. There are grounds, which Starmerism underestimates and undermines, for generalising a politics of health quite different from capitalist biopolitics. Its twin lynchpins, in opposition to the twin terms of Starmer's governmentality, would be to take sickness as real and socially caused, requiring care rather than punishment, and secondly to see sickness as a problem for our flourishing rather than for our usefulness to capital.

At the mere age of thirty-two, my body, marked by the intrusions of class power, is painfully catching up with me. Many of us suffer from forms of 'ordinary unhappiness'. Some of us suffer much worse. On my own estate, just an hour's walk away from Bentilee, you can see the melting pot of shit, precaritised jobs; appalling housing conditions; the ghosts of neoliberalism's wars in the form of drug addiction; and stark images of disorganised abandonment caught in the bonfires lit at night to warm the homeless and poor.

The past two decades of social struggle in Britain have often been concerned with defending what remains of the National Health Service and the broader welfare state. The politics of managed decline, privatisation and welfare authoritarianism have become sites of reactive campaigning which have sought to return the nation's health and social safety net to a long-abandoned past. Yet, if we are to escape this defensive and losing cycle, we must begin to put some flesh on the bones of what Artie Vierkant and Beatrice Adler-Bolton captivatingly term *Health Communism*.

In 1988, reckoning with the labour movement's isolation, Stuart Hall insisted that the Left learn from its enemies. Cognisant of a new realm of social identities and cultures forged throughout Thatcherite post-Fordism, Hall suggested that the labour movement should trade its 'negative' politics of 'contestation' over policy detail for an overarching account of the good society, fitted to contemporary structures of feeling, which could then more confidently ground a more radical set of policy demands. Thatcher framed the future of the NHS through enterprising principles and the 'politics of choice.' Hall argued that the Left should take up that fight and articulate its own vision of health, 'dramatising the NHS crisis in concepts Thatcherism has not managed to appropriate: democratisation, rights and the expansion of social citizenship'. Today, we must rise to this task and refuse the consolation that the coalitions of the past will suffice. The future of communist politics demands that we articulate a vision of health and welfare futurity constructed through a diverse array of social agents – nurses, GPs, the physically sick, the mentally ill, welfare claimants and taxpayers – who can actually see their needs and hopes communicated in the construction of a majoritarian vision.

This view of communist freedom should combine Frantz Fanon's psychoanalytic and political case (as David Marriott has put it) for 'repair within revolution' with Alberto Toscano's ruminations on 'dual biopower', wherein subaltern populations stitch together a collective project reappropriating control over their bodies from the state and capitalists. Marshalling Fanon's clinical practices and the Black Panther Party's free breakfasts and health clinics could perhaps provide us with the organisational and ideological inspiration to cultivate an insurgent moral economy from below. A social order whose pollution attacks our lungs, a working day whose rhythms exhaust our capacity to be fully present with loved ones after it's over, and the sense of self-loathing and wasteful existence deliberately propagated in humiliating Work Capability Assessments all make us *less than we might be.* In struggling to be fuller versions of ourselves, drawing the connections between our health and the health of the planet and its ecosystems too, we might find that a horizon of repair is (as David Scott points out in writing on reparations for slavery and colonialism) less invested in teleological stories of progress than past left vocabularies. The push for repair could combine a supreme norm of care (which is different from *growth*) with daily practices that instantiate and prefigure that norm, enacted by radicals in a mode that involves and empowers the sickly of the earth. But there are limits to such a community approach, where it works from below and leaves the grand heights up above (including most of the state) outside its reach. Building towards the democratic control of health and welfare, free at the point of use, shorn from the market, statism and means-testing, and in service of a liberated and healthy future for everyone, will almost certainly require a party.

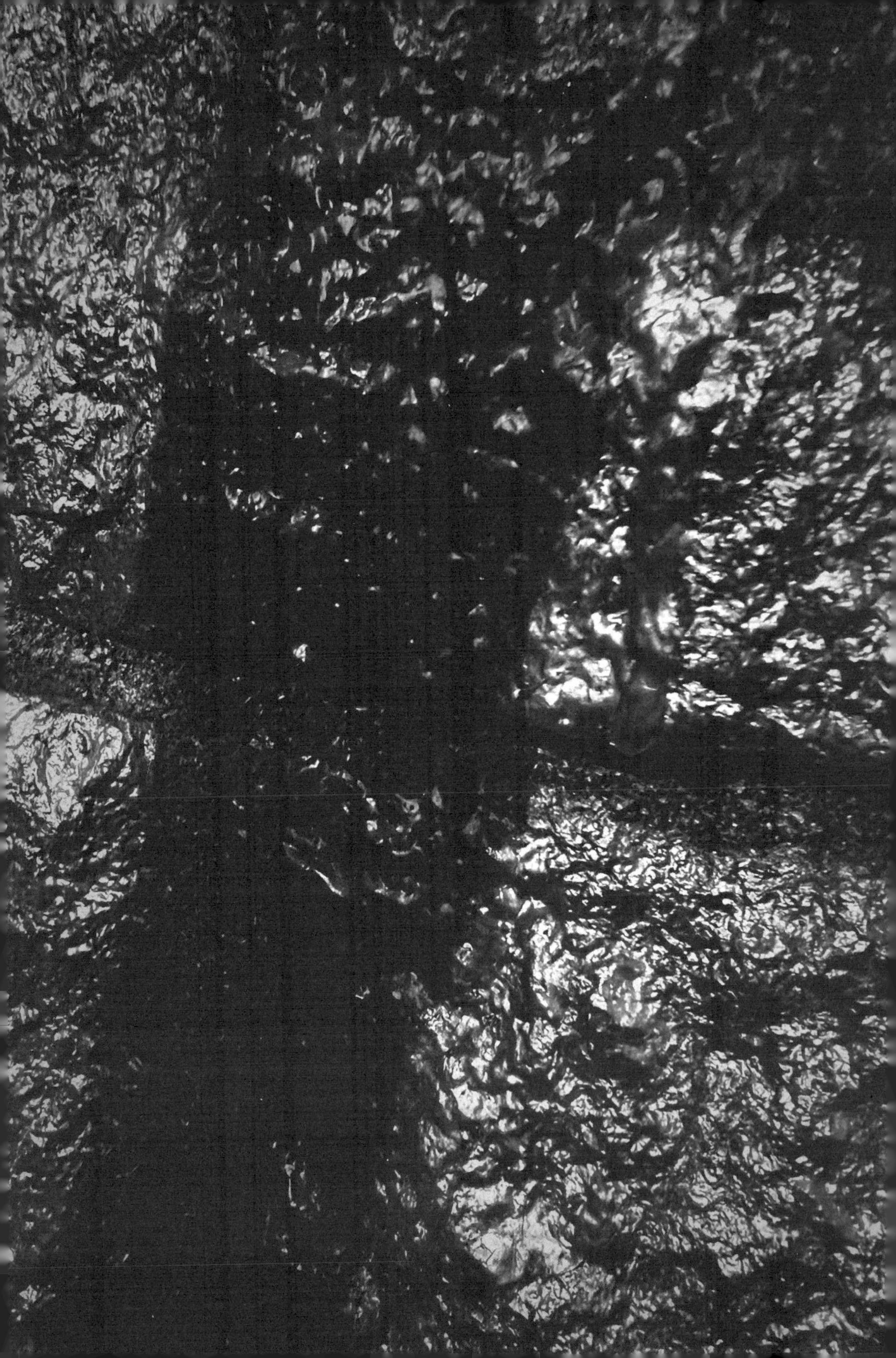

CHINA MIÉVILLE

# Beyond Folk Marxism: Mind, Metaphysics and Spooky Materialism

'Could we please hypothetically imagine that an actual paradigm shift takes place, and it becomes widely understood that materialism ... cannot account for the existence of consciousness, and therefore must be rejected as false. ... How would Marxist thought be affected if materialism was acknowledged to be incoherent?'
– 'Eunomiacus', Reddit, r/Marxism, 2023

Consciousness – does this need to be said? – could hardly be more important for Marxists[*]. As radicals for whom theory and practice must be inextricable, it has been key to our investigations, for purposes of analysis and intervention. *The Communist Manifesto*

---

[*] A short version of this essay was presented at the London Historical Materialism Conference in 2023. I am very grateful to all those respondents for their thoughts. Above all, I'm grateful to David Bentley Hart and Richard Seymour.

sternly demands of its reader consciousness appropriate to the epochal task of rupture. DuBois, Luxemburg, Lenin, Gramsci in hand, we strive to outline consciousness in its popular forms, to make sense of its contradictions and aporia, to diagnose its 'dual' nature, to evaluate its manipulations by and recalcitrance against ruling-class ideologies. Aided by insights from psychoanalysis, we consider how consciousness might change, and/or be resistant to the change desperately warranted. As historical materialists, we investigate consciousness in its complex relations with – to use the hoary and frequently unhelpful shorthand – society's underlying 'economic base'. Debates follow, such as those between (to put it crudely) 'spontaneists' and 'vanguardists', over how consciousness moves, for example, or between Maoists and Deutscherites over limits to conscious, voluntarist will. Such disputes all bespeak a shared key aim: consciousness's development, a striving to enrich its emancipatory content and form, to develop a class consciousness. The Left's familiarity with such issues might manifest in a scholarly deep dive into the hermeneutics of social structure and political agency, and/or in sobbing with frustration because one's uncle doggedly believes patently mendacious racist lies.

☭

Of course, what social theorists mean by 'consciousness' is generally different from what psychoanalysts mean, which is not the same as the usage of neuroscientists, itself distinct from that of philosophers, and so on, even if there is overlap and/or descriptions of similar or inextricable phenomena from distinct vantage points. What's notable is how little the underlying problem of consciousness *tout court* registers on the Left. That is, putting to one side its specifics and politics, *why is there consciousness full stop*? Why, and how, are any of us capable of self-reflective thought? Of experiencing emotion, ratiocination, preference, cold, whim, melancholy, joy? Anything at all? With important exceptions, for the most part the Left has remained untroubled by the voluminous and vexed ruminations on these issues. Untroubled and worse.

To be fair, the field is recondite and hard-going. Considering consciousness *au fond* necessarily tends to a level of abstraction that can feel far removed from urgent questions of *political* consciousness. And it's perfectly possible to work with sophisticated models of consciousness and its contestation at such lived day-to-day levels, never detained by wonder that we are conscious beings at all. Or wondering if indeed we are.

Historical materialism holds that people's material activities are at the source of their social existence. In what follows, Engels, who coined the term 'historical materialism', will come under critical scrutiny, so it's worth approving his own definition here. In *Socialism: Utopian and Scientific*, he describes

> the view of the course of history which seeks the ultimate cause and the great moving power of all important historic events in the economic development of society, in the changes in the modes of production and exchange, in the consequent division of society into distinct classes, and into the struggles of these classes against one another.

Hence, especially given transformative aspirations, the crucial place of class consciousness. It need not be the duty of a socialist to be interested in more abstract, fundamental questions of consciousness. None of us can investigate everything. Asked why and how are we conscious at all, the theorist of political consciousness may simply shrug and proceed on the basis that this fact is a given. And, in everyday life, it may be.

But of course connections must exist between the mystery at its most abstract and those sharper, pressing issues of concrete consciousness. And what won't wash is to suggest that the former question is irrelevant or unimportant, or to revert to a sneer. Let alone to simply assume or insist that the issue is solved *because something something materialism*. Strikingly, however, that is not only a typical response but, if anything, the default position. Far from agreeing to bracket the underlying question, for large swathes of the Marxist Left, especially the activist Left, some such answer is simply assumed. This is a tenet of what we might call 'folk Marxism'.

As a matter of intellectual seriousness, this should not be allowed to stand. An investigation could be diagnostically useful, uncovering a reliance of much actually existing Marxism on presumptions and inherited myths. If folk Marxism is wrong or inadequate in this particular case, what other 'obvious' presuppositions stand in the way of critical thought, and thus practice? Further, though this piece will only touch on these in passing, it's a contention here that there are in fact, inevitably, political and practical ramifications to such seemingly abstract philosophical questions. If nothing else, as Landon Frim and Harrison Fluss very shrewdly point out in 'Reason is Red' – from a philosophical position otherwise clearly at odds with what is advanced here – a Marxism that brackets metaphysics will always be 'question-begging', and 'always searches for a borrowed normativity not derived from "what is" but only chosen according to one's own whim'. Metaphysics is ultimately necessary fully to earn, rather than just 'borrow', our political ethics.

Folk Marxism misses what is at stake here. Which, beyond foundations of normativity, is what it is to be human, and the nature of reality itself.

☭

For the later Engels, in 1886's *Ludwig Feuerbach and the End of Classical German Philosophy*, philosophy is divided into 'two great camps': materialism and idealism. Marxism, of course, is firmly in the former. Engels approvingly cites Feuerbach:

> [T]he material, sensuously perceptible world to which we ourselves belong is the only reality; and ... our consciousness and thinking, however supra-sensuous they may seem, are the product of a material, bodily organ, the brain. Matter is not a product of mind, but mind itself is merely the highest product of matter.

Terminology is a minefield in this area. To complicate matters, some in the Marxist tradition, following Engels, use the term 'metaphysical materialism' disparagingly in distinction from a putative post-Engels holism notionally opposed to reductive and simplistic materialist theories, often called dialectical materialism. Though he did not use that latter term, Engels inaugurated this usage of 'metaphysical materialism', which even Helena Sheehan, otherwise a subtle defender of Engels from many brickbats, calls 'most unfortunate', using 'metaphysics' 'in a particularly eccentric way way that has been followed by subsequent generations of Marxists ... bringing serious confusion into the development of the tradition through his fixation on the terminology of dialectics.' Even more than Engels, Lenin, in *Materialism and Empirio-Criticism*, is the font of this confusing usage, as when he approvingly describes how Engels

> refutes and ridicules the dogmatic, metaphysical materialist Dühring ... To be a materialist is to acknowledge objective truth, which is revealed to us by our sense-organs. To acknowledge objective truth, ie, truth not dependent upon man and mankind, is, in one way or another, to recognise absolute truth and it is this 'one way or another' which distinguishes the metaphysical materialist Dühring from the dialectical materialist Engels.

But, though with different dynamics than its imagined 'metaphysical' other, such 'DiaMat' is itself also predicated on a fundamental ontology of matter, as Lenin's formulation makes clear. Such a grundnorm *is*, in usual contemporary philosophical parlance, a metaphysical materialism. This confusion is one route, within the shared sociolect of Marxism, by which vulgar and reductive materialism are often conflated with metaphysical materialism. In what follows, I use the term metaphysical materialism in its conventional philosophical sense.

In *A Dictionary of Marxist Thought*, Ralph Miliband calmly distinguishes different levels of ambitions for materialism.

> In its broadest sense, materialism contends that whatever exists just is, or at least depends upon, matter. (In its more general form it claims that all reality is essentially material; in its more specific form, that human reality is). In the Marxist tradition, materialism has normally been of the weaker, non-reductive kind.

But Miliband allows that the concept has been deployed in 'various ways'. Where '[f]or Marx's practical materialism, which is restricted to the social sphere (including of course natural science) and where "matter" is to be understood in the sense of "social practice", no particular difficulty arises' with the definition of matter. 'But from Engels on, Marxist materialism has more global pretensions'.

One doesn't have to sign up *in toto* to (or even claim entirely to understand) Reiner Schürmann's dense reading of Marx to share his frustration, in a lecture of 1977, not only over misreadings of Marx, in which 'reality' means 'matter', which 'totally miss' Marx's operations, but 'how frequent they are in Marxist literature!' Such 'pretensions' are now, while not universal, a Marxist common sense. And as is usually the case for common sense, they are an enemy to thought and rigour.

Sometimes a philosophical co-constitution of Marxist and some such metaphysics is explicit. Sean Creaven, in his 1999 PhD thesis and the book later derived from it, is unusually clear and adamant both on the distinction and the necessary 'exposition and defence of two kinds of materialism – ontological (or philosophical) and analytical-explanatory (i.e. anthropological and sociological)' as 'consistent with one another'. Indeed, more than consistent:

> The fundamental point of contact between ontological materialism and explanatory ... materialism is ... in the simple fact that the laws or tendencies of humanity's

> biological nature are basic to the laws of socio-cultural and socio-historical reality. There is, in short, a 'chain of being' extending from physico-chemical reality to biological reality and then to socio-cultural reality.

The connection, even when clearly made, is rarely so systematically argued. Alex Callinicos in *Marxism and Philosophy*, explicitly repudiating what he calls 'physicalism' – 'the demand for a reduction of the human sciences to physics' – describes an important sense not only in which 'Marxism is a materialism', but 'is "ontological materialism", or naturalism', according to which 'methodological principles relevant to the formulation and evaluation of theoretical discourses are the same in both the natural and the social sciences'. Sean Sayers, too, distinguishes 'physicalism' from 'a non-mechanistic and non-physicalist form of materialism', of which he sees Engels as a key developer. Further, he defends materialism, including Marxist materialism, as insisting that '[a]ll reality is material; there is nothing in the world but matter in motion'. Sebastiano Timpanaro, in 'Considerations on Materialism', combatively defends a totalising, bottom-up materialism, predicated 'above all' on the 'acknowledgement of the priority of nature over "mind", or if you like, of the physical level over the biological level, and of the biological level over the socio-economic and cultural level'. Timpanaro praises Engels (and latterly Lenin), for extending the, as he sees it, incomplete paradigm of Marx from a merely human theory into an overarching ontology.

> Marxism was born as an affirmation of the decisive primacy of the socio-economic level over juridical, political and cultural phenomena, and as an affirmation of the historicity of the economy ... If a critique of anthropocentrism and an emphasis on the conditioning of man by nature are considered essential to materialism, it must be said that Marxism, especially in its first phase ... is not materialism proper ... Even more than by Marx – though evidently not in dissent from him – the

> need for the construction of a materialism which was not purely socio-economic but also 'natural' was felt by Engels, and this was a great merit of his.

Of course, and crucially, there is no sharp line between such explicit articulations and the mere *en passant* statements of an assumed case. And it's precisely when argument is not deemed necessary that ideology is at its strongest. Justin Holt's introductory text, *The Social Thought of Karl Marx*, for example, devotes a chapter to Marx's materialism, merely glossing it briefly as a subset of 'a theory that considers the entire existence of people and the universe as physical matter'. *The Encyclopedia Britannica* describes 'the principles of historical materialism' as being 'laid out in Engels's 1878 book ... *Anti-Dühring*', thus locating the locus classicus of the approach in a text that in fact, and far more problematically, revolves around a metaphysical materialism (if not by that name). The predication of Marxism on metaphysical materialism is often not even stated, simply given – if sometimes hazily, possibly unconsciously – by non-Marxists and, more importantly, by many Marxists.

Such folk Marxism has an enormous influence on the culture of the Left. Where the elision of historical and metaphysical materialism is challenged, or even simply raised, the folk Marxist must defend it. When the Reddit-user 'Eunomiacus' put the question which is the epigraph to this essay, one respondent thundered: 'Without materialism, Marxism will lose its grounding and will become a swamp of reformism.'

☭

The issue of consciousness *tout court* has always been central to the ontological questions here, precisely because it is so evasive, particularly to materialism. Sayers, in his spirited if ultimately unconvincing defence of Engels, describes this as the 'old problems of the relation of the mental and physical', the fact that the '"psychological" standpoint cannot be captured in purely physical terms'. Thus it's on these grounds that the folk Marxist must engage.

There are very many examples out there of such folk Marxism, of which what follows are only a representative few. In 2021, the journal *Marxist Student*, an official outlet of the Trotskyist Revolutionary Communist International, pedagogically explained its position on 'materialism' thus:

> The major cleavage in the field of philosophy is over the question of the relationship between mind and matter. Materialists, such as Hobbes, Diderot, and Marx, argue that matter (e.g. the material world) is primary: the world around us exists, and it can be known. Moreover, they argue that there is no real distinction between mind and matter – just that matter organised in a certain way results in mind and consciousness.

In 'Marx and Historical Materialism', written for the activist group RS21, Rob Hoveman put it that 'Marx believed that human beings were part of nature, not beings placed on Earth by God', that though distinct from other animals, 'human beings as ... part of the natural world [were] beings who were wholly physical in nature'. And in such wholly physical creatures, 'quantitative change (such as the evolution of the brain) could turn into qualitative change (such as consciousness)'.

Tellingly, the title of Hoveman's piece, republished in the US *Socialist Worker*, was tweaked to 'Marxism and the Meaning of Materialism' – the important adjective 'historical' now lost, the text's elision between distinct kinds of materialisms was now negatively enshrined in the title. For Alan Woods and Ted Grant, in their 1995 *Reason in Revolt*,

> the great strides forward made by science ... provide striking confirmation of the materialist outlook. This is particularly the case in relation to the controversies over the brain and neurobiology. The last hiding place of idealism is under attack ... What we call 'mind' is just the mode of existence of the brain.

The antique 'mind-body problem', then, while hardly easy for philosophers of any stamp, particularly vexes metaphysical materialism. Historical materialism, meanwhile, must deploy its intense and necessary focus on the problematic of consciousness, its content and social traction. To the extent that the latter materialism is, per Timpanaro, a derived function of the former, this raises a profound difficulty internal to Marxism.

In response we tend to see the insistence on the distinction between, on the one hand, 'physicalism', or 'reductionism', or 'neopositivism', as the remarkable Marxist philosopher Evald Ilyenkov called his own foil, or 'mechanical' or 'mechanistic materialism,' or 'vulgar materialism', or even, confusingly, that so-called 'metaphysical materialism', from succulent, nimble, 'dialectical', worthy Marxist materialism on the other. In whatever nuances the various former might differ, their main role in these models is as the obverse of the desired 'non-mechanistic, non-reductive form of philosophical materialism' that Sayers credits to Engels.

This is an attempted inoculation against the antique canard that, in the ignorant swaggering words of one critic, '[t]he realm of pure human thought and idea is relegated by the Marxist to a state of jejune non-effectuality'. Engels himself, in his commitment to materialism, long ago preemptively countered that, insisting that he wasn't arguing that the 'economic factor is the only determining one ... systems of dogma also exercise their influence upon the course of historical struggles and in many cases determine their form in particular'. But what does – what *can* – this mean? In such a model, where does consciousness come from?

☭

In a classic exposition of Marxist psychology, Alexsei Leontyev, in *Problems of the Development of Mind* describes 'the transition to consciousness' as

> the beginning of a new, higher stage in the evolution of the psyche. In contrast to the psychic reflection

> peculiar to animals, conscious reflection is reflection of material reality in its separateness from the subject's ... attitudes to it ... The cause underlying the humanising of man's animal-like ancestors is the emergence of labour and the formation of human society on its basis ... The origin and development of labour, this first and basic condition for the existence of man [sic], led to a change in his brain

In *Activity and Consciousness*, Leontyev sees 'individual consciousness as a specifically human form of the subjective reflection of objective reality' and that it

> may be understood only as the product of those relations and mediacies that arise in the course of the establishment and development of society ... the study of the phenomena of consciousness ... allows us to understand them only on the condition that man's activity itself is regarded as a process included in the system of relations, a process that realises his social being, which is the means of his existence also as a natural, corporeal creature.

Compare this to Callinicos arguing – on the offhand basis of ontological materialism – against the reduction of the human sciences to physics, because 'what sets man [sic] off from the rest of the natural world is his ability to act upon and transform his natural environment' (an inflated distinction in any case), and that

> [o]n the basis of this metabolism ... there arise structures which in their complexity and capacity for internally generated transformation are unique to human beings.

Thus we're presented with consciousness as an evolved, intrinsically social phenomenon, and one that reacts back on the structures out of which it emerged. Now, this is not worthless. Particularly, this model can be foil to those – perfectly genuine – more mechanical traditions, Marxist or not, that implicitly or explicitly downplay (few would explicitly deny) interaction between 'consciousness' and the world, for a more simplistic unilinear theory, wherein consciousness 'reflects' material reality. One seminal such is Stalin's balefully authoritative 1938 'Dialectical and Historical Materialism', a vulgarisation of Lenin's already questionable approach to these matters. According to Stalin,

> Marxist philosophical materialism holds that matter, nature, being, is an objective reality existing outside and independent of our consciousness; that matter is primary, since it is the source of sensations, ideas, consciousness, and that consciousness is secondary, derivative, since it is a reflection of matter, a reflection of being ... Further, if nature, being, the material world, is primary, and consciousness, thought, is secondary, derivative; if the material world represents objective reality existing independently of the consciousness of men, while consciousness is a reflection of this objective reality, it follows that the material life of society, its being, is also primary, and its spiritual life secondary, derivative, and that the material life of society is an objective reality existing independently of the will of men.

The Leontyevian ruminations can be useful rebukes to such formulations. So far, so adequate. But however persuasive and useful they are, those ruminations are models, *depictions of* consciousness and/or its development in and as motion, of how it acts, is acted on and interacts, and by and with what. What they are *not*, however, are true theories of what consciousness *is*. To be fair, not for nothing is this known as the 'hard problem of consciousness'.

The paths of this hard problem are very well-trodden to those au fait with philosophies of consciousness, yet likely to be abstruse to the newcomer. This essay is written particularly for the open-minded non-specialist Marxist, perhaps especially if they're aware of having tamped down theoretical disquiet over some of these issues, for whom an introduction to the terrain and its stakes will be helpful. The text is dense with quotations, both to make the case that folk Marxism is a thing, and to underscore the scale of the issues it does not notice, or purports to have solved. I hammer in particular at that hard problem, to a degree perhaps obnoxious to those who know the debates. I do so hardly with any claim to solve it, but precisely because the key schism here is less between those with different suggested answers, than those who encounter it as the problem it emphatically and irreducibly is, and those who, for whatever reasons, shrug it away or make out no real there there. I hope those already familiar will be patient.

Though even for them it might be worth revisiting old ground. More so than with perhaps any other issue, it can take repeated encounters with the hard problem for it to even register as it should, as a fundamental epistemic issue – and thus a metaphysical one. And paradoxically, real advances in neuroscience may only increase that barrier. As one online commenter ('rustgarden') shrewdly puts it below a recent gloss on this issue by Bernardo Kastrup, '[t]he reality of the Hard Problem is going to become even more difficult to convey to people as technology finds more sophisticated correlations' between brain states and experiences – to the point where they might allow, for example, reasonable guesstimates of experienced sound from brainwaves. 'I expect that physicalists will soon point to examples like this to say that the hard problem has been solved, even though it still doesn't explain anything of how we could get quality from quantity.'

It might be after many such shrugs and wonderings about what the big deal is that one abruptly experiences the kind of crisis that Tad DeLay sees as crucial to critical thought, inaugurating the appropriate inability to explain or wave the explanatory gap between matter and consciousness away. Not merely formally to be familiar with the question, but, to deploy Heinlein's useful neologism for understanding powerfully, intuitively, and so deeply that the knowledge becomes part of you, to *grok* it, is to experience the debate as the existential question it is. When that explanatory gap is felt, the result can be wracking and exhilarating. (The philosophical thunderbolt that such a felt encounter with these issues occasioned in me has been reconfigurative.)

☭

To quote David Chalmers, who formulated the term, the 'hard problem' is that of

> how physical processes in the brain give rise to the subjective experience of the mind and of the world ... When I see ... photons hit my eyes – they send a signal that goes up the optic nerve ... This is how science might describe me from the objective point of view. But there's also a subjective point of view. There's what it feels like for the agent who is seeing the scene. When I see you, I see colors, I see shapes, I have an experience from a first-person point of view. There's something it's like to be me.

Predictably, the riposte 'What hard problem?' is not uncommon. It is a category error, claims Massimo Pigliucci. '*Why* phenomenal consciousness exists is a typical question for evolutionary biology', he writes. This leaves one with the ghastly sense that for him that is the *only* field for which it is appropriate, as when he question-beggingly insists that '[c]onsciousness is a biological phenomenon, so its appearance in a certain lineage of hominids seems to be squarely a matter for evolutionary biology'. And all that can be reasonably asked, he insists, is the nuts-and-bolts of how it works with regard to associated brain states.

[W]hat it is like [to be conscious] is like an experience ... It is obvious that I cannot experience what it is like to be you, but I can potentially have a complete explanation of how and why it is possible to be you. To ask for that explanation to also somehow encompass the experience itself is both incoherent, and an illegitimate use of the word 'explanation'.

To be clear, and bracketing all of Pigliucci's unwarranted assumptions, if this were to mean any such question is *beyond* what he calls the 'principle of scientific naturalism', by which he means metaphysical materialism (though the two are importantly not, in fact, necessarily coterminous), he might be making a plausible argument. But this is not his case, as his repeated analogies between the heart and, not the brain, but *consciousness* itself, show. 'If you were asking how the heart works, you'd be turning to anatomy and molecular biology, and I see no reason things should be different in the case of consciousness.'

Of course the hard problem is the fact that conscious phenomenal experience is *not* biology – certainly not as it is traditionally understood and scientifically studied in terms of causalities of matter and energy – even if it is predicated on or inextricable from it. No recourse to Searle can help Pigliucci: if it is in fact true that 'where consciousness is concerned, the existence of the appearance is the reality', this is precisely to restate the mystery, not to suggest that it can be tidied away as some 'experience' neither in biological science's purview yet not bespeaking any limits thereto.

What subjectivity is it, after all, that is there to experience the experience?

☭

Here, to sketch out the parameters of the field, a brief excursus on the controversial, criticised and much abused concept of the philosophical (or p-) zombie is necessary – and, at least for some of us, highly useful. This (admittedly, to the horror fan, poorly named) thought experiment is a creature physically, and in terms of all observable behaviour, identical to a human being, but without interiority and subjective experience – absent consciousness. A flawless biological automaton.

The p-zombie is a vexed creature. There are those (including me) for whom it is an invaluable heuristic, while for others it is a pointless and unhelpful chimera. To be clear, in brief defence of the concept, the claim is not, of course, that any such zombies exist (an oddly common misunderstanding), but that imagining them can help highlight what is at stake – which is precisely the subjectivity they do not have, and yet which no non-zombie interlocutor could know they lack. P-zombies illustrate that we can coherently imagine beings physically identical to humans and possessing and performing all the physical processes of human life, but lacking consciousness. Which *at the very least* implies that consciousness might involve non-physical properties or processes. In Michael Tye's words, '[t]he point is that the idea of a zombie makes sense, and it makes sense because of how we think of phenomenal consciousness.' Absent it, they would still interact with the world seemingly as we do, no less 'efficiently' and no less seemingly human.

Which is why, among the uses of this thought experiment is that it problematises the gestures at evolution or biology to deflate the hard problem. Contrary to Pigliucci's claim that consciousness's *'raison d'etre'* can ... be accounted for on evolutionary grounds', the *behaviour* we associate with consciousness can be so accounted, and is highly adaptive. (We'll bracket here the fact that 'adaptation' and the fact of the adapted/-ing subject raise major philosophical questions.) But *consciousness itself*, as Chalmers argues until he's hoarse, is not presumed in such adaptive zombie behaviour, nor can it be derived from it. If, as Pigliucci clearly believes, consciousness in this case is definitionally inextricable from the behaviour, that is simply to restate the problem as its own solution. If adaptive behaviour of a certain complexity demands consciousness, as is implied in Pigliucci's mention of a *'raison d'etre'*, two questions follow: why?; and much more tellingly, the hard problem itself – how does that 'necessary' consciousness arise from unconscious matter?

Meanwhile, Daniel Dennett's claim that any 'putative contrast between zombies and conscious beings is illusory', presented as if it bracingly upends a pointless paradigm, attempts to solve the problem by universalising zombiehood, and – though he would contest this – eradicating consciousness. (His claim that those who think they can imagine such zombies in fact cannot and 'invariably ... end up imagining something that violates their own definition' is related, but much more straightforwardly false.)

☭

The hard problem is one of what are called qualia: subjective, conscious experiences. Why is *any* physical state one of not just behaviour, but consciousness? How does one derive not merely the objective motion in brains that accompanies but the *subjective experience* itself from matter in motion?

In urgently trying to communicate this, scientists and philosophers often wax poetic – how do we experience and what is our experience of the scent of this rare flower, the taste of that expensive wine, the subtle hues of the sunset-lit other? 'There is a great deal to say for the view that accompanying every joy and, generally, every movement of consciousness, there is a closely connected but imperceptible movement of atoms in the cerebrum', as Erich Becher wrote in 1925. 'But joy is not this movement'.

It's no surprise that the agitated consciousness-theorist gropes for rare and splendid sensory events in the attempt to invoke appropriate 'thaumazein', the wonder that Aristotle saw as the root of philosophy, at our subjectivity. No less philosophically extraordinary, of course, is our experience of pulling on our pants, the desire to blow one's nose, the taste of cheap bread. We cannot but take ourselves for granted. But the fact of our experiences at all, our first-person subjectivity, if we are able to stop and consider them, are profoundly mysterious – particularly for the materialist.

Though Chalmers coined the term 'hard problem' in 1994, and has developed it and doggedly insisted on its centrality ever since, he was certainly not the first to note the issue. In 1714, Leibniz, in *The Monadology*, observed that 'perception, and that which depends on it, are inexplicable by mechanical causes'. He presented his now-notorious mill.

> [S]upposing that there were a mechanism so constructed as to think, feel and have perception, we might enter it as into a mill. And this granted, we should only find on visiting it, pieces which push one against another, but never anything by which to explain perception.

In 1865, the philosopher and historian of materialism Friedrich Lange declared a refutation of materialism 'to which there is no answer': 'Consciousness cannot be explained out of material movements.' Max Horkheimer in his 'Materialism and Metaphysics', underlines that 'this argument has been tirelessly repeated ever since the debate on materialism in 1854'. This he illustrates with a remarkable cavalcade of quotations from the nineteenth and early twentieth centuries, including those from Becher and Lange, above[†]. The foundations for this insight can even be discerned more than two millennia ago, in Aristotle's distinction in the *Generation of Animals* between all 'those principles whose activity is bodily' and which therefore 'cannot exist without a body' and cannot enter it from without, and 'reason' (or 'thought') 'alone', which is left 'so to enter and alone to be divine, for no bodily activity has any connexion with the activity of reason'. It is very old news, in the words of one of Horkheimer's sources Harmann, that materialism

> cannot only not prove, it cannot even suggest principles for understanding how a process in consciousness could derive from spatio-temporal processes in the nervous system, how even the simplest content of sensation really arises. Between the one and the other there is a gap which is completely impervious to reason, with no connecting link that we can discern.

---

† I'm grateful to Ray Brassier for bringing this to my attention. Small wonder that, for him, it is 'somewhat galling that David Chalmers's reputation as a significant philosopher rests on "discovering" a problem that was well-known to European philosophers a century before!'

This latter fact, as Pannekoek puts it in his perspicacious and exciting, though ultimately frustrating, 1942 piece 'Materialism and Historical Materialism', is that 'ideas are different from bile ... mind cannot simply be put into the same category with force or energy'. That this is a problem of kind is key.

☭

The inextricability of this hard problem with questions of metaphysics opens out into a vast debate. Robert Lawrence Kuhn, whose tv series *Closer to Truth* is an invaluable repository of open-minded discussion on these issues, recently published a book-length overview of the field, 'A Landscape of Consciousness: Toward a Taxonomy of Explanations and Implications'. Kuhn gathers nine broad explanatory paradigms – 'Materialism', 'Non-Reductive Physicalism', 'Quantum', 'Integrated Information Theory', 'Panpsychisms', 'Monisms', 'Dualisms', 'Idealisms', 'Anomalous & Altered States', and 'Challenge'. The first of these, Materialism, reflecting its state as the single dominant philosophy on this, and indeed on all scientific questions, hardly just among Marxists, is further divided into 10 subsets. Within each set and subset Kuhn includes several theorists and/or approaches, ending up with brief but lucid glosses on no fewer than *225* theories of consciousness.

This obviously ranges far beyond our scope here. For all the gallons of ink spilt, for all the vital distinctions within each camp, for all the tempestuous debates over the esoterica, there are essentially two and a half broad underlying metaphysics by which one can approach this issue. (And yes, for all those positions that claim to bypass this fundamental distinction, too.)

The first is ontological, metaphysical materialism of the type discussed above. This, the same model underpinning folk Marxism, is by far the most common view for scientists studying consciousness. Though substantially less dominant, it is – just – the majority view, too, among professional philosophers: according to the 2020 PhilPapers Survey of Anglophone academic philosophers, 51.9 per cent of respondents accepted or leaned towards a 'physicalist' – materialist – philosophy of mind.

The second metaphysical grundnorm is some form of idealist explanation. Here what this means is, to quote Chalmers again, 'the thesis that the universe is fundamentally mental, or perhaps that all concrete facts are grounded in mental facts'. A large number of the theories that Kuhn categorises using other terms – such as, for example, David Bentley Hart's monism – are, whatever their other specificities, predicated on a fundamentally idealist metaphysics.

Of course, for a folk-Marxist audience, the very term 'idealist' is an immediate red flag, and, indeed, self-evidently wrong. Without making any positive claims for idealism here, it's worth underlining the extent to which this nostrum is often predicated on ignorance and philosophical philistinism, and not only within Marxism. As Tom Rockmore puts it, many

> observers are clear that idealism has been overcome but unclear about what idealists believe. Thus [G.E.] Moore famously thinks that all idealists share the disbelief in the reality of the external world. The charm of this unqualified claim is only slightly tarnished by the inability to name anyone in the history of the tradition who has ever held it.

The remainder – that is, the half of a metaphysics – comprises substance-dualist explanations, for which, crudely, in a material universe, mental phenomena are irreducibly non-physical, thus distinguishing the physical brain from the thinking, feeling mind. Such dualism certainly works as a vague holding theory and description, one that evades the impasse of materialism and the scandal of idealism, but it's hard to conceive of a systematically dualist philosophy of mind, and thus of reality, in which one or other of the two poles does not ultimately assert ontological primacy. Whether or not it's true that nature, as has been said, abhors a dualism, certainly, as Hart insists, reason does. The simple fact that the two, mind and brain, are related – indeed, that any two phenomena in the same universe are related – militates against any such foundational dualism.

This is what Hart, in *All Things Are Full of Gods*, calls

> the *fallacy of terminal dualism* ... the mistake of thinking any dualistic account of the relation of mind to matter could constitute an adequate explanation rather than a mere deferral of the problem to another level of mystery ... in the end, a dualism can never be more than a provisional answer to any question; for two qualitatively different relata to be reconciled, there must be some broader, simpler, more encompassing unity in which they participate, some more basic ontological ground, a shared medium underlying both and repugnant to neither ... some metaphysical or logical medium that comprises them both in itself and provides the basis of their congruity. Only at that level can one hope for any sort of answer to the 'problem of mind.' All final answers are in some way monistic, or they aren't final.

In this sense at least Engels is clearly right about the two great camps. At a metaphysical level of high abstraction, it does, indeed, come down to idealism or materialism.

☭

Of course, those attempts to bypass this Scylla and Charybdis are common enough. Thus claim some proponents of sensorimotor theory, neutral monism, Structural Qualia, Integrated Information Theory, some versions of panpsychism, according to which consciousness is a fundamental, pervasive feature of the universe, possessed at least in inchoate form by all things, including inanimate objects. Most of the particularities of such theories is beyond us, except to stress that the claims of any or all such to evade that dyad – let alone to solve the hard problem – are not convincing.

Panpsychism in particular, to engage in another brief excursus, can exercise a powerful pull on those justly troubled by the 'hard question', and it comes in both self-styled idealist and physicalist versions. Thus for example Michael Tye turned panpsychist in part because phenomenal consciousness is 'apparently not admitting of borderline cases'. That is it either *is* or *is not* – drawing on the p-zombie, Tye is compelling against the counterargument that such consciousness might be 'vague'. Which is to say that it cannot rigorously be described as having evolved (a position related to a critique of 'emergence' developed below). Thus Tye was led to panpsychism as 'the best solution', 'to say that consciousness did not emerge and moreover consciousness is not reducible to anything physical ... [but] is a fundamental intrinsic feature of basic micro-entities. It was there all along at the absolute bedrock of reality'.

Of course, this raises very many other questions about the nature of such phenomenal consciousness at various levels of complexity and/or fundamentality, as Tye is clear. And more to the point, such 'materialist panpsychism' is simply asserted, and in no way more logically compelling than idealism: as Hart asks, why is it 'more coherent' if one 'phrases the matter in terms of mental "properties" inhering in matter', rather than saying 'that the "physical" or "material" subsists as a property of mind?' As the stopgap for metaphysical materialism as which it functions, then, the materialism of such 'materialist' panpsychism is not logically derived, but merely a rearguard expression of preference. Further, Hart points out:

> [I]f you're willing to concede that matter is already in some sense mind at this point we're discussing dispositions or potentials in matter so far outside the mechanistic paradigm [which is to say metaphysical materialism] that terms like ... 'naturalism' have been rendered otiose, since apparently they exclude nothing – except, perhaps, some hazy pictures of an anthropomorphic God and an ectoplasmic soul inherited from the religion of the nursery or the philosophy of Descartes. It seems rather pointless so vigilantly to guard one's metaphysics against incursions of supernaturalism in a world that can accommodate sentient sand. ... [Because] for panpsychism to serve as a

> truly physicalist rather than classically idealist theory, it would have to posit the presence of real agency all the way down ... [ and w]e're merely deferring the question of mind to the subatomic level.

The fundamental – Engelsian – materialist/idealist schism thus remains. All of which is why it isn't meant as a snide gotcha but with amused empathy to wonder if the title of Tye's essay – 'How I Learned to Stop Worrying and Love Panpyschism' protests too much. Smacking as it does of disavowed – and entirely appropriate – worry.

☭

How, then, do materialist theories of consciousness attempt to answer the hard problem? How can one make sense of that joy, say, not just as an inferable, socially contextual state in others but as an *experienced experience*, from a brain-state, and ultimately from physical atoms?

Most commonly by far, attempts from within metaphysical materialism are made by reference to 'emergence'.

Emergence is the model by which the properties of a complex entity are greater than, and distinct, from those of its parts and underlying strata. As the obverse of reductionism, it has been a useful resource to materialist theories of consciousness, among much else.

Helena Sheehan, in *Marxism and the Philosophy of Science*, describes 'Engels put[ting] the weight of his effort into differentiating between his materialism and theirs [his intellectual opponents], contrasting the new organicist and emergentist form of materialism with the old mechanistic and reductionist form'. S. A. Grave, in 'The Marxist Theory of Matter and Mind', of 1953, argues that

> [w]hat Marxist materialism does hold as a first principle is that mind is derived from matter. Matter is temporally and causally prior ... Mind (i.e. God) did not make matter ...

> Matter did make mind. The production of mind by matter is however 'dialectical' not 'mechanical' ... the emergence of life and mind from inanimate matter in progressive evolution is the emergence of radically new qualities wholly irreducible in nature to what has gone before.

Gail Edwards, decades later, in 'Putting Critical Realism to Work for Education and Revolution', drawing on the theories of critical realism, for which emergence is central, argues in similar fashion.

> Properties and powers can emerge from reality's underlying strata but are not reducible to them. People's liabilities and powers are not determined by their biology, for example. Human reasons, intentions and consciousness emerge from, but are *not* reducible to, neurophysiological matter.

Beyond Marxism, and with a rather deflationary sense of emergence, materialist and physicist Sean Carroll describes consciousness as 'one of these emergent phenomena that we find is a useful way of packaging reality'. For Mario Bunge's 'emergent materialism', 'mental states form a subset (albeit a very distinguished one) of brain states (which in turn are a subset of the state space of the whole animal)', emergent in that it is 'a property possessed by a system but not by its components'.

Emergence as a heuristic may well work as a 'thick description' here, in the sense used by Ryle and, especially, Clifford Geertz. It may, through a particular species of rich and granular description, vividly depict and contextualise the phenomenon of human consciousness, its historical, social and individual development, rise, and workings. What emergence is not, however, is explanation. It cannot answer the hard question. Further, it can only overcome the problems of metaphysical materialism by relying on gestural proclamations, vagueness, and folk-Marxist common sense.

Key to understanding this is the established distinction between weak and strong emergence. In the former, a system-level trait may not be obviously the result of its more fundamental components, but in principle, can be explained as such. In the latter, 'micro-level principles are quite simply inadequate to *account* for the system's behaviour as a whole', in Paul Davies' words. The emphasis is added to show: this is not merely a question of being an inadequate description.

As an illustration of emergence, Davies explains that while 'water may be described as wet ... it would be meaningless to ask whether a molecule of $H_2O$ is wet'. However, this is weak emergence: counterintuitive as it may be 'that the properties of two common gases, hydrogen and oxygen, can combine to form a liquid that is wet and a solid that expands when cooled', as Kuhn points out, 'physics and physical chemistry can explain all of this, in terms of atomic structures and bonding angles'. As Hart tartly observes, '[p]hysical properties derived from other physical properties – no great problem there. So long as this is all that's meant by "emergence," then the concept is as inoffensive as it is obvious.'

The qualities of consciousness, of course, are utterly different. But too often materialist and Marxist theorists act as if this is not the case. They segue blithely from examples of weak emergence to those of life, its own mystery, let alone consciousness, as if the materialist story of the latter is thus proved. Thus, from the remarkable (erstwhile Christian minister) Marxist John Lewis:

> Hydrogen is a gas, oxygen is a gas, but their combination in certain proportions is water. Organic substances have quite different properties from inorganic and yet may be synthesised from the inorganic. Protoplasm ... builds organic substances first into proteins and then into protoplasm which then exhibits the characteristics of life ... Life is simply the property of a particular pattern of non-living parts, but its reality and novelty are undeniable. ... [I]n the case of man [sic] we have ... foresight and *self-awareness* ... Marxism does not deny the reality of either life or mind. It asserts, however, that they are functions of highly organised matter on the organic level.

Decades later Sean Sayers would offer a similar narrative.

> [A]ll biological entities ... are made up of chemical constituents in the forms of atoms and molecules, and these in turn are composed of more fundamental physical particles. Nevertheless the concepts describing biological entities ... are distinct from, and irreducible to, the concepts and laws of physics. ... A biological organism is not a mere collection of chemical or physical constituents. ... Similarly the behaviour of an organism can be explained only in terms of laws governing the organism as a whole. ... Human beings are ... biological organisms. ... Nevertheless, human thought ... cannot be described or understood as such in purely biological, let alone chemical or physical terms ... To understand the activity of the brain, as the organ of thought, it must also be seen in its social and psychological context, in which the concepts and principles of neurophysiology are blind.

This last point is absolutely true. But it leaves the hard problem untouched, despite the claim that humans 'are made up entirely of physical, chemical, biological constituents'. The hard problem is a logical/philosophical problem. 'Historical, social and psychological context' is an invaluable thick description, but that logical gap it does not come close to filling.

Still less is the hard problem one of insufficient data. Because this is a problem of category, a 'fundamental epistemic question', in Kastrup's words, 'not merely an operational or contingent one', *no* amount of knowledge of the behaviour of particles either singly or in their interactions – nor of historical, social and psychological context – can possibly 'explain' consciousness in materialist or physicalist terms. This is not circular logic: it is not that consciousness is here *defined* as something beyond the purview of metaphysical materialism. Rather, if we accept the existence of consciousness (not a given, as will become clear), then it *is* inexplicable precisely according to the logic and categories espoused by metaphysical materialism (certainly absent such esoteric qualifications to the notion of 'matter' that i) the status of the resulting theory as 'materialist' is ultimately questionable, and ii) a whole host of new theoretical problems necessarily arise – see for example the brief discussion of panpsychism above). Recalling Pannekoek's bile, '[m]atter', in Colin McGinn's provocative formulation, 'is just the wrong kind of thing to give birth to consciousness'. That it does seem to give birth to it is precisely the difficulty. None of this is to deny the inextricability of brain and mind, nor to suggest that consciousness is free-floating from biology. Consciousness does in fact emerge, in one way, but this is clearly not 'weak emergence'. And 'strong emergence' *qua* theory cannot and, despite some protestations to the contrary by metaphysical materialists, never will explain it.

Worse, in Bentley Hart's words again, with my emphasis, this 'is a perfect example of precisely the kind of problem that vague talk of "emergence" only allows us to *evade*'. 'Emergence' is perhaps the most common wand currently available to wave to achieve such a trick, though it is only one of the available strategies. Others, not mutually exclusive, include italicisation, emphatic deployments of 'neither', 'nor', 'not only' and 'but both' or similar, and/or the fairy-dust of too-easily-invoked 'dialectics'.

'*Thought, mind,*' John Lewis insists, 'is not a substance added to matter, it is a *function* of a certain kind of matter.' Lewis is not the only writer who seems to believe that restating a problem with a flourish solves it. To take a more recent example, from one perfectly clear that thought 'cannot be explained in narrowly neurophysiological terms', the capacity of humans to self-consciously reflect, offers Sayers in 'Engels and Materialism',

> is only *relatively* autonomous from the natural conditions and social practices from which it develops and on which it is based. It is not a merely biological ability, but nor is it an ability that entirely separates us from the material world and transcends its processes. It is

> an ability which emerges and develops, gradually and by degrees, in the course of biological and historical evolution ... [Engels'] aim in putting forward the idea of a dialectic in nature is not to idealise nature, but rather to naturalise the mental.

The most systematic – and sometimes rich – exposition of 'emergentist Marxism', Creaven's, tells the same story with the same examples. Similarly inadequately to the hard problem. (It's telling that Creaven is heavily and explicitly indebted to Dennett, whose thin emergentism, to the extent that it is there, is nowhere near as usefully developed as Creaven's own, and whose theory of consciousness neither relies on nor validates such a model. And is, as we will see, for all its influence, hollow.)

Pannekoek saw the problem clearly from within Marxism, but ultimately failed to follow through on its ramifications. Instead, he ostentatiously wields dialectics in his own emergent story.

> It is metaphysical and non-dialectical to identify thought because it is the product of brain processes with the products of other organs, or to assume that mind, because it is a quality of material substance, is a characteristic quality of all matter. It is also false to think that because mind is something other than matter, it must absolutely and totally differ from it, that there is no transition to and connection with both so that a dualism of mind and matter, reaching down to the atoms, remains sharp and unbridgeable. From the standpoint of dialectics, mind incorporates all those phenomena we call mental which, however, cannot be carried beyond their actual existence in the lowest living animals. There the term mind becomes questionable, because the spiritual phenomena disappear gradually into mere sense perception, into the simple forms of life. The characteristic quality 'spirit', which is or is not there, does not exist in nature; spirit is just

> a name we attach to a number of definite phenomena, some of which we understand clearly, others only partly. Here life itself offers a close analogy. Proceeding from the smallest microscopic organism to still smaller invisible bacteria, we finally come to very complicated albuminous molecules that fall within the sphere of chemistry. Where living matter ceases to exist and dead matter begins cannot be determined; phenomena change gradually, become simplified, are still analogous and are yet already different. This does not mean that we are unable to ascertain demarcation lines; it is simply a fact that nature knows no borders.

In his fascinating and conflicted 1945 essay 'Le problème de la conscience dans la biologie contemporaine' ('The Problem of Consciousness in Contemporary Biology'), the extraordinary Marxist and surrealist Pierre Naville, as a deployer himself of dialectical techniques, was ruthless in diagnosing the anxiety of materialism that provokes such techniques, as well as their inadequacy.

> How can you reduce the miracle of a plant's growth, an animal's adaptation or a child's activity to the principles governing the clash of two balls? ... So what a relief it was when Bergsonian sophisms, which were destined to end up in the most uncertain theology, came to the rescue of failing idealism! People enthusiastically ran after mechanism and materialism, and confused the problem to their heart's content. But what is surprising, once again, is to see Marxists taking their place in the chorus, by the circuitous route of dialectics, which can do nothing about it!

Nor will the related process of focusing on praxis-as-materiality/materiality-as-praxis square this circle. To be emphatic: such an approach – as for example in Vygotsky's insistence that '[w]e need to concentrate not on the *product* of development but on the very *process* by which the higher forms are established' – can be invaluable. It enriches thick description against currents of Marxist (and other) reductionism, not least in seeing human consciousness as intrinsically historical and sociological. What it cannot do is unlock the hard problem. Tran Duc Thao's claim, in *Phenomenology and Dialectical Materialism*, that '[t]he notion of production takes into full account the enigma of consciousness' is an unconvincing claim in a mostly remarkable book, one clear about the scale of the problem.

In *On Marx*, Paula Allman suggests that Marx's theory of consciousness 'is actually a theory of praxis', and 'when people sensuously engage with the material world, their thoughts and feelings, their objectives and subjective responses, are produced simultaneously'. Presumably aware that the astonishing final three words in that passage somewhat apologetically wave away precisely the mystery, Allman allows that 'thinking in terms of Marx's theory of consciousness ... can be difficult to express in human language'. That is undoubtedly true. But to the extent that it purports to be a theory (rather, again, than thick description), this too is word magic, of an apophatic kind.

Hart puts the problem trenchantly in *The Experience of God* (a book that, the allergic reaction its title might provoke in folk Marxism notwithstanding, should be required reading for anyone concerned with materialism and consciousness). With particular regard to emergence, 'one is really just talking about some marvelously inexplicable transition from the undirected, mindless causality of mechanistic matter to the intentional unity of consciousness. Talk of emergence in purely physical terms, then, really does not seem conspicuously better than talk of magic.'

Particularly and particularly clearly with respect to consciousness, strong emergence tout court, Hart would later write, in *All Things Are Full of Gods*,

> would be the appearance of entirely novel propensities that are wholly unrelated to the properties whose conjunction resulted in them – rather like the chanting of certain words, conjoined to certain herbs and eyes

> of newt and the light of a full moon, producing a magic castle. If we properly distinguish weak from strong emergence, what we'll find is that instances of the former abound – ... nature more or less consists in them – but that instances of the latter are absolutely nowhere to be found, and that what might occasionally look like a case of strong emergence is actually a case of formal causation.

Though this claim is routinely contested on the Left, as Naville has the clarity to point out, it is logically incontestable that there is simply no way, without some intervening mediation, 'dialectics' or what have you notwithstanding, that consciousness can 'emerge' from inert physical matter that possesses no such implicit properties. This 'emergence' is lux ex tenebris – a vulgar idealism at the heart of notionally sophisticated materialism. The folk Marxist, indeed the folk materialist, 'answers' to this do not explain anything: they merely evade the question.

☭

With strong emergence banished, and if materialism, consciously or not, is predicated on metaphysical materialism – which it need not be – a current arises that Galen Strawson calls 'the most extraordinary move that has ever been made in the history of human thought'. This is the turn to eliminative materialism.

In the words of Paul Churchland, one of its most esteemed representatives, alongside his wife Patricia Churchland, '[e]liminative materialism is the thesis that our commonsense conception of psychological phenomena constitutes a radically false theory ... so fundamentally defective that both [its] principles and ... ontology ... will eventually be displaced ... by completed neuroscience.' This solves the problem by dispensing with emergence, *by dispensing with consciousness*. As Avrum Stroll puts it, 'The correct view ... according to eliminative materialism, is that there are no mental states in the folk-psychological sense.' For eliminativists, too, there is no hard problem – because there is no consciousness at all (certainly in the sense with which that problem is concerned). At least they, unlike Pigliucci and other 'what hard problem?'-ists keen to disassociate themselves from eliminativism, recognise that the subjective, interiority itself, cannot be compartmentalised off as irrelevant. It must be banished.

A few necessary caveats. There is, of course, no unanimity among the eliminativists on the exact parameters of their position(s). There's disagreement about who is or is not, precisely speaking, an 'eliminativist'. Is Dennett an 'eliminativist' or a closely related 'illusionist', and what, and how important and fundamental, are the distinctions? There are differences among these radicals over whether what are being 'eliminated' are 'propositional states' – the mental states expressed by verbs such as 'believe x', 'fear y', etcetera – and/or qualia. Dennett is particularly emphatic on that latter point: 'contrary to what seems obvious at first blush', he writes in 'Quining Qualia', 'there simply are no qualia at all'.

For Paul Churchland, '[t]he concepts of folk psychology – belief, desire, fear, sensation, pain, joy, and so on – await a similar fate' to belief in witches – 'elimination from our serious ontology'. Of course, such mental states *comprise* consciousness not merely as we understand but as we experience it. Still, some, such as Dennett, claim that they are not saying consciousness does not exist, but that they would undermine its fallacies of self, the 'Cartesian theatre', that it is 'not what it seems'. The latter claim, however, is either thin to the point of vacuous and obviously true – who would deny that there are mysteries to consciousness? – or 'strong', and false, and ultimately about the non-existence of consciousness *tout court*. No wonder there are less shy eliminativists, like Michael Graziano, for whom '[c]onsciousness doesn't happen'. On such a basis, Thomas Metzinger in *Being No One* encourages us to 'give up the idea that we ever had anything like conscious minds in the first place'.

> The illusion is irresistible. Behind every face there is a self ... An essence. But ... the brute fact is there is nothing but material substance: flesh and blood and bone and brain...

> You look down into an open head, watching the brain pulsate ... and you understand with absolute conviction that there is nothing more to it. There's no one there.

For Keith Frankish, '[p]henomenal consciousness is a fiction written by our brains'.

> It is phenomenal consciousness that I believe is illusory. For science finds nothing qualitative in our brains, any more than in the world outside. The atoms in your brain aren't coloured and they don't compose a colourful inner image.

One reason for eliminativism's vogue is doubtless because it is scandalous and exciting, *pour épater le mainstream*. As such, it might even operate in some version as a not-uninteresting philosophical provocation – Chalmer's p-zombies are, effectively, the subjects of eliminativism with enough insightless insight not to be fooled by their own supposed selves. Perhaps the most satisfying presentation of eliminativism is as the reveal in Thomas Ligotti's horror short story 'The Shadow, the Darkness', proving yet again that flawed or fallacious theories can be the bases of rich art. But beyond this bohemian disreputability, it is also true that part of the appeal of eliminativism, counterintuitive as it is, is that it is more rigorous *qua* materialist metaphysics than emergence or similar magic. Kastrup lays out Frankish's position as follows (emphasis in the original).

> 1) Material things, in themselves, have no qualitative properties (like color, flavor, etc.), only our perceptions of them do;
> 2) The brain is a material thing;
> From 1) and 2), the brain has no qualitative properties;
> 3) Experience is reducible to the brain;
> From 3) and 4), experience cannot entail qualitative properties.
> Ergo, phenomenal consciousness *cannot* exist; it *must*, instead, be an illusion.

This gloss of Frankish is highly critical, but it is not the logic of the argument that Kastrup contests, but its predicates. As Hart points out, '[e]liminativists grasp – as many materialists are unable or unwilling to do – that a truly consistent materialism must inevitably reach just such a logical terminus.'

☭

It's perhaps no surprise, then, that in the work of some of the more ruthless Marxist materialists writing on consciousness, a certain proto-eliminativism can be discerned. For the leftist neuropsychiatrist Peter Stirling, according to a personal communication, 'if you read about neuro-philosophy, one of the only people who makes sense and knows both fields and writes beautifully is Patricia Churchland'. Naville, eighty years ago, though he does not explicitly eliminate consciousness, is palpably theoretically uneasy about its existence. In a remarkable prefiguration of Churchlandian dismissal of 'folk psychology', he ruefully allows that 'confining ourselves to using a given of acquired language', 'we will continue to use' the word 'consciousness' 'and we will wait until historical progress perhaps allows it to be replaced by notions more directly inspired by the realities in questions'. To avoid falling back into idealism, for Naville, 'there is only one path left for objective psychology, the one opened up by behaviourism, which does not consider psychology as the study of "mental facts", even if they are determined by being, but as the study of observable behaviour' – stripped of any interiority. In this way, focusing on behaviour '[t]here is no problem of consciousness'.

'We know that the metaphysicians,' Naville writes, 'inconsolable at having been forced to divorce themselves from psychology, did not give up so easily. Bergson, one of the great modern renovators of metaphysics, started from the pseudo-"immediate data of consciousness".' But the point is that whatever its manifold mysteries, in its very strangeness, notwithstanding that we can be wrong about our own thoughts, in the fact that even if it does in fact comprise illusions *so too does it that subjectivity which can be fooled thereby*, this is not only our only access to any data whatsoever, but is, in fact, immediate data, too.

'[T]he existentialists and phenomenologists have quite simply resurrected the Cartesian Cogito, making it the starting point for a new ontology', Naville complains. But one certainly doesn't have to, and shouldn't, have a naïve pre-Freudian view, sans the unconscious, narrowly rationalist, etcetera, to acknowledge that consciousness is occurring. There is one thin sense in which we should, indeed, all be Cartesian: we might well quibble with the 'therefore' in *Cogito Ergo Sum*, but by virtue of quibbling with, or considering, anything at all, ever, the cogito stands. I – we – think. Neurological data are invaluable – indispensable – but they neither explain nor eliminate such qualia.

Where the eliminative considers a 'thought' or 'emotion' better expressed in terms of underlying processes, such qualia, *whatever* their associated brain states – and/or historical and social context – *are* phenomena, and irreducibly so. Consciousness. Which repudiates eliminative materialism. When Dennett describes the 'illusion of consciousness', this raises the question of what is being 'fooled' by that illusion, if not a consciousness?

In *Consciousness Explained*, he claims that

> When an entity arrives on the scene capable of behaviour that staves off, however primitively, its own dissolution and decomposition, it brings into the world its own 'good'. That is to say, it creates a point of view from which the world's events can be roughly partitioned into the favourable, the unfavourable and the neutral. As the creature thus comes to have interests, the world and its events begin creating reasons for it, whether or not the creature can fully recognise them. The first reasons pre-existed their own recognition.

Curiously, here Dennett almost precisely replicates, from a materialist ontology, the trick diagnosed by Thao in Heidegger:

> the actual problem posed by the structure of intentionality – to know that the world is ideally in my consciousness when I am really in it – finds its immediate solution ... by a simple reordering of words, transforms the expression 'the world in which I am' into a moment of myself [though, as above, for Dennett an 'illusory' moment] inasmuch as I am precisely being-in-the-world.

If, as Thao puts it in his earlier work, this is 'the magic of language', Dennett's is fairly crude prestidigitation. Of all the philosophical heavy lifting being asked of the words and formulations in Dennett's position – poor bloated 'good', 'favourable', 'interests' and 'reasons' – perhaps the most remarkable is that blithe 'creates a point of view'. Here, again, the problem is restated as if it were its own solution.

In such fashion, eliminativism thus throws up its own category errors and sleights whenever it must deal with the inescapable facts of thought, including about itself. (This is not quite the facile barb that if thought is an illusion so are the thoughts about eliminativism.)

Some of these, to be generous, might be explained away as ordinary-language shorthands, as when Patricia Churchland – by no means an unserious thinker – suggests in a 2018 interview that rather than 'free will' we should use the 'fruitful and rewarding concept' of 'self-control'. This she suggests because there are 'particular brain regions' that 'cooperate and interact in order to suppress certain impulses that would be unproductive, for example'. Such a model of course raises questions such as 'Unproductive according to what ends?' and 'Ends reached by what agent?', and indeed is predicated on a 'self' to exercise control. This may be merely a holding term, but that would be to attempt to suppress a subjectivity that can only always-already return. When Paul Churchland suggests that with the elimination of folk psychology '[o]ur private introspection will ... be transformed, and may be profoundly enhanced by reason', it's notable that the privacy and introspection of that private introspection smuggles subjectivity back in.

Repeating the same manoeuvre, this time as ludicrous farce, is Brian Tomasik's effort in 'The Eliminativist Approach to Consciousness' – as part of his commitment to 'effective altruism', no less – to describe embodying an eliminativist epistemology, which he calls the physical stance.

> Try adopting the physical stance as you go about your day. When you have a particular feeling or become aware of a particular object, think about what kinds of neural operations are occurring in your head ... My experience with this exercise is that it soon becomes less weird ... It feels more intuitive that, yes, I am an active, intelligent collection of cells whose sharing and processing of signals constitutes the inner life of my mind and allows for a vast repertoire of behaviors. Worries that I should be a zombie vanish, because I can feel what it's like to be physics for what it is. In fact, being physics feels just like it always did when I thought consciousness was somehow special ... Yes, the neurons in my brain are doing particular kinds of processing that other clumps of atoms in the world are not, and this explains why these thoughts show up in my head and not in the floor or a beetle outside. ... We can import some phenomenal-stance intuitions when thinking about what parts of physics we want to think of as 'suffering', but we don't trip ourselves up over trying to pigeonhole suffering as being something other than an attribution we make to whirlpools within the ocean of physics.

The risibly vulgar voluntarism here lies in thinking that despite the fact that, as Paul Churchland himself has it, 'folk psychology has enjoyed no significant changes in well over 2,000 years', you can think yourself out of this subjectivity, constitutive of human consciousness as we and the eliminativists know it, if you *try real hard*. Tomasik breezily disgraces the very philosophy he purports to practice in his own exposition thereof. He reduces eliminative materialism to 'believing in physicalism'. He seems not to grasp that those very moments of reflection he describes as his success are their own inevitable failure. To think oneself 'a chunk of physics' is still to think, and to have a 'oneself' to do it with, with the interiority and subjectivity eliminativism eliminates. Tomasik's banalised eliminativism slides into a distinct position: that 'being physics feels just like it always did when I thought consciousness was something special.' This is to return to a Pigliucci-ite 'what hard problem?' standpoint. Which, especially for a self-described eliminativist, immediately raises the question 'Feels like *to what?*'

In Richard Seymour's words, 'Eliminative materialism presupposes the very subject that it tries to eliminate: for there to be a theatre of consciousness which beguiles us with impressions derived from physical impulses there has to be an observer to be beguiled'. To quote Hart, at his most waspish,

> the arcane idea that somewhere out there, in principle at least, there exists an infinite narrative of physical particularities that could supplant all references to unified states of consciousness, without any empirical remainder – is not so much audacious as hallucinatory. At the apex of the mind, so to speak, there is the experience of consciousness as an absolutely singular and indivisible reality, which no inventory of material constituents and physical events will ever be able to eliminate. Here again, and as nowhere else, we are dealing with an irreducibly primordial datum.

☭

This is the 'qualiaphilia' criticised by Dennett – who disputes that qualia exist – and (though not from within eliminativism) by Ray Brassier. For Brassier, whose critical engagement is forbidding, the

> appeal to the self-evident transparency of appearance conveniently dispenses with the need for justification by insisting that we all already know 'what it's like' for something to appear to us, or for something 'to be *like*' something for us ... It is this seeming, and not its constitutive conditions, that has to be accounted for 'in its own terms' ... But what are 'their own terms'? Precisely the terms concomitant with the first-person phenomenological point of view. ... But how exactly are we supposed to describe appearance strictly in its own terms, without smuggling in any extrinsic, objectifying factors?

I want to suggest that this is an implicit and, in this discussion, common elision of *understanding* with *experience*. We see it also when Metzinger decries a sense of

> ongoing conspiracy in the philosophical community, an organised form of self-deception, as in a cult, to simply all together pretend that we knew what 'first-person perspective' (or ... 'consciousness') means, so that we can keep our traditional debates running on forever.

To argue that qualia and mental states, those definitional phenomena of internal subjectivity, are not merely sometimes mistaken in content or misleading in form but *do not exist* is to deny not the content but the fact of consciousness as it is experienced. To acknowledge this phenomenal experience is not of course to ludicrously suggest that all beliefs or feelings, including about oneself, are reasonable, or accurate, or adequate, or helpful. But some eliminationists, however, such as Michael Graziano, even more explicitly conflate that absurd conclusion with the critique of phenomenal consciousness itself – subjectivity. Consciousness is 'a mistaken construct'. 'He starts by talking about subjective experience – i.e. phenomenal consciousness, which is what science can't explain', Kastrup glosses, 'just to end up explaining something else entirely: our ability to cognise ourselves as agents and metacognitively represent our own mental contents.' Effectively this is to inflate the errancy or elusive nature of beliefs and feelings into the eliminationist conclusion that they are not 'really', in fact, beliefs or feelings. As Hart puts it with regard to Dennett, because no imagined subject

> has any infallibly direct access to his private intuitions, hence ... there are no qualia at all. But this is simply a non-sequitur. No one doubts that qualitative states of consciousness can be altered by changes both in the objects of perception or in one's organs of perception, or that they may not be constant throughout one's life; but that does not mean that such states do not exist.

Indeed, errancies, alterations and inadequacies are inextricable to phenomenal consciousness, and should be probed. This leaves space to make part of the exploration of actually-existing phenomenal consciousness ideology, the deep 'real abstractions' which structure the experiences of and consciousness in social life, and perhaps even also relationships between what Wilfred Sellars (an important figure to eliminativism) called the 'scientific' and the 'manifest image' of the world and humanity, including the latter's inadequacies and folk psychological aspects.

But the fundamental point about qualia is not that we already know 'what it's like' to experience them. Indeed, that is an extraordinary mystery. Rather, it is simply that it is *like something at all*. If that is true – and it is true – then eliminativism is false.

☭

So what now?

Metaphysical idealism of course remains a bogeyman for folk Marxism. Anecdotally, this is evidenced in the repeated and scornful deployment in Marxist spaces (echoing Einstein's uneasy response to quantum entanglement) of the adjective 'spooky' at the suggestion of any possible non-material elements to consciousness. A spectre is haunting materialism.

This is no surprise. And common sense, including Marxist common sense, will not help here. (When did it ever?) The thunderbolt of the hard problem is real, for all the various edgelord assertions that it is not a problem at all. But this is a negative satori for the materialist, and no particular positive paradigm leaps forward to solve the problem.

'I do not claim that idealism is plausible', Chalmers allows in his own long rumination 'Idealism and the Mind-Body Problem'. But he goes on. 'No position on the mind-body problem is plausible.' That indeed is the rub.

> Materialism: implausible. Dualism: implausible. Idealism: implausible …. None of the above: implausible. But the probabilities of all these views get a boost from the fact that one … must be true. Idealism is not significantly less plausible than its main competitors … there is a non-negligible probability that it is true.'

There are, if you like, no good options, certainly for the folk Marxist. This is one of those times when the task must be, in the words of a fashionable left injunction regularly intoned but rarely observed, to stay with the trouble.

☭

Of course one might argue that moving away from a metaphysically materialist theory of the mind needn't make a great difference to life 'as a Marxist'. As has already been argued, this is not an obligatory field of interest, and its absence as such need not cause any particular hiccups in the work of solidarity and activism, or intellectual or artistic pursuits. Three Marxists can act together in solidarity, can theorise and debate in comradely fashion on the Temporal Single Systems approach to the transformation problem, or the role of uneven and combined development to modern imperialism, or strategies for Palestine solidarity, while two fervently disagree on the metaphysics of consciousness, and the third doesn't care. Certainly, however, accepting the inadequacy of metaphysical materialism should impact work closer to that wheelhouse. One might suggest, for example, and for all Naville's concerns about this very move, that in placing centrally the conscious experience of the world, such a paradigm could usefully promote a revival of a Marxist phenomenology, say. A return, perhaps, to Michel Henry's *Marx: A Philosophy of Human Reality*, or Tran Duc Thao, whose text's dutiful stated commitments to metaphysical materialism are largely epiphenomenal to the succulence of the work therein. And the criticism of metaphysical materialist theories of consciousness here clearly has implications for knotted (and ill-named) questions of 'free will' and determinism and even ethics, among other areas, which are obviously relevant to Marxism.

Most directly of all, Richard Seymour, also quaking from his encounter with the Hart Event, has begun to produce remarkable pieces contesting any notion that such a philosophical turn is too abstract to much impact Marxism as theory or practice. In fact this essay is, to some extent, intended to serve as a post-factum philosophical ground-clearing for Seymour's recent work on a Marxist approach adequate to such consciousness of consciousness, in 'Marxism and Freedom'; 'Freedom and Consciousness'; 'Duel and Duality, or, Degrowth and Dialectics'; his extended series on 'How to Survive a Mass Extinction'; and the remarkable short piece 'Mailbag #2: Theological Remnant', all on Patreon.

☭

Of course the claims here should all stand or fall on their own merits. That said, Marxism – though, to be fair, hardly Marxism alone – is a field in which authority and permission have outsized weight. So the question of Marx's own position is important, and vexed.

How right is Etienne Balibar to say, in *The Philosophy of Marx*, that 'Marx's materialism has nothing to do with a reference to matter'?

With close reading and insight, Sheehan contends at length 'that Marx considered himself to be in accord with Engels in philosophical orientation and shared his explicit materialism and his conception of the dialectics of nature'. But this claim is ultimately unconvincing. Sheehans' citations of Marx's attention to technology and science are underwhelming on this point, unless metaphysical non-materialism and naturalism are automatically counterposed, which need not be the case. Her claim that 'Marx repeatedly stated his explicit adherence to materialism' is true, of course, but the question is precisely what materialism? She makes the important point that Marx did not disassociate himself from Engels' *Anti-Dühring*, with its explicitly metaphysical materialism, and indeed he read and commented on the manuscript. But it doesn't necessarily follow that this is evidence of his agreement therewith: George Kline has listed several other possible reasons for this absence of dispute, among them a disinclination to argue over abstruse matters; loyalty to a friend; and/or even a sense that Engels' work on this was too weak to be worth debating.

That last claim in particular seems a stretch. As well as commenting on Engels's work in these areas, he encouraged him towards the project that would ultimately become the *Dialectics of Nature*. And Marx himself certainly at times expressed views that seem to chime with Engels's project to extend their historic system beyond that sphere, or understand it as derived from beyond it: 'My standpoint', he wrote in the 1867 preface to the German edition of *Capital* volume one, for example, is one 'from which the evolution of the economic formation of society is viewed as a process of natural history'. But his own investment in these questions was never equal to Engels', and what's of even more importance is that *whatever* Marx thought of Engels' system, or thought he thought, if anything, while it is not irrelevant, is by no means the close of the debate. Marx is hardly the only thinker sometimes wrong about aspects of their own thought, after all.

It might mollify heresy-hunters to go back to Miliband's observations about the less ambitious materialisms in Marxism. We must remember that there have always been traditions and understandings of Marxism, including that of Marx, *not*, even explicitly not, predicated on metaphysical materialism, in sharp contradistinction to the more voluble and familiar folk Marxism. Leszek Kolakowski distinguishes Plekhanov from 'most West European Marxists' of his time, 'who saw no logical connection between Marxism as a theory of social development and any particular view of epistemological or metaphysical questions'. Terry Eagleton, in his recent book on the subject, *Materialism*, puts the matter simply and unapologetically: 'Historical materialism is not an ontological affair. It does not assert that everything is made out of matter'.

Max Horkheimer, in 1933, in 'Materialism and Metaphysics', which does not focus exclusively on Marxist materialism but does encompass it, and draws explicitly and fruitfully on dialectical methods, criticises 'most of the philosophical representatives of materialism' for 'starting with metaphysical questions and setting up their own theses in opposition to idealist positions'. By contrast, for Horkheimer, 'any interpretation of the materialist orientation of thought which sees it primarily as an answer to metaphysical questions will be unable to grasp those characteristics of it which are the most important ones today'. This philosophical humility was spurred in Horkheimer precisely by the intractability for materialism of the hard problem, as his extensive quotations illustrate. His position, in Marlte Frøslee Ibsen's words, is 'the meta-philosophical insight that human thought is always conditioned by the social and historical context from which it emerges' – a more humble historical materialism than metaphysical.

Such insights, of course, don't necessarily presume any particular positive alternative theories, but their rejection of metaphysical materialism is hardly unimportant. Particularly when a similar move is detectable in Marx himself.

In his 2018 piece 'Is Marx a Materialist', the philosopher, including of Marxism, Tom Rockmore, in a close examination, finds that Marx 'says little about materialism', and 'he does not use this term in standard fashion as an ontological designation for the building blocks of the universe'. He is clear that metaphysical materialism 'is unimportant for Marx but central for Marxism' – what

I've called folk Marxism. It's such an understanding that, in his introduction to Paul Reitter's 2024 translation of *Capital* volume one, leads Paul North to discern in Marx the position that 'materialism ... should ... mean neither the primacy of basic physical elements like atoms, nor the primacy of objects presented to human perception, but "sensuous practical activity by human beings"'.

Earlier substantial important work in the vein of Rockmore's includes Frederick Bender's 1983 'Marx, Materialism and the Limits of Philosophy' and Alison Assiter's 1979 'Philosophical Materialism or the Materialist Conception of History'. Marx's historical materialism, Bender writes, 'contains certain basic assumptions about man [sic], society, labor, production and nature', but is predicated on a 'social-historical, rather than philosophical, sense of the term "materialism"'. For Bender, indeed, Marx himself – if incompletely – in his *system* (which is to say, whatever he may have believed) repudiated ontological materialism and metaphysics *tout court*. For Assiter, similarly, Marx's materialism 'is not a philosophical materialism of any sort', 'is neither an ontological nor an epistemological theory, but is an empirical theory about human beings in history', which 'should be construed as a kind of "naturalism"'. Alfred Schmidt, in his brilliant and seminal *The Concept of Nature in Marx*, titles the trenchant opening chapter, and dedicates its textual and logical argument to presenting, 'The Non-Ontological Character of Marxist Materialism'. For Marx's model, he argues, it is '[n]ot the abstract nature of matter, but the concrete nature of social practice is the true subject and basis of materialist theory'.

Even Naville himself, countervailing his draw to a proto-eliminativism, at least glimpses an alternative, similarly anti-metaphysical, and thus as has been argued here more fruitful, way out of the impasse. His focus on 'behaviour' might diminish the importance of consciousness, but might also be, as he clearly hopes, a way to *bypass* the ontological questions it throws up: '[W]e consider it essential not to allow ourselves to be imposed upon by the great melodramas of metaphysics'.

The fact is that Marx, despite his background in philosophy, had no deep interest in metaphysics one way or another, particularly after the 1840s – again, whatever he may have thought he thought. His system was of a more limited kind. Kline, in his extremely important 1988 essay 'The Myth of Marx' Materialism', assiduously taxonomises Marx's uses of the term 'material', picking apart its various meanings, distinguishing Marx's uses from Engels', and persuasively denies that there 'is evidence of, or support for, a materialist ontology provided by Marx's colloquially "materialistic" turns of phrase'. Kline goes further, critically examining what he calls Engels' 'tendentious editing' of *Capital* volume one in its English translation, comparing it to the first French translation, with which Marx was closely involved, to underline misleading 'metaphysical' implications that Engels brought into Marx's text. Kline makes his conclusions as plain as he can:

> I am denying that Marx, even the youngest Marx, was a philosophical materialist, i.e., a theorist who develops or defends a materialist ontology, asserting the ontological primacy of matter and explaining whatever appears to common sense to be non-material (e.g., thoughts, feelings, values, ideals, structures, laws) as manifestations, functions, or relational properties of 'matter in motion'. Thus a less elliptical and more explicit, if also more unwieldy, formulation of my title would be 'The Mythical Claim that Marx Developed or Defended a Materialist Ontology'.

☭

Just as there is a cottage industry in Marxist attacks on Engels, so too is there in his defence, and, often concomitantly, in the minimisation of the distinctions between the two authors. No such police are needed here: Engels is indispensable to Marxism, often wildly ahead of his time, highly perspicacious. But his materialism was not identical to Marx's. It went further – too far.

Engels's apparently simple claim that '[m]atter is nothing but the totality of material things from which their concept is abstracted' provokes Sheehan's impressive exposition of a more nuanced Engels than is traditionally allowed, and chimes with a similar approach by Joseph Ferraro, in 'Engels as an Ontological Materialist', wherein he stresses elements of Engels' materialism not as reductive but as 'a general world outlook resting upon a definite conception of matter and mind' – at least potentially a less closed conception. Sheehan insists that for Engels, matter was not 'a *materia prima* ... a substratum', but 'an abstraction' that 'did not depend on a notion of prime matter'.

Still, and even where that might have led him in other directions, it is also the case that, in his own words, his materialism 'means nothing more than the simple conception of nature just as it is, without alien addition'. Lying in bed he announced to himself that 'the subject matter of natural science [is] matter in motion, bodies'. In his book on Feuerbach, Engels is clear that 'our consciousness and thinking, however supra-sensuous they may seem, are the product of a material, bodily organ, the brain'.

Ferraro emphatically denies that Engels is an ontological materialist, and he and Sheehan certainly complicate the story. But the most generous statement we can make is that Engels can be ambiguous. It would be tendentious to deny, at minimum, a strong pull towards metaphysical materialism in Engels, even if it is also sometimes countervailed. That this has been a seminal reading of his texts is not mere misreading.

And in any case, however generous one is inclined to be to him, at issue here is less what *he* thought, than the elision of historical and metaphysical materialism overall. To the extent that Engels may have avoided this, he was right. To the extent that he succumbed, he was wrong. As, whatever his responsibility for it, is folk Marxism.

It's no surprise that Engels, more than any other figure, haunts this problematic. The development of his metaphysical materialism was a multi-text project, of which the extraordinary, ambitious, insightful, tendentious and unfinished *Dialectics of Nature* remains a keystone. The sprawling debate around whether or not Engels' application of dialectics to and discernment of dialectical motion in nature holds up and/or is dispensable to Marxism continues. The problem, for the metaphysically materialist Marxist, is that neither Yes nor No is an adequate answer. 'On the one hand', to quote Seymour (in a personal correspondence), 'his extension of the dialectic to nature is "idealist". On the other hand, his critics are "idealist" because ... how can the dialectic apply only to human beings when humans are thoroughly material?' Thus Gramsci, taking Lukacs to task for his criticism of the dialectics of nature: '[I]f human history should be conceived also as the history of nature, how can the dialectic be separated from nature?' In fact, more than one solution to this conundrum is possible, from within historical materialism itself – but only at the expense of metaphysical materialism.

Some understanding of this, an obverse to folk Marxism, even survives in the swirl of what Brassier has called the 'online orgy of stupidity'. In response to Eunomiacus' question, certain Marxist interlocutors on Reddit were perfectly cheerful in proclaiming that 'materialism isn't necessarily an absolute metaphysical truth", or even that '[o]ntology doesn't matter at all.'

☭

Rather than anyone so admirably unflustered as these cheerful red Redditeers, who'd be justified in thinking this is an awful lot of sound and fury to argue for the obvious, these final remarks are addressed to my own past self and those in a similar place. Of whom I know there are many.

For a long time I proceeded according to folk Marxism, on the vague, gestural sense that historical materialism was undergirded by metaphysical materialism. This didn't, I hope, and doesn't, preclude having attempted worthwhile activism or writing. But it is not predicated on rigorous metaphysics. Which – as the anti-metaphysical historical materialists above might attest – is fine as far as it goes: but it is less so if it *believes* itself to be so predicated. And even in the best case, that can only go so far. Once you become interested in consciousness, then things tend to go bump in the night.

There is of course a rhetorical flex in claiming not to like the implications of your own analysis, but to push on regardless, because facts, famously, don't care about your feelings. With apologies, therefore, for any such seeming pose, I'll allow that when I first realised I'd argued my way out of a metaphysically materialist theory of mind, my resulting shakenness reminded me of CS Lewis describing himself at the arrival of his Christian faith as 'the most dejected and reluctant convert in all England'. Because such a position leads, as Richard Seymour has put it, to 'alarming things'.

But one can recover from shocks, and thrive in their aftermath. Now, when I shake at the implications it is with excitement

☭

To review, the key claims here are threefold, and negative: i) contrary to prevailing opinion, Marxist and not, metaphysical materialism cannot account for human consciousness: ii) contrary to a contrarian wing of radical materialist theory, consciousness exists; iii) contrary to folk Marxism, Marxist historical materialism need not be (and in Marx's writings is not, and given i) and ii) cannot be) predicated on metaphysical materialism.

What, if anything, one does with these data is left entirely open.

It's to be hoped that one result of the triple-claim above, for those Marxists who find themselves still worrying at these questions, is a diminution of a certain traditional philistinism with regard to and/or traducing of non-materialist metaphysics and theories. Idealism in particular – given the caveats about dualism noted above – is a vast and complex field, stretching back lifetimes and undergoing something of a renaissance. Fluss and Frimm are tenacious and thoughtful Marxist proponents of the importance of metaphysics, and my contestation of the materialist metaphysics they espouse is mostly from a position of comradely admiration. But their claim, defending Engels' materialism, not only that '[s]ubjective thoughts and ideas do not freely produce themselves, but instead are produced by and reflect the material world around us', but further that '[t]o say otherwise is to lapse into an irrationalist panpsychism, where a vitalistic spirit (not material cause and effect) is what animates reality', is a swingeing parody of much, let alone the best, idealist thought. Metaphysical idealism need not be anti-realist, scientifically speaking. It cannot be assumed away, nor materialism assumed, according to a mistranslation of scientific methodology into ontology (a mistranslation of which, to be sure, much modern science is guilty). When Creaven says, 'I take it that the lack of scientific support for any "mind-first" understanding of the universe is sufficient proof of the *necessity* of a materialist ontology of being', the emphasis is his, and startlingly weak logic. Subjective, Objective, Transcendental, Analytical, Absolute Idealism, among many others, and their associated figures, whether disputed or not, are all worthy of respectful engagement, beyond any traditional leftist snickering about ghosts.

Even more ripe for dismissal is the rote, still common Marxist accusation that metaphysical non-materialism has an inexorable gravitational pull to both irrationalism and political reaction, by a baleful chain, expressed by Lewis with vividly paternalist racecraft.

> The absence of materialism, let alone idealist metaphysics, opens the floodgates to every form of superstition ... Instead of seeking out the scientific causes of disease the man [sic] who believes in the supernatural may attribute it to black magic, or devils. ... Natives in Central Africa when they fail in their primitive methods of iron-smelting do not try to find out what technical error they have made, but attribute their failure to someone having bewitched them. ... Eventually science is held to be something blasphemous. ... If it should be contrary to the interests of any privileged section of the community to remove these evils, it will be seen how the superstition which paralyzes man's efforts serves their ends. In this fact we have, perhaps, one of the reasons for the revival of idealism in an age in which many social evils exist and in which the remedies at hand conflict with vested interests.... In sociology ... the interests of the privileged may be immediately threatened by sound social theory. In

that case it will be desirable that knowledge should be clouded and human power to interfere enfeebled. This does not mean, of course, that every idealist is consciously defending his cash interests or the interests of a privileged class, but it does suggest that in a society ruled by and ideologically dominated by such interests there will be a certain pressure or drift away from scientific social thinking and towards idealism, superstition and supernaturalism, and that the greater the danger of social change, the more widespread will superstition tend to become.

If not expressed in like manner, such a hermeneutic of anti-idealist suspicion vividly colours many folk-Marxist attacks. Also comprising such attacks, to be fair, is a considerably more reasonable anti-clericalism, and agon against certain forms of conspiracism. Because certainly superstition and 'irrationalism' *can* be, and often are, powerful engines of reaction, but their elision with metaphysical idealism is not only philosophically incoherent, but a political insult to the countless revolutionaries and comrades simply agnostic on metaphysical claims, let alone to those politically motivated in part by religious faith.

In his book on materialism, Eagleton opens his discussion of ontology with a typical provocation, bringing in one of the most celebrated – holy – ghosts of all. 'It is worth noting', he writes, 'that historical materialists need not be atheists, though many of them seem curiously ignorant of the fact.'

That ignorance is itself evidence of the tenacity of folk Marxism. Marx's atheism is well attested, of course, but was inflected less by metaphysical materialism than by a Promethean and even ethical anthropocentrism, an analysis and criticism of alienation. As Vanessa Wills puts it, quoting Marx himself, it was

> not primarily as an ontological stance on the existence or non-existence of God, but rather as part and parcel of a philosophical worldview radically committed to

> sweeping such questions aside, to ... centering the human perspective, to overthrowing 'all relations in which man [sic] is a debased, enslaved, forsaken, despicable being'.

A splendid and inspiring radical humanist urge, but one without much to say about origins or ontology.

This opens onto potential programs for further research far beyond these concluding gestures here. And if the recovering erstwhile folk Marxism sets out, as appropriate, with *docta ignorantia*, a new learned ignorance, they do not of course have to become a theist. Even if persuaded of the aporia of metaphysical materialism, it is perfectly possible to formulate, to quote the title of one of Helen Yetter-Chappell's essays, an 'Idealism without God'.

But with that in mind, and remembering also Chalmers' wry observations about the implausibility of all conceivable options to make sense of consciousness, one thing is undeniable. Once you've argued your way out of an ontologically materialist universe, of the many varieties of metaphysical idealism on offer, theism is probably not the least unlikely.

Of course, it also raises its own manifold problems, not least that of theodicy – evil. But of all Richard's 'alarming things' perhaps the most so is that theism also, in fact, solves an awful lot of problems that most other varieties of idealism retain. And it does so almost definitionally by fiat.

DANIEL ANDRÉS LÓPEZ

# The True Infinite and the Republic of Virtue

**What do Marxists talk about when they talk about love?**\*

> The philosophers have only interpreted the world, in various ways; the point is to change it.
> – Karl Marx, 'Theses On Feuerbach'

> theory also becomes a material force as soon as it has gripped the masses. Theory is capable of gripping the masses as soon as it demonstrates ad hominem, and it demonstrates ad hominem as soon as it becomes radical. To be radical is to grasp the root of the matter.
> – Karl Marx, 'A Contribution to the Critique of Hegel's Philosophy of Right'

Hitherto, Marxists have changed the world in ways that they did not understand, predict or desire. Regardless of how one feels about

---

\* For E.B.

the Soviet Union or the People's Republic of China, the obvious truth is that every Marxist current has failed to realise even its most minimum program. Marxist apologetics for this failure are usually moralistic and evasive, blaming defeats on other Marxists' failure to accept their specific brand of Marxism. Or perhaps claiming circumstances were to blame and future struggles will vindicate their true, revolutionary theory. Yet however much they change, changed circumstances never seem to demand that Marxism changes – at least not in its essentials. Thus clad in the conviction that theirs is the solution to the riddle of history, Marxists of various stripes stand chest-deep in the sea of current events and decry the rising tide. Such materialists, it seems, speak more from the heart than experience – and less to be heard than to drown out the crashing waves and their own doubts.

What Marxist accounts of the failure of Marxism avoid is introspection: consequently, Marxist rhetoric and analysis becomes predictable and dogmatic. In Hegel's language, Marxism is the thought of an ethical-political community that represents its purpose as a future both immanent and unrealised (revolution, communism, etcetera), knowledge of which is vouchsafed by 'lessons', unchanging and inherited. Their circularity is that of a 'bad infinity' that does not recognise its repetition. In Marx's language,

> just as they seem to be occupied with revolutionising themselves and things, creating something that did not exist before ... they anxiously conjure up the spirits of the past to their service.

Which is to say that, unlike Marx and Hegel, Marxists are traditionalists. This is why Marxist organisation and practice, too, like Marxist discourse, is repetitious and nostalgic. But their rhetoric notwithstanding, the Marxist movement is marginal. Perhaps this explains why, when Marxists talk about the organisations they build, they sound jealous. As Marx wrote, it is 'all the more clear what we have to accomplish at the present: the *ruthless criticism* of all that exists.' Marxism exists. It is not exempt. And as Marx also explained, being radical means grasping 'the root of the matter,' and 'the root is man himself.' It stands to reason, then, that we should start with Marx himself, and seek out his blind-spots and self-contradictions.

This is what lies behind the juxtaposition of the two quotes at the start of this essay, from 1845 and 1843 respectively. As Hannah Arendt observed in 'Karl Marx and the Tradition of Western Political Thought,' when we encounter in a great philosopher's work a flagrant and obvious self-contradiction – one they fail to notice themselves – it discloses the unthought essence of their idea, indicating both their motivator and their limit.

The first quote above, the famous eleventh thesis, disparages philosophy in the name of world-changing practice. The second quote promises the transubstantiation of sufficiently critical philosophy into a 'material force,' provided it can grip the masses by 'going to the root of the matter.' For the former, theory is impotent before practice. For the latter, practice grants radical theory potency.

Here, the antinomy between theory and practice is presented in a stark, dichotomised manner. So which is it to be? Or, are both claims true, the truth of each annihilating that of the other? If so, such unity of opposites implies a third, reconciling concept, namely, 'critical-practical activity' – more simply, 'praxis'. For Marxists, that usually means 'revolution': after all, critical-practical activity is also involved in cooking, playing guitar or writing poetry – but those aren't what Marxists usually talk about when they talk about what they love.

Praxis, in the Marxist sense, is the revolutionary reconciliation between theory and practice. But after the sublime zenith of revolution – about which Marxists speak most lovingly – the two poles fall apart again. So, bereft of the material force of the masses, those who hold on to the idea of praxis go forth again to seek the practice that completes their idea. For all their ardour, this search rarely goes well.

'The point is to change it', concludes every Marxist propagandist, having explained at length why members of a rival sect are not Marxists. Perhaps, then, the issue is not so much one of doctrine *per se* – at any rate, such disputes between Marxists typically go nowhere. Perhaps the problem is that disputation is what they regard as politics. It's not what they are saying, but that they choose to spend so much time saying it: maybe such repetition points to a problem of practice. After all, as Antonio Gramsci pointed out in his *Prison Notebooks*, 'the active man-in-the-mass' is frequently held back by a theoretical consciousness 'explicit or verbal which he has inherited from the past and uncritically absorbed'. Such consciousness 'holds together a specific social group … [and] influences moral conduct and the direction of the will', indeed, often powerfully enough to 'produce a condition of moral and political passivity'. What better account could there be of the deadening relation between theory and practice that afflicts the various Marxist currents and their most loyal proponents?

To revolution*ise* practice, then, it behoves us to remove theoretical roadblocks. The problem is that Marxists are only inclined towards theory insofar as it is confirmed by revolutionary practice. Which, although they speak of it lovingly, is something that the vast majority of them know only from books, articles and meetings – that is, theoretically.

The problem, then, is circular. And love forbids that the circle be broken.

So, instead, what if we follow it – what if we Return To Marx? After all, Marxists love returning to Marx. But usually they do so in the name of rediscovering the 'true' Marx, perhaps by emphasising one element of his thought (alienation, say, or the steam engine or the value form). Alternatively, they might pursue this by excluding 'sub-Marxist' aspects of Marx's oeuvre (say, pre-*Capital* or post-Engels Marx). Either way, the Marx to whom they return tends curiously to validate the outlook of their preferred sect or international. Any merits aside, such 'returns' are incomplete insofar as they ventriloquise Marx to legitimate contemporary Marxisms.

The obvious alternative is a Complete Return To Marx, one that excludes nothing and adds nothing. But the more seriously Marxists attempt this, the more they begin to resemble characters in a postmodern novel: must we really nod earnestly as a future presenter at Historical Materialism insists on the importance of *Herr Vogt*? Must we really include the long-lost 'Shopping List of 10 December 1854' in the *Marx-Engels-Gesamtausgabe*? Surely, the line must be drawn – but where?

Instead of this endless comedy, what I propose is a Speculative Return to Marx. Although I mean 'speculative' in the sense of Hegelian philosophy, I don't propose to deploy Hegel's method upside down, as Marx and the Hegelian Marxists have attempted. Rather, a Speculative Return to Marx should read his work as a conceptual whole, in light of its contradictions and their development through history, and in light of our own present vantagepoint. Because if Marx was right, the implication is that he grasped concepts that were true then and remain so now. And/but if Marx was right, then concepts are only true insofar as they change with history, past and present. We must read Marx, then, both conceptually and historically, in light of his time and our own.

Such an approach is part of what Hegel meant by speculation, and it presupposes the standpoint he first outlined in *The Phenomenology of Spirit*: that of philosophy. And before I am accused of divided affections, let us be clear that this standpoint isn't an external addition, but is implicit in Marx himself. Hegel was, after all, his first philosophical love.

The standpoint of speculative philosophy does not presume to educate Marx about those topics with which he deals most admirably, such as political economy. Nor does it claim political practice as the ground of its truth. Although acquainted with the fields, Hegel was neither an economist nor a revolutionary. Philosophy, in his sense, does not speak as a politician to the masses, nor does it presume to grant specialist knowledge. Instead, philosophy in the speculative sense is a discourse that cultivates our ability to reflect on the concepts that we use for the most part intuitively and uncritically. Speculative philosophy attempts to think concepts as such, as well as in their relation to the spheres of human experience and knowledge that condition and are reciprocally conditioned by them. It attempts to render explicit the unthought relations implicit in concepts that are presented immediately, and in abstract opposition to each other – for example, as Marx presents theory and practice in his 1840s writings.

The goal here is not to overturn Marxist concepts, but to elevate Marxist discourse to genuinely philosophical self-reflexivity, that its concepts may sustain their truth in contradiction. Marxists have no trouble speaking about what they love. But they do need to learn how to listen: to themselves, and, more importantly, to the reply of their beloved.

☭

Given its conceptual wealth, Marxism is a magnificent candidate for such a philosophical procedure. For the most part, however, Marxism has rejected philosophy. At worst, it has regarded philosophy as superseded, bourgeois and contemplative; at best, as a propaedeutic to historical materialism, or as a distant, secondary terrain for class struggle. Consequently, having discarded the sphere of knowledge most suited to cultivating conceptual self-reflexivity, Marxists have tended to develop and use their concepts myopically.

Sensing that they are sailing as ships in the night, Marxist theorists have often tried to materially anchor their concepts. But matter is *also* a concept, and like those it is supposed to anchor, it has a tendency to dissolve and give way to others. Some Marxists have tried other determinate material concepts in its place, including nature, economic statistics or class relations. But the problem is that these concepts only speak through people – that is, through those Marxists who articulate them. Consequently, Marxists purport to speak for reality when they nominate one 'material' substratum as essential – and in so doing, they substitute their concept for reality, misrecognising both. Their theory becomes an ideology masking unfree thought and practice.

Philosophy, by contrast, does not promise ultimate grounds or perfect practice. What it does offer is a vantagepoint from which we can re-cognise – that is, re-think – concepts and practices, precisely, in so doing, so as to de-fetishise them. In this way, speculative philosophy is as much a doctrine as it is a practice of knowing. It helps us grasp the concealed logic operating behind theory, to separate the rational kernel of Marxism from irrational chaff. Immanent critique is a cure by love.

When criticising Marx's dichotomies speculatively, the point isn't to come down on one side or another: rather, speculative philosophy grasps dichotomies from the point of view of what Hegel called the absolute idea, precisely in order to posit the truth of both sides in light of their opposition and mutual negation. The absolute idea is the totality of truth, both its result and its development. And because the absolute idea is life that knows itself as life, no attempt to articulate it finally can succeed. As Gillian Rose stated in *Hegel Contra Sociology*, to know the absolute is to fail to know it. As she explained,

> The absolute is the comprehensive thinking which transcends the dichotomies between concept and intuition, theoretical and practical reason. It cannot be thought (realised) because these dichotomies and their determination are not realised.
>
> Once we realise this we can think the absolute by acknowledging the element of *Sollen* [ought] in such a thinking, by acknowledging the subjective element, the limits on our thinking the absolute.

Absolute knowledge, then, is a kind of thinking that attempts systematically to know its own limit and, in knowing it, to transcend it. It is reason that has grasped its own concept, negativity, in relation to what exists. It is a true infinite; a circle whose completion is self-recognition and whose movement is non-identity. This is what Hegel talked about when he talked about love.

Marxism exhibits the same movement but without the subjective moment of self-recognition. Marxists relate negatively to what is, in the name of an 'ought' (revolution, communism, etcetera), but without grasping the determinate connection between what *ought* to be and what *is*. To be sure, Marx defined communism as the immanent result of proletarian class struggle. But as he soon added, it could only be realised insofar as the proletariat is organised into a communist party. Consequently, the communist 'ought,' depends on something contingent beyond what is; namely, Marxist organisation. The immanent result of proletarian class struggle, then, becomes a prophecy whose realisation depends on the Marxists themselves. After all, communism may be immanent to history and capitalism, but communist organisation is not. It depends on the political will of Marxists who choose to build parties. In this way, the Marxist 'ought' thus conceals a secularised political Calvinism: freedom is the immanent *telos* of hitherto history *only* insofar as Marxists carry out their predetermined duty.

In short, God is history, heaven is communism, Saint Peter is Marx – and only through his Party can the City of Man gain access to the City of God. In the meantime, the Marxists' faith leads them on a pilgrimage through this wearisome land. But this in fact begs the question: is it communism that Marxists love, or is it something else?

Listen as they answer. They sound like Christians – or, worse, Enlightenment humanists.

☭

The contradiction between is and ought, a component of the world that Marx sought to revolutionise, expressed itself in his theory and played itself out historically in the Marxist movement. This is why a full speculative re-reading of Marx would shed light on the genesis of each aporia, lacuna and miasma that has afflicted the Marxist movement, the sum of which may equal its pleroma. But that is well beyond my present ambition. My goal here, rather, is to prove the necessity *of* such a project, by intervening at the point of flagrant and obvious self-contradiction noted above: namely, the Marxist idea of praxis. That is why the backbone of this essay consists of a speculative rewriting of Marx's 'Theses on Feuerbach'.

The *Theses* are the most succinct, famous and dichotomous expression of Marx's idea of praxis. In rewriting the *Theses* speculatively, I have preserved the syntactic form of Marx's 'Theses', while transubstantiating their content in order to render their dichotomies rationally. Which is to say, it is an attempt to render neither theory nor practice singly or in priority, but both together and, simultaneously, in opposition.

For related reasons intrinsic to this project, I have replaced Feuerbach, Marx's polemical foil in the Theses, with Lukács, the preeminent Marxist philosopher of praxis. Because, to paraphrase Marx in *The German Ideology*, as far as Lukács thinks philosophically, he does not deal with praxis; and as far as he considers praxis, he does not think philosophically. Besides which, Lukács was the philosopher of Leninism. And Lenin is something else that Marxists talk about when they talk about love.

Marx, for his part, was a little more direct – when he talked about love he talked about Jenny.

A synopsis of my argument is as follows. 'The point is to change it' – yes, obviously. But from what and into what? Change results from action. Action is the determinate actualisation of will, and will is the activity of abstract negativity. Action intervenes in what is actual to negate what is in favour of what is not yet. The determinate content of action, therefore, does not emerge from the will – which is nothing – but from both the minds of actors, conscious and unconscious, and from the world, known and unknown, that acts through us, while we act on it. Studying *concrete* realities, actors and practices is something Marxists are good at. But it isn't enough to know specific actions and their specific circumstances; what is missing is an account of action *as such*. That is, what Marxist practitioners tend to lack is a rational *concept* of practical-critical activity. After all, Marxist opinions about what is to be done are abundant. Less so are Marxist reflections on the uncomprehended logic that has seen their action culminate in tragedy or comedy – or both – but never success. For Marxism to achieve such a standpoint, it's necessary to uncover a secret scandal – the covert relationship between Marxist practical-critical activity and capitalism.

As implied above, my hypothesis is that Marx radicalised bourgeois politics against itself by opposing civil society – the proletariat

– to the state – bourgeois right. This he did in the promise of the realm of genuine freedom – communism – over the reign of irrational necessity – the hitherto-existing history of class society. The problem is that he did not negate the negation, but instead posited communism as immanent to history *and yet* transcendentally beyond it.

While it might be a fine polemical stick with which to beat utopian socialism, communism, rendered as a beyond, *becomes a kind* 'thing-in-itself' of history that must be made 'for itself', by a process of infinite approximation – reform – culminating in a messianic leap – revolution. As a result of their faith in this political theology, the Marxist movement has failed to recognise how it reproduces the logic of bourgeois right against the bourgeoisie.

Every reformist betrayal and Stalinist crime was committed in the name of a transcendent ought, the free tomorrow of a liberated humanity. And the main historic achievement of Marxist internationalism in the Twentieth century was to aid in the creation of independent bourgeois nation states, albeit with red flags and capitalists who pay tax. Marxists do not love socialism as it is, but as it ought to be.

The utopian aspiration underpinning the effort at hand is a hope that Marxism, as a political culture, can be reformed enough to begin to recognise the hitherto uncomprehended political logic it has inherited from capitalism. Gillian Rose first proposed this in *Hegel Contra Sociology*: this essay is intended as a contribution to her 'Reformation of Marxism'. Consequently, it must also take an 'inwardising turn'; which is to say, I must give a self-account. My goal is to provoke Marxists to philosophical thought. I address the activists, the cadre, the intellectuals and leaders of the really existing socialist movement. My language is philosophical, and somewhat difficult. But it's nothing that Marx would have found challenging.

And out of respect for Marx, who did not bullshit, I will speak bluntly. Marxists: you want socialism to wash away the muck of ages, yet your movement is nostalgic. You denounce every injustice – but where do you articulate a concept of the good? What are your ethics? How do they inform a more just law than this, obviously unjust, one? If your idea of a good life is a society yet to be achieved, then what 'material' basis does it have in *this* society with its bad life? You affirm 'real' democracy but recognise no other legitimate politics than your own. You claim to represent the memory of the class – but at what point will its members remember their memory? And why does the putative memory of the proletariat so closely resemble the culture and thought of a movement that has been isolated from that proletariat for decades? You would propose a better social relation, and yet you resurrect twentieth-century political programs that either failed or produced tyrannies. More often than not, these days, your organisations fail: and less commonly now due to defeat or repression than thanks to sordid scandals and/or internecine sectarian conflict.

Marxists: you must change your lives.

The problem with Marxists is that their theory and practice are subjectively overdetermined by love for the small, sub-political ethical communities they build – communities that Marx disdained as sects – which sustain closed cultures and traditionalist hierarchies that are, in turn, sustained by closed and traditionalist Marxisms. If Marxists want to talk about their love for each other, they should just talk about love. Because mixing love and politics tends to make you a bad politician and a worse lover. Hannah Arendt understood how this goes, as she showed in a 1964 interview with Günter Gaus:

> The direct personal relationship in which one can speak of love, it exists, of course, first and foremost in actual love, and it exists in a sense in friendship too. Here a person is directly addressed, independent of their relation to the world. So we can say that people from quite different organisations can still be personal friends. But if one confuses these things, if one brings love to the negotiating table, to put it rather bluntly, I find that absolutely fatal. I find it apolitical. I find it world-less. And I genuinely find it to be an absolute disaster.

Still, consistency demands that I turn my criticism on myself. I, too, would rather talk about love. So why am I instead talking about Marxism?

Isn't it obvious?
Victory in the lead, with wings outspread – O Goddess
Hear me, and grant that my love prevail!

☭

**Thesis One**
The chief defect of all hitherto existing Marxism – that of Lukács included – is that spiritually self-certain, substantial, universal ethical life – that is, communism – is conceived only in the form of an ought, as abstract negativity, posited as the immanent yet indeterminate *telos* of history. Absolute ethical life is not posited from the standpoint of the true infinite – that is, from the standpoint of the absolute idea. Hence, in contradistinction with absolute idealism, Marxist materialism posited historical progress beyond capitalism either as a revolutionary advent, as reformist gradualism, or, at best, as the representative thought of the unity of theory and practice – that is, as a theory *of* praxis. This is because materialism, of course, does not know real, reflexive conceptual actuality *as such*.

Lukács wants sensuous objects, really distinct from thought objects. However, because he does not grasp the concept of action, he does not conceive of human activity itself as objective activity, only as such subjectively; theoretically. Hence, in *History and Class Consciousness*, he regards the theoretical attitude as ultimately that which actualises praxis, although it achieves this by *submerging itself* in practice. Thus, praxis is conceived in its totalising, historical, mythical manifestation, as an event, and thought is conceived in absolute abstraction from itself: that is, as absolute practice. The precludes grasping the significance of 'revolutionary' 'practical-critical', activity.

This is why Lukács's revolutionary theory has enjoyed no practical success, and his revolutionary practice led him to reconcile with state capitalist socialism.

ADDITION – THE HEART OF THE MATTER

Speculative philosophy is the standpoint of spirit that knows itself as spirit, which has won self-certainty by grasping its self-knowledge in light of both its content *and* logical form. 'Truth', as Hegel explains at the end of the *Phenomenology of Spirit*, supplies for this spirit 'the *content*, which in religion is still not identical with its certainty'. The materialism of revolutionary practice, by contrast, possesses the *content* of self-knowledge – absolute negativity – but not its logical form. Therefore, materialist hyperbole conceals uncertainty; its truth is not reconciled with its own shape, and its standpoint is that of secular political theology. The Marxist philosophy of praxis is a materialism that has its spiritual content *in-itself*, but not *for-itself*. Its thinking is a dream of 'matter'.

Matter is pure substance without determination; logically, it is the immediate idea of being posited with no relation to its boundary and limit. Matter is therefore equally pure form, which is nothing but the operation of abstract negativity: that is, thought. To posit matter in relation to its boundary, to what it is not, is to admit that matter is constituted by the idea: the result is either transcendental or absolute idealism. To the materialist, however, matter is just as material as the mind limited by it. 'Matter, matter everywhere', the materialist says – and blinks.

'The self-knowing Spirit', Hegel says, 'knows not only itself but also the negative of itself, or its limit: to know one's limit is to know how to sacrifice one's self.' From the point of view of matter, there is no limit, no determinate negativity. Consequently, without knowing themselves as spirit, the materialist cannot appreciate what they sacrifice by subsuming their thought under matter. 'Matter is in motion', claims the materialist. From where does it move, to where? When a materialist changes matter, from what does it change, and into what else? A lover's touch is as practical and material as their parting letter. Both confirm the 'this-sidedness of practice'. Material practice is also confirmed, when, in Catullus' words, 'the passing plough-blade slashes the flower at the field's edge'.

Matter is an idea, regardless of the adjectives that qualify it. Whether material is ultimately natural, economic or historic, because these materialisms derive their concepts from an external being – objective, in the case of nature, social in the case of economic and history – and not thought, they are pre-critical. Of course, if matter is an idea, then ideas are material. But if the mind of the materialist does not recognise its idea as idea, and instead names matter its master, it makes itself servant to a world (and a body) which speaks and acts through a mind that has little regard for itself.

What is more, when a materialist identifies their idea with the world, they represent the abstract universal substance of capitalist property relations – which reduces quality to quantity and content to form – as a secular metaphysics of matter. In theory and practice, their viewpoint is determined by the un-recognised content of its self-certainty, that is, absolute freedom; universal abstract negativity; pure thought in pure self-estrangement.

In the chapter of *The Phenomenology* on absolute freedom, Hegel warned of the consequences should such a materialism become legislator:

> This undivided Substance of absolute freedom ascends to the throne of the world without any power being able to resist it ... negativity has permeated all its moments ... In this absolute freedom, therefore, all social groups or classes which are the spiritual spheres into which the whole is articulated are abolished; the individual consciousness that belonged to any such sphere, and willed and fulfilled itself in it, has put aside its limitation; its purpose is the general purpose, its language universal law, its work the universal work.

The abstract universal freedom of materialism is the emptiness of the absolutely free self. As Hegel said in *The Science of Logic*, 'Spirit that were not idea, not the unity of the concept with itself, not the concept that has the concept itself as its reality, would be dead, spiritless spirit, a material object.' Materialism is a philosophy of death, not life. On a crisp, clear morning, the materialist steps out to light a cigarette after having informed against her lover to a party sub-committee.

## Thesis Two

The question of whether objective truth can be attributed to human practice is not a practical question, but a philosophical one. For practice to become reflexive and free, the subject of action must be able to give a rational – and therefore aporetic – account of their practice. Because practice must think the elements of abstraction and powerlessness, that is, of un-re-cognised illusion and contingency, both external and internal. Thus, the dispute over the reality or non-reality of practice that is isolated from philosophy is a purely pragmatic question, at once tragic, unfree and at risk of perpetuating domination.

### ADDITION – PRACTICE IS A BAD INFINITY

Practice achieves its self-certainty in successfully altering its object: that is, by negating it and demonstrating that object's finitude. The result is always not nothing: something. So, the more practice negates, the more practice posits other finite things to be overcome, again and again. The result is an endless succession of finite things. Practice itself is not exempt: every action has an end, at which point it ceases, making way for new practice. Practice consists in an endless succession of finite practices.

In Hegel's account in the *Logic*, the '*bad* or *negative* infinity … is nothing but the negation of the finite, which, however, re-emerges afresh and thus is just as much not sublated.' Insofar as thought establishes practice as the principle of truth, it posits the negation of finitude as an ought. The immediate thought of practice – assuredly 'this-sided' – is a bad infinity. A philosophy of practice is a philosophy of finitude. Although the practitioner may lose themselves in the empty joy of negation – consumption or critique, practical *or* verbal – when they pause, the 'sadness of finitude' creeps darkly into the corners of their vision.

Thinking that has not grasped the ideality of finitude may seek to delay or deny this by re-presenting its estranged concept – thought; the true infinite – as a thing-in-itself, or a transcendent beyond. Perhaps thought represents its own absolute negativity as some ancient arch-essence, or a universal a priori law of reason – or perhaps, as communism. These, however, are fetishisms, because they represent the form of self-consciousness – the negative idea – as an external limit that can be approximated, but not known or overcome.

Only thanks to self-consciousness does a living being maintain being-for-self: we desire our own form, our ideality; our self-identity in difference. Thus, our desire is also directed towards what we are *not*, which determines what we are. But when self-consciousness represents its limit as a transcendent beyond, it estranges its form and disavows its own ideality and negativity. Self-consciousness continues to desire, but now it does so only insofar as its desire is disavowed, and identified with an external object it takes to be infinite and its negative. One-sided and incapable of self-recognition, for the self-consciousness that lacks the self-certainty of the idea, desire itself becomes a bad infinity.

This shape of self-consciousness takes infinite flight from its other, the self-certain negativity of thought that *knows itself* as idea – and consequently, it regards such self-certain thought as sophistry. The price is unthinking practice: the will grasps whatever is first at hand, and changes it. (Even as such 'unthinkingness' is, of course, often accompanied by the species of external, dogmatic rationalisation that regards itself as thought.) The motion is thus doubled: the object and the thinking subject are rendered only as negative, and are void of determinate being. The immediate thought of practice is itself as empty and abstract as it imagines the idea to be.

Until this logic is grasped in and for itself, that is, in light of the absolute idea, the true infinite cannot be posed positively, either in theory *or* in practice. This would require that the ought be posited as a moment of what is. Instead, philosophy of praxis posits the ought as the abstract *negation* of what is, as the yet-to-be-actualised negation of capitalism: communism. 'In other words, this infinity expresses only that the finite *ought* to be sublated', Hegel writes in the *Logic*, adding that

> the progression to infinity stops short at expressing the contradiction that is contained in the finite, namely that it is *something* as well as its *other* and that it is the perpetual continuance of the alternation of these determinations each of which brings about the other.

The rhetoric of Marxist philosophy of praxis, that of Lukács especially, stops short at just this point – and so reveals itself as dogmatic. Its reasoning is sophistic, and conceals nothingness.

And yet, they think. Parmenides' words are good counsel for practitioners – today, Marxists, among others – who assert an estranged temporal locus and/or reified logic as grounds for their purpose:

> Look upon things which, though far off, are yet firmly present to the mind;
> For you shall not cut off what-is from holding fast to what-is
> For it neither disperses itself in every way everywhere in order,
> Nor gathers itself together.

☭

## Thesis Three
The speculative doctrine concerning the changing of circumstances and the upbringing of future generations recalls that actions change people, often for the worse, and that only via education can we attempt next time to change both circumstances and people for the better. Whoever changes the world is both educator and educated. For clarity in its concomitant purpose, then, this doctrine must, therefore, distinguish what is not known, what should be learned, who should teach and who would learn.

The oscillation, indeed, superposition of the changing of circumstances and of human activity or self-changing can be conceived and rationally understood only as the practical idea.

### ADDITION – WHAT IS NOT TO BE DONE?

Marxism poses the question 'what is to be done?', certain it possesses the only correct answer: the negation of the present state of affairs. Marxists declare that the educators must themselves be educated, but rarely count themselves among the former.

The proletariat does not teach anyone who will not learn. And learning means reflecting on practice by attempting to know and change *determinate* things. By grasping the determinacy – the finitude – of practices and objects, the practical consciousness learns to let them go and then to re-invest in new objects and practices, this time having learned. By reflecting on such a process, the immediate thought of practice itself may attain determination and, if so, having mediated the false infinity of practice, it may even grasp its concept. This requires not only uncertainty, but a capacity to apologise, to forgive, to mourn, and to re-cognise the unconscious subjective and objective determinants of our action.

All action is negation, and it all involves a temporary madness: to act is to give oneself over to an absolute moment in which will actualises intention, producing a deed which negates its object. In so doing, practice exposes itself to the contingency of an infinite totality of determinate past circumstances of which only a fraction can ever be known. To prepare for action, knowledge can, of course, be gathered – but at some point, we must act. The deed is a temporal cut opening a void. To approach it with certainty about its outcome – including when accompanied by rhetorical caveats – is to act blindly and madly.

When we act, we aim at a different future. Futures, however, are the projection of the present – for every facet of which, there is a future. All those facets of the present we know contain an unknown element, an element of non-being – and there are infinitely more facets that we don't know at all. So, for all the futures we suppose we know, there are infinitely more we do not. At best, the futures we intend are like prophecies: when they come to pass, we are astonished.

A decision hones the darkness of non-being – of the act and the present – into an edge whose razor-sharpness cuts infinite contingency into singular necessity. The act, then, is a violence that demands we sever those futures and pasts we thought we knew, as well as a thousand never-to-be-born futures and a million never-to-ripen pasts that we did not. From this contraction of uncountable contingencies, the vanishing finitude of a moment becomes a past necessity: a changed present emerges, and with it, a new infinity of possible futures.

And so on. There's no getting past this collision of time and being. But what we can do is think it. After all, the negativity of the act as such – the cut – is a precondition for the *determinate* act: the incision, the self-conscious act.

The madness of decision precedes ethics. Ethical action, therefore, is action that moves from madness to sanity – via recollection.

To return from madness to re-cognition, however, requires the work of mourning. Whoever acts must bid farewell to the infinite contingency of the present and future that their action negates. More importantly, after the act, we must mourn for the lost wholeness experienced in its moment of singularity, which is, no less, emptiness. This is why many refuse to act: they cannot bear to be absolutely whole, and thus empty and alone. This is also why some act compulsively: they cannot bear to be less than everything, so they sever whatever threatens their own empty wholeness.

The speculative unity of theory and practice requires re-cognition of the brokenness of all action. A view that denies action's aporetic character in the name of total knowledge of the past, present or future – mythology, dogma and eschatology – discloses an anxious will to mastery. The finite mediators between past and future – actors and their knowledge – are re-presented as a false infinite, which conceals the void with an image.

As Rose explained in 'Shadow of Spirit,' 'holy middles corrupt because they collude in the elimination of the broken middle by drawing attention away from the reconfiguration of singular, individual and universal that is at stake.' Having committed an unjust, unjustifiable action, the guilty practitioner preserves their holy wholeness – the vanity of their estranged negativity – by refusing to remember. Consequently, they cannot apologise: fearing their own absolute emptiness, they cannot face the absolute emptiness of their deed.

Yet a being that is absolutely whole is also incapable of acting – what is to be done by one who is all? The Olympian gods made decisions because they were plural; each was not whole. The God of the Old Testament was the God of his chosen people; he was not whole, but acted and was known in negative relation to other peoples and their gods. When the Christian God sacrificed his son, he became complete – and ceased to act. An absolutely whole being is absolutely empty, and voids do not make decisions.

To act – or to not act – is a decision made by a living being, between emptiness and wholeness, between is and ought. If we are to act rationally, we can only do so insofar as we re-cognise the moment of absolute emptiness, the abstract freedom of action, and return from it, to determination and concrete freedom.

If, as Nietzsche says, action requires forgetting, then learning requires memory. To mourn over an action we regret is the labour of the infinite: it proceeds through the re-cognition of what we represented as known, allowing us to realise what we have done. But such speculative reflection on an unjust action is not abject *confession*; it is a self-reflexive apology. It is not mediated by priests or party committees, but by interlocutors. And the half-light of the decision can only be illuminated by the light of speech and analysis shining back from the present. This makes the absolute negativity of the decision determinate, and reveals a little more of the world and ourselves in the hope that next time, we will act better – even if not, of course, perfectly.

This is why, in *The Phenomenology of Spirit*, absolute knowing occurs after the recollection of the passed shapes of consciousness. It's also why absolute knowing should be understood as an intellectual practice sustained by a culture that is implicitly speculative. 'Absolute knowledge', as Rose explains in *Hegel Contra Sociology*, 'is a path which must be continually traversed, re-collecting the forms of consciousness and the forms of science.' This returns consciousness to the present, the domain of absolute knowing. And from there, if it is your vocation, you may act again – but this time, having learned.

Marxism has yet to achieve any of this. What is to be done? Mourning what has been done.

☭

**Thesis Four**

Lukács starts out from the fact of his own religious self-alienation, but re-presents it universally: his own reification as that of the proletariat; his own abstraction as the reduction of the proletariat to the status of an identical subject-object; his own estrangement from the present as the flattening of time during the work day. His theology of praxis consisted of resolving this secular sociological diagnosis via messianic advent, presented as a theory of revolution.

The fact that this political theology detached itself from real politics and established itself as a purely intellectual breakthrough, with no practical dimension, can only be explained by the internal cleavages in its own concept. Which latter, therefore, must be understood in its contradiction, and reconciled philosophically. For example, after we discover the secret of Lukács's messianic image of praxis within the concrete, law-giving praxis of October 1917, the former must be de-fetishised theoretically, if it is to have practical import.

ADDITION – FICHTEAN MARXISM

In the 1928 essay 'Moses Hess and the Problem of Idealist Dialectics', Lukács argued that Left Hegelianism generally reverted to a Fichtean position, gaining superficial radicalism at the cost of utopianism. Insofar as this constituted a self-criticism, he was correct. In *History and Class Consciousness*, when Lukács was at his best, he even developed a kind of Fichtean Marxism, naturally, despite his best intentions and efforts.

But Lukács was different from Fichte insofar as he represented the identical subject-object as a historic *social class*, rather than as an originary ego. On such a basis he established the *ought* of proletarian praxis as a transcendent principle, opposed to what is.

Lukács wanted to see Bolshevik revolution win in Europe. 'What ought to be is', wrote Hegel in the *Logic*, 'and at the same time is not. If it were, we could not say that it ought merely to be.' By saying that Bolshevism *ought to be*, Lukács conceded that it *was not*. At the same time, by disavowing the ideality of this ought, he made it impossible to re-cognise the element within it of what *is*.

Because of this, Lukács's philosophy of praxis conceals a political theology ultimately grounded in the law of bourgeois property relations. As Gillian Rose explains in *Hegel Contra Sociology*, 'exchange and contract depend on making things which are particular and different formally comparable or abstract, turning them into value or price.' Consequently, 'exchange and contract depend on the recognition of formal equalities which presuppose lack of identity or inequality.' Commodity production and exchange underpins the formal universality of bourgeois law which recognises each individual as a bearer of identical rights, as formally equal. Lukács diagnosed the same condition as reification. The same formalism, however, underpins the indifference of the will, and is a real abstraction, vested in being itself, as much as in thinking, acting subjects. In the latter, it powers all action and thought, with no regard for their determinate content, and when absolutised, by its own logic unleashed, this indifference reduces subject and object to self-sameness, negating their determinacy. Lukács understood this well enough sociologically, and even to some extent philosophically. But he did not recognise the determinant actualisation of this logic within politics, the very sphere in which he hoped concrete freedom would emerge.

Rose explains the manner in which Fichte built a finite idealism of the deed on the basis of the abstract ego:

> For Fichte, the ego must posit a boundary because it is finite, but it is not limited by this boundary because

> the boundary is posited absolutely. The positing is dependent on the ego alone. Thus the boundary, which makes the ego finite, lies *wherever* in the infinite the ego posits it to be: it depends entirely on the spontaneity of the ego.

The boundary that Lukács posited was different, in that he identified it with revolutionary praxis. But if anything, this placed it even further beyond scrutiny. Like Fichte's ego, Lukács's subject-object of history posits its boundary absolutely: the realm of freedom lies on the other side of the revolution, where the proletariat is not.

To be more precise, what mattered for Lukács were the *moment* and the *decision*, which form the boundary between a reified, bourgeois society and one moving towards communism. According to the culmination of a dialectic between party and class, Lukács argued in *Defence of History and Class Consciousness* that the proletariat must make the decision to seize power in a revolutionary crisis: 'in such moments everything depends on class consciousness, on the conscious will of the proletariat. This is where the moment of decision lies.' Of course, he explained that this could only occur after a self-educative process of class struggle in which the proletariat grasps its role as subject-object of history, mediated by a Bolshevik party as an interlocutor. The problem is, it was Lenin who decided Russia needed an insurrection, and who convinced his party to lead the proletariat to make it. To be very precise, the Second All-Russian Congress of the Soviets enthusiastically ratified the October Revolution *after* it had succeeded. The 'ought' was before a vote decided that it ought to be.

As Rose explains, 'Fichte's absolute ego "demands the conformity of the object with the ego precisely in the name of its absolute being."' So too did Lukács's absolute subject-object – in reality, the party, representing itself as the proletariat – demand the conformity of the object – Russia – in the name of its universal purpose – communism. 'Essence', Rose continues, 'is the unity of absolute negativity (Fichte's absolute ego which bounds itself) and immediacy (Fichte's boundary). But neither essence nor immediacy have any determination'. The essence of Lukács's concept of praxis also lacked determination: an entire social class cannot make a decision. In its immediacy, too, his concept lacked determination: Lukács's philosophy of praxis had no practical impact.

To be fair, Lukács's account of the development of class consciousness was complex, concrete and mediated, as Merleau-Ponty was among the first to notice in the chapter on Western Marxism in *Adventures of the Dialectic*. However, lacking a speculative account of politics, Lukács's political theory was drawn almost entirely from the practice of Bolshevism. Lacking a standpoint from which he could re-cognise Bolshevik practice, he was unable to give a determinate account of the decision to seize power. Consequently, he represented past praxis as an infinite goal, and in so doing he masked its dichotomies – those of Leninism – dogmatically. As Rose wrote in *Hegel Contra Sociology*,

> [e]xternal reflection knows that it has posited determination, such as the distinction between finite and infinite, but leaves the determination as external. It does not claim to have determined the infinite, and contents itself with taking the finite 'as the first, as the real; as the foundation, the abiding foundation'; and not as the starting point of a negating reflection.

Lukács did not claim to have determined the infinite; he did not posit a new social law that could structure communism. Instead, he took the work of the Russian proletariat and the Bolshevik Party as the expression of the truth of history, and the foundation for a new communist law – but all without rendering these abstractions determinate through further 'negating reflection'. To have progressed further, he would have needed to de-mythologise the proletariat and party: that is, to posit their finitude. This would have required him to re-cognise Lenin's decision as the practical will of a revolutionary sovereign. Instead, he insisted that the *proletariat* decided, and did so in a way that was knowable and transparent in the moment of decision.

From there, on the basis of a misrecognised event, Lukács further misrepresents class consciousness as absolute knowledge, and as true beyond that event. Class consciousness, he argued in the eponymous chapter of *History and Class Consciousness*, corresponds to the 'economic and social position of the class as a totality', and therefore Marxist theory, as the intellectual expression of this consciousness, is 'not only able to refute a false one, but is also in a position to point to those moments of existence that spawn the incorrect theory.'

In the name of ideal class consciousness, Lukács thus collapsed the tension between the acting and judging consciousnesses, eradicating the broken middle between action and judgement, and, therefore, the possibility of their mutual recognition in otherness. In place of debate, there is the identity of the individual will, the 'I = I.' When a sovereign does this, it's dictatorial. When a theorist does this, it's dogmatic and solipsistic. Just as Bolshevism became incapable of recognising political difference, Lukács became incapable of recognising non-Marxist philosophy.

Lukács was always nostalgic – just consider his taste in literature, not to mention *Soul and Form*. After having invested his nostalgia in 1917, he became like a gambler trying to reproduce a winning bet; his was a tragic faith convinced it could beat the odds with a system.

'If ethical life is abstract', Rose wrote – and surely it was in 1923 – 'then it can only be recognised by recognising its abstractions, the cobwebs, and their determination. In this way actuality is recognised and another indeterminate, non-actuality is not posited.'

'Transformative activity,' she also said, 'acknowledges actuality in the act and does not oppose act to non-act.' Only the re-cognition of a law-creating decision as finite can produce a law that can leave space to recognise the other: that is, a law whose logic is truly infinite.

## Thesis Five

Lukács, not satisfied with abstract practice, wanted self-reflexive praxis. But he did not conceive of speculation – the activity of thought – in light of its concept, as the spiritual, rational idea.

ADDITION – THE LIFE OF THE MIND

The speculative idea is higher than practice. Yes, actions are infinite; decisions sever an infinite kaleidoscope of futures in favour of a new, indeterminate, boundless unfolding. Once the deed is done, however, it becomes immutable and self-identical. Other deeds may echo or follow it, and they may even negate the initial deed in a thousand ways, each mediated by that vast web of interactions and understandings. But the deed doesn't change.

Thought unceasingly changes. Not all thought is universal; not all thought recognises its ideality and participates in absolute knowing. Not all thought is free. But unlike deeds, some thought can remain identical while generating non-identity. Which is to say, speculative thoughts can live beyond their finite origins – and their authors often know it. Sometimes, they let on as much, with a wink or smile aimed at readers who also know.

Because Plato lent him a body of writing, when we read the *Phaedrus*, Socrates and the shining boy to whom he spoke of love come to life again in our minds – and, sometimes, in the vocation they inspire. They are reborn as us – as new minds rediscovering a forgotten truth – because we gratefully lend them a fraction of our lives, including when we disagree. And we receive much more in return: our souls recall themselves. This is both a secular critique of Plato's idea of resurrection, and its vindication. Socrates was correct to assert that philosophical lovers can be reborn to love again after a cycle of one thousand years: the mind of a philosopher can grow wings, he claimed, and Plato proved it.

To put it another way, the realisation that one has shared – or authored – a universal thought is, in Adorno's words, 'the happiness that dawns in the eye of the thinking person.' It 'is the happiness of humanity.'

Actions only live in this manner insofar as they are thought

– and even then, few remember the decisions of sovereigns and statesmen from Plato's time. Few, one day, will think about Lenin's decision. Yet, Socrates will live because, as he explained to his beloved, and as his beloved wrote, death is not the end, provided our knowledge is shared and resonates justly, beautifully and truly.

A soul scatters upon death: so too may a decision, for better or worse or both. But true thoughts are different. They recollect the fragments of their author's soul. They tread lightly: if thought births new action or thought, it is reborn, because of a truth and resonance that the living feel and know, for which they must take responsibility. Thoughts thus live with the living – and so long as the living learn, thoughts that are absolutely true flourish, both self-same and different. Like life itself.

☭

**Thesis Six**
Lukács resolves the ideal essence into a material, universal essence. But the idea is no abstraction arising from material being. In its actuality, it is spiritual self-knowledge; the logic of being that has been grasped in its essentialities in accordance with its immanent conceptual development through opposition.

Lukács, not entering upon a criticism of this genuinely speculative idealism, is consequently compelled:

1) To abstract from absolute knowing and to fix its 'material substratum' or essence as something that can be known in and for itself, by a practice that is also abstractly universal.

2) To see logic, therefore, as only being comprehensible as 'form', a self-referential schematic with an apparent separation from history that conceals Lukács's uncritical endorsement of irrationality.

ADDITION A – THE IDENTITY OF THE THEORETICAL AND PRACTICAL IDEA

Hegel begins the final chapter of the *Science of Logic* as follows: 'The absolute Idea has shown itself to be the identity of the theoretical and the practical Idea.' The practice of speculative thinking cannot resolve or end the aporia within the deed, but it does establish a rational vantagepoint beyond the dichotomies of theoretical and practical reason that allows thought to re-cognise this aporia that powers thought itself. This allows reason to think the decision after the fact. This won't change the Russian Revolution or re-write Lukács. But it can help to develop a speculative concept of praxis.

'Transformative activity', Rose wrote in *Hegel Contra Sociology*, 'acknowledges actuality in the act and does not oppose act to non-act.' To rise to this possibility, the representative thought of praxis must grasp the true infinite as the unity of the *ought* and the *is*, of the relation between finite being and its non-being, its limit, which equally determines its essence. This requires us to grasp the *ideality* of the finite and the *conceptuality* of our thinking and doing: this is the true infinite.

The absolute appears to consciousness dichotomised. Consciousness itself participates in this process of division, and indeed, divides itself into abstract moments: to re-cognise this is to grasp consciousness as self-consciousness. This is, in Rose's terms, a

> knowing which knows consciousness and its oppositions and is therefore comprehensive. This comprehension is not the concept which is opposed to nature or intuition, but the concept or Idea which includes the opposition between formal concept and its determinations.

The absolute idea does not replace life; it is life that has re-cognised itself rationally. It is life understood conceptually and is therefore the element in which concrete freedom can be thought. With the idea, we create the new. With the rational idea, we create the new freely.

When thought works through a past event, it must overcome the immediacy of that event in the present by mourning for that event's non-being; its finitude. This allows us to criticise the immanent limits of that event and to decide which aspects thereof we will preserve as lessons – which is also a negation. Thus we may reject, re-enact or simply discuss elements of the event, but whatever the case, there is no repetition of the event, and its afterlife, be it in thought or further action, is always different. The power of an event to generate the new – of finitude to give way to new finitude; the true infinite – is only foreclosed once and for all when we no longer think about it.

Death in general, is, for Rose, unthinkable. When we work through the death of the Russian Revolution, we in fact recover it *for us*. This is the only rational way in which an event can live again: it does so because we have negated its non-being through recollection, making it for us, investing it with *our* living thought and action. But this is to negate the event! Which is a cause for celebration: the re-cognition of death is always the cognition of life. Without the re-cognition of death and the recollection of what we have lost, now transformed and made our own, at the service of our lives, we walk among the antique ghosts of our own melancholy.

This is how we might gain our freedom with respect to history, to learn, and to knowingly create the new. It is the condition for free, self-given laws, because laws are the fixing in time of finite social relationships. And this is a labour that requires a living culture; self-knowing spirit is a social relation.

### ADDITION B – THE POLYRHYTHMIC POLYPHONY OF HISTORY

History is universal nostalgic imagery; the intellectual representation of objectively encoded memories, traditions, texts, artefacts, institutions and so on. A historian cannot make do without reason, and a rational work of history must undertake its labour of re-collection with reference to the genuine objectifications of past spirit, be they artefacts, texts or other mute sources. These are innumerable not only because of their multiplicity, but because there are so many which are unknown to historical thought. Such passed shapes of objective spirit possess innumerable meanings, some of which we articulate now, though always in ways shaped by our present.

To pretend the past speaks a simple truth is to host a séance. To declare the past has only one meaning is to drown out its cryptic traces and echoes with our own knowledge. Effectively, such an approach insists that our knowledge is perfect. And because our knowledge of the past is different from the self-knowledge of those who made the past, the idea of a single meaning to history inadvertently implies the absolute incommensurability of the past with present. This is to transform history into a soliloquy.

Instead, we must think the non-identity of the meaning of the past as we do the non-identity of the meaning of the present.

A good work of history accounts for its finitude, while a poor one presents its finite knowledge as infinite. This is the dogmatic secret of the 'materialist understanding of history', which uncritically projects this or that contemporary material essence – statistics, classes, social relations, etcetera – onto the past, and announces that it has resolved the polyphony of history once and for all into a single, correct narrative. In the case of dogmatic Marxism, this 'material essence' is almost always born of a lack that is experienced in the present; it's a variety of what Nietzsche termed 'monumental history' in his second untimely meditation. More sophisticated historical materialisms are superior insofar as they grasp the constitutive incompleteness of any historical account and seek to discover the covert links between the present from which they are articulated and the past they articulate. Nevertheless, without grasping the absolute present and the absolute idea as their temporal and logical vantagepoints respectively, they are only implicitly rational.

In his review of *History and Class Consciousness*, Bloch issued a friendly criticism of Lukács's attempt to contract the multiplicity of history into one moment of praxis.

> History is much more, quite apart from all the demands of the *omnia ubique*, a polyrhythmic structure, and not only the social extraction of a still hidden social humanity, but also the artistic, religious, metaphysical production of the secret transcendental human being is a thinking of being, of a new deep relationship of being. Certainly these new deep relationships and

> their objects are not sharply delineated from one another, but rather stand in a dialectical exchange, almost ceaselessly intersecting, mixing, merging, establishing the precision of the lower stage of being again and again in the higher one.

The light emanating from what Bloch so expressively termed the 'darkness of the lived moment' illuminates the polyvalent structure of the present *and* the past. He is right, then, to refer to the polyrhythmic structure of history.

The metaphor also suggests, correctly, that history composes in many keys at once, sometimes in harmony, sometimes in dissonance. This is to say that world spirit is not a single musician, or a conductor, but every player in every band – and their audience – all at once. The only way this might come to a final resolution or single meaning is in the silence of our self-annihilation – the cessation of the music of self-conscious life.

The gap that always exists between history as it was and history as we know it is a productive tension. A gap exists also in theology, between the representative image of the absolute, and its finite contents. Behind Christian dogma stands a dogmatic Church. Behind the dogmatic Marxist account of history stands a dogmatic Marxist sect or party. What they share is their insistence that there is no void between what they say and what was. Philosophy, by contrast, seeks to think this void and find a home in it. To fetishise a univalent historical narrative is to deny the void within the present, and to be unreconciled with it. It is to be buffeted by the polyvalence of the present and past while seeking assurance in a mythology. This estranges the present from itself by re-presenting it in mythic costume. Such a way of thinking cannot prevent the new from emerging, but forms a barrier to attempts to freely and rationally know the past or present, or to create the future.

If life, known conceptually, is the absolute idea, then Hegel's absolute must necessarily live within the absolute present. Consequently, *absolute knowing is practice* of spiritual knowledge that has endured the absolute temporal estrangement of historical thinking, and has returned to the present, having regathered within itself the shapes of past spirit. Its prize is the self-certainty of its own, living spirit. This knowledge is not an infinitised finite, as in historical mythologies: its movement of knowing is illuminated by the true infinite, which is present.

Every revenant emanates from a present diremption. To be free of nightmares, one should face them, and listen to what our unconscious says through them. To free our brain of the nightmarish weight of the tradition of all dead generations, we ought not flee from the past, presume to speak for it or deny it – which all amount to the same thing – but to converse with it as an interlocutor, listening and speaking in turn. This would be, in fact, a dialogue of the present with its own memory, with our objective universal unconscious. It is the condition for the free creation of a new, better future.

☭

## Thesis Seven

Lukács, consequent to all the above, does not grasp the concrete manner in which Marxism – which, as he acknowledges, represents the 'self-consciousness of capitalism' – is itself a moment of the present, one whose truth is not merely a negation, but also an affirmation, of a particular spiritual content within the social relations of capitalism.

### ADDITION – THE POLITICAL THEOLOGY OF FANATICISM

As we have seen, Lukács re-presented the infinite as praxis, and did so by mythologising an event, hoping it would recur. The deeper problem with this, as Hegel explained in the *Logic*, is that 'the affirmation of determinate being is lacking in it; the spurious infinite, held fast as only negative is even supposed to be not there, is supposed to be unattainable.'

Lukács committed his life to communism. But because he held fast to it as the immanent negation of capitalism, he deferred any concrete knowledge of its positive content indefinitely, rendering it unobtainable to the living. 'However, to be thus unattainable', Hegel continues, referring to the spurious infinite, 'is not its grandeur but its defect, which is at bottom the result of holding fast to the finite as such as a merely affirmative being.' Thus, Lukács's abstract commitment to communism concealed a faith in the finite affirmative being of really existing state capitalist socialism.

As the great twentieth-century socialist realist author, Henry Miller wrote, 'to be able to give oneself whole and completely is the greatest luxury that life affords. Real love only begins at this point of dissolution.' Lukács gave himself to an unknowable, infinitely distant future that he could only posit as the immanent negation of capitalism. In similar fashion, as Rose explained in *Hegel Contra Sociology*, because he elevated practical reason over the understanding, which he took to be finite, Fichte located the moral law of freedom not in nature or the ethical life of this world, but in an infinite will that postulates a supersensuous world. Consequently, the will to actualise the moral law of freedom depended, for Fichte, on conviction, faith, intuition, a decision and duty.

The quote with which Lukács announced his conversion to communism was telling on this axis: 'Even if God had placed sin between me and the deed enjoined upon me – who am I to be able to escape it?' Indeed, his leap was exemplary of the still largely unacknowledged and unthought leitmotifs of revelation, faith and duty within the Marxist movement. So, too, were his confessions and self-denunciations. Lukács was the Marxist Saint Augustine.

Faith and duty motivate communists to give themselves to an unknowable, transcendent *ought*. Whether faith and duty masquerade as sentimental humanism or scientific rationalism is beside the point: the ought is the negative determination of what is. Under capitalism, a transcendent ought thus betrays an uncritical affirmation of bourgeois right, and of the egotistical individuality upon which it is premised.

Communist faithfulness and dutifulness conceal the desire to be boundless and limitless; to dissolve into a perfect, absolute other. This apparent selflessness conceals an ego that wants to encompass the world, and that represents this desire as a universal moral law. It is a desire to submerge the self in the being of an absolute other whose determination as infinite *affirms the self* as infinite. Because this desired unity is infinitely distant – life within a future communist society – it is abstract in time and space, and conceals its finitude. It's a fantasy of absolute meaning and infinite pleasure without sin; the dream of a lover who will never fail the beloved.

Such a communist approaches the infinite by way of infinite duty. They ask themselves 'Am I good enough to be a revolutionary?', without pausing to consider what the question presupposes. To be redeemed, they sacrifice what is finite and this-worldly – they give time, labour, comfort, ambition, and sometimes even those they love. By giving themselves to a movement, communist fanatics flee their finitude, their particularity, and ascetically attempt to wholly identify themselves with their infinite lover – the party, which supposedly mediates between finitude and the transcendent infinite. Thus, the communist finds imaginary wholeness by submitting to a collective with a universal mission.

Insofar as they still enjoy what is finite and particular, it is concealed, discreet and shame-faced. In return, the party agrees to not love its members for their particularity, but for their abstract universality: that is, identically and equally, as comrades indistinct from each other. And this is what the ascetic communist desires: the abstract ego has found a way to love itself behind its own back. Asceticism is the debauchery of self-infatuation that can't face itself.

This love for a party – an earthly political community – is sanctified by revolutionary theory. The communist's desire to submit is echoed by the party's demand that the individual submit to its true theory: the full identification of one with the other is mirrored. Here, the unity of abstract individuals is guaranteed by a universal dogma: Marxism is the riddle of history solved – and the solution must be carefully monopolised. Witness this at Marxist meetings: the repetition of the same discussions, over and over. The point is not to learn, but to offer sermons and psalms affirming the community.

Parties and their knowledge, however, are finite. So, in truth, submission to a party usually amounts to submission to a charismatic leader or clique. This is a fleeting, decrepit joy, one that suspends the burden of separateness and offers a communism of disciplinary affect. This results in a suppression of difference: sometimes, members of a sect even take on the mannerisms or verbal tics of its leaders. In turn, such uniformity heightens the pernicious distance between the group and the world. The resulting rigid hierarchies breed subservience, resentment, spite, cruelty and intellectual mediocrity.

Occasionally the particular desire and pleasure that has been disavowed returns pathologically. Watch the communist moralists closely: they are often the most corrupt and abusive.

In the USSR, this was tragic in the true sense. Today, it is mostly comic, and insofar as it is tragic, it is so usually only for individuals whose self-sacrifice amounts to self-harm, if also, occasionally, the mistreatment of others. The freedom and love they seek become their opposites. This is because whoever desires absolute identity with their lover attempts to eradicate the difference between two which creates space for a third, shared imaginary – that is, for Eros. As Anne Carson observes in *Eros the Bittersweet*, Eros only exists

> because certain boundaries do. In the interval between reach and grasp, between glance and counterglance, between 'I love you' and 'I love you too,' the absent presence of desire comes alive. ... [I]t is only, suddenly, at the moment when I would dissolve that boundary, I realise I never can.

To demand the eradication of boundaries, as the duty-drunk communist does, is fatal to love: the dream of perfect identity is realised in the solipsism of the self. It's the tragedy of self-loathing narcissism that keeps loneliness at bay by controlling the lover.

The most valuable – and dangerous – element in this standpoint is the longing for infinity. When the desire for salvation via submission – the desire to be the object of the master's desire – becomes a political vocation that disavows concrete, extant, finite institutions, it can manifest as a desire for revolutionary terror.

Disavowed enjoyment reappears as cruelty; the fanatic's pleasure is betrayed by their lop-sided smirk.

☭

**Thesis Eight**
All social life is essentially ideal. All practices which lead representative thought to mysticism find their rational solution in the absolute idea as the identity of the theoretical and practical ideas.

ADDITION – TOTAL CONTROL OVER YOU

'Utopian consciousness', Bloch writes in his review of *History and Class Consciousness*, 'wants to look far into the distance, but ultimately only in order to penetrate the darkness so near it of the just lived moment, in which everything that is both drives and is hidden from itself.'

Insofar as the abstract, utopian consciousness declares that freedom is to be realised in a distant negation of the present, it represents its own disavowed, positive determinacy as an avowed, estranged image. What is positive and present is represented as a negative, that 'ought'. In addition to religious, such a stance has aesthetic dimensions. Insofar as the utopian consciousness flees its inner darkness via political activism, it subjects the world to its symptom. In so doing, it betrays that it seeks an infallible law that it may serve – and master.

Like all laws, this one is less infinite and absolute than initially supposed. That is to say, the utopian consciousness hides a self-given moral vocation behind a moralistic mask. The result is bad theatre and worse morality.

This goes some way to explaining the vanity of small differences prevalent within the Marxist movement – which relates to the world via a political aesthetic in order to mask its divided self. The result is capriciousness and hypocrisy: when the rhetoric of universal truth and justice mask psychological lacunae, because these lacunae are always idiosyncratic, the result is an idiosyncratic, intuitive and self-serving misrepresentation of truth and justice. In short, the utopian consciousness declares truth and justice to be what they feel like in the moment – claims dignified, of course, by various texts and rituals. If disagreement threatens the mask, the utopian narcissist re-casts the one who insists on dissent as a betrayer, enemy or monster.

This law demands submission – total boundlessness – of the other. It represents its particular lack as a universal law, and outrageously demands the other submit and abolish all boundaries, disavowing the petty authoritarianism of the command in the name of an idea as infallible as it is non-actual. What this lover really wants is to subordinate their beloved, and, as master, to be subordinated in turn. Should the beloved protest, the utopian consciousness threatens to punish them for disturbing their lonely enjoyment, by offering undivided company one day, and unbearable absence the next. It's a little game of *fort-da* characteristic of those who disguise emptiness with political masks.

When the beloved sees through the mask, the utopian consciousness is forced to choose between facing their finitude, or keeping the act going with those who confirm and conform to their self-image. Extras pass frequently through this lonely theatre.

Although art is not a cure – that's where psychoanalysis comes in – at least, when one expresses one's symptoms via art, as Julia Kristeva argued in *Black Sun*, there is less danger of direct violence and some possibility of meaning and renewal. Better – and more moral – to re-present the desire for boundlessness aesthetically: in, for example, a song.

This, however, requires the kind of mask that can be removed: in place of sanctimony, vulnerability shows its tear-streaked face. Afterwards, maybe recognition.

☭

## Thesis Nine
The highest point reached by practical materialism – that is, materialism which does not comprehend the ideality of practical activity – is the subsumption of the abstractly free individuals who

comprise civil society under the standpoint of the state, represented as a negative utopia.

### ADDITION – FANATICISM AND LOVE

When the unwept-for and unmourned past overwhelms the future, the result is despair writ large: joyful fanaticism. As absolute freedom, fanaticism is the indifferent will that immediately identifies itself with the world, and, owing to its inner emptiness and negativity, finds enjoyment in negating all. So it is that nihilism is at the core of messianism: abstraction annihilates the present in flight from an unconfronted past, in the name of a fetishistic future.

The antinomies of fanaticism – the present as abject and the future as perfect – survive only insofar as they're kept apart. But the commitment to redemption can only be realised insofar as the logic of despair is followed to the end. This reunites fanaticism's estranged dichotomies. When despair despairs of itself – which was Nietzsche's main injunction – the fanatic becomes bored. When dreaming of future enjoyment is no longer enjoyable, the present enjoyment that was disavowed or the cause of shame might be recovered instead. The result is concrete, particular self-knowledge and determinate regret. Where once there was metaphysical tragedy, now there is this-worldly comedy.

Faith – the bridge between despair and redemption – demands total self-emptying in preparation for grace. Rigorously applied, this movement of self-abnegation must also purge faith itself of egotism. But all faith is subjective; all faith is the worship of a graven idol. Faith is idolatry. After the renunciation of vain faith, there may occur a much more human dialogue between conviction and doubt.

Genuine love for a new future, which is always more than the present and past, spurs the realisation that faith in a negative utopia conceals a hubristic and vain projection of a present lack and unfreedom. But lack is equally the awareness of non-presence, and only one who is present and determinate can be aware of their non-being. It is with the recognition of particularity that satisfaction, however partial, becomes possible. Love for heaven – or even the abyss – is always rooted in the earth. Faith can thus only be united with its concept in the unfinished present: the coming of an incomplete messiah; the institutions, places, cultures and people we love.

Grace is the miraculous transubstantiation of despair into redemption. Descent, sin and self-abasement are grace's opposite motions. Yet, in grace, desire and sin are present as the positive absolute: sin reappears absolutely negated. Just look at Bernini's *Ecstasy of Saint Teresa* or the depiction of heaven and hell in the Cathedral of Bologna. And with the realisation that grace is libidinally charged, we are led to the domain of psychoanalysis proper: the unconscious. The love of self-abnegation and the desire for redemption must be discovered in a determinate, particular past: perhaps a childhood in which one became desolate with abandonment, to the point of resignation, after which the advent of the other appeared as a miracle. The desublimation of these moments opens a path to concrete relationships and human satisfaction.

This inner, psychological re-cognition is difficult, however, because it seems to risk corrupting the loved object: after all, in the salvific consciousness, the loved object is determined both as an absolute purpose and as radically distinct and distant. The desire for unity with God is the religious representation of the unity of these opposites; the desire for endless life is equally the desire for death.

If this limit can be thought and experienced conceptually, shy of actual death, it can motivate a return to life. The penitent fanatic may come to see that both they and their world are imperfectly redeemed. Suspended between heaven and hell, we are climbing Mount Purgatory – and at the pinnacle, we might find a garden of jagged stems, leaves and blossoms in all colours.

When the abstract alternation between nihilism and salvation becomes less interesting, through repetition, the rational self-consciousness may sublate despair, regaining its power of negativity in critique. Faith in heaven rediscovers its estranged love in a concrete, determinate life that flourishes freed of resentment. Surprised delight at the new replaces the impoverished ecstasy of salvation. Concrete sadness – which can be shared – replaces the solipsism and devastation of metaphysical tragedy. This sublation of grace allows one to comport oneself gracefully, and to receive and express the happiness and sadness of everyday life.

Instead of the loneliness of the false infinite, the fanatic becomes human again by loving finite beings in the knowledge that they will pass, and, when they do, by shedding tears of pain. Not alone, but with another who recognises that pain, and whose recognition facilitates self-recognition. Shared is the first smile that breaks through tears, and the first laugh to come after.

It is to walk with elated footfall to a lover's house, and to take deeper pleasure in every finite minute spent in their room, where time is, for a moment, infinite. It is to feel cold together before the heater has warmed space, to enjoy their cooking even when it hasn't lived up to their standards, to wake up together with the same hangover.

More fiercely do we fight for those finite beings we love knowing that they will be lost. More heaven do we find in finitude, knowing that in those glittering moments when two affirm their love for each other, going beyond their limits, they touch the infinite in the other's being. From this dance comes a fleeting third: Eros. And, now past, it is preserved as recollection, which is already negation. And perhaps also in literary representation:

It was a hand resting on a lover's calf, feeling her fine hair stand on end as time slowed for the first – but not the last – time.

It was when two lovers kissed under a humming orange streetlight; the stars held time still while a rift opened in the road and the earth freely gave its wealth as two incompletely divine beings joined the gods for a moment.

Once no longer a fanatic, one may learn to become a lover.

## Thesis Ten
The standpoint of Marxist materialism was that of the state; the standpoint of absolute idealism is absolute spirit, or, the spiritual self-knowledge of a culture that has grasped its concept.

ADDITION – TOWARDS A REFORMATION OF MARXISM

When Lukács intellectually reified the decision of the sovereign, he revealed a deeper truth encoded within Marx's failed critique of Hegel. This deeper truth – both crucial to Marx's breakthrough, and his limit – is that Marx articulated the political theology of the abstractly free state founded in bourgeois property relations. To grasp this insight, Marxism must reconcile the content of its truth with the form of its self-consciousness. That is, it must become *speculative Marxism*.

This reformed Marxism will re-cognise the historic and social determinants of its estranged truth insofar as it overcomes mythology, dogma and fanaticism. This will liberate us from the Marxist tradition, which presently hangs over the heads of Marxists not so much like a nightmare, but like a bored East German censor listlessly and inconsistently dictating what is or isn't permitted. In return for giving itself over to the absolute negativity of the speculative method, Marxism will re-collect its tradition, but in rational form, rather than as leaden inheritance.

The tradition will cease to be dead; it will become a self-certain culture that relates freely and critically to its patrimony. Reformed Marxism will contribute to a political philosophy of a concretely free state.

To speculatively affirm Marxism requires us to express its truth in light of its opposition. This, as Hegel explained in the *Logic*, is the nature of speculative thought,

> which consists solely in grasping the opposed moments in their unity. Each moment actually shows that it contains its opposite within itself and that in this opposite it is united with itself; thus the affirmative truth is this immanently active unity, the taking together of both thoughts, their infinity – the relation to self which is not immediate but finite.

So, what opposites are revealed by the speculative critique of Marxism? The Marxist critique of bourgeois politics asserts that the state is the false idealism of bourgeois civil society. This simultaneously posits civil society as substantial, and the state as insubstantial, thus implying the possibility of an ideal politics following the destruction of the state and the liberation of civil society. In this vision, communist civil society becomes absolutely positive as politics is diffused everywhere, no longer monopolised by a state that represents the domination of the bourgeoisie as a universal law of freedom. That is, in the Marxist vision, communism is the absolute immediacy of civil society, liberated from bourgeois rule by a state which is not a state; a state that has withered away.

This is why, ultimately, Marxism is anti-political: in communist civil society, the political sphere is supposed to be everywhere – and is therefore nowhere. This is indeed a liberation from every problem of politics: what need is there, in a society where politics is reduced to administration, for opposed parties?

Bourgeois politics also aims at the immediacy of civil society, but a civil society of commodity-producing and -exchanging property owners, which it realises via practical reason: bourgeois realpolitik. Marxism differs from bourgeois pragmatism in that it opposes the bourgeoisie, in the name of proletarian practice and realpolitik. To attain their desired civil society, the bourgeoisie needs to capture and run the state, or at least to outsource the job to suitable stand-ins. The Marxists understand that to abolish bourgeois civil society, their state must be abolished.

Yet because Marxists represent their vocation as that of the proletariat, and disavow any connection between their project and the bourgeois state and civil society they oppose, they neglect to think about how they could write a better constitution and laws. Instead, the major contributions to Marxist political theory have all centred around winning power, for the proletariat, of course – and its party. When Marx turned Hegel's *Philosophy of Right* on its head, he opened the way for a proletarian Machiavelli: Gramsci was to Lenin as Niccolò was to Piero Soderini.

If, however, we refuse to render communism as a transcendent and unknowable *telos*, then we can begin to articulate the positive content of communism. In fact, Marx already gestured to this in the *Economic and Philosophic Manuscripts of 1844*, when he suggested that 'crude and thoughtless communism' immediately negates capitalist private property relations by universalising them. By abolishing private ownership of capital and transforming the state into the universal capitalist, crude socialism both realises bourgeois civil society absolutely, and posits its other, the state, as immediately and absolutely negative. State capitalism, quite simply, is crude socialism. Capitalism was also crude in its early stages, and like it, crude socialism is something to be overcome. The genuine overcoming of crude communism – sophisticated communism, if you will – is *republican* communism. Crude, state-capitalist communism immediately negates bourgeois right by transforming the state into the universal capitalist. Insofar as it reasserts the right of the state over civil society, it is superior to the bourgeois configuration of law, which subordinates politics to a particular class, under the guise of universalism. But because crude communism does not permit a state capable of incorporating difference and mediation, it is incompatible with freedom, reason and democracy.

Crude communism is the immediate domination of a particular, national state bureaucracy, which is why it has always been politically inferior to bourgeois democracy. Republican communism, by contrast, re-cognises the elements of bourgeois right *within* socialism and communism, and thus, can reconcile with its own political logic. To win, Marxists must know and practice politics better than the bourgeoisie – *and* we must establish a freer state, that knows how to limit itself by instituting mediation and difference within its constitution and law.

Obviously, we'll still need to do away with the private ownership of capital. This will not be peaceful. However, these insights make possible a Marxist *Philosophy of Right*, without which the socialist movement has no grounds upon which to claim that it will establish a freer constitution, more rational institutions, or a more democratic, post-capitalist relation between civil society and the state. Without understanding the concept of right, Marxism has no right to articulate the law that can replace the law born of bourgeois property relations. In place of the primacy of practical reason, speculative Marxism will elevate the political experience of the Left to the status of spiritual self-knowledge. Armed with a concept of justice, speculative Marxism will contribute to drafting a constitution for the Republic of Virtue.

☭

## Thesis Eleven
The revolutionary Marxists have changed the world unfreely; the point is to change it freely.

ADDITION – MARXISM AND THE OUGHT

Marxists uniformly praise the eleventh thesis. Hegelians are not so thrilled. I mean, just read the original. It's patently obvious that Marx stops short at the 'standpoint of the ought'. This is precisely where Fichte went wrong, according to Hegel. When the Marxists go out to change the world, to borrow Hegel's words from the *Encyclopedia Logic*, a 'limit is posited, it is surpassed, then again a limit, and so on endlessly.' Marxist practice is repetitious, and the change they make is no change at all.

Instead of wasting our time with such 'empty and merely transcendent things', as Hegel describes the movement of finite beings, what philosophy should deal with 'is always something concrete and absolutely present': namely, the idea, which is infinite; and the true, as that which is in-itself infinite. That is to say, philosophy must grasp the *ideality* of the finite. As Hegel explains,

> [t]he ideality of the finite is the chief proposition of philosophy, and every true philosophy is for that reason *idealism*. The only thing that matters is not to take as the infinite what is at once made into something particular and finite in the determination of it.

What bearing could this have on Marx's famous eleventh thesis? It's simple. Hitherto, Marxists have changed the world, yes. But they have not done so rationally, freely or consciously. This is why, in the end, the way of the world won. And in turn, it changed Marxism, transforming it from a genuinely revolutionary mass movement into a vaguely ridiculous rump.

The problem isn't that Marx's criticism of Hegel was inept, although it obviously was. Rather, Marxism failed because it attempted something new. Marx believed capitalism had made it possible to achieve the historic *telos* of concrete, substantial, universal freedom. As did Hegel, for that matter. Only, Marx set about actualising this *telos* in practice, while Hegel quite consciously limited himself to philosophy. Well and good; nothing in speculative philosophy commands that a philosopher must make politics their vocation, but nothing in speculative philosophy recommends against it either. And in fairness to Marx, when all is said and done, the Hegelians can't claim to have penned the program of a movement that won labour rights, the welfare state and universal suffrage – not to mention the national liberation of millions.

To return to the point, after 180 years (if we mark 1844 as the birthday of Marxism), despite their dearly-held past triumphs, the Marxists have obviously and spectacularly failed. They have also failed to develop the intellectual tools – *concepts* – with which to discuss their failure. Most Marxist discourse is obscure, academic, pedantic and antiquarian. Some of them still genuinely believe mid-century British Trotskyism has the answers.

They need philosophy. They need it in order to understand the promise they offer the world in mythological form. They need it to elevate their political theology to self-consciousness: that is, to philosophy. They need it so they can critically sift through their legacy, taking responsibility for what they reject and preserve. They need it to make better decisions about actions they will take in the future. They need it to free themselves from the dead weight of their own traditions. In short, if Marxists want to change the world, they need to stop bullshitting and start thinking. They will soon find that theory and practice are not so sharply opposed as Marx and Lukács once presumed.

## Thesis Twelve

When he limited himself to eleven theses on Feuerbach, Marx stopped short at the 'ought' of praxis, and represented the practical idea as a universal anti-philosophy, instead of speculatively, in its connection with the theoretical idea. This led to two mistakes.

1. Marx announced that the role of philosophy had come to an end. Philosophers have disproven this by continuing to ply their trade. History has disproven it by making possible philosophical thinking. The end of philosophy is also disproven by Marx's own life work, which is implicitly philosophical. Had Marx announced that the role of philosophy had come to an end *for him*, he would have been on safer ground. And besides, when this or that Marxist argues that the historical rôle of philosophy has ended, one gets the feeling that they want to ban philosophy they disagree with.

2. By stopping short at the 'ought', Marx's theses concluded with abstract negativity. They did not rise to determinate negativity, which is equally the articulation of a new, *positive content*.

As the saying goes, *hic Rhodus, hic Salta*.

### ADDITION – AN ALLEGORY OF GOOD GOVERNMENT

This positive content of communism can only be known rationally by traversing the abstract oppositions of the representative thought of bourgeois society and its critics. In this essay, however, I have not attempted to do this. Rather, this essay is intended as a polemical prolegomena to such a task; as a *Purgatorio*. Consequently, it concludes with a vision of earthly paradise. This is apt because, shy of the actualisation of reason, knowledge of absolute ethical life – communism – must contain an element of the ought; of utopian representation. And because a speculative image ought to know itself as an image, it is allegorical.

The speculative utopia defends the best of *this* world, and even when fighting bitterly, it is restrained because it accepts its knowledge is aporetic, the result of having faced the negativity of its self-knowledge. None of this precludes action. However, whoever acts must be willing to hear judgement, to apologise, and to promise otherwise when they have been wrong.

The principle of a republic formed in the sunlight of recognition and concrete freedom should be the true infinite, in the shape of a substantial, self-certain spirit. Its *telos* is flourishing life, and it will sustain a many-sided, cultivated and active polity, in the Greek sense, only with the privilege of citizenship universalised. The true infinite, as a self-certain shape of spirit, is a world peopled by individuals cultivated towards self-reflexive thought, combined in communities, governed by freely self-given laws that may be tested, re-made and improved. It is a world of patiently built institutions that mediate the constitutive antinomies of our society and our soul, while refusing to conceal their aporias. It is a culture of philosophical knowing, of aesthetic experience and creation and of deliberative, restorative justice. It is life that knows itself as life. It is a dinner party shared with friends in which each contributes freely and gladly.

The point is to develop an economic law that abolishes the private ownership of capital and the exploitation of labour power by democratising ownership, production and exchange, granting us material security without ecological ruin, so we can lie on the grass, looking up at a leaf in a tree while it fractures into a thousand geometric facets, marvelling that such beauty can exist while realising that the universe sees itself through our eyes. The point is to cultivate people who will be generous and thoughtful as strangers, friends, lovers and family members; people who won't flee from the 'plagues of trouble' that, as Plato suggested in the *Phaedrus*, we inherit as children. The point is to build a society, political and economic, that grants us positive freedom: kindness and patience should govern our time, and generosity should govern our space. The point is to create structures that can bear our extremes, help us learn to mediate them, and, when we fail, deal with us respectfully and with care. The point is to build a polity whose constitution recognises the other in light of our own otherness, that upholds rights, not abstractly, but concretely, by recognising difference, while establishing customs, laws and democratic fora that can educate us as self-respecting, self-governing political actors. The point is to build a culture that will create architecture, music, poetry, literature, film

– and every other art – that reaches for harmony, rhythm, composition, images and language with which we might share with each other our experiences in both their darkest and most resplendent forms, so we may recognise each other. And so that our creations, images, echoes and imprints live beyond us, conversing with new generations who will wonder what life meant to us, that we would create works that live anew in their different-yet-similar hearts. The point is to create life that can value itself as life: culture.

A republic of virtue should eschew political perfection bought by resentful redemption, and instead together author laws, institutions and traditions that allow us to face negativity, subjective and objective, without denying brokenness; without abstract grounds and estranged ends. To consider our own voids, to cultivate the voices with which our unconsciouses might speak, in rhymes, dreams, images or analysis. To become better, not perfect. To step lightly when causing unavoidable pain – as when ending a relationship well – and to at all costs take responsibility for mistakes we have made. The Greek virtues of cultivation and flourishing, the Christian spirit of forgiveness and universal love, the Enlightened notions of reason and freedom, the socialist commitment to solidarity and equality, the avant-garde delight in subversion and free desire – united, extended to all and made concrete.

How better could we fill our time and space than by the light of our incomplete divinity, admiring the soft, wispy hairs on the back of a lover's neck as they lie in the mid-morning sun; and to wake them gently and see their first smile. Amidst the void, a garden.

Hitherto, Marxists have only dreamed of a republic of virtue.

The point is to awake and create one.

TRANSLATED BY MONICA LOUZON
SUSANA CALVO

# The Arrendatario

You're an expert at losing time. You feel like dying when the alarm clock sounds. You agonise as each one of those 'just five more minutes' passes. It doesn't matter how fast or slow you go. Your destiny remains the same: losing yourself in the social order, disconnecting from your essence. Calling yourself weak, a coward.

Every morning, in front of the mirror, you loose this monologue on yourself, on the woman looking back – trapped behind the glass, yet somehow the only one who's truly free.

When you gaze into the eyes of your baby, you feel alive. You can lose yourself in your daughter's smile. Even if you're crying from desperation and burnout. You punish yourself when she's sick, when you can't console her. Above all when you have to leave her in the arms of an extraño. You don't want that for either of you.

That's why you've rented out your life to some capricious rich guy: so you can squeeze the most out of each day. You find yourself watching as your life is broadcast through social networks. He'll go to work for you, he'll rise early to suffer for you. When it's his turn to swap into your class, he treats it like a game. Calls your existence pathetic, laughs at your salary, at your months of hard work that he purchased so effortlessly. He puts on your worn-out clothes, the ones that filled you with memories and didn't end up in the donation box. He laughs at your house, where neither hovercraft nor food deliveries – on the saddest days, not even food itself – will come.

But when it's your turn, you still get to take care of your baby. If you didn't, this experience would be too much.

You rejoice because of Clause Thirteen.

Normally, your little girl would be crying in a nursery while you worked, but instead you're holding her in your arms. You smile as she moves her little hands, blinking her eyes in the light. You contemplate how the arrendatario plays at being you, taking orders from your boss like a living robot.

You hug your baby, enjoying life without pressure during your turns. This – you're sure of it – is the way life is meant to be.

The arrendatario is so capricious. His sense of superiority, his entertainment, leads him to entrust you with the care of his own son.

> Clause 13B: For as long as the acquired experience shall last, the renter will not care for any child, including their own, be they biological or adopted.

His young son hinders him. He only had a child because the Estado required it.

You don't mind caring for the boy. You're still free.

You like his child's character: so studious, so responsible. You know an emotional void must be at the root of why the boy buries himself in books and memory implants. Banned as they are because they cause too much confusion, the implants remain in fashion with privileged addicts hooked on feelings.

You look at the screen where the arrendatario is, experiencing your boss's anger. Your boss: another idiot with a clouded mind. Your laughter makes your baby smile. Life is lovely when you aren't forced to exchange hours for money. Buying your own time has been your dream, as it would be for anyone – but for these rich bastards, that's not enough. They want to dominate. You let him.

The arrendatario rented out your life. He can do whatever he wants with it: defile it, taunt you, try to sneak into your inner circles. But he doesn't fit in with your class. His emotions give him away.

You watch your daughter growing happily, close to you. The two of you are so connected. When it's your turn, you pass the time watching her unbound red hair dancing in the wind until you grow sleepy. You don't want anything else.

His son is learning how to smile.

The boy brings you gifts on the appointed dates. He embraces you. You observe tenderly.

He has been distracted and sad lately. His father will return soon, the contract will end, and the arrendatario hasn't asked for more extensions. The man will be absent a while, recuperating his metabolic equilibrium, putting his body back together after it has been disrupted by your impoverished life.

You're sad too.

Your baby will spend hours in the arms of strangers. That's how it is when they sell their time, their own children held by more strangers. Not even studying makes sense anymore. There are machines out there that can do everything for us, including researching and advancing science – if we let them.

You smile.

If we all left our work to machines we could save the planet. Perhaps stop all wars. And poverty. And evil.

You laugh with your baby. It's so wonderful to watch her grow.

The doorbell rings. It's him.

You're nervous.

You open the door, knife in hand – at his son's throat, keeping the boy immobile.

The man seems to be trembling.

Go back to work for at least another three months, or you'll only see him in photos'.

The arrendatario raises his arms, begging for his son's life. You tell him to leave – his turn will begin soon. He goes without protest.

※

The boy gave you all the keys you needed for your new life: passwords for the banks, mailing accounts, and subscriptions to leisure platforms – and contact lists. You gave him the attention he needed.

He laughs. As you embrace, he asks: 'Did I do good, Mami?'

# About the Contributors

SUSANA CALVO (Madrid, 1978) earned her Bachelor's degree in Audiovisual Communication from the Universidad Complutense de Madrid. A voracious and omnivorous reader, Momo opened fantasy's doors for her when she was a child, and from there, she explored horror and science fiction. In February 2022, *El Yunque de Hefesto* published the Spanish-language version of 'The Arrendatario' ('Aquila tu vida'), which won the first Yunque Literary prize for science fiction. Her latest stories 'Nostalgia de bit' and 'Supervivente' appear in *Pulporama* #4 and #8, and you can read more of her stories at *Lektu*. Susana also enjoys sharing reviews on her social media.

JOSEPH DAHER is a Swiss Syrian socialist activist and academic. He teaches at the University of Lausanne, Switzerland, and the University of Ghent, Belgium. He is the author of *Syria after the Uprisings: The Political Economy of State Resilience*; *Hezbollah: the Political Economy of Lebanon's Party of God*; and *Marxism and Palestine*.

HAN DEE is a writer and PhD candidate in creative writing at Queen Mary University London. Their research is a non-fiction narrative centred on a near relative's experiences of incarceration in England's high-security psychiatric institutions 1972-2002: Broadmoor, Rampton and Ashworth. Han is a member of the Mental Health & Social Justice Network, Subtexts creative writers' group @subtexts_sed_qmul and TIAN – Transversal Institutional Analysis Network – connecting researchers, practitioners and organisers who study, invent, and reshape institutions: institutionalanalysis.net

REBEKAH DISKI is a PhD candidate at the University of Warwick and a teaching fellow at SOAS. She mainly writes and worries about labour and ecological breakdown, and the prospects for an eco-socialist future.

NICK DYER-WITHEFORD is author of *Cyber-Marx: Cycles and Circuits of Struggle in High Technology Capitalism* and, with Alessandra Mularoni, of *Cybernetic Circulation Complex: Big Tech and Planetary Crisis*.

JULES GILL-PETERSON is an associate professor of history at John Hopkins University and the author of *Histories of the Transgender Child* and *A Short History off Trans Misogyny*. She's also a member of the Death Panel podcast.

DAISY LAFARGE is a writer and artist living in Glasgow. She is the author of *Life Without Air*, *Paul* and *Lovebug*.

SOPHIE LEWIS is a writer and independent scholar living in Philadelphia. She's the author of *Full Surrogacy Now*, *Abolish the Family*, *Enemy Feminisms*, and the forthcoming *Femmephilia* (2026) and *The Liberation of Children* (2027).

DANIEL ANDRÉS LÓPEZ lives in Melbourne, Australia and is the author of *Lukács: Praxis and the Absolute*. He is a Commissioning Editor for *Jacobin*, lectures in political philosophy at La Trobe University and is working on a second book concerned with Gillian Rose and philosophy of love.

MONICA LOUZON (she/her) is a queer writer, translator, and editor from the United States. Her translations have previously appeared in *Apex* magazine, *Cosmorama*, *Futura House*, and others. Her story '9 Dystopias' was a Best Microfiction 2023 winner, and her speculative poetry was nominated for the Dwarf Stars Award. To learn more about Monica and her work, please visit linktr.ee/molowrites.

ANDREAS MALM is associate professor of human ecology at Lund University. His latest book, with Wim Carton, is *Overshoot: How the World Surrendered to Climate Breakdown*.

JONAS MARVIN is a writer and researcher, currently working on a book, provisionally titled *Disorganised Abandonment*, forthcoming In the Salvage Editions series with Verso. He also blogs at Marx's Dream Journal.

CHINA MIÉVILLE is a writer of fiction and non-fiction, and a founding editor of *Salvage*. chinamieville.net

ABDALJAWAD OMAR is a Palestinian scholar and writer who lectures in the Philosophy and Cultural Studies Department at Birzeit University. He writes for *Mondoweiss* and his recent publications include 'Shock without Awe: Zionism and its Horror' in *Radical Philosophy*, and 'Bleeding Forms: Beyond the Intifada' in *Critical Times*.

GHALYA SAADAWI teaches critical theory and art theory at Goldsmiths University and the Dutch Art Institute. Her first book *Between October and November* is forthcoming with Fitzcarraldo Editions.

RICHARD SEYMOUR is a writer and a founding editor of *Salvage*. He is the author, most recently, of *Disaster Nationalism: The Downfall of Liberal Civilization*.

DUNCAN THOMAS is a socialist and writer living in Glasgow. His work has appeared in *Jacobin*, *openDemocracy*, *Salvage*, and elsewhere.